Books of Merit

The Great Dominion

SELECTED WORKS BY DAVID DILKS

Curzon in India: Achievement (1969)

Curzon in India: Frustration (1970)

The Diaries of Sir Alexander Cadogan (ed.) (1971)

Retreat from Power (ed.), 2 vols. (1981)

'The Missing Dimension': Governments and Intelligence Communities in the 20th Century (joint ed.) (1984)

Neville Chamberlain: Pioneering and Reform 1869–1929 (1984)

Grossbritannien und der deutsche Widerstand (joint ed.) (1994)

Barbarossa: The Axis and the Allies (joint ed.) (1994)

David Dilks

WITH THE ASSISTANCE OF RICHARD DILKS

"The Great Dominion"

Winston Churchill in Canada 1900–1954

Foreword by The Lady Soames, D.B.E

Thomas Allen Publishers
Toronto

Library and Archives Canada Cataloguing in Publication

Dilks, David, 1938-
"The Great Dominion" : Winston Churchill in Canada, 1900-1954 / David Dilks ; with the assistance of Richard Dilks.

Includes bibliographical references and index.
ISBN 0-88762-162-7

1. Churchill, Winston S. (Winston Spencer), 1874-1965. 2. Churchill, Winston S. (Winston Spencer), 1874-1965—Travel—Canada. 3. Canada—Relations—Great Britain. 4. Great Britain—Relations—Canada. 5. Prime ministers—Great Britain—Biography. 6. Visits of state—Canada—History—20th century. I. Dilks, Richard. II. Title.

DA566.9.C5D53 2005 941.084'092 C2005-900056-2

Jacket and text design: Gordon Robertson
Jacket images: (Top) Lord of the British © Bettmann/CORBIS/MAGMA;
(Bottom) Parliament Hill, Ottawa, Canada (Fotosearch TR000416)

Published by Thomas Allen Publishers,
a division of Thomas Allen & Son Limited,
145 Front Street East, Suite 209,
Toronto, Ontario M5A 1E3 Canada

www.thomas-allen.com

Canada Council
for the Arts

The publisher gratefully acknowledges the support of the Ontario Arts Council for its publishing program.

We acknowledge the support of the Canada Council for the Arts, which last year invested $21.7 million in writing and publishing throughout Canada.

We acknowledge the Government of Ontario through the Ontario Media Development Corporation's Ontario Book Initiative.

We acknowledge the financial support of the Government of Canada through the Book Publishing Industry Development Program (BPIDP) for our publishing activities.

09 08 07 06 05 1 2 3 4 5

Printed and bound in Canada

"History with its flickering lamp stumbles along the trail of the past, trying to reconstruct its scenes, to revive its echoes, and kindle with pale gleams the passion of former days."

— From Winston Churchill's valediction of
Neville Chamberlain in the House of Commons,
November 12, 1940

Contents

Foreword

by The Lady Soames, D.B.E.

I am greatly complimented to have been asked by Professor David Dilks to write a Foreword to this new and important work, which I believe will be a notable addition to the already monumental corpus of writings about my father, Winston Churchill.

There are of course several full-length lives of Churchill, dominated by Sir Martin Gilbert's magisterial eight-volume biography, still unique in its field, as Sir Martin had the first and sole access to the Churchill Papers. Since 1995, however, the Churchill Papers, now in the keeping of the Sir Winston Churchill Archive Trust, and housed permanently in the purpose-built Churchill Archives Centre at Churchill College, Cambridge, have been open to the public. Consequent upon this, a steady stream of publications is emerging based on this massive archive which comprises over a million documents.

I believe that some of the most interesting books about my father are those which are concerned with some specific period of his life, or aspects of his talents and character. For me, contemplating his whole life is like gazing at a vast panoramic tapestry, and I find it infinitely rewarding to look at some area of the whole – as it were through a magnifying glass – when hitherto unnoticed details spring to life and colour. Such a book we have here in Professor Dilks's engrossing study of Winston Churchill's nine visits to Canada between 1900 and 1954, and the people with whom he had passing contacts or with whom he formed lasting relationships during the course of his travels in war and peace throughout the vast country he early came to regard as "The Great Dominion."

As a continuation of the lectures Winston had given in December 1900 in the United States, he made a whirlwind tour of Canadian cities, and I have found it fascinating to read the accounts quoted from various newspapers in Ottawa, Montreal, Toronto and Winnipeg of the effect upon the large and enthusiastic audiences, many of whose members had travelled very long distances to hear this speaker. He was twenty-six, of aristocratic-cum-American lineage, the son of a famous father, who as a cavalry officer and war correspondent had taken part in, and written books about, campaigns in Cuba, India and the Sudan. He had sprung to world fame by his adventures and exploits in the Boer War, and had recently been elected as a Member of Parliament. The *Ottawa Evening Journal* described him as "a tall, squarely built young man. He has the manner and appearance of an athlete. He is clean shaven and his face is rather youthful looking. . . . As a lecturer he is somewhat handicapped by a lisp." His athletic appearance was of course due to his arduous training in the cavalry and to his continued participation in polo. His remarked-upon lisp was, I think, a less conspicuous feature later on – I certainly have to be reminded of its existence – but is often greatly exaggerated by those who seek to imitate him.

It was while Winston was in Ottawa during Christmas 1900 that he met Mackenzie King for the first time. Born in the same year, and himself also on the brink of a political career which would see him Prime Minister of Canada for more than twenty years, Mackenzie King attended Churchill's lecture there, and called upon him the next day in his hotel, where he found him drinking champagne "in mid-morning." One can infer a degree of disapproval. But these two very unlike men over the years and despite various disagreements under the flail of war would become true friends, if not soulmates.

Nearly thirty years would elapse before Winston revisited Canada: in the late summer of 1929, liberated from the office of Chancellor of the Exchequer after the defeat of Stanley Baldwin's government in May, he decided to take a long holiday, and accompanied by Randolph (aged eighteen) and by brother Jack and his son Johnnie, he made a three-month tour of North America starting in Quebec. They travelled in the comfort of a private railway car and progressed westward, touring in the Rocky Mountains before descending to Vancouver, from where the party started on their travels in the United States. On his earlier visit to Canada, Winston had been very much a young man in a hurry – and on the make – seeking to establish financial security as he embarked on his political career. Now he was a politician of world stature, who had sustained dramatic ups and downs along the way, but during these weeks he was in holiday mode, and as he visited Montreal, Ottawa, Toronto, Calgary and many other cities, he made speeches free of charge; his interviews with the press were long and authoritative, and covered a wide spectrum of world affairs. While in Ottawa, Mackenzie King (now Prime Minister) and Winston saw each other again, and King invited the visitors to his nearby house and estate.

Winston's long letters home to my mother were full of enthusiasm for the beauties of the scenery, and appreciation of the spontaneously warm welcome he received from his hosts in each place. He admired Canadian enterprise, whether in lumbering and paper mills or on the vast wheat-growing prairies (where, he wrote to Clementine, "They have a new machine called the 'Combine' which not only cuts the corn, but threshes it"). In a moment of discouragement about home politics, and particularly about the future of the leadership of the Tory party, and greatly charmed by the unspoilt natural scenes and the scope of Canadian enterprise, Winston wrote, "I am greatly attracted to this country" and he even contemplated quitting "the dreary field [at home] for pastures new!"

I have found the chapters describing my father's visits during the Second World War to Canada particularly gripping: he addressed Parliament in Ottawa, and particularly important were the two Quebec Conferences in 1943 (to which I accompanied him as aide-de-camp) and 1944, when Churchill and President Roosevelt and their advisers and Service chiefs met. During the war Mackenzie King's working relationship with my father became increasingly close, and it is right that we should be reminded of the contribution Canada made in so many vital ways to the Allied war effort. She poured out her treasure in terms of valiant manpower, and the granting of facilities such as the air training schemes, and gave vast financial aid. Professor Dilks writes tellingly of "Canada's unmatched generosity, which continued throughout the war and into the peace."

Mackenzie King twice made wartime visits to England and each time came to Chequers (the official weekend residence of British Prime Ministers), where I had the pleasure of meeting him – he was always very kind to me. His diaries are illuminating, and show he greatly appreciated the informal and family atmosphere there: he liked my mother very much, and wrote her some charming thank-you letters. But he was a total abstainer – and was surprised and rather shocked not only by the amount my father drank, but also by the lavish supplies of alcohol hospitably on offer in our house. However, his undeniably spinsterish, prim character was offset by genuine warmth. From the beginning and right through their friendship, Mackenzie King's not infrequent disagreements with Winston's opinions or policies, and his disapproval of certain aspects of his character, were again and again rather touchingly disarmed by Winston's own warmth and charm.

Winston would visit Canada twice more after the war, during his last prime ministership (1951–55), and it is delightful to read the accounts of how he was welcomed as a well-known and trusted friend by the government, the press and the ordinary Canadian-in-the-street alike. On each occasion he was accompanied by Anthony Eden, the Foreign Secretary, his long-time colleague and generally perceived "heir apparent."

There was still much business to be conducted both in the United States and in Canada, principally on atomic research and development – for over all discussions lowered the chill cloud of the Cold War – but the intense pressure of the wartime visits was gone, as was the secrecy about engagements and movements, which had necessarily shrouded the programs in those years. Churchill's former colleague, Mr. Mackenzie King, had retired, and had been succeeded by Mr. St. Laurent, with whom Winston formed a friendly relationship; the Governor General was Field Marshal Earl Alexander of Tunis – "Alex" – an old comrade-in-arms.

In June 1954, Winston was nearing his eightieth birthday, and I find David Dilks's description of what would prove to be his last visit to Canada very moving. Churchill and Eden had arrived on June 29 from Washington, where they had spent a few days conferring with President Eisenhower, and they made a short visit to Ottawa before flying to New York to join the *Queen Elizabeth* for their voyage home.

During the thirty hours in Ottawa, Winston, apart from private talks with Mr. St. Laurent, attended a meeting of the Canadian Cabinet, held a long press conference, made a broadcast speech to the Canadian people and was guest at a large dinner. Wherever they drove, unusually large crowds turned out to cheer Churchill and Eden; a witness reported to a friend that Winston "reacted vigorously to his reception and was in magnificent form but he is now certainly an old gentleman." Although they could not know that this visit would be his last, there was an atmosphere of valediction as he made his goodbyes at the airport: although it was late in the evening, more than a thousand admirers had come to bid him farewell as he walked down the long, roped-back line shaking hands; "Tears ran down his pink old cheeks. Some in the crowd wept as openly and unashamedly."

Thus the leave-taking of the man who had first visited Canada as a sandy-haired young fellow fresh from his adventures in the Boer War, and on the threshold of his political career. He was received then with enthusiasm, interest and curiosity, and now more than half a century later he would make his farewell to the country he had come to think of as "The Great Dominion" with the mutual love, admiration and loyalty of tried and trusted friends who had walked a long road together in all kinds of weather.

Mary Soames

The Lady Soames, D.B.E.
February 2005

Principal Characters

ATTLEE Clement Richard, later 1st Earl Attlee (1883–1967); British politician; Chancellor of the Duchy of Lancaster, 1930–31; Lord Privy Seal, 1940–42; Deputy Prime Minister, 1942–45; Secretary of State for the Dominions, 1942–43; Lord President of the Council, 1943–45; Prime Minister, 1945–51.

BROOKE Alan Francis, later 1st Viscount Alanbrooke (1883–1963); British soldier; of Irish Protestant family and educated in France; commanded 2nd Army Corps, British Expeditionary Force, 1939–40; Commander-in-Chief, Home Forces, 1940–41; Chief of the Imperial General Staff, 1941–46, and Chairman of the Chiefs of Staff Committee, 1942–46; Field Marshal, 1944.

CHURCHILL Mrs. Winston, née Clementine Ogilvy Hozier, later Baroness Spencer-Churchill (1885–1977); married Winston Churchill, 1908; four children (three daughters, one son and a daughter who died in infancy); chairman, Red Cross Aid to Russia Fund, 1941–46.

CHURCHILL Randolph Frederick Edward Spencer (1911–1968); only son of Winston and Clementine Churchill; journalist; MP, 1940–45; war service in Western Desert, North Africa, Italy and Yugoslavia.

CHURCHILL Winston Leonard Spencer (1874–1965); educated at Harrow School and Sandhurst; elder son of Lord Randolph Churchill and his American wife, formerly Miss Jennie Jerome; soldier and journalist; MP, with brief intervals, 1900–64; left the Conservative Party for the Liberals, 1904; Parliamentary Under-Secretary of State, Colonial Office, 1905–8; President of the Board of Trade, 1908–10;

Home Secretary, 1910–11; First Lord of the Admiralty, 1911–15; Chancellor of the Duchy of Lancaster, 1915; Minister of Munitions, 1917–18; Secretary of State for War and Air, 1918–21, and for the Colonies, 1921–22; Chancellor of the Exchequer, 1924–29; First Lord of the Admiralty, 1939–40; Prime Minister and Minister of Defence, 1940–45; Prime Minister, 1951–55 (and Minister of Defence, 1951–52); Knight of the Garter, 1953; Nobel Prize for Literature, 1953; biographer of Lord Randolph Churchill (2 vols.) and Marlborough (4 vols.); author of autobiographical accounts of the First World War (5 vols.) and of the Second (6 vols.) and of numerous other works, including *A History of the English-Speaking Peoples* (4 vols.).

CLAXTON Brooke (1898–1960); Canadian lawyer and politician; served in First World War; MP from 1940; Minister of National Health and Welfare, 1944–46; Minister of National Defence, 1946–54; later Vice-President and General Manager for Canada, Metropolitan Life Insurance Co., and Chairman of the Canada Council.

COLVILLE John Rupert ("Jock") (1915–87); British diplomat; Assistant Private Secretary to successive Prime Ministers (Chamberlain, Churchill, Attlee), 1939–41, 1943–5; served with the Royal Air Force, 1941–43, 1944; Private Secretary to Princess Elizabeth, 1947–49; Joint Principal Private Secretary to Churchill, 1951–55; knighted, 1974.

DE GAULLE Charles André Joseph Marie (1890–1970); French general and politician; leader of Free French forces from 1940; President of French Committee of National Liberation, 1943–44; President of the Provisional Government of the French Republic, 1944–46; recalled to power, 1958, and President of the Republic, 1959–69.

EDEN Robert Anthony (1897–1977), later 1st Earl of Avon; British politician; Foreign Secretary, 1935–38, 1940–45, 1951–55; Secretary of State for the Dominions, 1939–40, and for War, 1940; Prime Minister, 1955–57.

EISENHOWER Dwight David (1890–1969); American soldier and politician; Commander-in-Chief, Allied forces, North Africa, 1942–44; Supreme Commander, Allied Expeditionary Force, Western Europe, 1944–45; Chief of Staff, U.S. Army, 1945–48; Supreme Commander, NATO forces, Europe, 1950–52; President of the United States, 1953–61.

ISMAY Hastings Lionel, later 1st Baron Ismay ("Pug") (1887–1965); British soldier and administrator; military service in India and East

Africa; Deputy Secretary of the Committee of Imperial Defence, 1936–38, and Secretary, 1938–40; Deputy Secretary (Military) to the War Cabinet, Chief Staff Officer to Churchill, as Minister of Defence, and a member of the Chiefs of Staff Committee, 1940–45; Chief of Staff to the Viceroy of India, Lord Mountbatten, 1947; Secretary of State for Commonwealth Relations, 1951–52; Secretary-General of NATO, 1952–57.

KING William Lyon Mackenzie (1874–1950); Canadian politician; grandson of William Lyon Mackenzie, leader of the abortive rebellion of 1837 in Upper Canada; Deputy Minister of Labour, 1900; elected to Parliament, 1908; Minister of Labour in Sir Wilfrid Laurier's Cabinet, 1909; leader of the Liberal Party in succession to Laurier, 1919, and held that post until 1948; Prime Minister (and Secretary of State for External Affairs until 1946), 1921–26, 1926–30, 1935–48.

MACDONALD Malcolm James (1901–81); British politician and diplomat; son of J. Ramsay MacDonald, Labour Prime Minister; Secretary of State for the Dominions, 1935–38 and 1938–39, and for the Colonies, 1938–40; Minister of Health, 1940–41; High Commissioner in Canada, 1941–46; Governor General of Malaya and Borneo, 1946–48; Commissioner-General in Southeast Asia, 1948–55; thereafter other high posts in India and Africa.

MORAN Charles McMoran Wilson (1882–1977), 1st Baron Moran; Royal Army Medical Corps from 1914 (Military Cross, despatches twice); Dean, St. Mary's Hospital Medical School, London, 1920–45; Churchill's personal physician, 1940–65; President, Royal College of Physicians, 1941–50.

PEARSON Lester Bowles (1897–1972); Canadian diplomat and politician; Minister-Counsellor, Canadian Embassy in Washington, 1942–45, and Ambassador, 1945–46; Under-Secretary for External Affairs, 1946–48; Secretary for External Affairs, 1948–57; awarded the Nobel Prize for Peace, 1957; leader of the Liberal Party and Prime Minister, 1963–68.

ROOSEVELT Franklin Delano (1882–1945); a distant relative of Theodore Roosevelt, 26th President of the United States; Assistant Secretary of the Navy, 1913–20; Governor of New York, 1928–32; 32nd President of the United States, 1933–45.

ST. LAURENT Louis Stephen (1882–1973); Canadian lawyer and politician; President, Canadian Bar Association, 1930–32; Minister of Justice and Attorney General, 1941–46; Secretary of State, 1946–48;

Prime Minister, in succession to W.L. Mackenzie King, 1948–57.

SMUTS Jan Christian (1870–1950); South African lawyer, soldier and politician; ministerial posts from 1907; commanded forces in British East Africa, 1916–17; member of the Imperial War Cabinet in London, 1917–18; Prime Minister and Minister for Native Affairs, 1919–24; Minister of Justice, 1933–39; Prime Minister and Minister of External Affairs and Defence, 1939–48; Honorary Field Marshal of the British Army, 1941.

STALIN Joseph (1879–1953); born in Georgia (Russia); an early convert to Marxism and the armed struggle; appointed Commissar for Nationalities and a member of the Politburo after the revolution of 1917; General Secretary to the Central Committee of the Communist Party, 1922, and the dominant force in the government of Russia after Lenin's death in 1924; Marshal of the Soviet Union, 1943; Generalissimo, 1945.

Abbreviations

C-in-C	Commander-in-Chief
CIGS	Chief of the Imperial General Staff
COS	Chiefs of Staff
CCOS	Combined Chiefs of Staff
MP	Member of Parliament
NATO	North Atlantic Treaty Organisation
SACMED	Supreme Allied Commander, Mediterranean
UN	United Nations
W.S.C.	Churchill

Code Names

Admiral Q/PQ	President Roosevelt
Anakim	Recapture of Burma
Anvil	Allied landings in the south of France, 1944 (later termed Dragoon)
Colonel Warden	Churchill
Culverin	Operations against Sumatra
Dragoon	Allied landings in the south of France, 1944
Dracula	Capture of Rangoon and severance of lines to Japanese bases in Siam
Habbakuk	Floating seadrome made of ice
Husky	Attack on Sicily, 1943
Octagon	Conference at Quebec, September 1944
Overlord	Invasion of northern France, 1944 earlier known as Round-up)
Pilgrim	Proposal for British occupation of the Canary Islands
Quadrant	Conference at Quebec, August 1943
Subaltern	Mary Churchill
Torch	Invasion of North Africa, November 1942 (previously Gymnast)
Trident	Conference at Washington, May 1943
Tube Alloys	Research on the atomic bomb

Introduction

For a long spell, British prime ministers were closely acquainted with Canada. Andrew Bonar Law was Canadian by birth; Stanley Baldwin had gone there as a young man seeking orders for his family company; Ramsay MacDonald valued his Canadian contacts and had given hospitality in London to Mackenzie King, a link of significance to both sides when MacDonald's son was British High Commissioner in Ottawa during the war; Neville Chamberlain toured Canada extensively in 1922, and was Baldwin's principal lieutenant at Ottawa in the negotiation of the economic agreements of 1932; Clement Attlee, Harold Macmillan, and Sir Alec Douglas-Home knew Canada at first-hand, and Anthony Eden took care to point out in his memoirs that for twenty years he had visited Canada more often than any country except France.

Winston Churchill's connection with "the Great Dominion," as he liked to call it, spanned more than half a century. At Winnipeg he heard the news of Queen Victoria's death. In Vancouver harbour he caught a lovely salmon. Near Banff he painted several pictures, two of which have lately been identified; at Halifax, showing a fine disdain for wartime security, he led a large crowd in singing on the quayside. At Niagara Falls in 1929 he regretted that he had not tried to buy a concession there in 1900; and when he took his daughter to Niagara in 1943 on their way to Roosevelt's home at Hyde Park, he rejoined, when asked whether he noticed any differences since his first visit, "The principle seems to be much the same; the water still falls over." At Toronto he acknowledged in 1932 his emancipation from the doctrines of free trade. At Ottawa in the dark days of 1941 he proclaimed his confidence in victory and in 1952 had to concede that the result of victory had been far less satisfying than all had wished. At Quebec in 1943, and again in 1944, he concerted with Roosevelt and the two countries' Chiefs of Staff the high strategy of the war.

Many of those images flooded into Churchill's mind in 1954 when, a few weeks short of his eightieth birthday, he spoke from the Château Laurier on his last night in Canada. He lamented that in all those years he had not managed to visit Fort Churchill, named after John Churchill, first Duke of Marlborough. Before more pressing cares intervened, Churchill had half-hoped to penetrate there after the Quebec Conference of 1943, and to show his wife and daughter the splendours of the Rockies and Lake Louise. In the event, he never travelled west of Ontario after 1929. All the same, his experiences at the turn of the century left upon Churchill's mind a conviction of Canada's spaciousness, so sharply contrasting with the throbbing, crowded life of Britain, which he never lost; and that impression deepened during his odyssey of 1929, when many of the uncertainties manifest at the turn of the century had been subdued.

Between Churchill's first visit and the second, Canadians had rallied in their hundreds of thousands to Britain's side and distinguished themselves on the field of battle, as the next generation was to do after 1939. Stricken like other agricultural communities during the Depression, Canada later saw her economy expand by leaps and bounds when, chiefly under the impetus of the second war, she became a major manufacturing and trading power; the armed services grew to a size and strength previously undreamed of; and she played no mean part on the international stage. A population of five million had increased within two generations to fourteen million; Churchill guessed correctly that in his grandchildren's time, it would rise to thirty million. Canada, he said in that broadcast of 1954, was a country that would certainly take its place in the first rank of sovereign communities:

> When all these hopes are fulfilled and all these glories come to you, do not forget the Old Land; do not forget that little Island lost among the Northern mists which played so great a part in your early days and now regards you with so much admiration and pride.

Of no other Commonwealth country did Churchill have this lifelong knowledge, or anything resembling it. He never went to Australia, New Zealand, Hong Kong, Malaya, Singapore or any of the British territories in Southeast Asia and the Pacific; he did not return to South Africa after 1900, or to the Indian subcontinent after 1899. As a young Under-Secretary he toured East Africa, but the enormous British possessions in West and Central Africa remained unexplored by him. Of course, much of this had to do with distance and transport. By contrast with these other lands, Canada lay six days away by liner or latterly a day by air. Moreover, Canada adjoined the United States.

On eight of his nine visits to Canada, Churchill travelled through the United States or went on to America once the Canadian part of his journey was complete. The conference with Roosevelt at Placentia Bay in August 1941 provides the exception. It is treated here as if the destination had been Quebec or Ottawa; after all, did not the Prime Minister and a few of his party scramble ashore in a deserted bay one afternoon? The government of Canada had no part in that meeting off Newfoundland; by way of compensation, so to speak, Mackenzie King's conversations in London immediately afterwards are included in Chapter Four.

Even those acquainted with Churchill's career are sometimes surprised to find that he travelled to Canada so often, and many works about him treat the fact as a mere appendix to his connections with the United States. I hope this book may show that there was more to it than that. My purpose has been to bring together accounts of each visit, letting Churchill fulfill a function for which he was uniquely qualified: to speak for himself. Around these records I have tried to provide a setting, in the hope that readers may feel inspired to pursue their own lines of thought and inquiry; even a large volume has to leave a good deal unsaid.

The substance of Churchill's lectures in 1900–01 and 1929 can be retrieved only from Canadian newspapers, for his own archive provides scanty information. From the beginning, he enjoyed a good hearing and a large following in Canada. By 1929, he found with delight an abounding friendliness and an enthusiastic response from almost all Canadian journals, including those published in French. In each city the audiences overflowed; time and again, demand for tickets was impossible to satisfy. Later, when Prime Minister, he was able to glory in the fact that twice in one generation the countries of the Commonwealth had fulfilled a prophecy which he had in his schooldays heard a distinguished Canadian venture: that if steps were taken to hold the Empire to the Crown, and danger struck at the heart and life of that Empire, Nelson's signal "England expects that every man this day will do his duty" would run not along a line of ships, but of nations.

The press accounts of Churchill's visit of 1929 would fill a volume by themselves, and the records of his wartime visits might require several, for the British exported to Quebec in 1943 and 1944 the men who directed the war in its military and diplomatic aspects, and both conferences coincided with external events of the utmost importance. To select a small fraction has been no simple task. However, Churchill's own example has helped. He was the only politician of the front rank who spent a large portion of the first war, and the whole of the second, in high office. In his magisterial accounts of both conflicts, he adopted the method of Daniel Defoe's *Memoirs of a Cavalier*; no model could have been more aptly chosen, since he was himself a cavalier to the core. The chronicle of great events, in military and political spheres alike, is hung upon the thread of one man's experience.

For Churchill's forays to Canada between 1941 and 1954 I have tried to follow the same principle, but with the important qualification that we now have access to material of which he was necessarily unaware: for examples, the records of the Canadian government, the private correspondence of Lester Pearson, the unpublished memoirs of Brooke Claxton. And then there is a document which does not fit easily into any category, the diary of Mackenzie King, blending most private musings with accounts of conversations and meetings. Churchill kept no diary, and normally recorded talks only if they required action. Time and again, King's diary recounts episodes of which we should otherwise know nothing. An absorbing book might now be written about the relationship between the two of them. Over a distance of more than sixty years, we can almost hear the sniff with which Churchill greeted the other's observation "The great thing in politics is to avoid mistakes," just as we imagine without difficulty King's sighs of disapproval as he read some vehement telegram from London and reflected upon Churchill's generous consumption of "stimulants."

King was no Pepys. He had directed that much of his diary should be destroyed at his death, and his executors deserve the thanks of posterity for their decision to preserve the whole. Politicians in parliamentary democracies like to hold power and win elections. Churchill did not fail to observe Mackenzie King's remarkable success in that respect; he heard

Roosevelt's repeated references to a long friendship with King and to the high reputation which the Prime Minister of Canada enjoyed in America. Churchill's attitude toward him and the new Canada became steadily more understanding and appreciative, even if King's inner demons would surface now and again and cause him to inveigh against British indifference to Canadian susceptibilities or Churchillian designs to deny Canada her full sovereignty. Of these outbursts Malcolm MacDonald absorbed the first blast, a role to which he was admirably suited.

Though Churchill could be brusque, bullying, offhand, dismissive, such moods did not last long, and were generally condoned and understood by people who appreciated how mountainous a burden he bore. He had great charm, the more powerful because it was not based upon vapid blandishments or the detested "official grimace." To exercise such charm upon the President was required in the interests of Britain and the wider world; no lover, Churchill would say with a twinkle, ever studied his mistress's whims as carefully as he studied Roosevelt's. He admired Roosevelt's political skills, loved his buoyancy and felt genuine pleasure when the President telegraphed to him, "It is fun to be in the same decade with you."[1]

Upon Mackenzie King, Churchill had no special need to practise such spells, but his respect for King stood high and grew during the war, while his admiration for Canada's conduct knew few bounds. Like almost everyone else, King was moved by the political confidences and private hospitality which the Churchills extended. We may say with confidence that no one but Churchill could have moved the sober Prime Minister of Canada to dance with him in the Great Hall at Chequers, and it is unlikely that anyone but Mrs. Churchill could have persuaded King to drink a glass of champagne by way of celebrating the successful conclusion of the second Quebec Conference.

With few exceptions, the documents printed in this book were written at the time. Some are included for the light they cast on Churchill's character and methods, relations with colleagues and view of the world. I have usually given preference to Churchill's own telegrams and speeches, and to those issues which preoccupied him while he chanced to be on Canadian soil. The printing in *The Second World War* of his minutes to ministers and military men provoked much irritation, for the replies were generally absent. I have tried to meet the point in part by placing his messages in context. Where a document is full – for instance, the record of his meeting with the Canadian Cabinet in 1952 – I have not repeated the sense in an editorial interpolation. Many of the documents are extracted from something longer; to avoid disfiguring the page, I have indicated omissions only within the selected passage. The texts retain their original spelling and punctuation, at the cost of occasional inconsistency.

In 1900–01, and more markedly in 1929, Churchill reproduced a good deal of material from one lecture to another. Much of this duplication has been omitted, at the price of distorting somewhat the record of a particular speech. Where the original seemed to be garbled or inadequate, I have once or twice taken a few words from another newspaper's record. Obvious mistakes have been corrected without comment; the *Winnipeg Free Press* for August 21, 1929, says "drawn inch by inch into the position of advocating our responsibilities towards Egypt" but this volume has "abdicating."

"Really, my dear, your handwriting is a disgrace," said Sir Winston Churchill one day to his Private Secretary. "It is like three spiders arm in arm . . . the one unbreakable cypher."[2] Mackenzie King would have been mortified, we imagine, if his own script had been so described. Let us say that it is often difficult for the inexpert to read, and even those preparing typed versions in later years have sometimes been baffled. During the war, King usually dictated his diary to the well-named Mr. Handy, but it is clear that the Prime Minister himself often had no time to check the result. I have accordingly made a considerable number of silent corrections. To take two from the diary of December 29, 1941, "thought Russia would hold out and afflict great damage" has become "inflict," and where the original says "to roll thanks off ships," there seemed little risk in substituting "tanks."

Following Churchill's own example, I have occasionally allowed idiosyncrasies in the footnotes and endnotes; the former identify individuals and events, the latter show where the documents are to be found. Two diarists cited frequently in this book started the war with one name and were eventually better known under another; Sir Charles Wilson became Lord Moran, and General Brooke by stages General Sir Alan Brooke, Field Marshal Sir Alan Brooke and eventually Lord Alanbrooke. In the hope of avoiding confusion, I have put "Lord Moran's diary" or "Lord Alanbrooke's diary" throughout. In respect of titles, I have also allowed some simplifications: Malcolm MacDonald held the office of "High Commissioner in Canada for the United Kingdom," but appears here as

"British High Commissioner in Canada"; and I have often used "Foreign Secretary" instead of "Secretary of State for Foreign Affairs." Readers in Canada will realize that the initials CPR may not be familiar elsewhere, and those in Britain that "Chequers" requires a sentence of explanation.

Editorial interpolations in the texts or between documents are enclosed within square brackets.

* * *

We may say of Churchill what was well observed of Einstein, that he possessed the authentic magic which transcends logic and distinguishes the genius from the mass of lesser men with greater talent. Anthony Eden, echoing Ben Johnson, described Churchill as "so rammed with life." Infuriating and overbearing he might often be, and variable in opinion, for he wrote and spoke copiously upon countless issues for some sixty years, and believed with the philosopher that a foolish consistency is the hobgoblin of little minds, with which a great soul has simply nothing to do. Challenged about changes of front, Churchill would reply, "I have often had to eat my words, and on the whole I have found them a very nourishing diet," and about his changes of party, "Any fool can rat, but I flatter myself that it requires a certain ingenuity to re-rat." Almost all those who worked closely with Churchill during the Second World War believed he was a great man; some grew to love him. With many millions at home and overseas, his zeal, candour, bearing and language created a bond which endured to his death and beyond. To adapt what Churchill wrote of his mother, the wine of life ran in his veins.

It would be pointless to pretend that there were no imperfections, and Churchill himself would have been the last man to expect such deference. Nor did unbroken harmony always prevail in the upper reaches of the British government, or between Britain and the Dominions. On the balance, however, the discords signified far less than the concordances. The countries of the Commonwealth and Empire were the only powers that fought from the beginning of the war in 1939 to its end in 1945. Without them it could not have been won; and that towering achievement, to which Churchill contributed more than any other individual, is not heightened by the brushing away of blemishes. As Dr. Johnson observed of his own *Shakespeare*:

> We must confess the faults of our favourite, to gain credit to our praise of his excellencies. He that claims, either in himself or for another, the honours of perfection, will surely injure the reputation which he designs to assist.[3]

* * *

I am deeply grateful to Sir Winston's daughter Lady Soames, who appears in these pages under the code name Subaltern, for writing so gracious a Foreword.

The late Sir William Deakin, friend and coadjutor of her father, compounded his countless kindnesses by commenting upon the text a few weeks before his death.

Many colleagues have helped me. Two of them deserve particular thanks: Mr. Boris Stipernitz in Ottawa and Dr. Liz Evans in London. Mrs. Lorraine Trickett has coped expertly with the secretarial side of the task. I am grateful to Patrick Crean, Pat Kennedy and their colleagues at Thomas Allen for enthusiasm and constructive support, and to Bruce Hunter for all his help in London.

My wife encouraged the enterprise in all manner of ways, not least by believing against the evidence that the mountains of material would one day be reduced to order. Our son Richard studied the documents, put many of them on disk and provided material for a goodly number of footnotes. He, like his parents, has often enjoyed the matchless hospitality of friends in Canada. We are all three of us glad of this opportunity to express our thanks, not least to the Churchill Societies in Edmonton, Vancouver, Calgary and Toronto.

February 4, 2005
David Dilks

1

Young Man in a Hurry: 1900–01

A FEW MILES FROM OXFORD lies Blenheim Palace, the gift of a grateful sovereign and nation to John Churchill, first Duke of Marlborough, who by military prowess and diplomatic stratagem had done more than any other man in Europe to contain French power. There Winston Churchill was born on November 30, 1874, the elder child of Lord Randolph Churchill (himself a younger son of the 7th Duke) and his American wife, Jennie Jerome. It was at Blenheim that Winston Churchill became engaged to Clementine Hozier; there he worked for months in the Muniment Room to gather material for the monumental *Life* of his great ancestor; and at Bladon Church, close to the boundary of the park, he was by his own wish buried. The chapel holds a small statue in marble of Marlborough's triumph at the Battle of Blenheim. To the one side sits Fame with her trumpet; to the other, adorned by angels' wings, we find History with her feathery quill; beneath, the long-tongued figure of Envy is crushed. Through sixty strenuous years, Winston Churchill sought and enjoyed fame; read, wrote and made history; and despised envy.

Small and often sickly as a child, he was generally unhappy at the several schools to which he was sent, and subjected to ferocious punishment. When he recalled late in life to a Canadian audience that, in December 1941, knowing what penalties the Japanese would soon exact in the Far East, he had felt "like one about to come under the lash wielded by a strong and merciless arm," he spoke whereof he knew. He yearned to be closer to his often disapproving father, a political figure of the first rank who combined radicalism with Toryism and briefly held the office of Chancellor of the Exchequer. His mother, he once wrote, "shone for me like the Evening Star. I loved her dearly – but at a distance."[1] It was perhaps from her and her American forbears that he inherited a taste for peril and gambles, a part of his nature not always dominant but never far below the surface. Like his father, he had a prodigious memory, which enabled him to recall without error everything from solemn poetry to music-hall songs. With a rooted aversion to Latin, Greek and mathematics went a natural ear for the rhythms of English. By a stroke of good fortune for him and for posterity, he came at Harrow School under the care of a teacher of English to whom he always acknowledged his indebtedness. While his contemporaries toiled at the classics, Churchill learned thoroughly the structure of his own language.

Destined for the Army because deemed unsuited for university, he passed with some difficulty into the military college at Sandhurst. There he loved the life and fared far better in examinations than at school. On his twenty-first birthday, in Cuba, he came under fire for the first time. Already he had created a pattern which prevailed for the rest of his life; he would seek adventure, court danger and then describe his experiences. Lieutenant Churchill returned from Cuba with the Spanish Order of the Red Cross and a fondness for siestas and cigars. He had already begun to write for the newspapers and it was still possible to combine military service with reporting, though the habit was heartily disapproved by many. He campaigned on the North-West Frontier of India and wrote a book; he played polo to high levels of distinction; conscious of his lack of university education, he caused his mother to send him many volumes, and modelled himself upon Gibbon and Macaulay. Having taken part in the last great cavalry charge of the British Army, at Omdurman in the autumn of 1898, he promptly produced another splendid work, *The River War*. During that campaign to reconquer the Sudan, he had acted as war correspondent for the *Morning Post* in London.

By the age of twenty-four, then, Churchill had seen something of life in four continents, and fought in three; but as he liked to say in later life to young men making their way in the world, "Napoleon took Toulon when he was twenty-four!" Lord Randolph Churchill had died after a painful decline some years before. The son never wished to be anything but a politician. He resigned his commission, came home, stood as a Conservative in Oldham and was defeated by a narrow margin. His mother, affectionate but hopelessly improvident, of whom it was said that life did not begin for her on a basis of less than forty pairs of shoes,[2] had remarried. Her son had little money of his own, and Members of Parliament were in those days unpaid. Undeterred, he set himself the task of building up a substantial sum in a short time.

When the Boer War broke out in South Africa, the *Morning Post* appointed him as its correspondent at the then-enormous salary of £250 per month. Within a short while, Churchill had run into a friend he had known in India, Captain Haldane, who was to take a party of men and a truck with a naval gun along the line from Estcourt toward Colenso. When the train was attacked, Churchill behaved with conspicuous bravery and by the luckiest of chances did not have his pistol when captured. Imprisoned in the State Model Schools at Pretoria, some five hundred miles north of Estcourt, Churchill argued that since he was a press correspondent, not a soldier, he should be released. Unsurprisingly, his captors retorted that a newspaper correspondent who took part in a vigorous military engagement had forfeited his non-combatant status. This was the point at which he decided to attempt an escape.

He succeeded, whereupon the Boer authorities offered a reward of £25 to anyone who could bring Churchill to them, dead or alive. Many years later, when Mackenzie King remarked that a price of £1,000 had been put upon the head of his grandfather after an abortive rebellion in 1837, Churchill reflected with amusement upon the disparity of value. Before this episode, he had been well-known, perhaps notorious to some. Now newspapers far and wide, not least the *Morning Post* which printed his own vivid despatches, celebrated his exploit. Like Lord Byron, he awoke and found himself famous.

After more months of campaigning in South Africa, but with no immediate end to the war in sight, he returned to England, published accounts of these latest adventures and won the seat at Oldham which had eluded him in the previous year. He found himself called upon to address great public meetings with the leading political figures of the day. Oratory was not an art which Churchill acquired easily. Command of the spoken word came to him far less readily than command of the written. He prepared elaborate drafts, which his Napoleonic memory enabled him to retain, and had a mild impediment of speech, which he strove to overcome. Fearful that if he lost his thread he might break down with nothing to say, he determined to conquer apprehension. Even after a lifetime's experience, he always preferred to have a detailed script and to open a debate rather than wind it up, so that he should not be called upon to respond without a text.

The despatches from South Africa had already brought in a substantial sum. If he were to live in modest style in London and sustain his new position in Parliament, he needed to earn more. Mastery of language, to which Churchill probably owed more than any other British Prime Minister, provided the answer. Once the election was over, he lectured with his lantern slides in every major British city, moving each day from one place to the next. In a single month, he made by these exertions nearly £4,000, keeping a sharp eye on the night's takings. Enticing offers had arrived from the New World. Without waiting to take his seat in Parliament, Winston Churchill set sail for the United States and Canada.

* * *

No drafts for Churchill's Canadian speeches survive. To judge from the newspapers, the essential content was the same as in England; a survey of the Boer War as it developed and the story of his own escape treated in that broad context. Introducing him to an audience in New York, Mark Twain said dryly, "Mr. Churchill by his father is an Englishman, by his mother he is an American, no doubt a blend that makes the perfect man. England and America; we are kin. And now that we are also kin in sin, there is nothing more to be desired. The harmony is perfect – like Mr. Churchill himself . . ."[3] By "kin in sin," he meant that the United States should not have gone to war in the Philippines, nor Britain in South Africa. It appeared many Americans shared at least the latter part of his opinion. Some lively exchanges ensued. Moreover, Churchill found the advertisements for his performances crude and offensive. The same agency was responsible for his lectures in Canada, and at least one of them had to be cancelled after a squall of accusations and counterclaims. Nonetheless, he hoped that the tour in Canada would prove more congenial than that in the United States; with good reason, as it soon turned out.

* * *

The *Ottawa Journal*, December 24, 1900

Winston Spencer Churchill has a very distinctive style on the platform. Like all English speakers he takes a little time to warm up to his subject and when he first begins he has the air of being a little uncertain as to what he is going to say. His language and gestures are of the simplest character but as he proceeds the simplicity takes on the appearance of the most subtle art, the gestures are seen to be perfectly appropriate to the situation described, while the hesitating delivery becomes a means to effects which even veteran lecturers would be glad if they could imitate. In a quarter of an hour you find the address throbbing with the mingled humor and pathos of all battle experiences worthy of the name; in half an hour he gives you the impression, boy as he seems, of a keen and resourceful intelligence not only familiar with the ways of the world, but also able to hold his own in it, and then you want to hear him to the end. It is a cleverly managed narrative throughout, for the lecturer's own problem is to weave his personal experiences into a narrative of the South African campaign in such a way as to keep his audience interested. That he did this last night was abundantly shown by the running fire of laughter and applause which divided his story up into sections, like so many audible punctuation marks. The above is the analysis of the *Boston Herald* on Winston Churchill's style.

[The war was widely seen as a test of Great Britain's willingness to stand up for the rights of her own nationals, in this instance the Outlanders. This was one of the chief reasons why all the self-governing parts of the Empire sent contingents to South Africa. Canadian volunteers fought with toughness and distinction; four won the Victoria Cross, no fewer than nineteen the Distinguished Service Order and seventeen the Distinguished Conduct Medal. In French-speaking Canada, opposition to the war was widespread.

The British and Imperial forces in South Africa suffered heavy losses in battle and from disease. They found themselves fighting a kind of war for which their tactics and equipment often proved unsuitable; the enemy, often outnumbered by ten to one or more, proved elusive.]

The *Montreal Gazette*, December 24, 1900

"Thank God, we are once more on British soil". This was the fervent ejaculation uttered yesterday morning by Mr. Winston Spencer Churchill, M.P., as he alighted from the Boston train at the Windsor Station. The now famous war correspondent looked a good deal beyond twenty-six years of age, when he first stepped from the car, but when the young Imperialist laid aside his heavy coat and hard black hat his general youthful appearance was most pronounced. Mr. Churchill is a typical Britisher, and is somewhat reserved at the outset, but he thaws out immensely as the conversation proceeds and is cordial in the extreme thereafter. While waiting for the departure of the Ottawa train, he expressed the intense pleasure he felt in reaching Montreal, saying that he anticipated a most delightful sojourn here. This, he added, was his first visit to Canada.

"You ask for my political convictions. Well, I am a Tory democrat. I won Oldham which has 30,000 voters and we polled about 26,000 of this number.* The constituency, as you know, is in Lancashire, and my electors are exclusively working people."

Then the member for Oldham referred naturally to events in South Africa. He did not feel at all alarmed as far as the military situation was concerned, and he quite concurred in the policy of sending more troops to the front. He could not say it was true, as alleged, that Lord Kitchener† had applied for a large additional force, but he believed that there was wisdom in sending out all the commander-in-chief might require. As for the number of British troops in South Africa, Mr. Churchill said he did not suppose there were more than 150,000 available. However, he declared that the sooner the war was brought to a final close the sooner the Briton and Boer would get down to the working out of their destiny in the new colonies.

PEACE DESIRABLE

Peace was also to be desired on the ground that law and order would then prevail in Cape Colony. As long as the Transvaal and Cape Colony existed as republics, so long, Mr. Churchill said, did they appear to Cape Colony as the centre of Dutch influence in South Africa, and with this feeling ever prevalent in the public mind there was naturally a deal of unrest abroad all over the country.

"Will they secure self-government very soon?" he was asked.

"It is the Outlanders in the Transvaal who will secure self-government for this,

---

* Oldham was a constituency which returned two MPs. W.S.C. and his Conservative colleague, who was not elected, polled just under 25,000 votes between them.

† Horatio Herbert Kitchener (1850–1916), later 1st Earl Kitchener, Sirdar of the Egyptian Army from 1892 and in command at the battle of Omdurman, 1898; Chief of Staff in South Africa, 1899–1900, to Lord Roberts, whom he succeeded as Commander-in-Chief there; later Commander-in-Chief in India; Field Marshal, 1909; Secretary of State for War, 1914–16.

in fact, was the cause of the war.* As soon as matters settle down the British will be in a large majority in the Transvaal, and it will be one of the most loyal colonies of the Empire. The Orange River Colony, on the other hand, will remain Dutch, its resources being largely agricultural."

"What do you think of the statement that De Wet† had a large force and 18,000 horses?"

"It is impossible to form any idea, but I may say that I always have my doubts when I hear of many Boers being killed."

He was particularly pleased to have the opportunity of bearing testimony to the bravery and general excellence of the Canadian troops in the field. Mr. Churchill had seen them at work several times, and General Smith-Dorrien** had told him of the heroic attitude of the Canadian soldiers who administered the coup de grace to Cronje's army prior to the surrender at Paardeburg.†† "They need no eulogy from me," he continued, "and the assistance Canada and the other self-governing dependencies of the Empire have rendered during the war can never be overestimated. The fact that Canada has given the world to understand that she is one with the Imperial authorities in matters pertaining to the colonial empire has, more than anything else, driven the idea of intervention from the mind of the European powers."

THE ARMY REFORMS

Mr. Churchill was also questioned as to the alleged inefficiency of the army, as at present constituted, and he replied, by an energetic defence of the British officers in the field. He considered it monstrous to bring such charges, for is not the casualty list a proof of the officers' bravery and devotion. There may not be many Napoleons

---

* 100,000 people (more than 75,000 of whom were British) who had come to the Transvaal since 1886, when new and immensely rich goldfields were discovered near Johannesburg. They were not permitted voting or other civil rights. Their petition for redress, sent to Queen Victoria, was taken up by the British government in May 1899.

† Gen. Christian Rudolph De Wet (1854–1922), in command of a small force, took more than a thousand British prisoners at Nicholson's Nek at the end of October 1899. On the capture of Cronje at Paardeburg four months later, De Wet became Commander-in-Chief.

** Gen. Sir Horace Lockwood Smith-Dorrien (1858–1930), commanded a brigade, then a division, in South Africa, 1900–01; later Commander-in-Chief, Southern Command, 1912–14, 2nd Army Corps and then 2nd Army, 1914–15.

†† Gen. Piet Cronje (1835–1911), a valiant South African soldier, who had helped to defeat the Jameson Raid in 1896, surrendered to Roberts at Paardeburg on February 27, 1900, with some four thousand men, after the Canadian forces had advanced close to the Boers' position. Ladysmith was relieved the next day. Paardeburg fell nineteen years to the day after the defeat of the British forces at Majuba Hill.

amongst them, he stated, but they did their work in a manner which could not have been surpassed by any other army in Europe. The organisation of the army in South Africa, he claimed, was perfect, but pausing, the member for Oldham said: "There are many reforms to be operated. I am pledged to my constituents and there are a great many members of the present House in the same position, and we are expected to see that certain army reforms are carried out." . . .

Mr. Churchill left by the 9.30 train for Ottawa, where he will spend Christmas Day with Lord and Lady Minto* returning to Montreal on Wednesday.

The *Montreal Gazette*, December 27, 1900

The twelve hundred odd people who filled the Windsor Hall last night to hear Mr. Winston Churchill lecture on the South African war, were disappointed if they attended anticipating any new light on that all-absorbing subject. Mr. Churchill imparted very little information that anyone who followed the news of the campaign, as it progressed, was not already possessed of, but nevertheless his chat, rather than lecture, upon some of the dramatic episodes of the past year was quite entertaining, even if the information contained therein was somewhat meagre. Lord Randolph's son has a very taking way with him, and after the first few sentences of his talk, caught the sympathy and interest of his audience, and retained it throughout. His humorous asides and running comment were not the least effective of his methods, in attaining this result, and that he knows how to get into touch with his hearers was incontestably proven last evening. He had the backing on the platform of a large body of influential citizens, but it is safe to assume that while their presence was a courtesy the lecturer appreciated, he is a young gentleman quite able to play a lone hand, when there is any occasion for it. . . .

As usual in Montreal, the audience arrived very late, for it was not until twenty-five minutes to nine that the Mayor came forward and introduced the lecturer in a few well-chosen words, in which he dwelt upon the interest Canadians had in all matters pertaining to the Empire as a whole, such as the subject Mr. Churchill was about to discuss.

The latter lost no time beating about the bush, but plunged at once into a spirited description of the wrecking of the armored train, in which incident of the war he cut such a conspicuous figure. He illustrated his remarks by some very fine photographs, and the kernel of this portion of his address was that the idea of an armored

---

* Gilbert John Murray Kynynmond Elliot (1845–1914), 4th Earl of Minto, Governor General of Canada, 1898–1904; Viceroy of India, 1905–10.

train was a ridiculous one against an enemy like the Boers, who unchivalrously declined to be bound by the rules of the game, and were impolite enough to tear up the railway track on which it was operating. The audience may have been curious on the point, but Mr. Churchill did not see fit to make any reference to his own actions in that warm little skirmish, contenting himself with remarking that the Boers got him before he could get away.

His description of the aspect of the war balloon hanging over Ladysmith as the prisoners were being carried past the beleaguered town was a fine little word picture, as was also the racy little sketch of the arrival at Pretoria and the incidents of their detention. . . . The escape from the prison was a breezy bit, eliciting loud applause, also the difficulties experienced, and the relief he felt when after, hungry with a twenty-four hours' fast, he stumbled on the house of the solitary Britisher, manager of the coal mine, where he was hid until he could be smuggled through to Lorenzo Marques in a train load of wool.

The description of the terrible day and night of Spion Kop* was perhaps the most eloquent portion of Mr. Churchill's lecture, for the story of how Thorneycroft and his men grimly hung on to that fatal hilltop was a graphic bit of work indeed. Incidental to it he advanced a theory for the failure of the manoeuvres there to secure what they aimed at, the relief of Ladysmith, that was about the only bit of real, fresh information contained in his lecture. It was that the failure hinged on a very simple thing, which he said only exemplified the awful luck which seemed to dog the Natal field force. The engineer officers in locating the trenches on the hilltop, in the night, owing to the darkness, placed them back too far, instead of where they intended to, right on the brow of the hill. By an outline picture Mr. Churchill made it clear how, owing to this blunder, the Boers were able to keep under cover until they were close to the British trenches and snipe the defenders.

The *Ottawa Evening Journal*, December 28, 1900

Churchill is a tall, squarely built young man. He has the manner and appearance of an athlete. He is clean shaven and his face is rather youthful looking, though his general stature to some extent contradicts this idea. As a lecturer he is somewhat handicapped by a lisp. He does not indulge in the frills assumed by numerous lecturers. He evidently does not make any pretensions to oratory. He simply tells his story of the war in a chatty, conversational style. At times, however, when occasion

---

* In the battle to hold this exposed hill, the British forces lost well over a thousand men, killed, wounded, or captured.

offers he imparts a great deal of vigor to his delivery, giving an impression of that amplitude of energy and determination without which he could never have won the reputation he did in South Africa. He speaks with an English accent. Churchill has been ridiculed for his alleged egotism, and many who heard him last evening will agree that his critics were not without some justification.

He has self-confidence and self-reliance, but more than that, he has evidently no mean opinion of Mr. Churchill. His subject matter as well as a number of remarks indicated that.

He showed a little nervousness in opening his lecture [at the Russell Theatre, Ottawa]. When introduced he promptly walked forward, put his right arm akimbo, placed his left against a high desk beside which he stood and without a word of "local" introduction began what was apparently the stereotyped form of his lecture. In a short time, however, he became more at ease. The position beside the desk was Churchill's position during the greater part of the lecture. He did not make many gestures. He emphasized his remarks in the main by sharp movements of the head.

The lecture itself consisted of a brightly told summary of the Natal campaign, Churchill's capture and subsequent escape from Pretoria, and Roberts' sweep across the Free State and the Transvaal to Pretoria. There was no waste of words. He spoke in short, pointed sentences. He also imparted considerable humor, largely of a sarcastic tone to his remarks. His bright sallies kept the house in good humor.

[Churchill in later life was apt to date his acquaintance with W.L. Mackenzie King to 1907 or thereabouts. It is clear however that they met in 1900. King was exactly of an age with Churchill. He had recently returned from academic studies in the United States, after taking a first degree at the University of Toronto, and had begun his career as a civil servant in a tiny department. Even at that stage of his life, King might not have been wholly disbelieving if told that he would one day be Prime Minister of Canada, or Churchill to think that he might inhabit 10 Downing Street. Neither could have imagined in 1900 that King would serve as Prime Minister of Canada for more than twenty years, carefully calculating in the later stages how many more days he needed to survive in office in order to surpass Sir Robert Walpole's tenure in Britain two centuries before.

We know only that Mackenzie King went to call upon Churchill, whom he found drinking champagne in mid-morning, and that he attended W.S.C.'s lecture in Ottawa.]

The *Globe*, Toronto, December 31, 1900

"The War as I Saw It" was the title of the lecture delivered in Massey Hall on Saturday night by Mr. Winston Churchill, M.P., soldier, war correspondent and author. Every seat in the vast hall was occupied, every person present anticipated an enjoyable evening, and no one was disappointed. Mr. Churchill is an extremely young-looking man, with a boyish face, fine features and a good voice. Both in features and platform presence and action he resembles his father, the late Lord Randolph Churchill. . . .

Mr. Churchill said that during his tour in the United States he had often been asked, "When will the South African war end?" to which he had in turn asked, "When will the campaign in the Philippines be over?" His questioners would answer, "Just as soon as the Filipinos realize that we are there to stay, and that further resistance to our forces is useless." "And that", I answered, "is exactly the situation in South Africa."

Speaking of his arrival in South Africa, Mr. Churchill said that the situation in the Cape Colony at that time was dark and critical, much more dark and critical than it is to-day. There were few troops, and the Boers had a numerical preponderance. Now there were thousands of soldiers on the spot, and where the Boers were once numbered by the hundreds and tens of hundreds, they were now numbered by the fifties. In regard to the condition of affairs in Natal he pointed out that the army of 12,000 men, originally intended for the defence of that colony, was cooped up in Ladysmith, and all that lay between the Boers and the rest of the colony was a little garrison of not more than 2,000 men at Estcourt. It was the duty of this garrison to make itself appear as large as possible, in fact to play a game of "bluff". And so reconnoitring forces and reconnaissance parties were constantly moving about around the town, and every day "the ridiculous armored train" made its journey along the single line running to Colenso.

"But there came a day when we bluffed once too often," said Mr. Churchill, and then he told, in graphic language, the story of the armored train disaster, as a result of which he and number of others were captured and sent on to Pretoria.*

The action or series of actions resulting in the capture and abandonment of Spion Kop was vividly portrayed. By means of a large scale map Mr. Churchill showed the immense importance of Spion Kop to both armies. Personally he was

---

* The *Globe* had commented on November 20, 1899, that a strict interpretation of the laws of war would justify the Boers in executing W.S.C., whose acts though brave had been very rash; while it was hardly expected that Joubert would inflict this extreme penalty, General Buller would no doubt experience much difficulty in securing the young man's release. A month later the world learned that Churchill had not relied upon the General's intervention.

of the opinion that had General Warren's* force pushed right on after crossing the river the result would have been different. "But," he said, "we dawdled, and while we dawdled the Boers dug. Had we pushed on immediately along the stretch of country from Acton Homes to Spion Kop, we might, and I believe we would, have been successful, though at a heavy cost." The capture of Spion Kop, the all-day fight, the frightful casualty list of 1,200 killed and wounded out of 3,000 actually engaged in the struggle on the position, and the gallantry of Colonel Thorneycroft, his officers and men, were sketched in graphic language. But while repulsed, the Natal army did not despair. The abandonment of Spion Kop was not the darkest hour for them: the darkest hour came with the withdrawal from Vaal Krantz† a fortnight later. "Then, indeed," said Mr. Churchill, "we gave up hope, believing, as many no doubt believed throughout the empire, that the gallant garrison at Ladysmith would be starved into a surrender worse than death. But we had not reckoned upon the superb military genius of Lord Roberts** and the iron determination of Sir Redvers Buller.†† We had forgotten for the time being, though history should have taught us better, that the British soldier, though often repulsed, is always willing and ready to resume the attack and carry it out to a successful issue." Then came the report of the relief of Kimberley and the news of Lord Roberts' advance. Once more the Natal army, with faith in General Buller strong as ever, started out on the great struggle, with its fourteen days of continuous fighting around Picter's Hill, which resulted in clearing the road to Ladysmith on the anniversary of the defeat of the British at Majuba.

Mr. Churchill then joined General Ian Hamilton's*** column, which guarded the right flank of Lord Roberts' army, on the wonderful march to Pretoria. He dealt briefly with the work of the column, paying a compliment to Gen. Smith-Dorrien's

---

* Gen. Sir Charles Warren (1840–1927), archaeologist and soldier, commanded the 5th Division in South Africa, 1899–1900.

† The position, found to be untenable under bombardment from Boer artillery at Spion Kop and Doornkop, was abandoned on February 7, 1900.

** Frederick Sleigh Roberts, VC (1832–1914), later 1st Earl Roberts, Commander-in-Chief, India, 1885–93, Ireland, 1895–99, South Africa, 1899–1900, and of the British Army, 1900–04.

†† Gen. Sir Redvers Henry Buller, VC (1839–1908), Adjutant-General, 1890–7; in command in South Africa, 1899, until the arrival of Lord Roberts; and then in command of Natal Army until October 1900.

*** Gen. Sir Ian Standish Monteith Hamilton (1853–1947), whom W.S.C. first met in India; severely wounded at Majuba Hill, 1881; commanded a division in South Africa and Chief of Staff to Kitchener there, 1901–02; Commander-in-Chief, Southern Command, 1905–09; commanded the Allied forces in the Dardanelles, 1915; a close friend of W.S.C.

brigade, in which were the Royal Canadians. The entry into Pretoria and the review of the troops by Lord Roberts were described. "I marked," said Mr. Churchill, "the British flag flying above the Presidency and I said to myself, 'Please god it shall never be hauled down again.' But," he continued, "I do not want to see it remain there unless it means justice, equal rights and freedom to all."

The best blood of the empire, he said, had been poured out in South Africa, but not in vain. He considered it the sacred duty of the statesmen of the empire to carry their policy in regard to South Africa to a logical and triumphant conclusion. They had gone so far on the journey, would it not be well to continue to the end? He spoke next of the sacrifices made by Canada in the struggle. Canada had drawn her maiden sword in an honorable way and in a righteous cause, gaining thereby a dignity and standing which many years of commercial progress and advancement in the arts of peace might not have gained for her. He touched upon the admiration and respect felt throughout all the army for the Canadians, and by the Canadians for the Imperial army officers and men. He also spoke in closing in terms of praise of Generals Botha,* De Wet and the dead Joubert.† There was no feeling of rancor in the army against these men, a fact which, he thought, augured well for the future of the unhappy country.

At the conclusion of the address Hon. Mr. Mulock** moved a vote of thanks to Mr. Churchill. The more the lecturer became acquainted with Canada, said Mr. Mulock, the less he would be surprised at demonstrations such as had greeted him. Canada had a deep and personal interest in the conflict, and the people of the Dominion hoped, with Mr. Churchill, for a bright future for South Africa. Mr. Mulock spoke of Canadian confederation, the confederation of the Australasian colonies, and expressed the opinion that in a few short years there would doubtless be a confederation in South Africa. Then the world would witness a spectacle such as it had never seen before: three great outlying empires, composed of self-governing colonies, all recognising and paying allegiance to Great Britain, and all united to her by the common love for British institutions, freedom and justice.

---

* Gen. Louis Botha (1862–1919), Commandant-General, Transvaal, and Commander-in-Chief, Boer forces, 1900–02; Prime Minister of the Transvaal, 1907–10, and of the Union of South Africa, 1910–19.

† Gen. Piet Petrus Jacobus Joubert (1831–1900), victor at Majuba Hill and of several battles in the early weeks of the war in 1899.

** William Mulock (1844–1944), lawyer, Liberal politician; Postmaster General, 1896–1905, and Minister of Labour, 1900–05; brought W.L. Mackenzie King into public life; Chief Justice of Ontario, 1923–36; Chancellor of the University of Toronto, 1924–44; British Privy Councillor, 1925; knighted, 1902. On Sir William Mulock's 100th birthday, King (then Prime Minister) took breakfast with him in Toronto. They toasted each other in orangeade.

W.S.C. to his mother, January 1, 1901[4]

Toronto

The lecture tour is by no means the success I had expected, although here in Canada there is a great deal more interest than in the States. Pond's terms are vy grasping compared to Christie's* and he has been vy foolish in selling for fixed sums to local agents some of the best towns. For instance he sold Toronto for 500 dollars (£100) and the takings at the door amounted to near £450, out of which on his arrangement I got only £70. Naturally I protested against this sort of thing and we had a most unpleasant squabble. He is a vulgar Yankee impressario and poured a lot of very mendacious statements into the ears of the reporters and the whole business has been discussed in whole columns of all the papers. Peace has however, been patched up on my terms, and I propose to go through with the tour. I had magnificent audiences in Montreal, Ottawa, & Toronto and had great success with them, but did not benefit financially as I should have done, for the reason explained. Had I been able to foresee all this I would not have come but would have gone on with my tour in England which was more pleasant & far more profitable. However I shall remain till Feb 2 (when I sail) – making £50 a night clear and perhaps a little more.

I have spent 4 days at Ottawa with the Minto's which days were so pleasant that I shall go back again at the end of this week for 3 days more. Pamela† was there – very pretty and apparently quite happy. We had no painful discussions, but there is no doubt in my mind that she is the only woman I could ever live happily with. . . .

I am not in the best of spirits – chiefly because my tour has not come up to my expectations – but I am looking forward keenly to the Parliamentary Session. Cassel** made a speculation for me the other day which resulted in a profit of £187.10. He is vy kind and his judgement is marvellously accurate.

---

* Mr. G. Christie's agency had arranged W.S.C.'s lectures at home in the autumn of 1900; Maj. J.B. Pond did likewise for this visit to the United States and Canada.

† Pamela Plowden (1874–1971), whom W.S.C. had first met in India. In 1902, she married the Earl of Lytton. She and W.S.C. remained lifelong friends.

** Sir Ernest Cassel (1852–1921), a wealthy financier and philanthropist who had known Lord Randolph Churchill well. For many years Cassel advised W.S.C. about his investments.

I hope my dearest Mamma to be able to provide for myself in the future – at any rate until things are better with you. If you can arrange to relieve me of this loan, with the interest of which I am heavily burdened – £300 per annum – I will not ask for any allowance whatever from you . . .

But what a lucky thing it is that I did not remain in the army, for I could not have retained my commission in either cav[alry] or infantry under the circumstances.

I am vy proud of the fact that there is not one person in a million who at my age could have earned £10,000 without any capital in less than two years. But sometimes it is vy unpleasant work. For instance last week, I arrived to lecture in an American town & found Pond had not arranged any public lecture but that I was hired out for £40 to perform at an evening party in a private house – like a conjurer. Several times I have harangued in local theatres to almost empty benches. I have been horribly vulgarised by the odious advertisements Pond and Myrmidons think it necessary to circulate – and only my cynical vein has helped me to go on.

[Whatever the reason, Churchill's ambition to marry Pamela Plowden had now paled. Lord Minto reported to Lady Randolph that everything seemed platonic between the two young people; but, as he confessed disarmingly, "I am becoming so humdrum that it is difficult for me to imagine that anyone ever had any other feelings than those of Plato."]

W.S.C. to his mother, January 9, 1901[5]

Ottawa

I shall be home by the 10th of February and am looking forward very much to the beginning of Parliament. I think troublous times lie ahead and the government will have to display an unusual firmness and courage if they are to preserve the confidence and support of the country. I have come back to Ottawa for three more days, but leave again tonight, and I have only eighteen more lectures [all but one in the United States] so that the worst is over. I have got to hate the tour very much indeed, and if it were much longer I do not think I would be able to go through with it.

The *Winnipeg Free Press*, January 24, 1901

Winston Spencer Churchill, M.P., the now famous war correspondent of the London [Morning] Post, addressed Monday the largest and most representative audience ever gathered together in the Winnipeg theatre. . . .

Mr. Churchill prefaced his address by alluding to the serious illness of Her Majesty Queen Victoria and expressing his doubts as to the propriety of holding such a meeting when the empire to which we all belong was on the verge of such an impending calamity. He then read the latest bulletin concerning the Queen's condition which indicated that there was a slight improvement.

The lecturer opened up his subject with a narration in an easy and colloquial style of the earlier events of the war which transpired after his arrival on the scene of action as the correspondent of the Morning Post. The operations from Estcourt by the famous armored train, which ultimately came to grief by venturing too far from home, his own capture and trip to Pretoria as a prisoner were then rapidly narrated. Reports of the war received in Winnipeg both then and now were apt to be colored somewhat on account of the channel through which they came. There was now, we may rest assured, no cause for alarm with Lord Roberts at the war office, Lord Kitchener at the war and the British army on the scene of action.

Several views of South African typical scenes and individuals were then thrown upon a screen, the first being a map of South Africa.

"Look closely at this," said Mr. Churchill. "It is a map of South Africa. It belongs to us."

This remark called for a regular storm of applause. Other pictures of Boer artillery and Boer men were then shown, accompanied by humorous comments from the speaker. The audience here began to feel that there was a vein of wit and originality in the speaker of an uncommon order and hung on his every word with closest attention. At one point early in his narration he stopped and remarked apologetically: "But I have told you all this story in a book* which it would be unbecoming for me to recommend or advertise here, but I earnestly hope each one of you will procure it and read it." . . .

Mr. Churchill related the story of his escape after showing a picture of the arrival of the group of prisoners to which he belonged at Pretoria. They were sent for safe keeping to the state Normal school, where almost the only break in the routine of life was a bottle of whiskey, smuggled in to them in the coat-tail pocket of the secretary

---

* Either *London to Ladysmith via Pretoria* (published in May 1900) or *Ian Hamilton's March* (October 1900).

of state. The officers much appreciated this – not the whiskey – the kindness of the secretary. Mr. Churchill then related the story of his escape, a narrative which proved of absorbing interest. On the evening of Dec. 12, 1899, he climbed over the garden wall of the Normal school while the secretary was lighting his pipe. He suffered one moment of intense anxiety when his clothes became caught in the ornamental work on top of the fence. He found his way to the railway track and stowed himself away in a freight car on the first train which went out. The train was evidently bound for some colliery as the freight was all addressed to the same place. He concluded that it would not be wise for him to visit the colliery and when some distance from Pretoria jumped off the train as it was running slowly around a curve. A wood near by afforded him shelter during the day, which he spent with nothing to eat but a chocolate. As he found this as a diet neither sufficiently varied nor liberal he concluded to try and board another train that night, but in this he was unsuccessful. After walking many hours in search of a Kaffir kraal he finally reached a dwelling, in which he decided to try and find food and lodging. When he obtained admission he found himself in the presence of the manager of the coal mine.

"I was riding on a train," explained Mr. Churchill, "when I was accidentally thrown off and hurt my shoulder very badly. I have lain on the ground unconscious for several hours and have come here for help and food. I am very hungry indeed." When his host had supplied him with food he looked steadfastly at his visitor and said, "I don't quite understand how you came to fall off that train."

At this Mr. Churchill decided to tell him all and answered, "I am Churchill, I have escaped from Pretoria, and if you will assist me to get to Delagoa Bay you will be handsomely rewarded. Money is no object."

At this his host turned and locked the door and pulled down the window blinds. "An action," commented Mr. Churchill, "not very reassuring to me." "Thank God you came here," were the words of his host, "I am your friend, but there is not another house for miles around where you would not have been taken prisoner if they saw you."

The lecturer then described how the manager hid him away for four and a half days in the bottom of a coal mine which was not being worked.*

"My only companions," continued the speaker "were numbers of white rats with pink eyes. However, I was furnished every morning with copies of Boer newspapers in which I read accounts of my own capture in different disguises each day. The Boers have been reputed to be an uncivilised lot, but in the respect of intelligent

---

* The manager, Mr. Howard, provided two chickens and a revolver. The chickens did not last long; the revolver did, for W.S.C. returned it in 1901 as a token of gratitude in an ebony box, together with a brandy flask. In 2002, the revolver fetched £32,000 at auction in London.

anticipation and fertile imagination I can say as a journalist that their newspapers are the equal of anything in the civilized world."

The speaker then told how he was placed on a train bound for Delagoa Bay in a car loaded with wool. On his safe arrival there he soon took passage on a vessel for Durban, and arrived in the British camp [at Chieveley, near Pietermaritzburg] in time to eat his Christmas dinner with Sir Redvers Buller. . . .

"Canada's part in the war has not been taken in vain, apart from the fact that the prestige of the empire has been sustained. Through her soldiers in Africa she has won for herself a dignity and a name among nations which otherwise she might not have attained in many years. There is, moreover, a sense of unity throughout the empire to-day, a common feeling between the rancher of the Alberta plains with the English farmer, that each belongs to the great British empire and the empire belongs to him. The quarrel of a hundred years has been fought out at last, and let us hope that the time is not far distant when the Union Jack will wave over a free and united South Africa."

In thanking the audience for their liberal applause and attention, Mr. Churchill said that he had been much impressed with the growth and prospects of this great city. Placed here by itself, hundreds of miles from any other city, it was distinctively the product of the great and fertile west. "The Canadian west is Britain's bread shop," continued the speaker "and when I go back I shall tell the electors of my constituency that I have spoken to those who supply them with their bread.

"I don't know why people who live in Winnipeg should call themselves Winnipeggers," he added. "I think a far more simple and appropriate name would be 'Winners.'"

This remark called for considerable laughter and applause.

W.S.C. to his mother, January 22, 1901[6]

Winnipeg

So the Queen is dead. The news reached us at Winnipeg and this city far away among the snows – fourteen hundred miles from any British town of importance – began to hang its head and hoist half-masted flags. A great and solemn event: but I am curious to know about the King. Will it entirely revolutionise his way of life? Will he sell his horses and scatter his Jews or will Reuben Sassoon* be enshrined among the crown jewels

* Reuben Sassoon (1835–1905), Jewish philanthropist and friend of the Prince of Wales.

and other regalia? Will he become desperately serious. Will he continue to be friendly to you? Will the Keppel* be appointed 1st Lady of the Bedchamber? . . .

I have had a most successful meeting at Winnipeg. Fancy 20 years ago there were only a few mud huts – tents: and last night a magnificent audience of men in evening dress & ladies half out of it, filled a fine opera house and we took $1150 at the doors. £230: more that is to say than in cities like Newcastle. Winnipeg has a wonderful future before it. At the back of the town there is a large wheat field 980 miles long & 230 broad – not all cultivated yet, but which will some [day] feed the whole of the British Isles. I called the town "Great Britain's Breadshop"; at which they purred. They are furiously British and a visit to them is most exhilarating.

The *Winnipeg Evening Tribune*, August 19, 1929

MR. CHURCHILL

BY W.J. HEALY†

For all his boyishness of face and figure and his restless cocksureness of manner as he faced the audience [on his visit to Winnipeg in January 1901], with a slender stick in his hand to use as a pointer in explaining the lantern slides, that young man of twenty-six, who looked younger, had already begun to succeed brilliantly in making himself a celebrated person. . . .

Before the curtain went up the lecturer looked through the peephole in it, and speaking to the manager of the theatre, who stood at his elbow, asked him for his estimate of the of the sum of money "in the house". To the present writer, standing in the wings, a Winnipeg lawyer and leading citizen who was next to him expressed disappointment on hearing the lecturer thus openly show his interest in the yield of cash to be reaped from the lecture. He had been looking at the lecturer through a glamor which surrounded him as Lord Randolph Churchill's son and grandson of the seventh Duke of Marlborough, the enchanting glamor of the Blenheim Palace background; but young Mr. Winston Churchill himself, though a romantically glamorous figure in that Winnipeg man's eyes, was realist enough to be above wanting to pretend that he did not want to get an idea of the amount of money gathered in the box office for the evening's performance. . . .

---

* Mrs. George Keppel (née Alice Elphinstone) (1869–1947), mistress of the new King.

† W.J. Healy (1867–1950), chief associate editor, *Winnipeg Free Press*, 1899–1918.

Mr. Churchill was in Winnipeg only for a day and a night. During the afternoon of his stay here he went to the Hudson's Bay Company's store and bought himself a coon coat, which he was wearing as he stood on the rear platform of the train for St. Paul next morning, waving good-bye to Winnipeg.

* * *

Lady Randolph Churchill liked to spend all the money readily to hand, and was not always averse to spending money still in prospect. These and other characteristics she shared with her elder son. When he reached England in mid-February 1901, he immediately sent his mother the sum of £300, with a charming and revealing note: "In a certain sense it belongs to you; for I could never have earned it had you not transmitted to me the wit and energy which are necessary."[7]

His recent books about the wars in the valley of the Nile and South Africa had sold well; his salary from the *Morning Post* had been substantial; to the profits of his lectures at home we must add about £1,600 from the United States and Canada. These were the main ingredients of the £10,000 of which Churchill had written to her on New Year's Day. He was entitled to be proud of this achievement, and we need not dispute his assertion that not one person in a million, starting without any capital, could at his age have earned such a sum in less than two years. Thus Churchill became independent as to money, and free to work at nothing but politics. He tells us that he handed the £10,000 to Sir Ernest Cassel with the instruction "Feed my sheep." This Sir Ernest did with prudence. The sheep did not multiply fast, but at least they fattened and indeed produced a few lambs. Churchill devoured the latter, and from time to time ate one or two of the sheep. In a few years, he had consumed most of the capital as well as the interest.[8] They were however the vital years, when he found his feet in Parliament and on the platform. By the standards of the political grandees, he was far from well off. All the same, he had a sufficiency and felt no inclination or need to economize unduly. Nor does he ever seem to have doubted that by exercise of his pen he could earn the substantial sums which his tastes for travel and good living required. As he used to remark, "I am easily satisfied with the very best."[9]

2

"Your Wonderful Canada": 1929

CHURCHILL'S FORECAST of "troublous times ahead" for the government was promptly confirmed. He took a prominent part in Parliament, spoke much at public meetings and found himself increasingly disenchanted with the Conservative Party. When the Boer War dragged to its conclusion in the summer of 1902, Lord Salisbury resigned as Prime Minister and was succeeded by his nephew Arthur Balfour, with whom Churchill had many lively jousts over the years but whose intellect and standards he admired. In the following year, Joseph Chamberlain left the government and campaigned for a policy of tariffs and protection, with preferences which he hoped would help both the cohesion and the economies of the Empire. By contrast, Churchill proclaimed in a pure form the doctrine of free trade that had long held sway in nineteenth-century England. He crossed the floor of the House of Commons in 1904 and joined the Liberal Party.

When Balfour's government resigned in December 1905, Churchill became, at the age of thirty-one, Under-Secretary of State for the Colonies and little more than two years later entered the Cabinet of H.H. Asquith as President of the Board of Trade. There, and as Home Secretary, he showed himself zealous for social reform, hostile to large expenditure on the Navy (in which attitude, as he later had the grace to admit, he was badly mistaken), and a doughty champion of the Commons against the House of Lords. No one assailed his former Conservative colleagues more wittily or trenchantly. Churchill had himself the great merit of not resenting hard blows received in Parliament or on the platform. Certainly he delivered enough of his own, and it is unlikely that he ever understood how deeply they were resented. Violent verbal swordplay was to him a natural recreation, to be forgotten within an hour or a day. Those more reticent by upbringing and less ready with words found his assaults wounding or offensive.

Even in that Cabinet of high talent, Churchill shone. The faculties and characteristics which distinguished his long career were already apparent: unwearying industry; a capacity to master sheaves of material, evidenced by his weighty biography of Lord Randolph Churchill; fertility of imagination, which manifested itself in numerous suggestions and schemes, not always confined to the affairs of his own office and not always practical (a colleague in a later administration remarked, "He laid eggs as rapidly as a partridge & if his nest was disturbed quickly started another, but the proportion of his eggs which came to maturity was small")[1]; a physical zest as abounding as his mental energy; genius in ambush of the unexpected word; vigour in pursuing the interests of his department and a readiness to take on the colour of his surroundings; skill in the division of his time and a capacity to concentrate unrelentingly upon the business in hand; efficiency in administration.

The Prime Minister had enjoyed a career of academic triumphs at Oxford and legal ones at the Bar, whereas Churchill might with justice have described himself as being educated in the school holidays and the hot afternoons of India. Asquith was deeply read in the Classics, stubborn resistance to which had been a marked feature of Churchill's schooldays, and in modern literature, of which his colleague knew little. While Churchill had to prepare public speeches laboriously and commit them to that wonderful memory, the Prime Minister could speak with distinction at a moment's notice. Though sometimes irritated by Churchill's incursions, or mildly amused by his schoolboy enthusiasms, Asquith advanced him to posts of the highest responsibility. This fact Churchill later ascribed not so much to any good impression produced by conversation or speeches as to his confidential writings about the affairs of state, for a carefully marshalled argument would often command Asquith's decisive support. "One felt that the case was submitted to a high tribunal, and that repetition, verbiage, rhetoric, false argument, would be impassively but inexorably put aside."[2]

The two were much thrown together in Parliament. Once, when the leader of the Opposition was speaking, Churchill fumed and said that he wished he had the ability to answer him; this, Asquith said with amusement, was the only modest remark he had heard Churchill utter. On another occasion, Churchill in presenting the Naval Estimates for 1913 delivered a magnificent speech, which Asquith said no one but he could have made.[3] To Asquith's daughter Violet, Churchill spoke in a cascade of spontaneous eloquence about the shortness of human life before declaring memorably, "We are all worms. But I do believe that I am a glow-worm."[4]

Here to all outward appearances was a man of abundant talent and exuberant energy, sure – in the eyes of many, all too sure – of his powers. Nowadays we know, as his contemporaries could not, of hesitations and self-doubt then concealed. Pamela Plowden, with whom he had spent those pleasant few days at Ottawa in 1900, had married the Earl of Lytton a couple of years later. She remained a friend of Churchill, of whom she said affectionately, "The first time you meet Winston you see all his faults, and the rest of your life you spend in discovering his virtues."[5] Some years later, he fell helplessly in love with Clementine Hozier, beautiful, slim, staunchly Liberal, independent of mind. Soon she was invited to Blenheim. The Duke of Marlborough, Winston Churchill explained to Miss Hozier, "is quite different from me, understanding women thoroughly, getting into touch with them at once. . . . Whereas I am stupid and clumsy in that relation, and naturally quite self-reliant and self-contained."[6]

They walked in the Rose Garden, for which assignation Miss Hozier arrived punctually and her husband-to-be did not. This was entirely characteristic of both; a year or two later, when Clementine said she was sure her husband would be late at the station, his Private Secretary replied, "Winston is such a sportsman, he always gives the train a chance to get away."[7]

To his future mother-in-law, Churchill wrote endearingly, "I am not rich nor powerfully established, but your daughter loves me & with that love I feel strong enough to assume this great & sacred responsibility; & I think I can make her happy & give her a station & career worthy of her beauty and her virtues."[8] The Prime Minister and his daughter received news of the engagement with apprehension or even disdain. Asquith apparently thought the marriage would spell disaster for both parties, while she remarked, "His wife could never be more to him than an ornamental sideboard as I have often said & she is unexacting enough not to mind not being more."[9] These judgments were comprehensively mistaken, as Violet Asquith soon recognized.

In 1911, Churchill became First Lord of the Admiralty, where in his usual style he absorbed himself in the administration and put every part of British naval policy on the anvil. His previous declarations in favour of economy were rapidly abandoned and indeed reversed; to his opponents a proof of inconsistency, to his defenders a timely recognition of increasing danger. The Royal Navy had by far the most powerful fleet afloat, a position which Churchill was determined to maintain and perhaps even improve upon. Some of his tussles with the Chancellor of the Exchequer, Lloyd George, were of an heroic nature and required political courage of a high order.

A good deal, much of it exaggerated, has been written about Churchill's spells of depression. While he was Prime Minister during the Second World War, when there was more than enough cause for depression, he exuded determination and confidence. Yet there had been a time in his earlier life when, as he expressed it, "the light faded out of the picture." This phase seems to have lasted two or three years and to have coincided in part with Churchill's tenure of the Home Office, where he hated the duty of deciding whether executions should proceed. When worried, he wrote down the main causes of concern, a technique which he always recommended to friends and colleagues. Once the list was made, it would be found that concerning two or three troubles nothing could be done anyway; perhaps two more were trivial; and attention could then be concentrated upon the two remaining.

Lord Beaverbrook once said that there were two Churchills, "Churchill Up and Churchill Down."[10] It helped, Churchill remarked long after, to talk to his wife about these phases of depression, and, as we now see, to write to her when they were separated:

"You know so much about me, & with your intuition have measured the good & bad in my nature. Alas I have no good opinion of myself. At times, I think I cd conquer everything – & then again I know I am only a weak vain fool. But your love for me is the greatest glory & recognition that has or will ever befall me: the attachment wh I feel towards you is not capable of being altered by the sort of things that happen in this world. I only wish I were more worthy of you & more able to meet the inner needs of your soul." "I am so much centred in my politics, that I often feel I must be a dull companion, to anyone who is not in the trade too. It gives me so much joy to make you happy – & [I] often wish I were more various in my topics. Still the best is to be true to oneself – unless you happen to have a vy tiresome self!" "I was stupid last night – but you know what a prey I am to nerves and pre-possessions. . . . I have no one but you to break the loneliness of a bustling and bustled existence." Or again, many years later, "of course I feel far safer from worry and depression when you are with me & when I can confide in yr sweet soul. . . . You are a rock & I depend on you & rest on you. Come back to me therefore as soon as you can."[11]

* * *

Churchill spoke from time to time on Canadian subjects, and renewed acquaintance in London with Mackenzie King. As First Lord of the Admiralty, he negotiated with Robert Borden, successor to Laurier as Prime Minister in Ottawa, whose government had offered to pay for three Dreadnoughts; the burden of Imperial defence weighing heavily upon the British, this prospect was most welcome. It was proposed that Churchill should visit Canada to complete the negotiations; then domestic difficulties there became apparent and the plan eventually failed in the late spring of 1913. The British naval estimates for 1914–15 were accordingly increased, and the building of two of the larger battleships was accelerated. When the crisis came in the summer of 1914, the Royal Navy was ready and powerful. Churchill deserves a good deal of the credit for that fact. He was at once appalled and exhilarated by the clash of arms. Some thought and said, at the time and afterwards, that he "enjoyed war." There was truth in that, but not the whole truth. Mackenzie King's diary for November 19, 1914, is near the mark: "I think there can be no doubt Churchill was glad to be a war [as against neutrality] Minister & wd. favour war, but he could never precipitate it."[12]

What he did desire most ardently was to abbreviate it. The first few months on the Western Front brought dreadful casualties for little gain. Churchill hoped that by naval and military action in the Near East it would be possible at once to defeat Turkey, help Russia, and undermine Austria-Hungary; hence Gallipoli and the Dardanelles. Much went awry, including Churchill's relations with the First Sea Lord, Admiral Fisher. What had been intended as an operation by land and naval forces became fragmented, and Churchill took the risk of persuading his colleagues that a strong naval force alone might prevail. While the outcome was uncertain, he said one night to Violet Asquith, herself a friendly witness, "I think a curse should rest on me – because I love this war. I know it's smashing &

shattering the lives of thousands every moment – & yet – I can't help it – I enjoy every second of it."[13]

Fisher resigned amidst recriminations. Churchill had not realized the inwardness of this situation; he was often too self-absorbed to take the measure of those with whom he had to work and liked to follow the principle of putting his faith in people unless he had good reason to do otherwise. "Poor Winston – there is a very naïve disarming trustfulness about him – he is quite insensitive to climatic conditions"; thus Miss Asquith at the height of the crisis.[14]

Her father felt that he must form a coalition government. The incoming Conservative members insisted that Churchill go from the Admiralty, chiefly, no doubt, because the Gallipoli enterprise had become bogged down at heavy cost and partly perhaps because his change of party and vehement assaults upon former colleagues had not been forgiven. Ejected from the Admiralty but still a minister, Churchill found himself well-informed but impotent as the Dardanelles enterprise failed. At the end of that year, 1915, he left the government and went to the front in France. There he experienced again physical danger, admired the unflinching fortitude of the soldiers and found an unexpected contentment. He confided to his wife:

> So much effort, so many years of ceaseless fighting & worry, so much excitement & now this rough fierce life here under the hammer of Thor, makes my older mind turn – for the first time I think to other things than action.... Sometimes also I think I wd not mind stopping living vy much – I am so devoured by egoism that I wd like to have another soul in another world & meet you in another setting, & pay you all the love & honour of the gt romances.[15]

When he set off for the war, he was leaving behind a political career apparently in ruins, a wife a good deal younger than himself, and three small children. "Above all don't be worried about me," he wrote to her. "If my destiny has not already been accomplished, I shall be guarded surely."[16] Churchill left the army in May 1916 and returned to London. The war continued unabated, at a frightful cost to each belligerent; Lloyd George replaced Asquith at the end of 1916, and a detailed inquiry into the Dardanelles expedition restored a good deal of Churchill's reputation. Resuming office in July 1917, he displayed his usual grasp as Minister of Munitions, collaborated fruitfully with colleagues in the United States, which had by then entered the war, saw at first-hand how near the Germans came to success in 1918 and did his utmost to ensure that the Allied armies were provided with the sinews of victory.

The six frustrated months which Churchill spent as a minister after he left the Admiralty in the spring of 1915 had convinced him that the separation of power from responsibility is, at any rate at the higher levels of government, a sure recipe for bad blood and bad decisions. As Prime Minister a generation later, he showed no enthusiasm for a War Cabinet the members of which would be free of departmental responsibilities and thus able to indulge in exalted brooding about the affairs of others. He had learned, so painfully that his wife once said she thought he would die of grief, that to attempt an enterprise of great moment from a subordinate position is perilous or even foolhardy. Interested though not instructed in applied science, ingenious and always searching for new weapons, he did a good deal to encourage the development of the tank; and he saw the amateur politicians, astonishingly, proved right in their insistence that the professionals at the Admiralty must adopt a thorough-going convoy system to reduce the immense damage which German submarines were inflicting. Here too was a lesson that he did not forget.

His wife's dignified demeanour in adversity and wholehearted belief in his star, his delight in the company of their children, had provided him with a solid rock upon which to stand; and in those months of distress after his departure from the Admiralty, he had taught himself to paint, and soon to paint well. He was always modest about his accomplishments as an artist. "I never had any real lessons, you know," he would say. Painting became the most enduring recreation of his adult life. He realized that even those who, like himself, are wholly absorbed in their daily work need a means of diversion, and came to associate painting with sunshine and holidays, a change of scene, conversation and conviviality of an evening after the light had faded. He loved the bright colours and recognized with pleasure that this new pastime brought him an intense appreciation of landscape and buildings. Friends noticed with some surprise that while at the easel he remained silent.

In 1919, there being no longer any need of a Ministry of Munitions, Churchill became Secretary of State for War and Air, and in 1921 Secretary of State for the Colonies. Those few years after the war proved a time of mixed fortunes. Churchill tried to strangle at birth the new regime in

Russia or, as he called it with rhetorical flourish, "the foul baboonery of Bolshevism." His colleagues in the Cabinet, weary of warfare, heavily oppressed by debt, doubtful of the whole enterprise, dissented. The Irish troubles were resolved in part by a treaty in which Churchill played a substantial part. A welter of claims and counterclaims in the Middle East caused him to convene a conference in Cairo. When Mrs. Churchill accompanied him on a visit to the Pyramids, he fell off his camel. "How easily are the mighty fallen," she said. Her husband, offered a horse, replied with finality, "I started on a camel and I shall finish on a camel."[17] Some of the consequences of the settlement there endure to this day. It is unlikely that a better one could have been made, and no one could have reconciled all the claims or met all the grievances. Churchill had always supported the Balfour Declaration, looking to the establishment of a Jewish homeland, and returned with that conviction reinforced. He remained a convinced Zionist for the rest of his life.

* * *

The young man who heard Churchill speak in Ottawa at Christmas 1900 had by now become leader of the Liberal Party and Prime Minister in Canada. Mackenzie King's diary for September 17, 1922, records that he reached Ottawa that morning by train. A cable from Churchill was brought to him in the railway carriage. An acute crisis had blown up suddenly in the Near East. A victorious Turkish army, under command of the dashing soldier Ataturk, who had helped to defeat the Allied forces in 1915, had reached the Dardanelles and confronted the small British force still stationed there. On behalf of the Cabinet in London, Churchill suggested that the Dominions might send contingents of troops. Alas, a communiqué had been issued in London before the Prime Ministers in the Dominions had received the telegram.

Churchill had thought that because of the immense sacrifices made by Australia and New Zealand at the Dardanelles in 1915, the offer of military contingents from them would carry special weight; and the messages sent to Canada and South Africa were identical with those despatched to the two Pacific Dominions. He soon recognized that the handling of all this might have been a good deal better.

Mackenzie King replied promptly that no contingent would go from Canada without the summoning of Parliament. New Zealand and Newfoundland (then not part of Canada) did indeed offer to send troops. The Prime Minister of Canada was correct in judging that the Turks would climb down before long, and mistaken in believing that the whole business was mostly an election manoeuvre by Lloyd George and his colleagues. The crisis lasted for several weeks. When King received a message from London early in October, which suggested that Constantinople might soon be the scene of massacre and pillage on a huge scale, he recorded: "It is a serious business having matters in [the] hand of a man like Churchill – the fate of an Empire! I am sure we have done right & aided the cause of peace by holding back."[18]

In the event, war did not break out; but it had been a close-run thing, and the fissures in Britain's coalition government widened. It depended upon Conservative support, which was largely withdrawn in October. Lloyd George resigned, and a general election followed. At the crucial moment, Churchill was taken ill with appendicitis. He was able to go to his constituency only a few days before the poll and, after violent scenes at his election meetings, was defeated by a large majority. The Conservatives under Bonar Law took office; and Churchill observed ruefully that he found himself without an office, without a seat, without a party and without an appendix. The Liberals suffered from acute internal dissensions. For the better part of two years, Churchill lacked a parliamentary seat; he stood as a "Liberal Free Trader" in 1923 and lost, and early in the following year as an "Independent anti-Socialist" but was defeated by the tiniest of margins. Stanley Baldwin had become leader of the Conservative Party and Prime Minister in 1923. He lost office in that autumn, but returned a year later, having abandoned for the moment a policy of protection and tariffs. This opened up new possibilities and enabled Churchill, still a devoted free trader but a strong opponent of Socialism, to find a place within the Conservative ranks. He was adopted for a safe seat in the autumn of 1924 but had not even rejoined the party formally when to the general amazement (not least his own) he was appointed Chancellor of the Exchequer.

Few read the news with greater surprise than the Prime Minister of Canada, who had been told by Baldwin in the previous year that Lloyd George, Churchill and Lord Birkenhead were "the three most dangerous men in the Empire"[19]; and now Birkenhead was Secretary of State for India, and Churchill at the Treasury. There he spent the better part of five years. His tenure is perhaps best remembered for Great Britain's return to the Gold Standard in 1925, a step taken with many misgivings but firmly supported by the Bank of England and most orthodox opinion. Britain's debts were enormous, in consequence of the war. International trade, upon which Britain depended more than any other great power, was already severely disturbed. Making only minor exceptions, Churchill adhered to the practices of free trade, and the government was in any event obliged by its election promises not to tax imports of food. Though the margin for manoeuvre was small, major reforms were undertaken in the fields of pensions, medical services, local government and much else; most of this was made possible by collaboration between Churchill and the Minister of Health, Neville Chamberlain. Churchill rationed the spending of the armed services strictly; those services worked on the rule, rolling forward until countermanded, that the British Empire would not be engaged in war with a first-class enemy for at least the next ten years. At the time, this belief was shared by most and certainly by Churchill, who was soon to justify it with vigour to Canadian audiences.

Unemployment remained obstinately high, especially in the old staple industries; many of their export markets had gone beyond retrieval. Baldwin set himself and the government the task of seeking a measure of peace and good feeling at home. When the process was interrupted by the General Strike in the spring of 1926, Churchill stood out for a stiff attitude until the strike itself could be broken. While his attitude was in substance that of all the members of the Cabinet, his expression of it lacked nothing in vigour. Many in the trades unions and Labour Party already regarded him as an enemy, and now found that opinion confirmed. Though the General Strike itself turned out to be no more than a ten days' wonder, the bitter dispute in the mining industry continued for many months. If the economic damage was great, the political and social harm lasted longer.

On the declaration of the Strike, Mackenzie King had recorded that "for Churchill I feel a scorn too great for words. He has been the evil genius in this." But that was far too harsh a judgment, as King himself probably recognized; and in the autumn of that year, when the Prime Minister of Canada was in London for the Imperial Conference which declared that the Dominions were wholly autonomous and in no way subordinate, Churchill said how pleased he was with Baldwin's support; no other man would have taken him into the Cabinet without knowing him and the Prime Minister "thought things out carefully and was sound and safe in his judgement." These harmonious relations lasted more or less intact for several years. As for his own methods of administration, Churchill explained to King in the same conversation, "It is all done for me by excellent men; I seldom write a letter; a man at the head of a department should have a clean desk and have time to think; this was impossible if there was much correspondence to be attended to."[20]

That description would have caused some skepticism among his leading colleagues, whom he addressed on a wide variety of subjects in his inimitable style. When every allowance is made for Churchill's capacity to delegate, and his own wholly exceptional powers of concentration, we may still marvel at the scale and excellence of his literary output. In 1923–24, when he was not in Parliament, his earnings reached the figure of £16,448.[21] This might equate in today's money to £400,000 or more. Once he took office, such a feat could not be repeated. All the same, he continued to write about the war, placing his own tumultuous experiences in a wider setting. By the spring of 1929, no less than five volumes of *The World Crisis* had been published. The last had taken less than a year; and although it is true that Churchill had good help, the essence of the work was unmistakably his. "I am immersed," wrote the aged Lord Balfour, "in Winston's brilliant Autobiography, disguised as a history of the universe."[22] This is perhaps Churchill's best large work of literature, less partisan than *Marlborough*, more tightly written than *The Second World War*; it is not "history," in the sense of assembling documents from all quarters, balancing and appraising. Nor could it be; for the events described were recent, and much of the raw material long remained unknown. However, it is a contribution to history of the first water; generous in most of its judgments, not afraid to place events on a scale of importance and individuals on a scale of merit, and full of the insights which, since human understanding is almost always limited by experience, come to those who see great affairs at first-hand and have the brains to understand what they have witnessed.

Churchill's thoughts now turned again toward the biography of John Churchill; in the political world, everything depended upon the outcome of the general election held at the end of May 1929. Baldwin's government was defeated by a middling margin; the Labour Party was now the largest in Parliament, though it still depended upon Liberal votes for a majority; and Ramsay MacDonald duly replaced Baldwin as Prime Minister. Churchill began work at once on *Marlborough*. He signed contracts to write articles at handsome rates. In short, he intended to recruit his fortunes by writing, a process more necessary than ever because he had a growing family and, after 1922, an expensive new possession. The death of a distant cousin had brought Churchill a substantial legacy, which enabled him to buy a country house of his own. He had fallen in love with Chartwell Manor in Kent, near enough to London but far removed from all the bustle of the city. The place cost a small fortune to rebuild and run. Mrs. Churchill feared the financial burden, with good reason, whereas her husband remained confident that with pen and tongue he could keep the family in style.

Nearly five years at the Treasury would have taxed the energies of any minister. Britain's burdens, the pressure for economy, the industrial dislocation, the desire for expensive new strokes of policy, all were great. With hindsight, Churchill might have thought himself fortunate in the moment of his departure, since the Labour government was shortly to encounter conditions far worse than those which had afflicted the Conservatives. He wasted no time in pointless regrets. "What fun it is to get away from England," he wrote to Lord Beaverbrook, "and feel one has no responsibility for her exceedingly tiresome and embarrassing affairs."[23]

He generously agreed to give a series of speeches without fee in Canada. Almost thirty years had passed since the lectures about Spion Kop, Mafeking, and his escape from Pretoria. Here was a new opportunity to see a country that had grown in population, stature and confidence, and rallied nobly to the Allied cause in the war. He could then, given the long parliamentary recess and the electorate's decision, travel back through the United States. What was more, this would be a family expedition; Churchill and his much-loved brother Jack, with their undergraduate sons Randolph and Johnnie, left Southampton on August 3.

* * *

W.S.C. to his wife, August 3, 1929[24]

Canadian Pacific
Empress of Australia

My darling one,
It was not without some melancholy twinges that I watched the figures of Diana & Sarah* disappearing on the quay. All departures from home even

---

* The Churchills' two elder daughters, born in 1909 and 1914 respectively.

on pleasure are sad. The vessel drifts away from the shore & an ever-widening gulf opens between one and the citadel of ones life & soul. But most of all I was distressed to think of you being lonely & unhappy & left behind. . . .*

We are plodding across a calm Channel & this goes to you from Cherbourg. I expect to do a lot of work – Certainly 2 articles before landing: & to read copiously into Marlbor.

I think of you at each hour, where you will be & how you will look. I long to see you smiling & sedate – taking things coolly & gathering strength. Send me a wireless to mid-ocean to tell me how you are getting on.

With tender love

Your devoted

xxxxx W.

W.S.C. to his wife, August 8, 1929[25]

Empress of Australia
Rimouski

My darling,

We have had a wonderfully good passage with only one day of unpleasant motion. The ship is comfortable and well-found, and we have splendid cabins. We have just passed the Straits of Belle Isle, and tomorrow night will arrive at Quebec. It was pleasing this morning to see the green shores of Labrador after six days of grey sky and sea. A few moments ago we passed the point on which the "Raleigh" was wrecked two years ago, and the little island with a lighthouse on it on which the two Germans descended after the first flight† across the Atlantic from East to West. The boys were called by the Captain at 6.30 am to see a large iceberg – 160ft. high – which we passed at no great distance. They did not, however, wake me, which was a pity. . . .

We are now in the great inland sea between Newfoundland and the mouth of the St. Lawrence. It is calm and bright, and getting steadily warmer. . . .

---

* Mrs. Churchill had been seriously unwell in 1928, and had just undergone an operation for tonsillitis. To this letter W.S.C. appended, as he sometimes did in writing to his wife, a sketch of an amply proportioned pig.

† This had taken place only the year before, in April 1928.

I have been reading a good deal on 'Marlborough'. It is a wonderful thing to have all these contracts satisfactorily settled, and to feel that two or three years agreeable work is mapped out, and, if completed, will certainly be rewarded. In order to make sure of accomplishing the task within three years instead of leaving it to drag on indefinitely, I am going to spend money with some freedom upon expert assistance. . . .

I have done nothing so far about preparing speeches. It will be better to see what the atmosphere is on landing, and I shall have all Sunday and Monday morning before my luncheon speech at Montreal. I have, of course, got some ideas already formed.

I have not yet seen the text of the Egyptian Treaty. What lies Henderson* told in the debate persisting that no negotiations had been going on, when almost immediately the whole is published cut and dried! I predict with certainty that the plan of fortifying ourselves on the canal and leaving Egypt to go to hell will never last, will be followed by disorder and degeneration, and will lead to our resuming an abdicated responsibility, possibly after serious bloodshed.

My darling I have been rather sad at times thinking of you in low spirits at home. Do send me some messages. I love you so much & it grieves me to feel you are lonely. I should greatly like to make a fine plan for October. But you must get fit & well. Tender love my sweet Clemmie, from yr devoted loving husband

W.

[The recall of Lord Lloyd† as High Commissioner in Egypt had been announced toward the end of July, the new government in London having required his resignation. The Foreign Secretary denied that any change of policy was intended; the Prime Minister assured the House of Commons that no new treaty would be concluded with Egypt without the consent of Parliament and the Dominions, an important qualification, which recog-

* Arthur Henderson (1863–1935), Labour politician; member of the War Cabinet, 1916–17; Home Secretary, 1924; Foreign Secretary, 1929–31; President of the Disarmament Conference at Geneva, 1932–34.

† George Ambrose Lloyd, 1st Baron Lloyd (1879–1941); Governor of Bombay, 1918–23; High Commissioner for Egypt and the Sudan, 1925–29; Colonial Secretary in Churchill's administration, 1940–41, and Leader of the House of Lords for a few weeks before his premature death.

nized the special importance of Egypt and the Suez Canal to Australia and New Zealand, but which also offered the governments of South Africa and Canada the opportunity to become involved if they wished.

The draft treaty stated that the occupation of Egypt by British forces would end; an alliance would be established between the two countries; Britain would be allowed to maintain armed forces in the Canal Zone; the protection of foreign interests and minorities in Egypt would be the business of the Egyptian government. In the end, the treaty did not come into effect, chiefly because no Egyptian government could be found with sufficient authority to carry through these terms.

Further East, the future of the naval base at Singapore, which had been proceeding by slow stages for the previous five years, was again in doubt.

In 1929, international affairs looked peaceable enough, and to most Canadians, half a world away from Suez and Singapore, such subjects must have seemed remote and academic. A dozen years later, when Churchill came to Ottawa just after Pearl Harbor and immediately before the fall of Singapore, everything would bear a different and deadly aspect; and the polite pretence that Singapore constituted no threat to the Japanese had long since been exposed, for there was no other first-rank naval power against which the base could be useful.

On board *Empress of Australia* was L.S. Amery, Churchill's colleague in the Cabinet from 1924. They had known each other more than forty years, since Churchill shortly after his arrival at Harrow had thrown Amery into the swimming pool; a gesture which the other, small of stature but even then of impressive muscular development, had returned with interest. Learned and tireless, Amery had been a loyal disciple of Joseph Chamberlain from those heady days when tariff reform and imperial preference first convulsed British politics. Holding simultaneously the Colonial Office and the Dominions Office, he had been driven to distraction and the verge of resignation by what seemed to him Churchill's faddish adherence to free trade and refusal to support even inexpensive measures of Imperial development. In private, they remained intermittently cordial. To Amery, it seemed that Churchill could think only in phrases, which might be countered only by equally striking phrases. When Amery said that he did not know whether he might have been wiser to follow his instinct and leave the late government, and that anyway he would not be muzzled any longer, Churchill "was very friendly about it, and only said that if I got my way he would retire from politics and devote himself to making money.

He had been all he ever wanted to be short of the highest post which he saw no prospect of, and anyhow politics were not what they had been." Churchill asserted that the statesmen of the previous generation, even though the issues they faced were admittedly less titanic, had been greater men than their successors. He began to undress for bed. Amery replied when asked why he was smiling, "Free Trade, mid-Victorian statesmanship and the old-fashioned nightshirt, how appropriate a combination." All this convinced Amery of a view he had long held, that "the key to Winston is to realise that he is mid-Victorian, steeped in the politics of his father's period, and unable ever to get the modern point of view. It is only his verbal exuberance and abounding vitality that conceal this elementary fact about him."

When they discussed their life at Harrow, W.S.C. remarked that he had always had the greatest sympathy for convicts and as Home Secretary had striven to reduce their sentences, since he had himself undergone eleven years of penal servitude in the schools of Britain.

On the next evening, when the two former ministers talked about the Dardanelles, Churchill remarked in jest that his only consolation was that God, wishing things to be prolonged in order to sicken mankind of war, had interfered with the project that would have brought the struggle to a speedier conclusion. Churchill's other evidence for the existence of a deity, Amery's diary relates, was the fact that a hell was certainly needed for Lenin and Trotsky.*]

The *Toronto Daily Star*, August 8, 1929

VERSATILITY OF GENIUS EXPLAINS FASCINATION OF WINSTON CHURCHILL

BY R.E. KNOWLES†

Winston Churchill is the most nearly universal genius in captivity. And "captivity," as applied to Mr. Churchill, is no idle word. For he was actually, during the Boer war, a common prisoner – if this bird of so brilliant plumage can ever be common, or, for

---

* Leopold Charles Maurice Stennett Amery (1873–1955), MP for the same constituency in Birmingham for thirty-four years from 1911; active and knowledgeable in many spheres; First Lord of the Admiralty, 1922–24; Colonial Secretary, 1924–29, and Dominions Secretary 1925–29; Secretary of State for India and Burma in Churchill's administration, 1940–45. For his discussions with W.S.C. on this voyage, see L.C.M.S. Amery, *My Political Life*, vol. 2 (London, 1953), pp. 510–11; M. Gilbert, *Winston S. Churchill*, vol. 5 (London, 1976), p. 339.

† Rev. Robert Edward Knowles (1868–1946), Presbyterian minister and later lecturer and journalist; special writer, *Toronto Daily Star*.

that matter, can ever be bereft of that larger liberty of which stone walls or iron bars do not bereave the highest type of genius.

Which very type is Mr. Churchill's own. All that has come to him – of inspiration, experience, triumph, mastery – he has not sought. It has simply come, as breezes seek aeolian wires. . . .

I first began to study this untamed spirit, this democratic aristocrat, this elfin prodigy at whose christening all the fairy god-mothers seem to have been in such a spendthrift mood, exactly twenty years ago. It was in the House of Commons that my eye first caught the strange fire in his own, first rested on that eagle-like brow, even then about as bald as an eagle's, that carelessly dressed stocky form, that aura of some unearned increment of power which we call genius for want of a better word.

Upon that occasion he was in tense and ejaculatory conflict, a sort of short sword encounter, with Lloyd George,* the two thrusting and parrying in a swift "question-hour" dialogue which was the finest exhibition of mental and verbal tennis it has ever been, or is ever likely to be, my privilege to enjoy with both eye and ear. Lloyd George had by far the finer sweep and power – but Winston drew blood far oftener, though his sabre could not cleave to the bone like the other's.

Twenty years later, just about two months ago, I heard him again, saw him again, felt him again – before a 10,000-soul audience in Liverpool.†

He passed within a foot of me – I had a seat on the platform – as he made his way to his chair, the Countess of Derby on his arm. He had changed. That majestic cerebral dome was unthatched, lines had come to abide on the former boyish face, and a portliness not exactly fitting to such a superior kind of sprite rather belied the tenuous wiry agility which had so in other days impressed me.

And his speech was all but innocent of the power of that earlier hour . . . he was not agile, nor scintillating, nor even uniformly coherent. He contrasted the liquor revenues that swelled his exchequer with the boot-legging profits that "the intolerant and tyrannical government of the United States" had turned in to their secret coffers. He spoke of Hon. J. H. Thomas** as having put over "a dirty pact with the

---

* David Lloyd George, 1st Earl Lloyd George (1863–1945), Chancellor of the Exchequer, 1908–15; Minister of Munitions, 1915–16; Prime Minister, 1916–22.

† Churchill spoke there on May 27, just before the election, condemning Labour's program as one of promises, plunder and taxation. As for Ramsay Macdonald's record, it had "chiefly consisted in unexampled desertion of this country in every crisis of her fate." According to *The Times* of May 28, it was Philip Snowden, not J.H. Thomas, who had in mind "some dirty Parliamentary deal" with the Liberals.

** James Henry Thomas (1874–1949), General Secretary, National Union of Railwaymen, 1918–24, 1925–31; Colonial Secretary, 1924, 1931, 1935–36; Lord Privy Seal and Minister of Employment, 1929–30; Dominions Secretary, 1930–35.

Liberals." He referred to his adversaries in terms of unqualified opprobrium, quoting his own father (to whom he constantly referred as "Lord Randolph Churchill") who once described the Liberals as possessed of a "savage lust for office and an insatiate greed for power." Like many a lesser debater, he made the fatal mistake of atoning for weakness of argument by strength of statement. . . .

Closing, let me quote what I regard as the two finest specimens of his oratory, packed with thought and aglow with a rare power of expression. The first, so cognate to this age and its basic problem goes straight to the vital point as to the rights of property, especially of hereditary property. Churchill said: "Respect for the rights of private property cannot be secured, and ought not to be expected, unless property is associated in the minds of the great mass of the people with ideas of justice and reason." The present Labor government should paste that extract in its collective hat.

And another of Mr. Churchill's great utterances, spoken in defence of his transfer of allegiance from one party to another, was to this effect: "Some men change their principles to fit their parties – others change their parties to fit their principles."

And, by the way, though in far less majestic vein, the finest compliment of recent times paid to the ex-chancellor of the exchequer was from the lips of the new lord privy seal, the old railroader, Rt. Hon. J. H. Thomas. This gentleman said the other day: "When I heard that Mr. Churchill was about to start on an extended trip across the Atlantic, I said to myself: 'Jim,' said I, 'You're sure of your salary for six months longer anyhow – Winston's going to America.'"

The *Toronto Daily Star*, August 10, 1929

So far as the Labor government was concerned, he [Churchill, in an interview at the Château Frontenac, Quebec] said it would remain in office as long as it behaved itself. If it adhered to radical and liberal policies its tenure would continue, but just as soon as it tried to put into effect purely socialistic doctrines its regime would come to an end. Britain, he said, did not wish to be disturbed.

Mr. Churchill is not disposed to over-emphasize the gravity of the Lancashire cotton strike.

"I do not believe it will be too bitter," he said. "They are such very fine people in Lancashire. You remember how during the American Civil war, they faced penury and starvation rather than abandon their convictions on the evils of slavery?

"There is so little to divide in the British cotton industry. For so many years the Oriental market has absorbed the greater part of Lancashire's innumerable looms. Now the Oriental market is disintegrating. Japanese competition and the Indian nationalist policy of home production of coarse fabrics is cutting to the bone."

But Mr. Churchill was ready with a solution. It lies, he believes, in the production of finer and better materials than the Oriental makers can produce.

"But what about Oriental cheap labor?" he was asked. "I am no believer in cheap labor," was the instant response. "The cheapest labor you can secure, slave labor, is the most uneconomic and the least productive. No, instead of cheap labor, I believe in highly paid, skilled labor, turning out under modern methods of mass production vastly more and vastly better material than your cheap labor will or can produce. I am not a technician, but I can, I think, see the answer in finer cloths, perhaps a cotton with a thread of silk in it. In the finer fabrics, we still have predominance; we are not yet a back number."

There was equal incisiveness in response to a question about British relations with Russia.

"What's preventing trade with Russia?" he asked. "The United States has always had the right idea there. You come and do business with us if you want to, but on the basis on which everybody else does business. Russia will, of course, be delighted to trade with us so long as we do not ask her to pay for what she buys. Why should we make special concessions to people like this, and hold down to strict business principles other countries which are civilized and have striven and are striving to make honorable payments for business honorably done?

"What have we done where Russia is concerned? We have vacillated here and vacillated there. When there was a Soviet headquarters in London, there was a great outcry to kick them out. When we did kick them out,* there was a great outcry about that. We should have had – should have – a plain, simple straightforward policy toward these people and adhere to it."

Mr Churchill is not a believer in the nationalization of natural resources, at least so far as the coal mines of Britain are concerned. He does not believe even in the idea of the purchase by the state of the royalties in the mines.

"It means simply the taking over by the state of many of the anxieties of private ownership," is the way he expressed it. "There is a spirit of syndicalism among the miners which believes that mines should belong to the miners. No, there cannot be any provision for dealing with nationalization under any budget. That would have to come in the form of a separate bill before parliament."

He did not believe that such a policy in such a bill would meet with general public support.

---

* After a raid in 1927 by the police on the London premises of Arcos, the Soviet trading company, and of the Soviet Trade Delegation, diplomatic relations with the U.S.S.R. had been broken off; they were shortly to be resumed by the new Labour government.

"Will there be abandonment of the Singapore naval base?" Mr. Churchill was asked.

"I hope not," was the answer. "The dominions have contributed more to that project than the mother country. Would it be honorable to take the people's money and then not to deliver what that money had been paid to provide? My own view of the Singapore base always has been that it is more important as, what I might call, a link of empire than in its military aspect, and that its significance is political rather than military. As such it seems to me very important indeed."

Mr. Snowden's* two-fisted opposition to the Young reparation plan at The Hague came in for ungrudging support.

"I have all along held and have always expressed the view that no government should be bound by the findings of the experts," Mr. Churchill said. "Naturally I approve any stand which opposes further unloading of unfair burdens on British shoulders. I think I made that abundantly clear in the past. So far as I have been able to follow events I believe Mr. Snowden is speaking clearly."

Randolph Churchill's diary, August 11, 1929[26]

Château Frontenac, Quebec

From our window we can see at night the Rothermere† paper mills all lit up. Papa said apropos of them, 'Fancy cutting down those beautiful trees we saw this afternoon to make pulp for those bloody newspapers, and calling it civilization.'

The *Toronto Daily Star*, August 12, 1929

Mr. Churchill was in his (colored) shirt sleeves, slippers still in evidence [at the Château Frontenac]. I sat at one end of a long sofa, Mr. Churchill sat on the other end, also in an arm chair, also on a rocking chair, also on the corner of one of the tables – that is, when he was sitting at all, since most of the time he was pacing up and down the room, a dynamo of unresting energy. . . .

"Go ahead," were Mr. Churchill's marching orders.

---

* Philip Snowden (1864–1937), Chancellor of the Exchequer, 1924, 1929–31.

† Harold Sidney Harmsworth (1868–1940), Viscount Rothermere, had created with his elder brother, Lord Northcliffe, a large and prosperous chain of newspapers.

"Very good – last night your son Randolph told me that your principal physical exercise is bricklaying. Is this, or is it not, a 'terminological inexactitude'?", these last two words constituting one of the phrases that made Winston famous.

The ex-chancellor grinned almost delightedly, for every man loves to hear one of his own phrases, especially via one of his own children.

"Well, no, I rather fancy Randolph's just about right. I used to play polo a great deal – but I'm older and heavier now, and it doesn't fit in as well as it used to. So, about the bricklaying, I welcome every form of sedate exercise, bricklaying among them, that helps keep me fit."

"Do you enjoy relaxation, Mr. Churchill?"

"Of course I do. Do you know that, for nearly 25 years, ever since 1905, I have been entrusted with high office. And high office means hard work. I can't tell you what this trip to Canada means to me."

"Speaking of high office, Mr. Churchill, I have a happy omen to reveal to you. It has to do with this very room."

"'This room,'" echoed the statesman, "what on earth could this room have to do with me?"

"Well, exactly one year ago this very month I interviewed Mr. Ramsay MacDonald* in this same suite 1301. And, within a twelvemonth, Mr. MacDonald was made prime minister of Great Britain. Why not the like for you?"

"Tut, tut," broke in this master of the English language, "what on earth put that into your head?"

"Well, Lord Queenborough for one thing."

"What has Queenborough to do with it – or to say about it?"

"It was less than a fortnight ago, in the Ritz at Montreal, that his Lordship spoke about you and the premiership – and he said a man would be a fool to bet you'd never be prime minister of Britain."

"All very good for a bit of chaff," said the far-seeing man, his forth-faring eyes fixed on my own as he spoke, "but such a thought never crosses my mind."†

"Don't you think No. 10 Downing Street would be a lovely place to live?"

"No, I don't," with great downrightness. "I've lived next door to it long enough to know. My word, but this taste of freedom is good," as he stopped in his to-and-fro career and gazed from the open window at the infinite watery beginnings of the

---

* James Ramsay MacDonald (1866–1937), Prime Minister, 1924, 1929–31, 1931–35 (of the National Government); Lord President of the Council, 1935–37.

† This is what W.S.C. might have called an inexactitude; see the letter to his wife of August 27 on pages 100–1.

noblest gulf on the planet. "There are two things I have my mind set on now – one is to have a jolly good rest, the other to learn all I can about your wonderful Canada and her place in the imperial plan." . . .

"Pardon my digression, Mr. Churchill, but do you ever regret that you didn't give your life to literature?"

This time the statesman-soldier-orator-author wheeled round and stood still in front of me. "Why should I regret that?" he asked.

"Well, sir, to be frank – perhaps bold, for I fancy you don't care for compliments – I would say, and far better judges think, that your after-the-war book is the greatest thing of that kind yet written. The last chapter of 'The Aftermath', good critics think, will belong to the generations. And what I meant to ask was, do you not think a great pen might do a greater lifework than an eloquent voice and a political genius?"

I was a little embarrassed by the long interrogative. But Mr. Churchill took the theme very seriously. "That's an old subject of debate," he replied; "perhaps what you say is true – though I'm not prepared to admit that I have either the one faculty or the other in any high degree. If I were to pronounce one way or the other I'd say I was much more at home with a pen than on the platform. To speak in public takes a great deal out of me, I never excelled as a platform speaker."

From this view I ventured to dissent. I observed that, so far as I could judge, leaving out Mr. Lloyd George, the people of England would be divided as to whether the palm for political oratory, should best go to Lord Birkenhead* or to the gentleman I was then addressing.

"No, no," Mr. Churchill said in answer, "Birkenhead is infinitely ahead of me in that regard."

W.S.C. to his wife, August 12, 1929[27]

Mount Royal Car
Canadian Pacific Railway
In the train at Quebec

The whole situation and aspect of Quebec on the St Lawrence River recalls nothing so much as the Firth of Forth viewed from Linlithgows† home. The

---

* Frederick Edwin Smith, 1st Earl of Birkenhead (1872–1930), barrister and politician; Lord Chancellor, 1919–22; Secretary of State for India, 1924–28; intimate and valued friend of W.S.C.

† The 2nd Marquess (1887–1952), who became Viceroy of India in 1936 and served there until 1943; he lived near Edinburgh.

water channel is about the same, but of course, a great fresh swiftly flowing river. The vegetation and appearance of the banks is exactly like Scotland. There is even an enormous cantilever bridge like the Forth Bridge, but with only two spans. We visited the bridge and walked over it. It is a fearsome height from the water so that the largest ships can go underneath.

Sunday we lunched with the Lieutenant-Governor,* a charming French Canadian who had been a distinguished Judge. He had read my war books and was very complimentary. A number of the *élite* of Quebec were present and made themselves very agreeable. After lunch a magnificent thunder storm

'Like water flung from some high crag,
The lightning fell with never a jag,
A river steep and wide.'†

Randolph was disappointed that it did not come nearer. It stopped all the trams, & the electric lights went out. The air which had been oppressive and muggy before has since become cool and fresh. Considerable state & formality attaches to the representative of the Crown and we were in our Sunday best for the occasion.

Late in the afternoon, when it had cleared up, we took an open motor car and went off twenty miles into the blue. I wanted to see the country at close quarters and nibble the grass and champ the branches. We saw hills and forests scarcely trodden by the foot of man, every kind of tree growing in primeval confusion and loveliest Scotch burns splashing down to rivers. We passed many lakes full of fish. Randolph expressed a desire to buy a piece of land and renounce society and ambition and settle here, building his own house. We have not, however, taken any final decision on this pending a view of other sites. We stopped at a little bungalow where four or five motor cars were assembled and found it a Country Club for fishing with twenty members in modest circumstances – quite Arcadian! Nothing would serve, when I was recognized, but to produce Champagne and the warmest of welcomes. We dined in the hotel.

---

* Henry George Carroll (1866–1939), Canadian barrister and politician; Lieutenant-Governor of Quebec, 1929–34.

† From Coleridge's *The Rime of the Ancient Mariner*; the first line should read 'Like waters shot from some high crag.'

I spent several hours on Sunday morning dictating my speech for Montreal on Tuesday. It is no use trying to say too much or pack too many topics into one occasion. They all seem to think here that Max's* campaign is most mischievous and will set back the cause for which he is fighting. The Twickenham election is a forerunner of what would happen in every constituency if we let ourselves be lured into it.

Amery made himself most agreeable on the boat and has since given an interview here, (perhaps the result of my arguments) strongly criticising the Empire Free Trade Campaign. I have been warned to be most careful about what I say, as fiscal matters may well become the issue of a general election sprung at short notice. The question is how Canada should reply to the American tariff, which is most cruel upon them and their agricultural products. Mr. Mackenzie King, for the Government, advocates finding new markets; Mr Bennett,† the Conservative and Protectionist Leader, presses for a new retaliatory tariff. Above all things I must keep clear of local politics....

The difficulties are to appreciate the immense size of this country which goes on for thousands of miles of good fertile land, well watered, well wooded, unlimited in possibilities. How silly for people to live crowded up in particular parts of the Empire when there is so much larger and better a life open here for millions. Half the effort of the war would have solved all these problems. However, the world is known to be unteachable.

The Vice P[resident] of the CPR has lent me his Secy Stenographer for the trip. This is a gt boon as I don't know how I shd dictate correspondence, telegrams, etc without this help....

PS. We are now in our [railroad] car on the way to Montreal through vast lush country following more or less the course of the St Lawrence. This

---

* William Maxwell Aitken, 1st Baron Beaverbrook (1879–1964); born in Canada and made his first fortune there; MP at Westminster, 1911–16; proprietor of the *Daily Express*, *Sunday Express* and *Evening Standard*; Minister of Aircraft Production, 1940–41; Minister of Supply, 1941–42; Lord Privy Seal, 1943–45; Chancellor of the University of New Brunswick, 1953–64. He had launched a vigorous campaign under the banner Empire Free Trade, which bade fair to split the Conservative vote in many constituencies. The support of the Conservative Central Office had been withdrawn from the candidate in Twickenham, who won by a narrow majority.

† Richard Bedford Bennett, later 1st Viscount Bennett (1870–1947); member of the Canadian House of Commons, 1911–21; Leader of the Conservative Party in Canada in succession to Arthur Meighen; Prime Minister of Canada, and Minister of External Affairs, 1930–35.

car is to be our home for three weeks so we have been unpacking all our clothes and arranging them afresh. When we leave the car we shall only take a suitcase each. The car is a wonderful habitation. Jack and I have large cabins with big double beds and private bath rooms. Randolph and Johnnie have something like an ordinary sleeping car compartment. There is a fine parlor with an observation room at the end and a large dining room which I use as the office and in which I am now dictating, together with kitchen and quarters for the staff. The car has a splendid wireless installation, refrigerators, fans, etc. We will certainly need this last. It is about as warm as a very hot English day but the air is cool and personally I do not mind the heat. But I can see that the journey will be laborious, & we shall I expect have enough of our land yachts before we are finished.

[W.S.C. and his party had inspected closely the site of the battle of 1759 in which James Wolfe (1727–1754) had secured victory over Montcalm's forces on the Plains of Abraham at Quebec. Wolfe was born at Westerham, very close to Chartwell. Churchill liked to take Canadian friends, including Mackenzie King, to see this house. When *A History of the English-Speaking Peoples* was published many years later, Churchill recounted Wolfe's reconnaissance of the river at night; his recitation of Gray's *Elegy*, with the line "The paths of glory lead but to the grave"; the landing of Wolfe and his men and their climb up the cliffs to the Heights; the defeat and death of Montcalm; and the last words of Wolfe himself, who expired as he knew victory was sure, "Now God be praised, I will die in peace."]*

Randolph Churchill's diary, August 12, 1929[28]

We arrived at Montreal at 6.30 having travelled about 180 miles from Quebec. We attended a dinner at the Mount Royal Club which included the fifty most prominent business men in Montreal which is a city with a population of considerably over a million. Mr Beatty† the Chairman of the CPR presided and Papa made an extremely effective speech of about thirty-five minutes which was well-received. He spoke without notes and

* Vol. 3 (1956), p. 129.

† Edward Wentworth Beatty (1877–1943), Vice-President of CPR, 1914–18, President, 1918–43; later knighted; Chancellor of McGill University, Montreal, from 1921, and director of various companies.

without preparation and proved what I have always believed that the effect on the actual audience is far greater if the delivery is absolutely spontaneous. Of course for a speech to read well long preparation and even notes are essential, but after all the influence the speech has on the audience is the primary consideration. I think Papa is gradually coming round to my point of view and is relying less and less upon notes. John Morley* once said 'Three things matter in speech – who says it, how he says it, and what he says, and of the three the last matters the least.' How true.

[Churchill had long believed that no British political party could declare its intention to tax food and hope to win a general election; Baldwin's loss of office in 1923 had given point to this message. Equally, the British could scarcely ask Australia and Canada to throw away tariffs and allow their growing industries to be exposed to a killing competition. These arguments found acceptance in 1929, though less readily than in earlier years; for the United States and other powers plainly had no intention of adhering to free trade. The irrational exuberance of the U.S. stock market was to implode within a few weeks; the fragility of the European economies took a little longer to become obvious; the collapse of international trade and domestic confidence, in every part of the world, soon followed.

In one Canadian city after another, Churchill put forcefully the propositions that of all the powers, the British Empire most needed peace and that prospects for concord between the nations were most promising. The first argument was emphatically true, for there was no power in the world less adequately armed, in relation to its risks and responsibilities, than the British Empire; and since the Dominions were entirely independent of Britain in their policies and budgets, the imbalance was compounded. Churchill himself, in his period as Chancellor just concluded, had squeezed the armed services severely, a policy which those who remembered his expansive days at the Admiralty before the war found hard to understand or sometimes to forgive. His first speech, at Montreal, made a virtue of these economies.

Repeatedly he spoke of the wonderful, almost mysterious, nature of the association which had brought men from all over the world to uphold

---

*Viscount Morley (1838–1923), distinguished Liberal politician, biographer of Gladstone and much admired by W.S.C., of whom he had been a Cabinet colleague before the war.

the common cause during the war, half a million of them from Canada. He was to dwell upon the same subjects in much the same language, with redoubled cause, during the next war. In several speeches he gave figures for the rebuilding of Britain's foreign investments and her steady repayment of enormous war debts. Almost every oration contained a robust defence of Britain's progress in education, health, sobriety. The only speech of which we have a complete record is that given at Toronto, printed in the Empire Club's *Addresses*. Otherwise we have to rely on Canadian newspapers and a handful of notes preserved in Churchill's papers, endorsed in a slightly despairing way by one of his staff: "Nothing was strung together; some numbered pages, some not. But all that came back have been put in here."*

Some of his themes varied according to location. In Montreal, he described the position of France in relation to Germany. At Ottawa, knowing that questions of Imperial preference loomed large in Canada and that a general election could not be long delayed, he made sure he said nothing to offend Mackenzie King. At Toronto and points farther west, he referred often to Egypt and Singapore, pointing out their significance to the Empire and urging the Dominions to have their say.]

The *Montreal Gazette*, August 14, 1929

Probably no previous speaker [to the Canadian Club in Montreal] had an audience of such proportions. Ballroom, Rose Room, galleries, corridors and platforms were filled in every available niche where a chair could be placed, and yet hundreds who had come to hear the famous statesman were turned away. Loudspeakers enabled thousands to hear the speech in addition. . . .

Mr. Churchill, who was received with long and prolonged applause, the audience rising to its feet, said:

I have come to Canada to learn from those men who are making and guiding the destinies of this country, what their problems are, what their anxieties are, what their hopes are, and how they think we in the Mother Country can best help and cooperate in the fulfilment of their desires.

I have come to study in particular the economic position and the means whereby we may promote not only the general volume of trade, but inter-Imperial trade. . . .

---

* The notes are to be found at Churchill College, Cambridge, CHAR 9/88B.

I had also undertaken at your invitation to make several, and in fact quite a lengthy number of speeches as I travel through your wonderful country; and in these speeches I shall try so far as I can, to make a more or less continuous statement of our joint interests and affairs primarily conceived from the point of view of a member of the British House of Parliament.

And here in Montreal, in this great city, I would begin with the first and greatest of the joint interests of the whole of the British Empire – I mean the maintenance of world peace. There is no other association in the world among men that has so great an interest in the maintenance of peace as the widespread community of the British Empire.

We have a greater need for peace than any other state; we have all that we need in lands and fame; we have all that we want in natural resources; we have potentialities in the British Empire sufficient to absorb the whole energy and genius of its many peoples for generations and even centuries to come. All we require is the reign of peace and law and that confidence which comes from the reign of peace and law; and therefore, Mr. Chairman, I rejoice – I think we can all rejoice – that the state of the world at present is so peaceful and that its mood and temper is so pacific.

I read the other day that Mr. Hoover,* President of the United States, said he thought that the outlook of the world was more peaceful than it had been for 50 years. And only a few weeks ago I was talking to that venerated and venerable statesman – the most venerable and venerated statesman in this Empire – Lord Balfour,† whom perhaps some of you know (applause); and I heard him say that although there were many dangers which naturally confronted the present generation he was happy to think that the danger of a great war between the civilized powers was not among them. And I think, gentlemen, we may take as a starting point in our political thought at the present time, a solid, practical assurance, that we have before us a prolonged period of peace. At any rate that is where I begin the study of political questions.

From peace our minds naturally turn to disarmament and I think the British Empire has set a good example in that; the British army is reduced to less than it was, less than the little army that we had before the war. The air force is not half the strength of the air force of our nearest neighbor and good friends. Even in the sphere of the navy, that vital foundation of the whole unity and life of the British Empire,

---

* Herbert Clark Hoover (1874–1964), President of the United States, 1929–33.

† Arthur James Balfour, 1st Earl of Balfour (1848–1930), philosopher and statesman; nephew of Prime Minister Lord Salisbury; succeeded his uncle as Prime Minister, 1902–05; W.S.C.'s successor as First Lord of the Admiralty, 1915; Foreign Secretary, 1916–19.

even there we have made the greatest reductions which have taken place since the war, and we have agreed to the principle that Great Britain and the United States shall be equal powers upon the sea.

Oddly enough, however, the only disputes which have troubled the world in the last few years have been disputes about disarmament. There is even a danger that the process of disarmament may be delayed by the eagerness of its advocates; and as long as nations are alarmed and suspicious, as long as they are harassed by fear, they will not disarm; and if while they have these alarms and suspicions pressure is put upon them to make them disarm, then resentment is created; suspicions and alarms are increased and the very process of disarmament is retarded.

Every nation has its own problem of national security to face and very little is gained when other nations who have not the same dangers to face or the same problems and difficulties, who have not been through the same experiences, try to solve the problems of particular nations for them. Take for instance the case of France. France is a very good instance to select. It is very easy for British and American opinion to point the finger of reproach at France because of the size of her standing army, and suggest to her its rapid reduction. But how much and how very different we would feel if we were Frenchmen dwelling side by side with a mighty nation whose military manhood was already at least double our own, by whom we had been twice invaded within living memory. Should we not be inclined to regard the reproaches of those who had no share in these perils, well meant as they might be, as an interference with our own vital security?

The French feel differently about it, and we must be very careful in all these questions of disarmament to carry the public opinion of every country affected with us in the step which has been taken in common. I do not believe myself that France would be willing to reduce her army to such a point that nothing stands between the French people and fresh invasion except the good will and good faith – which I do not impugn – of their German neighbor; and I am not at all sure that if the French were to disarm completely, thereby placing themselves in a defenceless position – I am not at all sure that the peace of Europe would stand upon a more secure or solid foundation than it does today. (Applause).

The only way to promote disarmament is to develop confidence and good will between all nations, to develop alternative forms of national endeavor in commerce, science, and trade; and if you wish to promote disarmament in Europe the key to that is the good relations and growth of common interests, particularly commercial interests between Germany and France. In this way, gentlemen, old quarrels and old animosities will fade and will be forgotten in the growth of new interests and co-operation.

We see great dangers – there are undoubtedly great dangers – in nations drawing generation after generation immense tribute from Germany, the result not of the fertile and reproductive investment in capital but as a penal consequence of defeat in war. This is, of course, familiar ground; you are all aware of the main arguments upon this subject. I only tread upon it in order to vindicate the policy which has been adopted by Great Britain with the object of giving the fairest chance to the growth of friendly confidence and co-operation between France and Germany, between those tremendous nations whose quarrels have so often devastated Europe and have finally affected the whole world and whose unity would make the solution of the European problems incomparably swift and easy. . . .

And here in Montreal in the magnificent Dominion of Canada which the whole Empire regards with such deep affection and pride, here in this great city I claim on behalf of the central government which must necessarily take the initiative and bear the greater part of the burden in conducting the foreign affairs of the Empire, I claim that our European policy since the war has been loyal, faithful, far-reaching and humane. . . .

You have made great progress. I come back after 29 years to Montreal, 29 eventful years, and I find that the city of Montreal is five times as large and probably 20 times as wealthy as when I left it last, only a little more than a quarter of a century ago. Of course, in an old country, a country which is densely populated, whose natural resources have long since been discovered, and measured, it is not possible for us to rival such a rate of progress. We cannot attempt to do so. Nevertheless, I feel, when I come here, that I have a right to tell you I come as the representative of one progressive, developing, expanding community, to land upon the shores of another.

How splendid is our common inheritance. It was with a thrill that after crossing for several days the great wastes of the Atlantic, I landed in a new world, in a new hemisphere, and found myself at home.

After crossing a quarter of the globe I found myself with friends, fellow citizens with laws and institutions with which I have been all my life familiar, a great community acknowledging allegiance to the same Crown, and proud of their associations with the same Flag.

It was with added pleasure and pride that for the first time I set foot in Quebec, the Capital of French Canada. What better feature could you have to represent the genius of the British Empire, than this large, powerful, thriving French community with their own traditions, their own history, their own language, dwelling happily and in perfect freedom within the confines of a British dominion. . . .

It is the set and fundamental policy of the British State, and of the British Empire, to foster and to seek by every means in their power the growth of friendly and kindred relations with the United States.

You have been pioneers in this good work. The marvellous spectacle of a frontier of 3,000 miles, unguarded, the facilities of inter-communication which exist, the confidence which prevails mutually ought to be the model – as they are the examples to every nation standing side by side in any part of the world.

The association, friendly, warm, affectionate association of the British Empire and the United States will give to the whole world the same assurances of prolonged peaceful development as is to be achieved in Europe by relationships between Germany and France. These are high objects. But I say let it be an equal association. Let us work together, these two gigantic powers of human society, let us walk together side by side as equals, aiding and perhaps guiding the world in the solution of the problems of the future.

That we can do so long as we remain, and only so long as we remain a United Empire founded on freedom and faith, and facing and sharing fair and stormy weather hand in hand.

The *Ottawa Morning Journal*, August 15, 1929

THE POSITION OF FRANCE

In his speech before the Montreal Canadian Club on Tuesday, Mr. Winston Churchill said something that the peoples of the British Empire should remember. Discussing disarmament, he remarked that it was all very well for other nations to point the finger of reproach at the great magnitude of France's standing army, but that it should be remembered how France had been invaded twice in the present generation.

That is a very pointed reminder – particularly for Canadians. We here in Canada do not know, have never known, what invasion means. Our land has not felt the tramp of foreign soldiery, we have not seen our churches and altars destroyed, our women held captive, our soil torn up by hostile cannon, our cities laid waste by the sword. Because we have not had the anguish of such things, because we have lived at peace with our neighbors for a century, do not bear upon the face of our country the deep scars of invasion, we find it hard to understand the point of view of France. Too often, perhaps, we actually disrespect it.

But it should not be so. France, surely, cannot be expected to regard disarmament in the light that we regard it. She cannot be expected to forget 1870, to forget Alsace-Lorraine, to forget Rheims and Verdun. No century of peace stands between her and her mighty neighbor; no mighty ocean separates her from the peril of aggression. To disregard these things, to disrespect France's memories and misgivings, to rail at the armies she maintains for security – such things are not sensible. They not only disregard grim and terrible realities; they make more difficult that bond of sympathy and understanding which, more than anything else, is essential to the great end of disarmament and peace which all well-wishers for humanity have in view.

Mackenzie King's diary, August 14, 1929

Kingsmere*

Churchill went over with me the lines of his speech for tomorrow. I found myself in agreement with his point of view as to wisdom of avoiding rigid agreements in Naval armaments etc., but [word illegible] rather the attitude & atmosphere for doing what each "wished" to do. On Empire Trade I could see no objection to his view of letting business men see what they could do, & report to Govts. for their action. He sees very little from an Economic Conference.

In the woods Churchill was keenly interested in the construction of dams, though the walking was bad he was greatly taken with the little property. We went over all save the farm. He liked the small cottages & lakes. Stayed till 5 o'clock.

Randolph Churchill's diary, August 15, 1929[29]

Ottawa

In the evening we dined with Sir Robert Borden,† who was PM for nine years. About fifteen people including Mackenzie King who I think is one of the most delightful men I have ever met. He was very kind to me, and took great trouble to be agreeable.

[This warm feeling was reciprocated, for Mackenzie King's diary records that he had been quite charmed by Randolph Churchill, "a fine looking

---

* Mackenzie King's house and estate near Ottawa.

† Sir Robert Laird Borden (1854–1937), Prime Minister of Canada, 1911–20; delegate to the Paris Peace Conference, 1919.

young fellow & most intelligent & clever." Three days later, however, the Prime Minister pointed out to the Governor General (whose reactions are not recorded) that the use by British visitors of the Lieutenant-Governors' residences across the continent "was likely sooner or later to raise a question looking to the abolition of the whole lot."

Churchill had originally intended to give perhaps half a dozen speeches in Canada. In the end, so insistent were the invitations, he delivered no less than twelve, and several other less formal addresses. Some were arranged by the National Council of Education and the Overseas Education League, which under the inspiration of a remarkable Canadian, Major F. J. Ney, had for years been bringing distinguished speakers to Canada; Churchill asked that the proceeds should be given to the furnishing of the Canadian Teachers' Hostel in London. As his letters show, he felt for the moment no anxiety about his finances; apart from large payments for his articles and the new book on Marlborough, there was another unexpected bright spot. Montreal, he told his wife in distant England, bought six hundred copies of *The World Crisis*. Even better, his contract stipulated that he should be paid at once for such sales. "If this keeps up we shall make an unexpected profit. . . ."[30]]

The *Ottawa Morning Journal*, August 15, 1929

OTTAWA'S DISTINGUISHED GUEST

Mr. Winston Churchill, presently Ottawa's guest, is one of the stormy petrels of British politics. But Canadians can salute Mr. Churchill as somebody more than that. Journalist, author, soldier, politician, orator, Mr. Churchill is one of the most extraordinary, one of the most salient figures of our time, a man who has impressed his personality and genius not only upon the British Empire but upon the whole structure of the world.

Mr. Churchill, it may be, has temperamental defects which deny to him the highest in statesmanship. It has been written of him that he has no moorings in political conviction, that he is a chameleon in politics, that he boxed the political compass and will continue to box it, that in a word, he is one of those extraordinary opportunists who, all down through time, have been found in the story of politics.

Whether such claims are true or false, matters little. The salient feature about Mr. Churchill is that he is Mr. Churchill, that he is something and somebody different, with his own distinctive intellect and genius, his own outlook and methods, his own compelling, vivid and colorful personality. He is no man's pale shadow; not even the shadow of the great Randolph, his father.

No living man has done such varied things, no man has done more things well, none has had more of romance and adventure.

[The newspaper also paid an eloquent and well-informed tribute to Churchill's part in the Irish settlement of 1921, under which the Irish Free State came into being.]

The *Ottawa Morning Journal*, August 16, 1929

Mr. Churchill was greeted with loud applause as he rose to deliver his address. "I am delighted to come to Ottawa, and most grateful to you for your cordial welcome," he said in opening.

"I am very glad to see here my old friend and former colleague, His Excellency,* whose long training and experience in every sphere of Imperial affairs, and also in the democratic arena of the British House of Commons, has enabled him to render such valuable service during his tenure of office in this country."

"And I am glad to sit next to my old friend, Mr. Mackenzie King, your Prime Minister, with whom I have, ever since the year 1907, been brought repeatedly in contact in matters of national or Imperial importance. And also to find at this board Sir Robert Borden, who played so great a part in the crisis of the war, and whom I first remember when he came to the Admiralty in 1912 with the offer of a powerful contribution to the British Fleet. . . ."

"The aim of every British Government since, and indeed, before the war, has been to remove stumbling blocks from the path of British and American friendship. One after another these obstacles have been got out of the way. Ireland with its long trail of troubles and misunderstandings, has passed altogether out of the sphere in which it could be the cause of conflict or ill-will on this side of the Atlantic."

Mr. Churchill added that the Anglo-Japanese Alliance had been happily merged in the wider agreement affecting the peace of the Pacific Ocean.

"The war debts have been settled in accordance with the wishes of the United States," continued the distinguished statesman amid loud laughter, and applause.

---

* Freeman Freeman-Thomas, Viscount Willingdon (1866–1941), Liberal MP and junior minister before the war; later Governor of Bombay and of Madras; Governor General of Canada, 1926–31; Viceroy of India, 1932–36; an earldom was conferred upon him in 1931, and a marquessate in 1936.

"Whatever we may think of that settlement so far as it affects the general interests of Europe, so long as we ourselves receive from Europe what we have paid, or are to pay, to the United States, it clearly is not a matter which has any direct influence upon our affairs or feelings.

"The only live issue that remains is the question of naval agreement. That is a very difficult topic and one upon which it is essential any discussion should be cool and frank and matter of fact.

"The great question we have to ask ourselves is: Will a new naval agreement make things easier? Will it bring about a reduction of the expense of armaments? Will it lay the naval controversy at rest?

"The Washington agreement of 1921* was a great decision of policy for which the Government of which I was a member bears its responsibility. I, myself, looked upon that agreement with faith and hope. But I must confess, looking back on it, I am sometimes inclined to wonder whether it has not done as much harm as good to Anglo-American relations.

"There certainly have been considerable disputes about who got the best of it," continued Mr. Churchill. He said the only cause of friction between countries and people which had so much in common had been the points connected with the working of that naval agreement.

Mr. Churchill said the Washington agreement dealt only with the battle fleets. "A new agreement will have to deal with cruisers, torpedo and all sorts of craft and must be a more complicated affair," he said. Ships varied so much, like human beings. They differed in size, speed, armor, guns and in age. Modern appliances, and the opinions of experts upon the value of ships also differed according to times and circumstances.

"It seems to me, at any rate, that we are opening up a field of almost infinite technical discussion with immense possibilities of misunderstandings, and especially if we try, as perhaps it is our duty to try, to regulate the whole of the minor construction of the two countries in accordance with some rigid treaty.

"There is another aspect. The situations of Great Britain and the United States are entirely different.

"I ask myself whether this diversity of conditions is understood fully by our friends in the United States and whether it will receive fair recognition in the proposals which, perhaps, they will have to make to us. If these fundamental differences in

* Actually of February 1922; it provided for some naval disarmament and laid down ratios of strength in the larger battleships between the United States, Great Britain, Japan, France and Italy.

circumstances do not receive such recognition then it seems to me a fair agreement will be very hard to reach.

"And if an agreement were reached on paper without the real assent of the nation on either side, then I fear as the years pass by it might open up again those suspicions which it is our common object to sweep away from the English-speaking world.

"I question very much if a rigid agreement will lead to further reduction in expense.

"If Great Britain, with all her special dangers and pre-occupations, is to fix a maximum for herself, which must take into consideration all tendencies, even remote tendencies, European or Asiatic, and she has to declare what her maximum must be, necessarily it will be very high.

"And I do not see where the burden is going to be lightened. See how badly the Washington agreement has worked about the limitation of what we call light cruisers of 10,000 tons, and eight-inch artillery. Before that was agreed to, no one had ever thought of building a light cruiser of such size as that. But ever since then, the whole tendency has been to build only vessels of that immense size, vessels I may say that, from the point of view of naval architecture, I believe are a most unnatural, unreasonable, and inefficient expression of the naval science. But all the nations of the world have in their navies large numbers of cruisers, old and small, which are wearing out and which from time to time they are replacing owing to the fact that the maximum has become the minimum and that this 10,000-ton, eight-inch-gun cruiser idea has been started. . . .

"I would prefer that both powers [the United States and Great Britain] should go each their own way in amity and peace, acting independently, and building only the fewest possible ships they require for their own vital security.

"After all we are not alarmed or offended if the United States build vessels its rulers think necessary for its security. We are sure they will not be used against us. . . .

"Now I turn to another delicate topic," said Mr. Churchill, "delicate, and one nearer home. What are we going to do for Empire trade? How are we going to increase its volume and its value? How are we arranging to handle profitably large, and larger, blocks of each other's business? That is a vital question to which all minds should be turned at the present time. So far as we in Great Britain are concerned we cannot tax imported food. It would be idle and fatal for any party to handicap itself with a burden of that kind, in presenting itself to the judgment of an immense electorate which has been recently augmented by millions of consumers. We cannot do that.

"On the other hand you cannot be expected, nor Australia, to throw down those protective barriers behind which your industries have grown up and flourished, and expose those industries to the rigorous and severe competition of our long-established and organized industries in the Motherland.

"But there may be other ways of obtaining the object we have in view. . . .

"Can we not all agree to regard the British Empire as an economic unit? Not necessarily an exclusive economic unit, but after all it should be self-conscious of its economic unity.

"Has not the time come for a very forward step?

"I have a modest proposal to make, a humble proposal, but very practical, I think. I do not wish to meddle in any way in Canadian party politics. That is not my intention. Speaking of British politics I would say, let us try to drag this issue of inter-Imperial trade out of the arena of party politics and party scores, lift it onto a higher and more reasonable platform.

"It seems to me the question ought to be examined as a business proposition. Let there be a conference, not of politicians, but of leading business men of the British Empire who are making and guiding the development of the great Dominions, and who are at the head of the largest industries in Great Britain.

"Let these men meet together in the first instance and study this question, not as a party matter, but as a question to be studied on its merits to see how we can handle our affairs and do the best for each other.

"That is the proposition. Let British political parties stand aside in a benevolent spirit while this investigation proceeds and until we have the best advice that can be given us from the experts, with a plan covering the whole Empire for the expansion and fertilization of Imperial trade. Let us know what these men would do if, for instance, they were a board of directors managing the greatest merger the world has ever seen. Parties could then consider the matter.

"Then would come a time for the Imperial Conference to say to what extent they could utilize the results of such a comprehensive survey of the problem. Very frequently when these conferences meet, those problems come to the front but we lack the experience of these business men which ought to be preliminary to parliamentary discussion.

"I am known generally as taking the free trade view. I believe I am not thought to be as orthodox as I once was because I imposed some duties of a protective character as Chancellor of the Exchequer. In the main, I still approach this question along the lines of the old orthodox economists. Still I say that is a question which transcends economic doctrine. And if there were a plan made of economic and useful service, I cannot believe it would be turned down because it did not conform to doctrinaire economic principles.

"The decision taken in the next few years may be vital for the drawing together of the bonds between the nations of the Empire and the furtherance of Imperial trade.

"I rejoice to be free just now," he said. "Instinct has led me to come to Canada, for once again it seems to me that Canada holds the Vimy Ridge* for the British Empire." (Loud applause.)

"This time it is with bloodless effort and without the horrors and guilt of war.

"Canada is in the foremost situation. She not only holds the position for the British Empire. She holds it for wider interests still. The ties which join this great country to the Mother Country are more flexible than elastic, stronger than steel and tenser than any material fabric known to science. These ties unite the old world to the new, they are the only ties across the Atlantic, strong enough to prevent in some future generation any antagonistic groupings by continents and nations. Canada bridges the gap between the old world and the new, and unites the world with a new bond of comradeship.

"The British Empire has survived its many perils because its own special interests have again and again, on many occasions, been found to be for the higher interests of the whole world.

"It is around that Empire that our thoughts centre today and I will make no excuse for using the oldest, most well-worn and truest of maxims: 'United we stand; divided we fall.' Divided we fall in shattering ruin first, and afterwards drift and disperse in feeble dissipation.

"United we are sure of a foremost place in the onward march of men," concluded Mr. Churchill, amid loud applause.

The Prime Minister took the first opportunity he said to assure Mr. Churchill how heartily the Government and people of Canada welcomed him to the Capital and to the Dominion.

"We welcome him for his great personality and remarkable ability. But above all for his great services to the Empire and the world at the time of the world's great crisis," said the Prime Minister. "His career is one that fills the minds of men, communities, and of nations with admiration. It is a source of pride to us that he should, with his first free moments, come to Canada to give us the benefit of his great experience.

"He may feel quite confident," added the Prime Minister, "that he has not said anything that will be taken exception to by any party in this country. If his addresses throughout the remainder of his tour in Canada are as carefully worded there will surely be only thanks to him for them," concluded the Prime Minister.

---

* The Canadian Corps of four divisions under Lieutenant General Byng (later Lord Byng, Governor General of Canada) took Vimy Ridge, north of Arras, in April 1917.

Mackenzie King's diary, August 15, 1929

Churchill made a very good speech, touching just the two themes Naval parity U.S. & Grt. Br. & Inter-Empire trade, closing with a very fine & very true peroration re "united we stand, divided we fall" re British Empire. The speech was very carefully prepared, notes quite complete and as I could see 'exact' in his own handwriting. He told me he dictates his books, then revising often 6 times, tries to get copy quickly into print for revision. Says his books "The Crisis" have paid well £40,000, thus far. Out of books made the wherewithal for public life.

After the luncheon, I took him & his brother & the boys over the Houses of Prlt. Churchill was visibly deeply impressed by the memorial chamber, read all the inscriptions and tablets. Also much enjoyed the visit to the Carillon, views from tower & our Council Chamber, he took pleasure in being seated in my chair at the Council table & in the H. of C. Throughout his visit yesterday & today he was exceedingly pleasant & companionable. A fine mind, nice nature. . . .

Read aloud to Joan & Godfroy* last night last chapter of Churchill's "Crisis" – very fine writing.

W.S.C. to his wife, August 15, 1929[31]

Ottawa

Our journey continues most interesting and stimulating, but it is also, as I cabled you, extremely strenuous. I have made two full dress speeches, one at Montreal and today here in Ottawa. I took a great deal of time and trouble over them on account of the unfamiliar atmosphere and also because of the delicacy of the topics. The audiences were very large and overflowing and most enthusiastic.

I have been every where welcomed in the warmest manner. Men who I have not seen for thirty years, but whom I ran across in my wanderings come up in twos and threes at every place to shake hands. Today a former Sergeant of the Engineers, who helped me in 98 make my plans for the

* Mr. and Mrs. Godfroy Patteson; Joan Patteson was King's closest confidante for the last thirty years of his life.

battle of Omdurman for the "River War,"* held me up in the street, introduced himself and presented me with a box of excellent cigars for use on my journey. He was in quite humble circumstances and I was greatly touched. . . .

The immense size and progress of this country impresses itself upon one more every day. There are now nearly ten million people here, and there is no doubt that in the next twenty-five years this number will be, at least, doubled. The sentimental feeling towards England is wonderful. The United States are stretching their tentacles out in all directions, but the Canadian National spirit and personality is becoming so powerful and self-contained that I do not think we need fear the future. . . .

Randolph has conducted himself in a most dutiful manner and is an admirable companion. I think he has made a good impression on everybody. He is taking a most intelligent interest in everything, and is a remarkable critic and appreciator of the speeches I make and the people we meet. Jack and Johnnie are enjoying themselves thoroughly. I am a little tired this evening after the speech and worry of preparing it. We travel tonight after dinner to Toronto which we reach at seven A.M. tomorrow.

The *Toronto Daily Star*, August 16, 1929

The famous British statesman when asked as to the old land [British] methods of dealing with the "Red" menace showed he had been reading Canadian newspapers. He knew about the "battle of the bandstand" at Queen's Park [Toronto] on Tuesday night.

"I see you've had a bit of a row here. What did they do? Did they actually hold a meeting?"

He was told that police did not let the Reds get that far – that they were not allowed to reach the bandstand.

"And did they use their truncheons? And chased them out of the park?"

Yes, they chased all the Reds and all the citizens. . . .

"Now, what would you do in England in such a situation?"

"Well, of course I don't want to meddle in your local affairs," said the former lord of the British admiralty. "But over there it is quite legal to hold a meeting. That is, if they first give notice to the police."

---

* W.S.C.'s two volumes on the campaigns in the valley of the Nile, published in 1899, immediately before his capture in South Africa.

Then after a pause he went on:

"It is quite legal for them to make a demonstration. When they hold a demonstration the police walk along with them to see that order is maintained.

"They can even run a candidate if they like."

"And if they talk sedition?" suggested The Star. "What then?"

"Ah, that is a different matter," smiled Mr. Churchill.

"But they are a poisonous breed," added the statesman, "though that also is another matter."

The *Globe*, Toronto, August 16, 1929

MR. CHURCHILL'S QUEST

Mr. Winston Churchill visits Toronto today. This distinguished Empire statesman comes to Canada primarily for the purpose of studying ways and means of increasing intra-Empire trade. He could hardly have come at a more propitious period. At no previous time was there as evident a desire on the part of Canadians to divert to British markets, at home or abroad, as many as possible of the purchases now being made in the United States. For the second time since the war the neighboring Republic proposes to erect greatly heightened barriers against Canadian products.* Canadians, regardless of their theoretic low-tariff or high-tariff predilections, are unwilling to sit passively by while trade doors are slammed in their faces. They are literally being forced to the conclusion that they must look for future business to those of their own kith and kin.

The *Montreal Daily Star*, August 16, 1929

CHURCHILL AND THE WASHINGTON CONFERENCE

There is something tonic and wholesome in the intervention of Mr. Churchill in the honeyed Anglo-American naval pourparlers† that are now in progress. As we have ventured to say from the first, it is not enough for Mr. MacDonald and Mr. Hoover to be in favour of a naval agreement. Mr. MacDonald must bring Mr. Churchill with him and Mr. Hoover must bring the American Senate.

---

* American tariffs, already substantial, were soon to be increased under the Smoot-Hawley Act, 1930.

† These progressed sufficiently for Ramsay MacDonald to visit the United States that autumn for talks with President Hoover, and led eventually to the London Naval Treaty of 1930, which limited construction of cruisers and provided for a "holiday" until 1936 in the building of larger battleships.

The root-cause of our present trouble over this question of naval parity is the fact that the Washington agreement left certain features of naval power unregulated, and so provided tinder for the ever-ready torch of international jealousies, suspicions and even fears. . . . If we are to have a new agreement, it is absolutely essential, as Mr. Churchill suggests, that this paper pact must be supported by "the real assent of public opinion in each country. . . ."

It is probable that we may credit Mr. Churchill with a flash of literary exaggeration when he says, speaking of the Washington Conference, that "on looking back, he begins to wonder if it did not do as much harm as good to Anglo-American relations." No one should know better than Mr. Churchill just what dangers that Conference averted. American feeling at that time – right after the wave of positive suspicion and even antagonism toward her late Allies that swept the United States during the ferocious anti-Versailles Peace Treaty campaign of the Harding election – was ripe and ready to be stampeded into a demand for "the greatest navy that has been. . . ."

If it had not been for the truce proclaimed when the Washington Conference was summoned, there is hardly a doubt in the world that the American Republic would have set itself to build a bigger navy than the British – seeking not parity but frank superiority. They had the money – they had the material – they know how to build those intricate machines we call warships. Great Britain was war-wounded, weary and burdened with debt.

Nothing but the Washington Conference saved us – and the world – from that disaster. It is true that we have had some bickerings since over the application of its principles. But what are these when compared with what we would have had if the British people had been asked to sit still and watch a rich rival take from them by sheer power of gold the command of the sea? Would the British people have sat still? Mr. Churchill knows more about that than any overseas observers can. But if the British people had sat still and watched another nation get into its grip such superiority at sea that ever afterward the British Empire would only exist on American sufferance, it would be the first time in a long history that they ever exhibited such sublime self-abnegation.

W.S.C.'s address to a joint meeting of the Empire Club, the Canadian Club and the Board of Trade at the Royal York Hotel, Toronto, August 16, 1929

British Imperial Interests

I am going to speak to you to-day upon some subjects of general interest to patriotic British citizens in every part of His Majesty's domain. Let me begin by saying what I said at Montreal, do not form too gloomy an opinion of the strength and prosperity of the Mother Country. . . .

Peace, I believe, is securely established, and I think Mr. Hoover was quite right in saying the prospects of peace were better than they had been for fifty years. Peace, I mean, between the great civilized nations of the world. I do not mean what disturbances may occur in barbarous parts of the world where the Russian Bolsheviks come in contact with other nations; but as far as the great civilized powers are concerned, I believe the foundations of peace are stronger now than they have ever been in our lifetime. . . .

Our first security under Providence, and our righteous behaviour, is the Royal Navy. We have long enjoyed the naval supremacy of the world. We did not abuse that supremacy . . . when the 20th century dawned it was the British Navy that proved the sure shield of freedom and civilization, and it was the British Navy that enabled the great republic of the United States to bring its influence to bear upon the closing phases of the war. . . . There never were two nations, two countries, more differently situated and circumstanced from the point of view of naval danger than the United States and Great Britain. The United States is almost a continent. It possesses within its bounds everything that is required to minister to its prosperity and life. We are a small, densely populated island with the need of importing three-quarters of the food we eat across salt water, and most of our raw material; and we are also the centre of an Empire which circles the globe, the only material connection between the component parts of which is the uninterrupted passage of ships across the seas. We are close to Europe, involved in all its dangers, though we keep as clear of them as we can, whereas the United States may rejoice in having thousands of miles of ocean between her and any enemy or danger, however speculative or impossible that danger may appear. I say there is an immense disparity of conditions between the two parties in this matter; and to apply a mere cheap logic, numerical parity to conditions which are in themselves so fundamentally disparate is not to arrive at what I am willing to arrive at, what I think we are entitled and justified in seeking, namely that the British Empire and the United States should be equal powers upon the sea; we should not arrive at that goal, the true goal, but arrive at the position where under the pretense of a power equality, Great Britain would be in fact relegated to permanent inferiority on the seas. That is a result, I earnestly hope, we may avoid. . . .

There is another instance where subversive activities inside the British Empire tend to work injury to our imperial interests. I take the case of Egypt, and I am sure you would wish me to say a few words upon that burning topic to-day. Let us look back and see why it was we went to Egypt. We went to Egypt because Egypt was in a state of chaos and bankruptcy and languishing under a harsh Oriental despotism. We went to Egypt because Egypt had always been to a very large extent a matter of European and international concern. The men of every race in Europe have connections and business interests in Egypt, and the condition of chaos in that country was intolerable. But if any country went there, it was most necessary that the predominant power should be Great Britain, because of the Suez Canal which is our vital connection with India and with Australia and New Zealand. We went to Egypt, and nearly fifty years have passed since we went. Every phase of Egyptian life has been improved. The cruel tyranny has been lifted from the Egyptian peasant; their water supplies have been enormously developed; the wealth of the country has gone ahead always, the wealth of this country, the oldest in the world, has gone forward almost as if it were in the new world, in Canada. A marvelous work, to which we are entitled to look back with pride and satisfaction. Our responsibilities in Egypt are direct. We have responsibilities for the protection of foreigners, of foreign powers; we have a responsibility for the protection of minorities.

All these responsibilities have been accepted by us before all the world, and I ask this: No one can say I am an enemy of self-government, I have been responsible myself for actually conducting through the House of Commons the two most daring experiments in self-government that any country has made – the Transvaal Constitution in 1906, and the Irish Free State Constitution in 1921. I ask myself gravely, are the Egyptians more capable of giving good government to Egypt, of creating those conditions of stability and order in Egypt which Europe requires, than they were in 1881? Certainly in so far as we have handed over in late years services to the Egyptians, for them to administer, and have withdrawn the guidance of parliamentary control, we have seen a marked deterioration in those services, whether they be services of irrigation or of other forms of public work throughout Egypt. And I am bound to say that it is only four years ago that the conditions in Cairo were those of incipient disorder of a very grave kind; murder and conspiracy were rife, and foreign communities expressed the deepest anxiety as to their personal and individual security.

Well, what is it that is now proposed? It is proposed that the British garrisons should be withdrawn from Cairo and Alexandria, they should evacuate those centres of control where they served as the foundation for a beneficent and ameliorating influence upon Egyptian affairs, that they should be withdrawn and that we should dig ourselves in along the Suez Canal, leaving Egypt to go if she pleases to wrack and ruin, and that at the same time we should forbid any one power to come effectively to her aid. I know well that this policy has come into force by gradual steps during the last eight or nine years, and I must admit that the late government went a long way in this direction. But when we survey the position as a whole, when we look at the scene in its full compass and extent, I am bound to say I feel the gravest misgivings about the proposals which have recently been made. It seems to me a weak policy, a selfish policy, and in a sense a dog-in-the-manger policy; it is certainly a melancholy abdication of duty which we owed not only to the citizens of the various states of Europe, but which we also owe to the Egyptian peasantry itself, and I cannot believe that such a policy, if it should be adopted, will be found to have a permanent continuation. Parliament has yet to decide, and it has been definitely promised by the present British administration that the Dominions shall be consulted. Australia and New Zealand have a vital interest, because the Suez Canal is the actual channel of communication which joins them to the Motherland and Europe, and they have a right to be heard because it was Australian and New Zealand troops which defended Egypt and held the line of the Canal against the Turkish invaders. Gentlemen, the British Government has promised that the Dominions shall be consulted and that Parliament shall know what their views are before it has to take the decision which will be asked of it in the autumn. And I would venture to say this: it seems a long way from Toronto to Cairo, but Canada has an interest as a partner in the Empire in the decision of these great matters. Anything that happens injuriously to the interests of Australia and New Zealand must affect Canadian interests and Canadian sentiment. Anything that affects the welfare of the whole affects the welfare of every part. Canada should have her opinion upon this subject of Egypt too.

Now I come to another stage in connections between the Mother Country and Australia, I come to Singapore. What is Singapore? It is a resting place, a fuelling place, for the British Fleet, to enable the British Fleet to go, if need be, to the rescue of Australia and New Zealand. That is what Singapore is for and that is the only thing it is for. People have suggested that it is a menace to Japan, but we always have the most friendly relations with Japan. No conceivable quarrel could arise between us and Japan. But our Empire must be buckled together by some effective lines of communication, and unless the British Fleet has this half-way house where it can rest and refresh and base itself, the contact is lost between Australia and New Zealand, and the Motherland and the rest of the Empire. Australia and New Zealand and the Straits Settlements and Hong Kong have made contributions to the building of this harbour, which exceed those which the Mother Country has made up to the present time. And I say to stop that work, to arrest this task in which the Empire has been engaged, just because there is a change of Government in the Mother Country, would be a disastrous set-back. We all remember what the Anzacs did in the Great War. And you, many of whom no doubt served in the Canadian Corps, you know what a comfort it was to find those valiant troops not far away, and ready to come into action in aid of the Canadian Corps. They came to our aid, and I say we must make sure that if they were in trouble, if anything arose which endangered those communities far away in the Pacific, under the Southern Cross, we must be sure that we could come to their aid with all the strength that we could muster.

I spoke at Ottawa yesterday upon Empire trade. What can we do to make more of it, to keep more business, to make business flow more easily, within the circle of the British Empire? What can we do to make the Dominions of the Crown more consciously a single economic unit? And even perhaps, to some extent, and as far as possible, a single fiscal unit? That is an urgent question. You know from your own experience how important it is that we should find means of handling large blocks of each other's business, much larger blocks than we have heretofore. . . . I proposed yesterday, and I repeat it here, that the leading business men, the great captains of industry, four or five men, who would be judged to be the outstanding figures in developing the economic life of Canada, or of Australia, or of South Africa, should meet together with the leaders of British industry, and that they should quietly and soberly examine the whole problem upon its merits, without any thought of party politics or what party is going to get the credit of it. . . . Let us push forward and tackle the difficulties by practical methods. After all, look what difficulties we have overcome in the past. When I was a schoolboy at Harrow I heard a lecture from a countryman of yours, I believe he came from this city, Sir

George Parkin.* He lectured on the subject of Empire Unity and Federation, and I sat, a little boy in an Eton jacket, and listened to his words. I remember that he said that at the Battle of Trafalgar, Nelson had set the signal flying "England expects that every man this day will do his duty." Oh, he said, if you take the steps that are necessary to bind together and hold together the great Empire to the Crown, and if at some future time danger and peril strikes at the heart and life of that Empire, then the signal will run, not along a line of battle ships but a line of nations. That is what Sir George Parkin said. I did not see him for 25 years or more and when I saw him it was at a banquet – not so large as this, indeed, but one of those great celebrations held to rejoice that victory had been won in the greatest of all wars, and that peace was now restored. And I went across the room to him and I said do you remember the words you spoke thirty years ago in your lecture, and he remembered that. All his dreams had come true, the dreams and hopes that no one would have dared even to breathe in many quarters before the war have been accomplished as actual facts. Miracles, as they would have been regarded by Victorian statesmen, have happened as the inevitable results of circumstances. The Empire has passed through the fire of war; the signal for help, the signal to arms was prepared along a line of nations which surround the world; and if ever again a peril loomed upon us we are confident it would be repeated again.

The *Globe*, Toronto, August 17,1929

MR. CHURCHILL IS RIGHT

Mr. Churchill has made his promised speech on Egypt. The visiting British statesman has come right to the point. He fears that the contemplated treaty constitutes "a melancholy abandonment of our duty to Egypt." He urges Canada to advise the Motherland against any weakening of the defenses of one of the most vital arteries of Empire.

Canada's course in the matter should be clear. As far as the Government of this Dominion is entitled to express an opinion, the urge should be for maintaining Empire communications in all their present strength. But it must be remembered that the Motherland alone has hitherto carried the entire burden of the defense of

* Sir George Parkin (1846–1922), protagonist of the Imperial Federation League; Principal of Upper Canada College, Toronto, 1895–1902; later Secretary of the Rhodes Scholarship Trust.

Egypt and of those vast portions of the Empire held in trust. Canada cannot talk too vehemently about maintaining the present defenses without inviting the obvious retort to help carry the burdens.

In a long career devoted to the State, Mr. Churchill has made occasional mistakes. But some of his most brilliant and permanent services to the Empire have been in strengthening the British position in the Near East. His warnings with regard to Egypt are worth heeding. His suggestions in this direction are worthy of the support of the Canadian people.

[The *Toronto Daily Star*, which generally upheld the Liberal government's view in the largely Conservative province of Ontario, entered a sharp note of dissent. Under the signature of Thomas Wayling, who was thought to receive more than occasional confidences from Mackenzie King, the newspaper stated that as consultation in respect of Egypt would mean responsibility, Canada had no desire to be consulted; since she was not directly interested in Egypt, she would not accept consultation.]

The *Ottawa Morning Journal*, August 20,1929

In his speeches before Canadian Clubs Mr. Winston Churchill is living up to his reputation for being unorthodox and audacious. Speakers before Canadian Clubs are not supposed to talk politics. Mr. Churchill, maker of his own laws, meets this rule by a skilful attack upon Mr. Ramsay MacDonald's naval reduction policy and a much more open and fierce assault upon the proposals regarding Egypt. It is transferring a British political platform to the hospitality of the Canadian Club.

Mr. Churchill, of course, is privileged to believe what he likes about the United States debt settlement, about the Washington Disarmament treaty of 1921, about Mr. MacDonald's proposals regarding naval reductions and Egypt. Seeing, however, that these things are matters of acute political division in Britain, Mr. Churchill might easily have refrained from discussing them in a non-political arena over here.

Canada is not a good place for Mr. Churchill to select for a belittlement of what was done in Washington in 1921 or to raise objections and doubts about what Mr. Hoover and Mr. MacDonald are trying to do now. There are too many people across the line ready to pounce like hawks upon anything that he says which may serve as ammunition for them in their "Big Navy" campaign. Mr. Baldwin, Mr. Churchill's chief, would be a little more cautious.

Saturday Night, Toronto, August 24,1929

BY A.R. RANDALL JONES

The speaker who presented Rt. Hon. Winston Churchill to the great Toronto gathering assembled in his honor on the 16th August certainly made no mistake in singling out his courage as the most salient feature of that Corinthian character. For, more than any living public man, he has exhibited that double sort of courage, so remarkable and so rare – the courage of daring and the courage of fortitude. Some people may dispute his possession of some qualities, and others of others. But his fearlessness is indisputable. . . .

It is strange how a man usually seems destined to follow his own early characteristics all his life long. It is a quarter of a century since I last heard Mr. Churchill speak until I listened to him, the other day, in Toronto. Twenty-five years ago he was just leaving the Tories and joining up with the Liberals. The rather piquant semi-insolence of the young aristocrat who was flirting with democracy has been exchanged today for the poise of the man-of-the-world statesman – for *poise* accompanied by *avoirdupois*. For his waist is much less slim than in the early days of the century. The aptitude for the terse and telling phrase still marks his public speech, but what was, in his salad days, a patent trick of phrasing – a sort of oratorical legerdemain – has ripened into literary artistry of the very first order.

There are few living men more adept at making an appeal to the intelligence of an audience and he has an unerring instinct for framing it on popular lines. That gift has always been his since the time when he first preached the gospel of Tory democracy from the platforms of Oldham. He has always loved the manipulation and the multiplication of words, but with the years he has increased his vocabulary as greatly as he has improved his style.

That style to-day is superb. I have never heard any speaker to equal him in the massive march of his utterances with their notable breadth and perfection of literary form. In every way he has grown greatly as an exponent of the oratorical art, but, in all main essentials, his oratory of to-day is just the same in kind as it was when he first entered public life. In the same way, he still retains the physical characteristics that then proved such a boon to the political caricaturist – the stoop of the shoulders, the protuberant eyes, the head thrust forward, the mobile play of facial expression, denoting, at one moment, a solemnity little short of portentous, and, at the next, an almost boyish spirit of fun. . . .

Long before he was thirty years of age, Mr. Churchill had seen life in four continents and had fought in three of them. Such experiences give a man something about which to write, and he knew how to write them. He has, all his grown-up life, had good, first-hand stories to tell – and they have lost nothing in the telling. Indeed, it is at least arguable that supreme as he is as a platform orator and as a Parliamentary debater – in the opinion of many good judges he is the most powerful controversialist in the present British House of Commons – he excels quite as much as a writer as he does in either capacity.

Thirty years and more ago he was being paid by London newspapers at rates that were the envy and the despair of the majority of first-class professional journalists. More than twenty years ago he wrote the biography of his father* – the book which first gave him definite rank as a man of letters as distinct from the "journalist-novelist" which was the position he had previously held in the writing world. For this work, which has been described as an "act of filial piety" he is said to have received the sum of $50,000. Which is a good deal more than most of us receive for any "acts of piety," whether filial or otherwise!

The *Toronto Daily Star*, August 17, 1929

Twenty-nine years ago, the British statesman visited Niagara Falls. He walked down a step-ladder to a perilous ledge somewhere under the roaring waters, and thought it all very awesome and very dangerous.

To-day he paid his second visit and found the step-ladder gone, and in its place an elevator. Where there had been a perilous ledge was now a long, winding tunnel, one hundred feet below the river.

"Ah, that's better," as he noted the change. "How time alters things. If I had only thought of this thirty years ago, if I'd only got the concession, I'd be a millionaire. One dollar a visitor – suppose there were only 100,000 visitors a year – that would mean more than 30,000 pounds, and it takes only about four people to operate the thing. Yes, I missed my chance – I might have been a millionaire.

"I was scared last time," he said. "There was no protection."

The *Montreal Star*, December 28, 1929: from an article by W.S.C.

We leave Toronto in the Canadian Pacific car which is to be our home for some weeks to come, and plunge out on a 1,200 mile swoop to Winnipeg. The fertile,

* *Lord Randolph Churchill*, published in two volumes, 1906.

cultivated lands of Ontario, rich in fruits and vegetables, studded with hamlets and farms – regions definitely subjugated by man, perennial fountains of commerce and agriculture – are left behind us. The train entered a vast "No Man's Land". Hour after hour, for hundreds of miles, we traversed scenes of savage but desolate beauty. One rocky wooded hill succeeded another in every direction, and in their recesses were innumerable lakes.

Here and there a swift-flowing river, packed with floating timber, gave some evidence of structure and activity; but for the rest it was a wild tumult of ground, stern and lonely. Even along the railways scarcely a dwelling could be seen. We are crossing a petrified sea whose waves were rocks, whose foam was forest. I could not imagine how anyone except the Indian hunter traversed these wilds on foot, where valley leads to valley and range succeeds range in seemingly endless succession. A wild beauty haunts these solitudes, so plentifully supplied with water, so clothed in forests.

Very early in the morning we are at Sudbury, at the extreme north of Lake Ontario. I looked through my window into the paling dawn, and saw the flames of furnaces and the pouring smoke of chimneys dotted here and there to the horizon. These harsh regions are now the centre of great mineral wealth. No one can tell what wealth they hold; but here, at any rate, is one of the world's finest deposits of nickel and copper. The conductor, seeing me peering through the window at the bleak panorama, interjected, "Here's where all those great fortunes have been made in the last few years. Yes, Sir! This is International Nickel."

All day long we journeyed through uninhabited lands of monotonous beauty, and as evening fell the train skirted the northern shores of Lake Superior. The limpid waters, clear and blue, of a mighty inland sea, fringed with rocky islands and marvellously tinted by the sunset, greeted the eye. The train winds for a hundred miles or more along the shores of the lake. One could see the rocks, worn smooth by the winter storms of ages, running deep down into the clear water. Here and there a hamlet, a few fishing boats, and to the north the same wonderful unending alternation of lakes and mountains.

With the night we arrive at Fort William. It is a tremendous piece of machinery for storing and embarking grain. Miles of enormous elevators, a good harbour, a fleet of grain ships, deep water communications with all the great lakes, with all the great cities on their shores, with canal systems constantly improving, with the St. Lawrence River, with the ocean, with the world; a fountain of food, as yet the unique outlet of the Manitoba wheatfields.

The *Winnipeg Tribune*, August 19, 1929

BY C.B. PYPER

There is no mistaking him. See him on the platform of his private car, dressed in a light-grey suit, with a long cigar in his mouth, plump, round-shouldered, round-cheeked, his head thrust slightly forward, and you recognize him at once. See him on the station platform, hatted, his hands thrust into his overcoat pockets, his cigar still in his mouth, talking to policemen, talking to strangers, buying a few cigars in a drygoods store, looking inquisitively in at the lunch counter, and you recognize him again. There is the hat. It is the hat of the caricature. It is an ordinary hat, but his is no ordinary head. His head would give an appearance of uniquity – pardon the word – to any hat.

See him stand with his hand on the rail as the porters shout "all aboard." "I never get on until the train starts," he explains. That is Winston all right: Winston the bad boy, Winston the audacious.

He is not quite so audacious when being interviewed. He is courteous and affable, but a little cautious and not altogether artless. . . .

"What sort of a meeting am I going to have in Winnipeg this time?" he asked.

I told him the seats were sold out in a few hours.

"What sort of audience will it be – mostly men?"

I told him there would be lots of women, and, reminding him that he had once suffered much extremity during the struggles of the suffragettes, asked whether he had any opinion to give now on the question of women and the vote.

"Well, they've got it," he grinned. "They've got it." He grinned again. That was a fait accompli, a question that could trouble him no more.

He considered a moment. "Women are a very great help in politics," he said. "Liberal women, Conservative women, Labor women – they all help their parties immensely."

I said I was going to ask a personal question, but that he and Napoleon had taught me the value of audacity. He leaned forward and listened attentively.

"You may possibly be prime minister of Great Britain," I said.

"What is that?" he asked.

"You may possibly be prime minister," I repeated.

"No," he said.

"Well," I said, "we in Winnipeg and Canada are interested in your chances. Your reputation with us is that of one of the most brilliant brains in the political world but you have the additional reputation of being somewhat erratic."

"It's not true," he said, with a grin.

"Could you give me something to prove to the people of Winnipeg that it isn't true?"

He grinned again, and reflected. "You can't disprove some things. A man must be judged as a whole."

"Another personal question," I said. "Some boys wonder whether they would rather be famous writers or heroes whom writers would write about. You have been both. Which gives you the greatest satisfaction?"

He hesitated, then grinned again. "Actions are greater than words, you know," he said.

"What was the greatest thrill in your career?" I asked.

"The mobilization of the fleet for war," he replied, without hesitation. Nothing in his Spanish war, his South African war, his Indian campaign or his Omdurman campaign had thrilled him like that. "There was nothing like the Great War," he said. . . .

"I'm glad I've met you, Mr. Churchill," I said, "because I've always admired you and once hated you."

"Tell me when you hated me," he said with a smile.

"I'm an Ulsterman," I said.

"Oh, but the Ulster people have forgiven me," he said eagerly.

"Not altogether," I said.

"Yes," he said. "The last time I was in Belfast I got a tremendous reception, an overwhelming reception. That was in 1925, after the settlement. I've always stood for Ulster since the treaty. . . .

I forgave him, too. It would be hard to help forgiving Winston.

The *Manitoba Free Press*, August 20, 1929

"I am here to see your country and the men who are making it, and to find out how we can help you and help each other," declared Mr. Churchill, on his arrival [at Winnipeg] yesterday.

"Sit there," he said, pointing to a chair facing him, "I'll give you five minutes – now what would you like to know?" He pulled on a black cigar, which he manipulated deftly between his teeth, sank a little deeper into his chair, half closed his eyelids, and was "ready to go."

"The trend of British politics?" he repeated. "Well, the Labor government is in office, but not in power. They can do anything that they can get the Liberals to approve of – further than that they cannot go. Their power is limited to the length the Liberals are willing to go with them."

"The Liberals will go along with them considerable ways, and no doubt a great many things will be done of which we do not approve, but if the Labor government attempts any extreme social legislation the Liberals will not support them, and as you know, they are entirely in the hands of the House of Commons."

The Labor leaders were not anxious to put on extreme social legislation, Mr. Churchill intimated, and the number of educated men and level-headed thinkers among them would make them see the folly of such legislation. The government did not want to enact such legislation and would be glad of an excuse for not doing so. He approved of Mr. Snowden's efforts to secure a modification of the Young plan, but hoped that Mr. Snowden would not create unnecessary offence by his manner. Mr. Snowden's manner was somewhat "rasping," Mr. Churchill said, and foreigners might not understand it as well as it was understood in the British House of Commons. . . .

Mr. Churchill did not think that an outbreak of hostilities in the east, between Russia and China, would have any effect in Europe or on this continent. It might cause anxiety in Japan, but none among the Anglo-Saxon races.

[The same journal pointed out that the Churchill of 1929 was by no means the Churchill of *Liberalism and the Social Problem*, published twenty years earlier. He had moved far to the right; but whether he had grown wiser as he grew older, or had shed the generous impulses of youth and come to see merit in the existing social order, scarcely mattered, since his changes of view had been made sincerely and not from motives of expediency.]

The *Manitoba Free Press*, Winnipeg, August 21, 1929

"Let us beware of subversive propaganda which dresses itself up in the guise of pacifism and philanthropy, and which aims to coax the British Empire to give up its rights, to give away its interests, to let down its friends, and to part with some of its vital securities," declared Mr. Churchill. "Let us beware of these. . . ."

But there was a danger nearer home, said Mr. Churchill, in which subversive methods were in process. This was the menace of Communism. The British Empire was particularly obnoxious to this organization because of its traditions, its tolerance, its freedom of speech. All these were always obstacles to the progress of Communist doctrines. Consequently the British Empire was selected as a chief object of attack of the diatribes of Moscow. The methods of the Communists had all been carefully charted and laid out in their textbooks, as carefully and precisely as a medical prescription. Wherever there gathered together two or three Communists there was a germ cell.

"I say that in all these different spheres, whether it is in standing up for our rights, in our dealing with foreign nations, in carrying forth our mission in the Orient and bringing there a higher state of well being, we must have confidence in ourselves. We must be sure of ourselves both at home and abroad. We must respect with confidence the old British invocation: 'Britons hold your own.' We can meet all our difficulties if we hold together. . . ."

There is no over-lordship of the one part of the British Empire over another. Equal for all. The Empire belongs as much to Canada and Australia as it does to the Mother Country.

"It is your Crown, your Empire, as much as it is ours, and we are sure that you will guard and cherish it as we have always tried to do. There is no obligation on any one partner to give anything to any other, or to the common cause, but for that very reason every person, every part of the Empire, as it becomes more wealthy will be looking around for gifts to bestow.

"Let the slaves rage variously among themselves. We understand; we know. They tell us that such a system, based on freedom, cannot work, and will not last, but it does and it has lasted; also, that it would never stand a shake, but it has stood the most terrible shake, storm and convulsion. . . .

"I come here tonight to make my small contribution. What can an individual do to help? Do not let anyone underrate what any man or woman can do. The power and influence of a person is enormous. It is a matter in which individuals can play a part.

"The ordinary citizen, living a life that is a credit to his city and country, is helping to further our best ideals, and by that fact the greatest purposes of our universe will be achieved," Mr. Churchill said.

"It is indeed a thrill to find myself in Canada again after so many years. You who have gone back to England and landed at Southampton must have felt that same feeling and when you've looked around you you've been able to say, 'I belong here. Here are my own people, my sisters and brothers, and there, hurrah, is the Old Flag flying.' And in the centre of our affairs is the golden circle of the crown which links us all together with the majestic past that takes us back to the Tudors, the Plantagenets, the Magna Charta, Habeas Corpus, Petition of Rights, and English common law – which links us inseparably over all those massive stepping stones which the people of the British race shaped and forged to the joy, and peace, and glory of mankind."

The *Manitoba Free Press*, Winnipeg, August 22, 1929

It is a very large, congenial, warm, and brilliantly-colored audience to meet and listen to a picturesque, unusual, and brilliant gentleman. Mr. Churchill comes out in the conventional uniform of all conspicuous politicians: black coat, winged collar, grey striped trousers, and a link or two of thin gold shining on the black background of his waistcoat. He has the round, plump, little-Jack-Horner sort of face you might find on a friendly gnome in the depths of an enchanted forest. He sits down beside Archbishop Matheson,* whose purple apron glows royally in the footlights' soft glare. . . . And out in front the house is full, right up to the gallery's torrid roof; with Union Jacks draped in red and cobalt splashes on the balcony rails. When Mr. Churchill comes in everybody rises, and cheers abound.

He steps forward and the gnome in him comes right out and looks Puckishly into the crowded dark of the theatre. Clutching both coat lapels high up near his collar, he begins to speak, in a thin refined voice touched faintly with a dainty little lisp, and not wedded too uxoriously to the final English aspirate. "The Empire has come through the fiah, intact, united, stronger than ever," etc. He goes on to assure us that Great Britain was never so full of progress as she is today – and that while unemployment is a grave social problem it is not a national crisis. He says this firmly; his voice takes edge and puts on challenge; the gnome is suddenly a figure of menace, the humorous tabby, we perceive with a thrill, is a stalking feline. This pleasant explanatory gentleman is one of the Imperial personalities, and a world figure of the most formidable character. This was the man who unleashed the British sea power in the World War; who wrestled with the force and intelligence and frustration of a Titan over the expedition to the Dardanelles, and who rode out and survived the post-war typhoons of British politics. There he was, exactly like Low's cartoon of him, down on the stage beside the table, telling us with his light voice how Winnipeg had grown amazingly in thirty years and how unfortunate the people were who lived beside the Russian bolshevists. There, indeed, he was. A world figure before the war, and a world figure still, and speechmaking the least of his extraordinary accomplishments and activities.

In the pre-war missions to Germany when the English were exploring the possibilities of war and peace with the German Government, Churchill was on the delegations. There was he, on the Walker stage, criticizing the Egyptian treaty, but where were the potentates of Potsdam and the Wilhelmstrasse with whom he had consulted? William, out of spiked helmets and uniforms, combing his beard in Doorn; Bulow vanished; Bethmann vanished;† the great Germanic dream a realized madness now fortunately past. Our speaker was associated in the dealings of war lords and the rulers who decide the fate of nations. Great personages, tremendous episodes, irre-

---

* The Most Rev. Archbishop Samuel Pritchard Morrison (1852–1942), Anglican primate of Canada, 1909–30.

† The exiled Emperor William II of Germany, and two of those who had held the office of Imperial Chancellor.

trievable astounding decisions; wealth in its astronomical dimensions; power in its extreme expansions; these were the counters in the game Churchill played as an adept.

There was an unfortunate Mr. Young somewhere who had made a speech distasteful to our speaker. He would deal with Mr. Young. The thin voice was suddenly exciting. He had mounted a horse, and flashed out a sabre and whirled off Mr. Young's head by the simple inflexion of his tones. Here was the famous Winston, the hero of a hundred high dramatic scenes and misadventures.

He had contended with the great eccentric Lord Fisher,* the pride of the British Navy, and ousted him. He had stood up to Kitchener – the massive British military monument in the War Council, and had outfaced him, and had retained his respect. He had gone down in the rancorous political dirk-work which ushered in the first coalition government; he had come up again in the extravaganzas of the post-war politics; and gone down again to bite the bitter dust of defeat; and come back again to be Chancellor of the Exchequer; and was now in opposition but in good fighting order and with all his weapons shining.

He was speaking without exertion, giving us good advice. "Do not permit subversive pacifist and defeatist ideas to take lodgment in your midst." Spurn the suggestion that the relationships between Great Britain and the United States are such as will provoke war. "The maintenance of peace is the greatest object of the Empire." "We covet no one's land." "We are jealous of no other country in the world." "How beneficent have been the results of British influence on Egypt." "British influence, mark, not rule. British rule would have given still better results." It is all so good, too, for the native races. The pit applaud the assertion. He warns us against the Communists, and ends with a reference involving "the joy, the peace, the glory of mankind." Very loud and continued applause.

Churchill has the British statesman's peculiar appearance in its most marked degree. The appearance of pleasing oddity, of simpleness, of innocence, of naivete. It is a curious mask. The Germans at least scowled and strutted, and clanked; but the British Imperialists look like the Cheeryble Brothers. And the more gnomelike they seem the more desperate they are. Behind Winston Churchill are the fighting stocks which come down through the stormy years: adventurers, pirates, seamen, soldiers of fortune. Winston himself has all these traits; they are his blood-gift from his ancestors, and they form the contribution he himself has made to England; and which he hopes to add to quite considerably in the future.

---

* Adm. Lord Fisher of Kilverstone (1841–1920), First Sea Lord, 1904–10; brought back to the Admiralty by W.S.C., 1914, but resigned after disagreements with him over the naval action in the Dardanelles, 1915.

The *Winnipeg Evening Tribune*, August 21, 1929

TWO POSSIBLE PREMIERS

BY C.B. PYPER

The audience in the Walker theatre last night had the opportunity of seeing a budding statesman try his prentice hand in public under the watchful eye of his experienced and distinguished father. The youth was Randolph Spencer Churchill, son of Rt. Hon. Winston Churchill, grandson of Lord Randolph Churchill, and descendant of a long line of warriors and statesmen.

Young Churchill was perhaps the most interesting thing in the meeting. A good looking boy, with Winston's lips and eyes, and a straight nose that descends in the Greek line from the forehead, he sat on the platform with the distinguished guests, the perfect type of the well-groomed English public school boy, a young diplomat in the making.

In the earlier part of his meeting he divided his attention between his father's speech and a friend or friends in the audience, leading the applause loyally for that and sending nervous little smiles down to this or these. As the father came near his peroration, however, the son began to get busy. Out came a pencil and paper, and he made notes industriously for some minutes.

The purpose of this was apparent when Archbishop Matheson announced that the son would reply to the vote of thanks to the father. The boy rose and stood, notes in hand, before the audience, a huge audience for a boy to face. Swaying slightly as he stood, he delivered his speech in a clear, cultured and flexible voice.

It was a nicely phrased little speech, thought out and delivered with the great seriousness of boyhood. Like his father, he said, he had come to Canada in search of knowledge, and like his father, he had been astounded. The audience applauded and laughed. Winston applauded and laughed, the boy smiled and continued.

The laughter continued, hearty, friendly laughter. Nothing more friendly could be imagined, but for a boy making a maiden speech in intense seriousness, it was just a little embarrassing. He had his say to say, however, and he was going to say it; this was his opportunity to practise and he was going to use it.

Winston's face was a study. His laughter turned to a smile and then the smile faded away. He looked up thoughtfully out of the corners of his eyes at his son – so I have seen John Redmond* survey an enthusiastic Irish orator in the Queen's hall

---

* John Edward Redmond (1856–1918), born in Dublin and a champion of Home Rule for Ireland within the Empire; MP at Westminster for the better part of forty years.

– a little resentful, perhaps, of the laughter, a little fearful for the boy. He looked as though he would have liked to pull the tail of his son's coat and whisper: "That's enough for this time, Randolph; wind it up now and sit down." Randolph wound up for himself and sat down amid renewed laughter and applause, a little flustered, a little doubtful whether this was what he had striven for.

He had done well for a beginner. These first speeches are terrible things and he had not broken down or faltered. He had gone through with what he had set out to do. More experienced speakers than he have difficulty in stopping at the proper time. Besides, when he had finished his speech, he was more experienced than he had been. This was not so much an attempt to impress a Winnipeg audience as an effort to perfect himself in the arts of the platform. That is how statesmen train themselves in Great Britain.

His father had to go through a difficult period of training. Afflicted with a slight impediment in his speech, he practised assiduously to conquer the lisp that made itself apparent in his sibilants. It is said that at one time he so prepared his speeches as to avoid sibilants as far as possible. On his way home from the South African War, when his thoughts were turning from battlefields to political platforms, he astonished his fellow passengers on the boat by haranguing the waves at length. So Demosthenes – a pebble in his mouth – practised, so practised Cicero; practice is no less necessary for the orator than for the golfer.

The lisp, which is scarcely noticeable in his ordinary conversation, was distinctly noticeable in his speech. His voice is pleasant and clear, though not powerful, and he has a peculiar little rising inflection at the end of a clause that strikes quaintly on the ear. He stands in an easy and natural attitude and uses few gestures, now pulling the lapels of his coat in the Balfour style, now spreading his hands in front of him in a quiet style of his own.

The interest lay, however, not so much in the speeches as in the speakers. It is still within the bounds of Winston's ambition to be premier, and it is still within the bounds of possibility that he may achieve it. It is within the bounds of possibility that his son, with a little more practice, may be able to move his audience to seriousness or laughter at will, and may himself become prime minister. The meeting last night may turn out to have been a notable occasion for the people in the theatre – they may have heard on one platform two members of one family, father and son, both with the premiership in their knapsacks, so to speak.

The *Winnipeg Tribune*, August 21, 1929

CANADA'S EMPIRE

It is like a breath of fresh air to find today a statesman who does not apologize or appear to apologize when he uses the word Empire as applied to the association of British nations and their colonies and dependencies. It is an Empire still. The pattern is new in the world's history, true. Its joint heirs are the seven free nations rendering allegiance to the Throne. It is not a question of conquerors and conquered. But it is an Empire nevertheless, and the only one which survives.

It is a source of worthy pride to Mr. Churchill, this magnificent engine of peace and progress. It has great traditions, running far back into the centuries. It has made the greatest contributions that have been made to the cause of human liberty and civilization. Today it is majestic in its strength, a marvellous instrument for the development of civilization. Why should it not be equally a source of pride to every Canadian? Why should not every Canadian share equally with Mr. Churchill concern for the well-being of the whole and every part of it? It is our Empire too, a heritage offering possibilities of service to mankind immense in their scope.

If Mr. Churchill has any underlying motive in visiting Canada at this time we judge it to be to awaken in the Canadian people the sentiments of pride in their Imperial inheritance and desire to assume fully the responsibility and obligations of Empire citizenship. It is a purpose worthy of his brilliant talents. Canadians, joint heirs to the traditions that have followed the Union Jack to every corner of the globe and have there assisted in setting up the institutions of freedom and justice all the rest of the world envies, have not yet learned to think Imperially. It is their part to speed the day when every part of the Empire will compete in rendering to the whole the full yield of all the talents it can muster.

The *Manitoba Free Press*, Winnipeg, August 22, 1929

The speech in the Walker Theatre was a consummate expression of a set of opinions deeply and strongly held. That Mr. Churchill spoke what was in his mind with directness, force, and even passion, was a compliment to the great audience which listened to him. Quite possibly there will be criticism of this frankly partisan discussion of questions which are controversial; and especially of his tendering of advice to the Canadian Government in the matter of Egypt; but this will be beside the point. Last year there was similar criticism of Mr. Ramsay MacDonald for outspoken utterances while he was on his Canadian tour. Canadian audiences do not particularly want to hear amiable platitudes about non-controversial topics when British public men of first rank come to visit us; rather they want the vital issues which influence British public life brought home to them.

The *Leader*, Regina, August 22, 1929

"A startling contrast to the scenes we passed through two days ago," Rt. Hon. Winston Churchill remarked to a Leader-Post representative yesterday morning as he glanced from the window of his private car which was conveying himself and the other members of his party to Regina. "This is very different from the country north of the Great Lakes, which is impressively beautiful but fierce."

A broad expanse of plain, studded with poplar and willow bluffs and small sloughs which teemed with wildlife, and with fields of stooked wheat stretching to the horizon! This was the introduction of the British statesman to Saskatchewan. He has never been here before, for when he came to Canada 29 years ago Winnipeg was the most westerly point of his visit. . . .

After the little party of four had left the car to be greeted enthusiastically by the Reginans who had gathered on the platform to welcome the notable Old Country visitors, the Leader-Post man was interested to note several books lying on a table, which it may be presumed form the literary fare of Mr. Churchill and his brother, son and nephew, during the long rail journey across Canada.

Some of their titles were: "Overtones of War" by Edmund Blunden; "Three Centuries of Canadian Story" by J. E. Wetherell; Richardson's "War of 1812"; a volume of Macaulay's History; and Taverner's "Birds of Western Canada." The last-named volume, generally considered to be the most comprehensive work on the avian population of the Canadian West, was presented to the visitors while they were in Winnipeg.

There was also a slim volume setting forth in detail the activities of Winnipeg's Anti-Mosquito Campaign. Obviously some thoughtful person, knowing Mr. Churchill to be a keen student of war, had made him a present of this work on insecticide in the hope that he would find its contents engrossing and instructive.

The *Morning Leader*, Regina, August 22, 1929

"Our president [W.S.C. said in his speech at Regina] has recapitulated in a long succession all the public offices which I have been called upon to hold in Great Britain during the last 35 [25?] years, and I am sure if you run your mind back over what he has said you will readily understand the feeling which arose in the Mother Country, that after such long and arduous toils I was entitled to a period of rest. You know what public opinion is.

"From time to time in our country even the best governments fail to meet what are considered to be the needs of the times or the wishes of the electors and these intervals, variously termed as great revivals of national conscience or lamentable aberrations on the part of the democracy, these changes afford a welcome opportunity to public men who have been long in the collar pulling hard along a rough road, very often through stormy weather, to have a rest and to see the world, and in the case of British public men an opportunity at once of seeing the world and the Empire which spans the world. . . .

"We are all members of one family, and anything that affects one part of that family reacts on the other members. I was impressed with the manner in which you sang "O Canada" at our opening today. It is an inspiring thought, your great confidence in the Empire.

"I think of the Imperial conference of 1926. It gave a new constitution in a shape which all can understand and with which anyone would find it difficult to quarrel. Under that constitution every self-governing part of the Empire is of equal status. Some are larger or more powerful than others, but their constitutional status is equal. We have His Majesty's government in London. You have His Majesty's government in Canada. All these bodies are equal in status, rights and independence, in their direct relation to the Crown. A most remarkable development of constitutional evolution.

"So let us go ahead together. You drive your furrows in this great land and make it fertile, make cities of power and science, make the resources at your disposal draw forward the chariot of development. Cast your eye across the Pacific and the Atlantic where people, too, have their place, and, hand in hand, let us advance, seeking peace, envying none, fearing none."

The *Morning Leader*, Regina, August 23, 1929

Mr. Churchill's eloquent and fervid words in regard to the feeling of common citizenship which should grip all people in the British community of nations were of the type that should help to attain that end. Probably no Regina audience has ever heard from the lips of a statesman of the Old Land such impressive words in this connection. Their weight lay in the standing of the statesman himself and in his emphasis upon the full measure of equality readily vouchsafed to every nation in the British Commonwealth.

[In Saskatchewan, the Liberals had just been defeated after nearly a quarter-century in power. At Regina, Churchill met the Premier, and next day, at

Saskatoon, the triumphant leader of the Conservatives, who feared that the crafty Liberals might yet detach a few Independents and thus continue in office. "What fun they have in these rising towns and fast developing provinces!" Churchill reflected. "All the buoyancy of an expanding world and all the keenness of the political game played out with true Eighteenth Century rigour!"][32]

W.S.C. to his wife, August 22, 1929[33]

My darling Clemmie,
I intended to begin this letter while we were still running along the north shores of Lake Superior, but we have been travelling so incessantly, I have to speak so often & have had to meet so many people, that five days have slipped away.

First of all we traversed the more populated and well cultivated regions of Quebec and Ontario. Then, leaving Toronto on our long forward bound of twelve hundred miles to Winnipeg, we passed through an enormous region of rocky hills covered with birch and pine and interdispersed with innumerable lakes of every size. This vast area of grimly beautiful but inhospitable country divides the fertile settled east of Canada from the great central wheat belt. The railways pierce through it the only channels of communication. But fortunately this vast tract now appears to be rich in minerals; nickel and copper mines of world wide fame of an immense value are now coming into play. For the rest there is nothing that could live here but the roving Indian or wild animal.

At Winnipeg begins the corn belt and thence westerly and northward stretches about five thousand square miles (a square mile is eight times as large as Chartwell!) of deep loam soil, once the bed of a lake far mightier than Lake Superior capable of bearing crops thirty of forty years running without manure. Thenceforward we are in an ocean of corn fields. As far as the eye can reach, on every side nothing but waving corn with tiny farmsteads dotted about salutes the eye. They have a new machine called the 'Combine' which not only cuts the corn, but threshes it, pouring a stream of golden grain into an enormous container, from this it is immediately removed by motor vehicles to the elevators which tower up along the railway lines; and thence to the grain ports at the head of Lake Superior. The farmer whose machine we saw at work told us that he and his son had reaped and threshed seventy acres the preceding day. The introduction of these new machines since last year has dispensed with the need of employing 20,000 men, and consequently has closed another avenue to the employment of English labour. Farming here is very much like manufacture; not a horse is used on the modern farms, and chauffeurs and mechanics, rather than farm labourers, are what are really wanted.

Tomorrow we arrive at Edmonton, the Capital of Alberta, and thereafter leave the corn belt for the rising slopes of the Rocky mountains. This region, twenty Switzerlands rolled into one, also stands between us and the beautiful and luxuriant Pacific Coast.

I have had to consent to no fewer than ten public speeches, six of which are over, Montreal two, Ottawa, Toronto, Winnipeg and Regina. The meetings have all been crammed to overflowing and everyone of consequence of all parties, classes and religions have attended. The Toronto luncheon was attended by three thousand of the keenest looking fellows I ever saw; the broadcast was probably listened to by many thousands. I was fairly well satisfied. I took a great deal of trouble about my earlier speeches, but am now working over old ground as in an election campaign.

At Winnipeg we were taken charge of by a Mr Richardson,* who is the leading grain merchant. A very good specimen of a new world business man, the owner of immense properties and undertakings from nickel and copper to a fleet of thirty-seven aeroplanes. We saw the Winnipeg Wheat Exchange where frantic dealers screamed and gesticulated as the telegrams from all the world recorded the ceaseless fluctuations of wheat prices. We are led to believe it would be wise to buy wheat for October delivery at $1.50 and that such an operation would probably be rewarded by .50¢ profit in a few months time. However we have no funds for such a venture.

We made an expedition from Winnipeg, back two hundred miles along the line to Kenora the Lake of the Woods, with three or four of the magnates including a Vice President of the Railway, who came in another private car. This lovely lake is their country club and playground. It is more than one hundred miles long and forty broad, and this expanse of clear water is dotted with islands, twenty or thirty thousand they say. Several hundreds of these have charming summer dwellings in which the victors of the mart of Winnipeg relax and disport themselves at the weekend. Between them scud motor boats of alarming speed whose fierce furrows

---

* James Armstrong Richardson (1885–1939), financier, grain merchant and founder of Western Canadian Airways.

toss the canoes of the Indians (real) about like corks. This was a day you would have really enjoyed. We scoured the lake in the fastest of all motor boats. The boys bathed and did surf riding. We lunched expansively in a palatial Peter Pan Bungalow while the wireless recounted the ceaseless patter of the movements of the Winnipeg Grain Exchange. Any of these islands could be made into a most beautiful summer residence and Randolph and I have given notice of our intention to buy one unless on our journeys we see something we like better. The brilliant aspect of this lake has left a strong impression on my mind and some day I shall have to show it to you.

If our trip had been arranged for purpose of pleasure we should certainly have stopped three or four days upon the Lake of the Woods and given Winnipeg, Regina, Edmonton and Calgary only the favour of inspection from the train. It would, however, have been impossible to see and learn the country without visiting these brand new cities which have sprung into vehement existence as the result of the discovery that wheat can be grown right up to the Arctic Circle. The frozen north in its brief five months becomes a very volcano of food. Most cordial welcomes and warm demonstrations of loyalty to the Empire have greeted us at all these centres. They are so glad to see someone they have heard about, and although it is a worry and a burden I am satisfied that my speeches are a contribution to the common cause.

I had almost forgotten to tell you that we spent the morning at Niagara Falls now two thousand miles behind, that the river was exceptionally full, that the falls were magnificent and at their very best, and far more impressive than when I saw them thirty years ago. We went under them in a tunnel with openings scooped out to see the foaming waters shearing downwards, and we went across the great whirl pool in a frail aerial car borne by wires six hundred yards long. This looked alarming but was really quite safe.

This is now our seventh successive night in the train and tomorrow will make an eighth. The car is very comfortable. Although the baths are very short by lying back with one's paws in the air, a good dip can be obtained. The heat is not really severe, indeed it is only when the car is standing on a siding that there is any discomfort.

Tender love my darling, from your somewhat harassed but ever devoted W.

The *Ottawa Morning Journal*, August 23, 1929

CHURCHILL TRYING TO CAUSE MISCHIEF

LONDON PAPER HOPES CANADIANS ARE ABLE TO ASSESS REMARKS

LONDON, Aug. 22. – With regard to the comments of certain Canadian newspapers on the speeches of Rt. Hon. Winston Churchill, former Chancellor of the Exchequer, in Canada, tonight's Star says: – "We know our Winston better than Canadians and Americans know him and can make allowances for the depth of feeling engendered in him by what he considers the injustice done to 'my friend Lord Lloyd' (who recently resigned as High Commissioner to Egypt).

"His attempt to rally the Dominions against the Egyptian settlement is undoubtedly mischievous but Canadians should themselves be able to assess it at its real value. They have had experience before of the ex-Chancellor waving the flag frantically before their eyes in the Chanak affair.

"That was when he was in office and if he failed then he is not likely to succeed now that he is out of office. It is merely the ebullience of the irresponsible boy who is still behind Mr. Churchill's 55 years."

The *Edmonton Bulletin*, August 24, 1929

HOTEL CROWDED AS EX-CHANCELLOR IS SPEAKER AT LUNCH

TELLS THRILLED LISTENERS OF EMPIRE'S MIGHT – STRIKES OPTIMISTIC NOTE – CROWD FLOWS OVER INTO TERRACE

More than 1,000 people thronged the main dining room, corridor and terrace of the Macdonald Hotel at noon Friday to hear Rt. Hon. Winston Spencer Churchill, P.C., M.P., ex-chancellor of the exchequer, guest of honor of the City of Edmonton, deliver an address that thrilled his listeners.

Praise of Canada and its progress, the place it was undoubtedly destined to hold among nations of the world; the British Empire, its achievements and advances, and above all, the little island kingdom, Great Britain itself, were subjects which he dealt with. Time after time bursts of applause would interrupt him as some particularly telling phrase was spoken.

Great Britain, always the same, always in the van of progress towards world peace and settlement, its progress since the war and its present condition proved the contention, stated Mr. Churchill, that England today was stronger than ever and still the greatest power the world has ever known.

ROOM FILLED LONG BEFORE START

Half an hour before the luncheon was scheduled to start the big dining room was well filled, while at 12:30 there was not a vacant chair, either in the dining room or corridor. At the conclusion of the luncheon proper, many of the tables were removed to make way for chairs of those unfortunate enough not to have gained admittance to the dining room.

On the terrace were several hundred more citizens. These listened to the address by means of a loud speaker provided by the provincial government. The address was also broadcast by radio. . . .

CANADA'S ADVANCE

"No part of the world shows more marked advance than Canada," he said. "Thirty years ago there was a feeling of despondency. That it would not hold together as an economic unit; that it would resolve into its various elements. But these problems have passed away.

"Canada, from coast to coast, is joined. It has become an effective and political entity, a nation from Atlantic to Pacific and has come into its own. It has the chance of building one of the greatest states known."

Not only had the west advanced, said Mr. Churchill, but also in those regions where agriculture is not possible, mining had been developed. Alberta had a great deal to be proud of, and thankful for. No other communities, he thought, had been so helped by science than the central portions of Canada. Distance has been annihilated and the motor car, telephone, aeroplane have completely changed the character of agricultural life. He trusted that they were grateful for the help science had accorded them.

Continuing, Mr. Churchill said that the British had always developed the habit of self-criticism. There never was a time, when the country was not going to the dogs, but it was well that this impression should not go abroad.

The *Edmonton Bulletin*, August 24, 1929

Perhaps the most interesting feature of Mr. Churchill's address was the insistent note – which ran all through it – that Britain is progressive and progressing, not decadent and tottering to the fall. Canadian readers learn much of Britain's domestic troubles, and seldom get a glimpse at the other side of the picture. Against all the talk of unemployment it is reassuring to be told that more people are at work in the old lands than ever before and at better rates of pay; that industrial and trading conditions are definitely on the mend; and – on the authority of a former Chancellor of the Exchequer – that Britain has re-established itself as the greatest creditor nation in the world. This is good news, for reasons both sentimental and practical. In stressing these facts before Canadian hearers Mr. Churchill is doing a service to both Britain and Canada. It is a cheering message and one to inspire confidence, and told in a way to cause it to be remembered.

The *Calgary Daily Herald*, August 24, 1929

"It is so fresh and beautiful out here."

Puffing away contentedly at an enormous black cigar, Rt. Hon. Winston Churchill, former chancellor of the British exchequer in the Baldwin government, made this remark as he stepped off his private car in the C.P.R. depot at 9:20 o'clock Saturday morning, and a moment later he was formally welcomed to this city by Mayor F. E. Osborne.*

Clad in a heather-colored suit and the famous old grey hat, the distinguished British parliamentarian looked a picture of health in spite of his strenuous trip across Canada. After a number of local men had been introduced to him, he strode across the platform and looking westwards towards the mountains, exclaimed: "What a glorious day! I can just see the peaks of the Rockies from here. It must be wonderful to be in the hills today. . . ."

With the introductions over, the British visitor asked Mayor Osborne if the visit to the oil fields was going to be undertaken as scheduled, and he seemed quite pleased when the mayor replied they were ready to start at any minute.

"They talked so much of forest fires last night that I did not know whether we would be able to go today," Mr. Churchill said.

The mayor replied that shifting winds during the night had swept the fires back over the burned out area and the danger to Turner Valley and the ranch lands beyond the valley had been averted.

"I'm jolly glad to hear that," Mr. Churchill said.

Mr. Churchill then asked if it would be possible to secure an open car for him in preference to a closed one.

"I want to see every bit of the country. I've heard so much about this wonderful province of Alberta that I don't want to miss anything." Someone suggested that an open car might be a rather dusty proposition.

---

* Frederick Ernest Osborne (1878–1948); ran a large bookstore in Calgary, of which he was Mayor, 1927–29.

Taking another healthy puff at his big cigar, Mr. Churchill said that he didn't mind the dust in the least. . . .

"I am looking forward to my sojourn in Alberta. One hears so much about this province, with its wheat fields, its oil resources and its mountain beauties. It does one good to get into the country and with such glorious skies overhead, I am sure I am going to enjoy every minute of my stay."

Randolph Churchill's diary, August 24, 1929[34]

Alberta

I happened to say (after seeing the Calgary oilfields) that it was a depressing thing to see all these oil magnates pigging up a beautiful valley to make fortunes and then being quite incapable of spending their money, and went on to criticise their lack of culture. Instantly Papa flared up, 'Cultured people are merely the glittering scum which floats upon the deep river of production!' Damn good.

W.S.C. to his wife, August 25, 1929[35]

On E. P. Ranch,
High River, Alberta

The Alberta Government entertained me at dinner in the evening [of August 23]. . . . We had cold water and boring speeches. Some kind friend, however, put something better in my tumbler.

That night (Friday) we travelled on to Calgary where we were met by the Mayor and leading citizens including Mr Carlyle* who manages the Prince of Wales' Ranch.† He told us the Prince wished us to come out and stay the week end here. So we motored through the Calgary oil fields, sixty miles, to the 'EP' (Edward Prince) ranch. The oil fields are a remarkable sight. They have hung fire for twelve or fourteen years and are now developing rapidly. The heads of the principal company conducted us around and gave us lunch. The whole valley is dotted with structures shaped like

* William Levi Carlyle (1870–1945), who had spent his earlier career largely in the United States as an expert in livestock and agriculture.

† The future King Edward VIII; after his abdication in 1936, Duke of Windsor.

the Eiffel Tower, and are 120' high. These are the derricks from which the boring down to the oil is made. They have to pierce down a mile to reach the lime stone in a kind of honeycombed cavern in which the immense volumes of gas have lain untouched for three or four hundred million years at least. The gas is under pressure so great that they have never dared to bridle it for measurement. It is so many degrees below zero that when it reaches the surface all the pipes, which are laid to carry it, are heavily frosted with snow. Out of this gas they make petrol and what is left warms the city of Calgary forty miles away. However, the city can only take half, so the rest burns to waste, roaring out its enormous flames eighty or ninety foot high and imparting to the landscape a truly Satanic appearance. I went into the whole process in detail & could now write a fairly lucid article on it. I am thinking of buying a thousand pound share in one of these companies, if all my enquiries are satisfactory....

We spent a most peaceful Sunday in this wild place, twenty or thirty miles from anyone. The house is simple but very comfortable and the weather divine. We went for a long ride all morning on sure-footed ponies galloping up and down the hills and obtaining wide views of rolling fertile country on wh every kind of crop & stock can be produced, and under which may lie fiery fortunes. The panorama of the Rocky mountains rises along the Western horizon in endless serrated ridges to grey blue peaks forty miles away, five thousand feet above this place and nine above the sea. In this vast labyrinth of mountains we shall spend the next week and then descend upon the Pacific. Randolph is in the seventh Heaven and is looking extremely well. He sleeps ten hours in every day, and eats enormously and rides as long and as often as he can. He is growing vy big & strong. I notice it. He is keeping his diary with great regularity, but he will not let me see its contents.

[At Calgary, Arthur Meighen, who had been Prime Minister of Canada a few years before, paid a glowing tribute to W.S.C. He was to preside when Churchill lectured at Toronto in 1932 and twenty years later attended the banquet in Churchill's honour at the Château Laurier. The citizens of Calgary gave Churchill a fine Stetson, which he kept for the rest of his life and was fond of wearing in his (and its) old age. The hat was sold recently in London for £9,400.]

The *Calgary Daily Herald*, August 26, 1929

"Thirty years ago, men traced the geographical formation of Canada on the map, pointed out her enormous spread of land and her small population, and said that a country of this size could not endure and progress under these conditions. Today, thirty years later, the voice of the pessimist has been silenced. With her agricultural and mineral wealth and her great northland only partially developed, Canada has taken her place among the nations of the world and her march of progress will go on."

This tribute to the Dominion of Canada, voiced by Mr. Churchill, brought an enthusiastic outburst of applause. The famous British visitor also paid a great tribute to Calgary and the province of Alberta in general. . . .

"I have witnessed the trend of Canadian national life and I am convinced that it is beyond the possibility of future catastrophe," Mr. Churchill said. "Thirty years ago I witnessed the beginning of a march to the west. Now that march is continuing. All this region is the home of a sturdy race and from this sturdy race will spring a future generation which will add to Canada's laurels.

The future will witness a great march to the north.

"Calgary," said the speaker, "has proved a wonder and delight to me. The city is in the process of a wonderful development. I congratulate the city upon its achievements and those achievements are an augury of what the future has in store.

"I witnessed good crops, heard that the farmers were to get good prices for their grain, saw for myself the remarkable oil development – all with a sense of satisfaction."

The political and social status of Britain stood ahead of every country in Europe. . . .

"I am sure that the working classes will eventually cast aside that barbarous delusion, Socialism, which has been imported into Britain from such unhappy countries as Russia and Germany, which do not know our political freedom. British security will not be fatally reduced because of it. We can trust the people and need never doubt the English democracy."

The *Calgary Daily Herald*, August 27, 1929

CALGARY HEARS FAMOUS STATESMAN

Many citizens who were privileged to hear Mr. Churchill's address at the civic luncheon yesterday must have experienced a sense of profound surprise. Here was a man who has given and received many hard knocks in his long public life, who has earned the reputation as a skilful controversialist, who glories in forensic battle with an enemy from whatever quarter, who spoke quietly, convincingly, and with a ring of deep sincerity.

His address was a model of lucidity and compactness. Known as one of the finest of parliamentary orators, he did not resort to the arts of the spellbinder nor seek momentary applause. He weighed each word carefully. He spoke with directness, and at all times with deep feeling which stirred his huge audience to a high pitch of patriotic feeling. Behind his quiet tones there was in evidence the authority and the power of eloquence which in the past have swayed huge gatherings of his fellow-countrymen. Hereafter whenever his name is mentioned, those who heard him at the civic luncheon will have a new conception of the remarkable qualities and virtues which have produced one of the most outstanding statesmen in the British Empire. . . .

His utterance was a stirring and memorable one. His words created a profound impression, all the more because of his high standing among Empire statesmen. He sounded a call to all men of British strain to remain true to the fine traditions of the race from which they spring.

W.S.C. to his wife, August 27, 1929[36]

Banff Springs Hotel

My darling,

I have longed again & again for you to be here. There have been days wh you wd have enjoyed beyond measure, & sights to see & people to please the cat [Mrs. Churchill]. But then there have been many more days wh wd simply have flattened you out. We have never ceased travelling, starting, stopping, packing, unpacking, scarcely ever two nights in any one bed except the train; & eight nights running in that. Racket of trains, racket of motor, racket of people, racket of speeches! I have made 9 & have 2 more. It has been a whirl: & on arriving here last night after the motor drives of 80 miles with a long speech at Calgary between then, I decreed a halt. So we stay here 36 hours in this magnificent hotel with every comfort – an outdoor swimming pool kept at 90 ° and riding – & I am going for the first time to try & paint a picture. I went to bed at 10 utterly tired out: & have just wakened at 7.30!

I have been wonderfully received in Canada. Never in my whole life have I been welcomed with so much genuine interest & admiration as throughout this vast country. All parties & classes have mingled in the welcome. The workmen in the streets, the girls who work the lifts, the ex service men, the farmers, up to the highest functionaries have shown such unaffected pleasure to see me & shake hands that I am profoundly touched; & I intend to devote my strength to interpreting Canada to our people & vice versa; & to bringing about an even closer association between us.

Darling one, our affairs have gone pretty well. Since we left Quebec till now (a fortnight) we have had no expense of any kind; and apart from this hotel & perhaps another at Vancouver I doubt if we shall have any for some weeks. It is astonishing to be picked up & handled in this way. However I regard 11 speeches as a substantial offset: & indeed may claim to have worked my passage. How I have wanted you!

On the other side of the account I have written one article for Nash & one for Answers for £750, have sold 1,200 extra copies of the Aftermath (so far), in Canada £250, have made another £250 with Vickers in London: & £2,000 wh Sir H. McGowan made for me by investing in Electric Shares & have contracted to write 10 articles on Canada & U.S. @ 250–300 each. I hope to make some successful investments here & in U.S.; & am glad to be able to find a little capital for that purpose. So you do not need to worry about money. The more we can save the better, but there is enough for all of us.

Darling I am greatly attracted to this country. Immense developments are going forward. There are fortunes to be made in many directions. The tide is flowing strongly. I have made up my mind that if N[eville] Ch[amberlain]* is made leader of the C[onservative] P[arty] or anyone else of that kind, I clear out of politics & see if I cannot make you & the kittens a little more comfortable before I die. Only one goal still attracts me, & if that were barred I shd quit the dreary field for pastures new. As Daniel Peggotty says "There's mighty lands beyond the seas". However the time to take decisions is not yet.

Randolph Churchill's diary, August 31, 1929[37]

At 12 o'clock we set out on an expedition to the glacier. Papa came out looking magnificent. Jodhpur riding suit of khaki, his ten-gallon hat, a malacca walking stick with gold knob, and riding a pure white horse. We

* Arthur Neville Chamberlain (1869–1940), Director General of National Service, 1916–17; Chancellor of the Exchequer, 1923–24, 1931–37; Minister of Health, 1924–29; Prime Minister, 1937–40; Lord President of the Council, 1940.

rode up to the Lake of the Clouds and then on to the edge of the moraine where we had lunch at 2 o'clock. We then rode on after seeing two marmots very tame and peaceful about eighteen inches long. Arrived at the glacier. Papa, Johnny and I climbed all over it – Papa with especial vigour.

W.S.C. to his wife, September 1, 1929[38]

Canadian Pacific Railway
En route to Vancouver

I have some news which will interest Mary.* First of all we have encountered bears. We were motoring along when suddenly at a turn in the road, bears were seen approaching at no great distance. It was in fact a she-bear attended by two large cubs. We stopped the motor alongside of them. The she-bear reared up on her hind legs in what looked at first a menacing attitude, but it turned out that she was not at all hostile, but was in fact only begging for biscuits, for which purpose she was accustomed to waylay travellers passing along this road. Alas we had no biscuits; so the she bear climbed upon the wooden balustrade by the side of the road and walked along it as on a tight-rope, while the two cubs turned somersaults on the opposite bank – all evidently offering an entertainment in return for food. Luckily at this moment another motor car arrived with plenty of biscuits, so the bears were fed quite delicately from hand to mouth and thoroughly photographed, and we resumed our journey. . . .

We also made the acquaintance of two other wild animals. The first is the 'chumpwick' as I call it, or the Chipmunk as it is properly named. This is a little squirrel about a quarter the size of our squirrel, but beautifully marked on its sides with black and yellow stripes, and in manner lively and confiding. These charming little animals soon become tame, and at the Tea House above Lake Louise they came in twos and threes and ate crumbs out of our hands, putting their little paws on our fingers and then sitting up and eating their food in the prettiest manner.

Finally on our way to the Glacier we lunched in a valley of stones out of which there appeared not only Chipmunks but three Marmots. This animal looks like a Beaver and is about two to three feet long including the

---

* The Churchills' youngest daughter, born in 1922.

tail. It wears Iron Grey fur down to its waist turning to Reddish Auburn to its tail, which is Black. He lives among the rocks and has disguised himself to look exactly like them. He is possessed of a great curiosity which led him to pry upon us as we picknicked, and he, too, allowed himself to be fed, although quite wild. The only Butterflies seen are – first the Camberwell Beauty, which is as common here as it is rare in England, the Clouded-Yellow, the larger Tortoise Shell and several kinds of Fritillaries. As we get further south we shall no doubt see many more varieties.

After the meeting at Calgary, which was great success, we motored eighty miles to Banff, the road gradually leading us into the hills and the hills gradually rising into high mountains amid which we were finally completely enclosed. Banff has a gigantic hotel placed amidst very striking scenery. Here we rested for a day and then started on a three day motor tour of about three hundred miles. The first night we spent at Radium Hot Springs. Here the water bubbles out of the rock hotter than you can bear. It is caught in a large swimming bath made by the Government; it is strongly charged with Radium, and 750,000 gallons pour out every day. It is the same sort of water as that recently prescribed for you. We bathed night and morning in the open air swimming bath, which was about as hot as a real hot bath. One felt almost too languid to swim but afterwards it is refreshing. The second night we slept at Lake Emerald after a fine drive along the sides of precipitous hills, across foaming torrents and through the magnificent gorges. Lake Emerald has an extraordinary colour more Turquoise or Jade than Emerald. Its water is Opaque like Jade. This is due to the muddy glacier streams by which it is fed. Around rise splendid glaciers and mountain peaks on every side. We slept at a Bungalow Camp maintained by the Canadian Pacific consisting of clusters of neat bungalows supplied with hot water and electric light and every comfort. I painted three pictures which give a very inadequate idea of the great beauty of this spot.*

The third day we went on to Lake Louise visiting en route the Yoho Valley. The scenery was most grand and awe inspiring. We also visited the Takakaw waterfall which leaps like a mighty horsetail out of a narrow cleft in the mountain side large as a river, and 1,200 feet high – a wonderful sight! In the evening we reached Lake Louise, where there is another enormous

* For these pictures, two of which were previously thought to be of scenes in northern Italy, see D. Coombs, *Sir Winston Churchill's Life through his Paintings* (2003), p. 120.

hotel. Its front is of forbidding aspect, but on walking through it a truly enchanting scene is revealed. Another green Lake of wide expanse surrounded by enormous precipices and with a wonderful line of snowclad peaks and glaciers in the centre. I longed for you to be with us at this point and at Emerald, and really I think I must some day persuade you to come. Now that I know the ropes I could plan the tour without any of the undue fatigue of some of our journeys. We could only spare one day amid the comforts and the beauties of a spot which in all of my travels I have never seen surpassed. That day, however, I spent in painting a picture which gives some idea of the colouring, and thereafter we all rode up to the glaciers. Two hours ride through forests and along rather dizzy mountain tracks brought us to the Plain of Six Glaciers, and here Randolph, Johnnie and I walked across the largest glacier right to the foot of the rock wall. Although these mountains are not above eleven thousand feet high and only six thousand feet higher than the hotel, their precipices are so sheer and their silhouettes so jagged, that they make an impression at this point more remarkable than anything I have seen in the Alps. On the glacier we were in a vast arctic cathedral surrounded by ice and walls of rock three or four thousand feet high. No more perfect Alpine scene exists than this though it is but two hours ride from a Ritz hotel. No wonder Lake Louise is becoming one of the most famous pleasure resorts on this continent!

Today we are making our last railway journey in the car. We are running at this moment along the Fraser River, a broad and winding torrent of clear Green water rolling, like us, down to the Pacific ocean.

[After the assembly had partaken of what Randolph Churchill described as "the most disgusting cold buffalo . . . ushered in by the singing of Rule Britannia," his father addressed an audience of seven hundred at New Westminster, near Vancouver, on September 2. When Churchill had last been in Canada, he told them, the future of the country was in doubt and many people believed that the east and the west would break apart; whereas now they were buckled together from ocean to ocean by two great railway systems and Canada was growing by every known test. A feature of the past thirty years had been the movement to the west; the future would see Canada going northward. He dwelt again on the intangible ties of sentiment, tradition, loyalty and sympathy, prospering only in an atmosphere of freedom, which held the British Empire together.

This was something which "foreign observers have never been able to comprehend."

Speaking at Vancouver ten years to the day before the outbreak of the Second World War, he once again declared the prospects for peace to be secure.]

The *Vancouver Sun*, September 4, 1929

"In Toronto [Churchill said at Vancouver] I gave a warning that this policy of evacuating the British troops out of Egypt would be attended by misfortune in the east. Confirmation has come.

"What more glaring example could we have of the effect of signs of lack of will power in the central government than the outbreaks of pillaging, rapine and slaughter in Palestine?*

"That is a bloody foretaste of what may be expected in the whole Nile valley and on a vaster scale throughout our whole Indian dependency if the guiding hand of Britain and its signs of power, without which the guiding hand could not effect its purpose, were stricken away.

"The British people should have confidence in their mission, not to enrich themselves out of subject peoples, but to bring the blessings of order and government into countries torn with religious and racial factions.

"Let us have confidence to give effect to that mission. Let us not give ear to those counsellors who advise meeting our problems by laying down our responsibilities and by ignominiously withdrawing to leave these peoples exposed to the horrors of internal strife.

"Palestine belongs to two races—the Jews and the Arabs." The Jews have at least as good a right there as the Arabs, and there is no reason why the Arabs should resent the arrival of larger numbers of Jews to develop the country.

"The Jews have done the Arabs no harm. They have increased the prosperity of the country, and are developing its wealth. They have made homes and farms out of the desert by their energy and the wealth they have brought from Europe and America. The only result to the Arabs has been wealth, wages, improvement in living and lifting the country from the squalor of centuries.

* After months of tension, serious anti-Jewish risings had taken place. The local police force being unable to contain the violence, troops and warships were sent. About 120 Jews and 180 Arabs were killed.

"The Jews are there as a result of the promise of this country. I am certain no party will fail to vote the necessary men and money to see that the word of Britain is kept and that order is restored."

[At the end of August, Snowden had agreed to a settlement of the reparations question, the French government having abandoned its insistence on the Young Plan. On paper, the terms looked well enough; in practice, they were soon to be swept away in the cataclysm of the early 1930s. Meanwhile, it had been agreed to evacuate the last of the Allied troops from the Rhineland, thus removing any physical security for enforcement of the peace treaty of 1919. This was hailed as a notable political achievement.]

The *Daily Province*, Vancouver, September 4, 1929

Mr. Churchill's new stand on the reparation question as enunciated Tuesday night brings him almost to the identical position taken by Hon. Philip Snowden in Parliament just before the recent election. To those who remembered the Snowden incident and the late Conservative cabinet's adhesion to the principle of the Balfour note, the speaker's statements were just short of startling.

The conclusions reached at The Hague conference, the former chancellor thought, were very satisfactory. He agreed that no British government could have accepted the Young plan as it stood, and that Mr. Snowden had been right in both his stubborn resistance and his final concessions. The amount involved in the concessions was not great enough to justify setting back the whole resettlement of Europe.

"Nevertheless the principle of the Balfour note has been impaired," he continued, "and we can no longer say that we are obtaining as much from Europe, including arrears, as the United States would receive from us. I have always recognized that some small concessions, such as Mr. Snowden made, would be necessary. It was my intention, however, if I continued in office, to take the opportunity afforded by any deviation from the principle of the Balfour note to restate that principle in terms more advantageous to Great Britain.

"It should have been made clear at The Hague – and I sincerely hope it was – that the Russian debt to Great Britain of nearly £600,000,000 stands outside the self-denying limitation of the Balfour note. France and Italy should have been invited to agree to this as an offset to fresh concessions we have made.

"Although no doubt a settlement of the Russian debt may seem remote and speculative, it is by no means impossible. If in ten or fifteen years' time Russia wishes to resume the garb of civilization, and effects a debt settlement with her creditors, the

British taxpayer should receive the relief therefrom. The Hague conference was the moment for obtaining this necessary assent of France and Italy to the restatement of the British position, and I hope it has not been overlooked. . . ."

[In the last part of his speech, W.S.C. discussed the outlook for Canada.]

"Today East and West," he continued, "are buckled together from ocean to ocean by two great transcontinental railway systems. The country is growing by every test that can be applied. . . ."

In Vancouver there was a special reason, he said, to plant hopes on the harvest, for this city, with all of the gathering force of the continental belt behind it, can not fail to find a way on the Pacific to greatness.

"The war," he continued, "which devastated Europe and scarred the world, also halted the expansion of Vancouver. Like other cities, you sent the flower of your manhood to fight overseas, but there was more than that to check activity. In Canada, cities saw not the fiery face of war as those cities in France and in some parts of England. There was no excitement of bombardment or bombing here, but only the cold chill suspension of activities and the sapping of prosperity of this city for welfare and service to the common good.

"Now, however, let us move forward together with the other parts of the Empire into the sunlight of victory street."

The *Daily Province*, Vancouver, September 4, 1929

CHURCHILL

You can agree with Winston Churchill or you can disagree with him, and you can do one or the other with a frankness which answers to his own, but what you can not do is to find him negligible and pass him by. All the audacity of his famous breed rang in the periods of his speech last night, and all the intelligence of the Churchills informed its precise and faultless phrases. He, the late chancellor of the exchequer, said the apt word in praise of Philip Snowden, his successor. He, the ex-minister of a defeated government, knew how to pay his respects to the new government without derogation from the things which belong to an undefeated conviction. It was Mr. Churchill who once said that Labor was unfit to govern. He did not say it last night; perhaps he will never feel like saying it again. But if the time comes, or if he ever thinks it has come, we may be very sure that Winston Churchill will not shrink from the challenge. This is the son of the man who said, "I will not be silenced."

The *Daily Colonist*, Victoria, September 6, 1929

Mr. Churchill was given a tumultuous reception when he arose to address the vast audience [at the Empress Hotel, Victoria]. Waves of applause and cheers greeted him, and it was nearly five minutes before he was able to make himself heard above the deafening welcome. During the ovation, Mr. Churchill smiled broadly, and gave indication that the warmth of the greeting by the assembly had touched him noticeably.

"I am a traveler who is finishing today what is to me a most memorable and thrilling journey across the Dominion of Canada," stated Mr. Churchill, in opening his address. "I am also finishing what has certainly been a serious task – making the sixteenth public address I have given in Canada in the last month.

"Where else could I look for a better climax and culmination of my tour than here in Victoria, where I am reminded on every side of the small island from which I started out. Your green lawns and sturdy oaks, and hearts as British as the oaks, all remind me of the Mother Country. . . .

With a reconciliation, a community of interests and a better understanding between France and Germany, all other difficulties in Europe will fall into lesser importance," he said. "We have succeeded in the Treaty of Locarno in binding together these two nations, and have brought them into a more solid comradeship in the future.

"We are anxious that Germany should resume her place in the family circle of Europe, and that has been achieved. Not that we did that at the expense of the Allies, with whom we stood side by side during those long years."

Mr. Churchill said the British policy in Europe had been clean, clear and consistent, and aimed only at the general interests of that continent.

Turning to the British policy in the East, the speaker claimed the course which Britain has pursued in the Pacific in the past ten years would bear the closest scrutiny of historians.

"We have very old and highly valued associations with Japan. I have always found my confidence in the Government and people of Japan strengthened by their conduct, in peace and in war," declared Mr. Churchill, amid cheers. . . .

The speaker considered the British Government and the Foreign Office is entitled to credit for the skill displayed in dealing with the baffling changes in the Chinese situation. In the past four years the situation has been completely transformed. The Chinese have sickened of the false Russian guides; they have seen the gulf of Communist annihilation to which they were being urged, and they have turned towards and have trusted the British Government," Mr. Churchill stated.

"Not only were patience and skill shown, but an element of firmness was needed. Firmness is always necessary in dealing with Oriental peoples. A force sent from England had arrived in the nick of time to secure safety in Shanghai, and to show that the force of right sometimes is necessary to be sustained by the right of force."

Mr. Churchill said the trade and economic advances of China must "carry your prosperity to higher levels than yet attained.

"The Pacific Ocean is coming into its own. The shores of America and Asia are being brought closer together, and you must be the channel through which the ever-growing cornfields of Canada must discharge their products to the people of the Orient. . . ."

"Let us be of good cheer," said Mr. Churchill. "Let us have confidence in the future."

Mr. Churchill mentioned that at the outbreak of the Great War he sent the following message to the Commander-in-Chief of the Grand Fleet, the skilful and trusted admiral, Lord Jellicoe, "Take up your great task in buoyancy and hope. We are sure that all will be well."

"The nations not so blessed as thee,
Shall in their turn to tyrants fall,
But thou shalt flourish, great and free,
The hope and envy of them all."*

Mr. Churchill quoted in conclusion, amid ringing cheers and applause.

Randolph Churchill's diary, September 6, 1929[39]

We are now on the ship bound to Seattle, American soil and Prohibition. But we are well equipped. My big flask is full of whiskey and the little one contains brandy. I have reserves of both in medicine bottles. It is almost certain that we shall have no trouble. Still if we do, Papa pays the fine, and I get the publicity. But we have a second line of reserves. We questioned the Chief of Police in Vancouver as to the best arrangements to be made and he said he would telephone and have some put on the train at Seattle. We asked him who would see to it. His reply shows how graft-stricken the US is: 'The police'! He knows the Chief of Police at Seattle, and he will readily oblige. Of course it is the Federal Police who are really

* A verse from "Rule, Britannia," much loved by W.S.C.; the quotation as printed here is not entirely correct.

responsible for drink, but still one cannot conceive of a situation like that in England.

W.S.C. to his wife, September 12, 1929[40]

New Place,
Burlingame, California

Canada improved in interest as we went West. British Columbia is a wonderful possession. . . . We were everywhere received with "Rule Britannia" and great demonstrations of Imperial patriotism. The one spare day we had was delightfully spent at a great lumber camp. An athletic youth shinned 190 feet up a giant tree and, hanging on by a loop of rope around his waist, hewed 60 feet off the top of the tree. He looked tiny at that awful height and I had many qualms. He wished to stand on his head on the bare summit of the tree pole in conclusion. It took all my authority to prevent this fearsome exhibition.

They cut the great trees, 200 or 300 feet high, without ropes of any kind and make them fall within an inch of where they wish. The devastation of these beautiful trees was sad to see.

The Chief of Police,* a remarkable character, escorted us everywhere. He was twenty-five years in the Metropolitan Police and received the freedom of the city of London, retiring on his pension. He came out to Canada and worked as a laborer or at any odd job, but last year the Mayor of Vancouver, a very fine fellow† – won his election on cleansing the local police force, whose condition was putrid; so they took our friend from his task as daily laborer and made him Chief Constable with plenary authority. In three months he cleaned up the whole situation, sacked forty principal officers, purified the moral atmosphere of the town, caught murderers and thieves in all directions, terrified others out of the district. They enforced the liquor laws with brilliant financial results to the State. He is therefore omnipotent, and all misdoers and grafters, however high in place, stand in terror of him. . . . He, the Chief Constable, is likely to be moved on to the control of the liquor law of British Columbia at a salary of $12,000. a year.

---

* William James Bingham (1875–1946), Chief Constable of Vancouver, 1929–31.

† William Malkin (1868–1959), philanthropist and businessman; Mayor of Vancouver, 1928–30.

Not bad within a year of getting $3.50 a day. He saw we were well provided with liquor – on the principle I suppose of not muzzling the ox etc.

We reached Victoria in Vancouver Island (which is as big as England) by a beautiful voyage in a perfectly appointed ship through an archipelago of delicious inlets. Victoria is English with a splendid climate thrown in. Sentiment, vegetation, manners, all revive the best in England.

A splendid old Scotsman, Mr. Randolph Bruce,* who landed forty years ago with £1 in his pocket and is now very wealthy, is Lieutenant-Governor. He entertained us in royal state. We were played into and through dinner by a Highland Piper and were much petted by all parties. I addressed an enormous luncheon, 700 or 800 men, the cream of Victoria, for an hour. Thanks were proposed to me by the Dean – a foolish Cleric with Socialist leanings who asked a number of cheeky questions† and maundered on unduly. So I put up Randolph to reply and he, in a brief, admirably turned debating speech of five minutes completely turned the tables upon the Dean, to the delight of the audience and also to their amazement. His performance not only showed his curious facility for spinning words but gave proof of great poise, judgment and tact. He knew exactly how far to go and how to win and keep the sympathies of this audience. I could not have done it so neatly myself.

* * *

The Churchill troupe now paid a visit to W.R. Hearst at his bizarre residence in California. Perhaps a little against expectation, Churchill liked Hearst, observing with some awe that he controlled newspapers which sold fifteen million copies a day and enjoyed an income of $1 million a year. With Charlie Chaplin, Churchill sat up until three in the morning and promised to write the scenario for a film if Chaplin would play the part of the young Napoleon. Reaching Chicago at the beginning of October and releasing Randolph and Johnnie for their return to Oxford, Churchill was

---

* Robert Randolph Bruce (1863–1942), Lieutenant-Governor of British Columbia, 1926–31; Canadian Minister in Tokyo, 1936–38.

† According to Randolph, the Dean asked his father three questions: "If he ever becomes Prime Minister, will he make me Archbishop of Canterbury? Does he intend to go into business with Lord Birkenhead? Is he still a member of the bricklayers' union?" Not surprisingly, Randolph "immediately saw the opportunity to make a hit."

joined by Bernie Baruch; the two had been fast friends for years, from the days when Baruch had been particularly helpful as Chairman of the War Industries Board in Washington and Churchill was Minister of Munitions.

He had already reported cheerfully to Clementine upon his improving financial prospects; in a matter of three weeks he had made profits on shares of more than £5,000 and received an advance of £6,000 for *Marlborough*, together with royalties and payments for articles amounting to nearly £4,000. Nor was that the end of it, for he then contracted to write twenty-two articles, all to be completed within a few months.[40] They would entail "heavy work on return," but bring in something like £40,000; which was just as well, in view of events about to occur.

It was always said of Churchill that he "made things happen." He loved to witness great events for himself, from a position as nearly central as possible. Even he could not have foreseen, still less wished, that the very day of his arrival in New York, October 24, would signify the beginning of the Great Crash. Though thousands of millions of capital value were annihilated in a week or two, Churchill was nevertheless sure that the disaster marked only a passing episode in the history of the United States. "Under my very window," he recorded, "a gentleman cast himself down 15 storeys and was dashed to pieces, causing a wild commotion and the arrival of the fire brigade. Quite a number of persons seem to have overbalanced themselves by accident in the same sort of way. A workman smoking his pipe on the girder of an unfinished building 400 feet above the ground blocked the traffic of the street below . . . the crowd, who thought he was a ruined capitalist, waiting in a respectful and prudently withdrawn crescent for the final act."

A stranger, recognizing Churchill as he walked down Wall Street at the worst moment of the panic, invited him to enter the gallery of the Stock Exchange. In place of the pandemonium he anticipated, Churchill viewed a scene of calm and order. The rules forbade running about or the raising of voices. "So there they were, walking to and fro like a slow-motion picture of a disturbed ant heap, offering each other enormous blocks of securities at a third of their old prices and half their present value, and for many minutes together finding no one strong enough to pick up the sure fortunes they were compelled to offer."[41]

Largely on account of his recent speculations, Churchill had lost more than £10,000. Characteristically, he told his wife the grim news there and then when she met him off the boat train on November 5.[42]

3

New Directions: 1932

Churchill's losses in the crash had been so substantial that his beloved Chartwell was largely closed that winter; only the study remained in use, and at the weekend he would join his young daughter Mary at a cottage by the kitchen garden. It might be thought that to lose office and a large fortune would bring low spirits; but if the black dog of depression did come, his visits were not prolonged.

In 1930, there died the two men whom Churchill later described to Mackenzie King as those whom he missed most, F.E. Smith and A.J. Balfour: "The former, habits very bad but brilliant intellectually. The latter, almost ascetic in his life, spiritually minded; a lofty character."[1] Balfour, whom Churchill had often assailed with vigour in earlier years, faded away in old age, and of him Churchill wrote perhaps the noblest passage in *Great Contemporaries*; Smith (in later life Lord Birkenhead) expired young, exhausted by his own excesses. He had been one of the few who could exercise a restraining influence upon Churchill's impetuosity. "Last night," wrote Mrs. Churchill to Birkenhead's widow, "Winston wept for his friend. He said several times, 'I feel so lonely'."[2]

Churchill dictated articles and books; as he used to say with a smile, "I live from mouth to hand." He busied himself with bricklaying, painted pictures and supervised all manner of works on the estate, including the building of a lake and the swimming pool. Soon normal life resumed at Chartwell, which required a staff of sixteen: eight indoor servants, two secretaries, three gardeners, a chauffeur, a bailiff for the farm, a groom.

When Churchill left the Treasury in the summer of 1929, he had held office with comparatively short intermissions for nearly a quarter-century. Despite his denials in Canada, he would have liked to become Prime Minister, while recognizing that such an event was unlikely. He had but recently returned to the Conservative Party; and many of his colleagues in the former administration, while admiring his talents and oratorical powers, found him mercurial and unreliable. One of them, who as First Lord of the Admiralty had suffered much from Churchill's relentless pursuit of economy, recorded, not long into the new Parliament, "It is very hard to hold him to an arrangement he has made & if he wants to get out of it he is not scrupulous. I should have expected him to be good in Opposition in the House, but he is disappointing – possibly because he has generally managed to change on to the victorious side & so has had little practice."[3]

The Labour government had come to office with high hopes and much talk of reducing unemployment. Philip Snowden, Churchill's successor at the Treasury, held views about financial orthodoxy which would have commanded the respect of Mr. Gladstone himself. Churchill once wrote, perhaps with some sorrow, that all Chancellors had yielded themselves, whether spontaneously or unconsciously or reluctantly, to the compulsive intellectual atmosphere of the Treasury. But with the advent of Snowden, the High Priest himself entered the sanctuary. "The Treasury mind and the Snowden mind embraced each other with the fervour of two long-separated kindred lizards, and the reign of joy began."[4]

It became plain that an economic catastrophe was being visited upon every part of the world. The economy of the United States took many years to recover; the banking systems of Central Europe proved fragile; the reparations payments so recently reduced and agreed still looked too heavy for Germany to bear; and by tariffs or other means many countries sought to protect their own economies. Although the British, with relatively minor exceptions, had retained free trade, it became only too apparent that the process was a one-sided affair. To Baldwin, Neville Chamberlain and most of the leading figures of the Conservative Party, many of whom had been tariff reformers since the early years of the century, the opportunity beckoned. It seemed more than likely that a measure of protection of the home economy, with some preferences for the countries of the Commonwealth and Empire, would become practical politics and perhaps quite soon. That prospect presented Churchill with a dilemma of an acute kind, for he still believed in the merits of free trade and it was only the temporary abandonment of protection which had enabled him to serve as Chancellor.

He also knew that Baldwin and the others were willing to make a substantial move in the direction of self-government for India. Churchill, as he expressed it long afterwards, believed that the Opposition should confront the Labour government on all great Imperial and national issues, and identify itself with the majesty of Britain as in the days of Disraeli and Salisbury; whereas Baldwin seemed to feel "that the times were too far gone for any robust assertion of British Imperial greatness."[5]

The issue is not a simple one, and the customary dismissal of Churchill's views as merely outmoded or reactionary is unjust. Over India, not free trade, he deliberately detached himself from his former colleagues. In January 1931, with the Labour government's economic difficulties mounting by the week, Churchill decided to leave the Opposition front bench. Since he disagreed strongly with his colleagues upon the grandest issue of Imperial policy and continued to do so until the summer of 1935, it was clearly right and creditable that he should leave their company. Churchill was not excluded by the Conservative or any other party from the National Government soon to be formed; he had excluded himself.

By now well embarked upon the research for *Marlborough*, for which he had recruited an able team of assistants, Churchill produced perhaps the most attractive of his books, *My Early Life*, dedicated "To A New Generation." He recaptures the cast of mind, even the language, of his youth, from early childhood to manhood. At the age of seven, going to school with dread, he learns that "O mensa" is the form to be used in speaking to a table. He blurts out "But I never do," only to be informed that if impertinent he will be punished very severely. "Such was my first introduction to the Classics from which, I have been told, many of our cleverest men have derived so much solace and profit." We see in our minds Churchill as a young officer in India, devouring the whole of Gibbon, moving on to Macaulay, Plato and Aristotle, Malthus and Darwin. "It was a curious education. First because I approached it with an empty, hungry mind, and with fairly strong jaws, and what I got I bit; secondly because I had no one to tell me: 'This is discredited . . . .' I now began for the first time to envy those young cubs at the university who had fine scholars to tell them what was what. . . ." And then there was the matter of whisky, which until his time in the blistering heat of the North-West Frontier Churchill had not been able to drink. Other than tea, the soldier could have tepid water, or tepid water with lime juice, or tepid water with whisky. By the end of five days' campaign, Churchill found that he had overcome his repugnance. Nor was this some momentary achievement; "To this day, although I have always practised true temperance, I have never shrunk when occasion warranted it from the main basic standing refreshment of the white officer in the East."[6]

Even the rigorous Chancellor of the Exchequer was driven to unbalance the budget. The cost of unemployment benefits, paid at the most modest of rates, rose inexorably as trade and confidence declined. Initiatives here and palliatives there failed. It is impossible not to sympathize with the predicament of a government caught in such a tempest, or with the distress felt by Labour ministers who on the one hand had to confront these intractable realities of economic life and on the other could hardly bear to think of imposing further sacrifices upon the working classes. The Cabinet broke up late in August 1931. Churchill was painting in the south of France and did not think it worthwhile to return at once to London. The crisis was judged so grave that only a coalition of the main parties could meet it. MacDonald accordingly remained Prime Minister, though almost all his leading Labour colleagues went into Opposition; the Conservatives under Baldwin supported the new National Government, as did most of the Liberals.

One of the principal purposes of the new administration was to uphold the Gold Standard, to which Britain had returned under Churchill's own impetus only six years earlier. In the event, the pressure proved too great; the Gold Standard was abandoned; the National Government determined to hold an early general election, each of the main parties putting forward its own manifesto; the Conservatives stated that they would press for a balanced budget and a tariff against imported goods. The result marked the most startling landslide in British parliamentary history, for the National Government came back with 558 supporters – of whom 473 were Conservatives – whereas the Labour Party had only 52. The landscape of politics had changed, and quickly. Established features had vanished as if in an earthquake; for example, the Liberal Party, only a few years earlier in triumphant command of political life, had subsided. Most members of the former Labour Cabinet had lost their seats. The value of the pound was no longer tied to gold, and no one could divine the outcome.

In his own election address, Churchill had stated, "As Conservatives we are convinced that an effective measure of Protection for British industry and British agriculture must hold a leading place in any scheme of national self-regeneration." The same document referred to the attempt to pay "those accursed War Debts and Reparations" across the "almost prohibitive tariffs," that is, the tariffs imposed by the United States.[7] To that country Churchill was eager to return. Much had happened since those tumultuous days in October 1929, when vast fortunes had crumbled away in days. The American economy had been ravaged; agriculture and manufacturing alike had suffered; unemployment had reached unprecedented heights; a Presidential election was soon due. What better moment to recapture the habits of 1900, and deliver a series of lectures, moving on each day from one city to another, but this time rather better rewarded than in 1900? The lectures were guaranteed to bring in at least £10,000, and a series of articles about his American experiences an even larger sum.

An obstacle loomed up. In old days, income tax had stood at modest levels. In 1931, by contrast, high incomes were heavily taxed. Churchill himself could hardly complain of this, since he had so recently been Chancellor of the Exchequer, but he had no desire to pay exorbitant sums. Would your alguazils, he asked his former Private Secretary at the Treasury, consider the proposition that the lecture fees should be separated from his profits as an author and journalist? Even P. J. Grigg, later to be Finance Member of the Government of India, Permanent Under-Secretary of State at the War Office, and, from 1942, Secretary of State for War in Churchill's administration, may have had to glance at his dictionary for a definition of *alguazil*: "a constable or an officer of justice in Spain" or "a mounted official at a bullfight." Doubtless Churchill intended the latter meaning. The alguazils were unanimously of the view that the lecture fees must be aggregated with his other profits in calculating liability to tax. Protesting, he asked Grigg to put an additional point to the alguazils:

"The act of delivering a lecture is not literary but histrionic in its character. It is a physical and psychic exertion of which most literary men or journalists would be incapable, a certain standard of quality being essential."[8]

Churchill found with chagrin that the profits from speaking would so raise the tax on the rest of his income that he would receive little more than two-fifths, but somehow the difficulties were met. Accompanied by his wife and daughter Diana, he left for America. Crossing the road in New York, he was nearly killed by an oncoming car. After a week in hospital, he immediately dictated a lengthy article, sold in London for £600 and in the United States for $1,500. "I rather plume myself," he wrote to Randolph with satisfaction, "upon having had the force to conceive, write and market this article so soon after the crash. I received a great price for it, but find it very dearly bought."[9] He even applied to his intimate friend Professor Lindemann for a mathematical calculation of the impact. The reply came by telegram from the south of France:

> COLLISION EQUIVALENT FALLING THIRTY FEET ON TO PAVEMENT EQUAL SIX THOUSAND FOOT POUND ENERGY EQUIVALENT STOPPING TEN POUND BRICK DROPPED SIX HUNDRED FEET OR TWO CHARGES BUCK SHOT POINT BLANK RANGE STOP SHOCK PRESUMABLY PROPORTIONAL RATE ENERGY TRANSFERRED STOP RATE INVERSELY PROPORTIONAL THICKNESS CUSHION SURROUNDING SKELETON AND GIVE OF FRAME STOP IF ASSUME AVERAGE ONE INCH YOUR BODY TRANSFERRED DURING IMPACT AT RATE EIGHT THOUSAND HORSE-POWER STOP CONGRATULATIONS ON PREPARING SUITABLE CUSHION AND SKILL IN TAKING BUMP[10]

So severe a crisis depressed even Churchill. His wife wrote to their son: "Last night he was very sad & said that he had now in the last 2 years had 3 very heavy blows. First the loss of all that money in the crash, then the loss of his political position in the Conservative Party and now this terrible physical injury. He said he did not think he would ever recover completely from the three events."[11]

Half recovered, he returned to America toward the end of January from convalescence in the Bahamas, where even "the most lovely tints of blue and green and purple" had not tempted him to paint. From some five weeks of lecturing he earned more than £7,500. In these speeches, he appealed for a closer union of the English-speaking peoples against Communism and the disintegrating forces of a disunited Europe. He saw two imminent forces in the shaping of mankind's destiny: Communism and the English-speaking ideal of individualism. He spoke enthusiastically about the results of the general election in Britain, which he described as a grand vote and good for the country. He dwelt upon the "horrid fall in world prices" and did not believe that the United States would consent to lower tariffs in reciprocity with Britain. As for the recent Japanese attack on Manchuria, he declared in Washington, as he was about to do in Toronto, that the British Empire was not going to be drawn into war to protect China, and denied any obligation under the Covenant of the League of Nations to fight for China; rather, the British people favoured the cautious policy adopted by the American and British governments alike. He expressed strong opposition to home rule or Dominion status for India. He discussed disarmament, but chiefly in terms of navies and armies, with little reference to air power.

It was now time to cross the border, for a most attractive offer had arrived from Toronto. According to the information of *The Times*' chief correspondent in Canada, Churchill was paid a fee of $2,500 for his lecture by Simpsons, one of the leading department stores.[12] This is not impossible, for he had earned on average $1,300 for each lecture in the United States, and most had been delivered in halls far less capacious than Maple Leaf Gardens. Arthur Meighen was to preside; good seats cost between 50¢ and $1, and the 48th Highlanders' Band would play.

Churchill arrived on March 2 and stayed at the Royal York, then proudly advertised as the largest hotel in the Empire.

* * *

The *Globe*, Toronto, March 3, 1932

SNAKESKIN SLIPPERS REMIND CHURCHILL REDS ARE REPTILES

"Shrubbery," Mr. Churchill said, "obstructs the view." He moved a bowl of flowers from a table in the centre of his sitting-room at the Royal York Hotel, sat down beside the table and began to talk.

Mr. Churchill's face is round and pink. His hands are square and pink. His hair, what remains of it, is gold – an astonishingly bright gold. His cigar is long and black. . . .

It must be a pleasant thing to be Mr. Churchill: to be unvexed by doubts; to be undismayed by circumstance; to know the right answer to every problem that troubles a troubled world; to command that treacherous jade, the English language, and hold her obedient to command. . . .

The man who was Britain's Secretary of State for War from 1918 to 1921 can see no immediate threat of war on the world's horizon in 1932, not even from Russia. "I don't know that there will be another war. I never said there would be."

Russia?

"A Government in the position of the Russian Government is capable of destroying all private industries in every other country, whatever it chooses to turn its baleful blast upon. No tariff is a barrier against Communist dumping," Mr. Churchill said, and did not smile. Mr. Churchill's bedroom slippers are of snakeskin. He fixed his eyes upon the toe of the top one. "Reptiles," he said, calmly, and without heat. "Every Communist is a reptile. . . ."

"I would not say that free trade is done forever; I would say that protection is to be given a fair trial. The country wants it," the man who was once Mr. Lloyd George's second-favourite free trade orator declared. "What is the use of going on mumbling the politics of twenty years ago? Change comes. Old sayings, old circumstances, all our fads and pomps must give way."

"On an absolutely international view," tariffs were not the ideal solution for the world's problems. An ideal world, Mr. Churchill thought, might well be a free trade world.

"But an ideal world isn't the world in which we live," he said. "And if nations are going to shut themselves in pens, well" – the Churchill smile irradiated the Churchill features – "well we have a pretty good one in the British Empire."

"Put a ring fence around the Empire," is Mr. Churchill's advice to the Empire statesmen destined to meet at Ottawa next July.

"Only a two or three per cent tariff" should make the encircling fence, he explained. Inside it and over it every Dominion would be free to make its own tariff bargains. But, "I'd like to see that girdle put around."

From W.S.C.'s draft press release for his speech in Toronto, March 3, 1932[13]

"For many years . . . I was a Free Trader; but the march of events and the state of the world has convinced me of the necessity of a fundamental change in our outlook. I am going to urge in the House of Commons that, now we are embarked upon a protectionist policy, we should give it a fair chance, and a scientific application, and not halt, with weak compromises, between two systems. We should take our steps wholeheartedly, and apply, with courage and logic, our new system to every aspect of imperial economic life.

The enormous blessings of British rule in India had been inadequately repaid by the Indian political classes which did not represent the vast mass of the Indian people, of whose true interests the Imperial Parliament was the inalienable guardian.

"I have always urged . . . firm, sober maintenance of British authority, and have opposed dividing the imperial responsibility of the Government of India with Gandhi and his disloyal Congress. I have always predicted that no serious disturbance will attend the firm, just assertion of law and order. I rejoice that, since I left home, the British Government have adopted fully and resolutely the course which, at some personal exertion, I urged continuously upon them."

No serious difficulties had attended that course. On the contrary, the realities of Indian life and the loyalties of its Princes and Peoples were now given a chance to assert themselves.

Our position in Egypt was also still intact, and the British troops were still in Cairo. "You may be sure," said Mr. Churchill, "that the new Parliament will not tolerate any tampering with that situation."

A strong British Navy was as essential to the existence of the British Empire, and to the peace of the world, as a strong French army was to the existence of France and the peace of Europe. The war in China, with all its dangers and horrors, would never have taken place if the British Navy had not been unduly weakened. He thought the U.S. were beginning to realise the mistake they made in cutting down the British Navy when they saw the overweening power they had conferred upon Japan over the whole of the Far East.

The *Globe*, Toronto, March 4, 1932

"Mark you, England's weakness is the world danger, and the strength of the Empire guarantees world peace." Winston Churchill said many things besides that when he addressed a Toronto audience in Maple Leaf Gardens last night, but he said nothing else quite so much as though he meant it.

Right Hon. Winston Spencer Churchill, P.C., M.P., variously at various times the Conservative Chancellor of the Exchequer, Coalition Secretary of State for War, Liberal First Lord of the Admiralty, and Free-Trade Little Englander, is now a British Imperialist, and a British Imperialist by conviction. Ask any of the six thousand people who listened and applauded last night while Mr. Churchill spoke about the Empire, if you doubt. They'll tell you.

"Rule Britannia" was the music to which Mr. Churchill entered the Gardens. "Almost a forbidden tune recently," Mr. Churchill remarked and after a tussle with the microphone swung into his speech.

For the world's economic ills Mr. Churchill prescribed an immediate international monetary conference – a speedy and general remonetization of silver – a decision to look facts in the face in the matter of reparation and war debts, and a tariff-united British Empire.

For the "world" peace he prescribed a strong British Empire working in partnership with the United States. For a strong British Empire he prescribed a light, encircling tariff girdle to be fitted at Ottawa next July. For India, he prescribed firmness and fairness. For Russia, quotas and embargos. And Mr. Churchill is confident that all his prescriptions are on the way to being filled. "Watch the new Parliament in England" Mr. Churchill said. "It's the best Parliament we will ever have. It is an Imperial Parliament."

Sustained applause followed his final words: "If it is in our power to make the next five years almost a dream in material and ethical achievement within the Empire, never must our children reproach us with having passed such an opportunity away."

Mr. Churchill paused in full flight to drop a few rose petals on the grave of the late Socialist Government of Great Britain.

"That blight," he said, "is now removed," and passed on to the tomb of Free Trade. For seventy years, he said, Great Britain had kept the Free Trade flag flying. Her reward had been to see foreign tariffs raised high and higher against her. "But," said this whole-hearted convert from the free trade faith: "Ladies and gentlemen, those days are gone."

He stopped to poke a little fun at Mr. Stimson,* who now, in face of Japan's aggressive attitude, threatened to revoke the self-denying naval ordinance which the United States promoted, and which we agreed to for the sake of a quiet life.

Mr. Churchill paid the tribute of a sigh to the Statute of Westminster.† It was "the end of a regrettable chapter in the Empire's history – a laborious attempt to express freedom in the musty language of a statute. Freedom by itself is not enough, we must have comradeship as well."

At the end, the English statesman looked into the future. "It may well be," he said "not in our time, perhaps, or in our children's time, but it may be that the influence of Canada may yet lead to a reunited association of the English-speaking people of the world."

Mr. Churchill, in suggesting closer relationships between Canada and the West Indies, declared: "You should cast your bread upon those Southern waters. It will come back to you before many years, not alone in trade, but in strengthening the elements of your own nationhood." And, in a vibrant passage, which was punctured with general applause, the speaker added: "We're not going to have Canadian and Australian wheat or Dominion timber supplanted by importations from Russia. But Russian dumpings of raw materials are only a prelude to the throwing down of

* Henry Louis Stimson (1867–1950), U.S. Secretary of State, 1929–33; Secretary of War, 1911–13, 1940–45.

† Of 1931; which recognized in law the status of the self-governing Dominions and their control over their own constitutions.

masses of highly manufactured products for any price they will fetch. Tariffs, however high, are no security against this menace. We must proceed by embargo and quota to deal with Russia. We must not hesitate to say 'Take your timber back. We will not accept the product of slave labor.' Nor must we hesitate to say 'Take your wheat cargoes back to the Black Sea and feed your own starving people.' I declare to you with all the emphasis at my command – let the Empire take the lead, whether the rest of the world is ready immediately to follow or not."

Mr. Churchill said: "No single nation – not even the United States – was strong enough to deal with the monetary problems. Action, to be effective, must be international." He urged an immediate international conference upon the monetary position, with the object not only of arresting deflation but of restoring price levels which yield a fair return to the primary producer. He expressed the hope that a clearer understanding between Great Britain and the United States would precede – and accompany – such a conference.

"Britain and the United States are the two outstanding creditor peoples of the world." "They have only to agree between them upon a policy to make their opinions rule. If they would only act and keep together they could quickly revive the purchasing power of the East."

As an interesting example of the deflation process, in its power to be hurtful to the unprotected primary producers in rural Canada and elsewhere, he gave the case of a farmer in Manitoba or Ontario. "When I was here some three years ago, that grower had to plow a furrow, say, 1,000 yards, in order to pay so much on a loan or mortgage. Go to him today and you will find him plowing between 1,400 and 1,500 yards to pay the same charges.

"Continue to destroy international trade," he said, "and later inevitable steps – including general debt repudiation – and you would soon reduce this world, with all its knowledge and science and boundless possibilities, to the barbarism and barter of the dark ages."

"Not less important to the British Empire is the forthcoming Ottawa Conference,* where fiscal unity is to be the theme," he declared. "It is my earnest hope that all men of goodwill throughout the Dominion will collaborate from their respective stations at this grave and cardinal moment. The watchword must be, 'The British Empire first, and last, and all the time.'

"I regret," continued Mr. Churchill, "that a Colonial Conference is not being held at the same time; or, at least, that important delegations representing the Crown colonies will not be present at Ottawa, in order that all the possibilities of Empire may

* Held, on Canadian initiative, in July and August 1932.

be explored. Perhaps it is not already too late. The Dominion of Canada is incomplete without the tropical and semi-tropical regions of the West Indies, which are her hothouse and winter garden.

"Hitherto the Crown Colonies of Great Britain have been thrown open to the commerce of the whole world, as freely to foreigners as to ourselves. There has been no return of reciprocity," said Mr. Churchill, and at this point came the ringing challenge: "The time has come to put a girdle around the Empire estate. It might, in the first instance, be a light and flexible girdle, but a girdle all the same, and within this economic girdle many special commercial ties should be developed by agreements and intra-Imperial commercial treaties.

"The growing strength of the British Empire would not make for war – it would as definitely make for peace," said Mr. Churchill, who, as political philosopher momentarily, added: "It is when Empires begin to break up and fall to bits; when their approaching dissolution fills the air, that appetites are excited, ambitions roused, and plans of aggression and partition are set on foot." The prime cause of the Great War had been the decay of the Austrian and Turkish empires. When a great organization was healthy and vital, tranquillity and progress could go forward together.

"I hope and wish to see the British Empire strong and united – not in foolish rivalry with the United States," added Mr. Churchill, "but for the very purpose of promoting closer friendship with them. This is a time both for resolve and hope. For too long, much too long, have we been fussing and worrying about relaxing the bonds of Empire; for too long have we been busying ourselves in cutting away the old ties and symbols that united us.

"For too long have we been dutiful servants to the fads and moods of the legalists and pedants. The Statute of Westminster marks the end of that chapter. Under Sinn Fein Irish and Dutch South African pressure, the Empire constitution had been stated at its loosest and weakest. Nevertheless, I do not fear the results of what has happened. Freedom is the very essence of our association.

"But now," concluded Mr. Churchill, "I feel that the tide is on the turn. The centrifugal forces have had their day – and it is now the turn of the centripetal. The period of cutting away is over. The period of building has begun. The inherent strength of Britain has been and is today enormous. Her sound institutions, her loyal people, her unrivalled marine, her vigorous industries will now have a fair chance. The days of self-abasement are over. There is a stir and a hum throughout the Empire which, rising in growing chorus, will drown the discordant cries and yells of our internal foes and weaklings. The Mother Country has revived! She is gathering her children around her and, hand in hand with Canada, will lead the Empire and the world out of the gloom of panic and depression into the sunlight of prosperity."

[Even before his visit of 1929, Churchill had thought of "putting a girdle round the Empire" as a theme for his speeches in Canada. But the time was not then ripe. By 1932, all was altered. Churchill abandoned free trade without painful pangs. To his opponents, that was a further proof, if one were needed, of inconsistency; to Churchill, it meant simply a recognition of facts. As he put it to his interlocutor from the *Globe*, there was no point in mumbling the politics of twenty years before.

For the moment, then, he sloughed off free trade as a man might thankfully get rid of a heavy overcoat in a heatwave. It is also noteworthy that despite the economic collapse in Europe, the turbulence within Germany, the Japanese assault upon Manchuria, the detachment of the United States from collective security, Churchill said that the watchword must be "The British Empire first and last and all the time"; in other words, the building up of the Empire's cohesion had the first claim on Britain's attention. Moreover, the election in the autumn of 1931 of what W.S.C. believed to be an "imperially-minded parliament" had changed that context out of recognition; the subtext was that such a parliament would be firmer than that of 1929–31 about Egypt and India. He conceded openly that, while the territories of the colonial Empire (as distinct from the Dominions) had been freely open to the trade of all, Britain had found "no return or reciprocity."]

The *Toronto Daily Star*, March 4, 1932

When Mr. Churchill spoke about the virtues of fiscal protection, he was applauded. He was so eloquent, and so persuasive, that I joined in the applause myself. I had forgotten, for the moment, that I was listening to a man who used to make famous speeches in which he extolled free trade. I had forgotten that, at the very outset of his speech, he had explained carefully, and lucidly, too, how post-war tariffs had paralyzed trade, plunging Germany and her creditors into the present economic morass. "A nation can pay its debts only with goods, done up in bales or boxes," he said. He made it very clear – at first. He did not explain why the United States, with its policy of high tariffs, is in a state of economic stagnation while Great Britain, which can scarcely feel, as yet, the effects of her new fiscal policy, is represented to-day by economists and statesmen, to be the most prosperous country in the world. I hate to mention these things, but Mr. Churchill's oratory last night put them right out of my head until I got out into the open air.

The *Ottawa Evening Journal*, March 5, 1932

Canada was once again on Vimy Ridge – on the Vimy Ridge of the Empire. The struggles of the Great War were over. The Empire was coming back into its own; and the nations of the Empire stretched out their hands to Canada "to lead not only our own Empire but if necessary the whole world out of the depression." So declared Rt. Hon. Winston Churchill, former British Chancellor of the Exchequer, at a luncheon given in his honor today by Prime Minister R.B. Bennett and attended by parliamentarians of all groups.

"Let us make quite sure," the British statesman declared in ringing utterances of confidence in the result of the Imperial Conference to be held in Ottawa in July next, "that given as we are this priceless opportunity our children will have no cause to say that we had the chance and threw it away."

The time had come, Mr. Churchill declared "when we should adopt the principle of special advantages in Empire trade, fostering it not only by tariff bulwarks but by special commercial treaties."

Continuing, Mr. Churchill stated: "We have the feeling that in a very short time we shall have the most brilliant opportunity of writing history for the British Empire, of showing a true British Empire, in July next, when the Imperial Conference meets in Ottawa."

There was an entirely new outlook in the British Parliament. It was a Parliament complete in its loyalty and absolutely unhampered by pledges. Thousands after thousands of people unemployed had "trooped" to the polls in the last election, Mr. Churchill said, "and voted against the dole because they believed the country needed it."

He had been a free trader for many years, Mr. Churchill remarked, and he wished to say that everywhere during the last British election when the supporters of the National Government were put the question by the electors as to whether they would vote for a tax on food one answer was given. "Everywhere we gave the answer, 'Certainly, if we think it is good for the Empire as a whole.'"

He went on:

"We have to think, in speaking of the coming conference, what our people will think of this conference 50 years from now. We owe it to our ancestors, we owe it to those who fought in the World War. We have the opportunity of doing something that will be here when we have passed away and that I think is the atmosphere in which this conference will take place."

Mackenzie King's diary, March 5, 1932

Lunched at Govt. House with Churchill. . . . I rather dreaded the venture, but it turned out to be quite the most pleasant and profitable visit to Government House since His Excellency [the Earl of Bessborough, Governor General]'s arrival. . . .

We talked in the presence of His Ex. re the forthcoming conference. I told him I thought all centralizing efforts wd. be a failure, that a decentralized Empire was the only form it could take. . . . We wd. never agree to any central council regulating tariff or other affairs. . . .

We got on to the Byng incident. Churchill said quite openly Byng had made a mistake, his mistake was not in refusing dissolution, that he had a right to do – (I agreed, though at his peril if [the] other man could not govern) the mistake was in not giving me dissolution when Meighen was defeated. I agreed and sd in the campaign I put the blame on Meighen for permitting Byng so to do. . . .

On the Conference it was clear Churchill did not feel much wd. be accomplished from the economic side, though he said the present Govt. wd. go almost any length to get results. He agreed with me that "locked" preferences to use his own expression wd. not work out, that "voluntary" preferences alone wd. avoid friction & the difficulties that wd. arise as govts. succeeded govts. I told him I was certain that was the only basis on which trade within the Empire cld. be fostered. To remember too US was a neighbour we had to regard. She had never taken exception to voluntary preference, or what we wanted to do within Empire – she might take exception to something that made it impossible for us to change our tariff at all & other countries as well. I said the tory party [in Canada] wd. never let Br. mffrs. [manufacturers] compete in this country with Canadians, & it was Br. mffrs. England was alone concerned with. If Bennett tried to throw the mffrs., the mffrs. & his party wd. throw him.

[In the same conversation, King explained why he thought the forthcoming Ottawa Conference a mistake. Churchill ought to lead a real Liberal Party, King said; to which Churchill replied that he had "inclined more to the right as he got older – but was glad to be out just now, he had had a row with Baldwin & could not stand Ramsay, never could." He conceded that Mackenzie King had been right about the Chanak affair ten years before and spoke "in an exceedingly nice way of myself, said we were old & close friends, that in Britain I was held in high regard by the best people of the country."

The reference to "the Byng incident" requires some elucidation. More than thirty years before, after his escape from Pretoria, Churchill had told General Buller that he would like a commission in one of the irregular corps being improvised after the series of British defeats in "Black Week," but could not relinquish his contract with the *Morning Post*. "All right," said Buller at last. "You can have a commission in Bungo's regiment. You will have to do as much as you can for both jobs. But you will get no pay for ours." Churchill agreed instantly.[14] "Bungo" was Col. Julian Byng, who appointed him assistant-adjutant – the self-same Byng who later commanded the Canadian forces in France and became Governor General. Quite apart from the constitutional issues, Churchill had his own reasons for a special interest in the events of 1926.

The Governor General in those days fulfilled the delicate task of representing in Canada not only the sovereign but also the British government. Following the election of October 1925, Mackenzie King no longer had a majority, but was able to continue in office with the support of some parliamentary allies. After a scandal involving corruption in the Ministry of Customs and Excise, the Liberal government lost two votes on questions of procedure. Lord Byng refused Mackenzie King's requests to consult the British government and to dissolve Parliament, inviting the leader of the Conservatives, Arthur Meighen, to form a government. This Meighen did; his party held 116 seats against the Liberals' 101, and the new administration looked as though it might survive for some while. Parliament, having passed a motion of censure against King's government, then defeated Meighen, and had thus achieved the remarkable feat of voting down both the Liberal and the Conservative governments.

Byng thereupon granted Meighen's request for a dissolution but only, it appears, after turning down the latter's suggestion that King should again be summoned. At the election, the Liberals won a comfortable majority. King thus returned for a second spell as Prime Minister in 1926, and when in London later that year, learned of Churchill's view: that Meighen after his own defeat in Parliament should have advised the Governor General to send for Mackenzie King, and that Byng was much to blame for not having done so. He expressed gratitude that King had neither attacked Lord Byng nor brought the British government into the imbroglio.[15]

Shortly afterwards, it was arranged that the British government would in future be represented at Ottawa by a High Commissioner.]

Memorandum by Lord Bessborough of a conversation with W.S.C., March 6, 1932[16]

Rideau Cottage,
Ottawa

Confidential.

Winston Churchill, who has been here for the week-end, took a great interest in the "Byng Case" – particularly in the question whether Lord B.* was right, in 1926, in granting to Meighen† a dissolution which he had shortly before refused to Mackenzie King, in the first year of a new Parliament, when it was actually only eight months old.

Winston takes the view that a dissolution is only natural and normal if it takes place towards the end of the statutory life of Parlt.: that a dissolution at any earlier stage is abnormal: that it involves the country in great expense and disturbance: and that the Prerogative of the Crown exists in order that the Crown may refuse such a dissolution, even though it be recommended by the Prime Minister, when the Sovereign (or his representative) is not satisfied that the utility of the Parliament of the day is exhausted.

Holding this view, Winston considers that Lord B. was right in refusing a dissolution to King, in that the latter recommended it at a time when Parlt. was only eight months old: that he was right in calling upon Meighen to form an Administration: but that he was wrong in granting a dissolution to M. only a few days later, having refused it to King so short a time previously. Lord B., in Winston's opinion, should have accepted Meighen's resignation, and then, having sent for King again, should have granted to the latter his original request for a dissolution: for, by that time it should have been clearly evident to him (Byng) that the utility of Parlt. was exhausted, no leader having been found who had the confidence of a majority in Parlt.

---

* Lord Byng of Vimy (1862–1935), had commanded the Canadian Army Corps on the Western Front, 1916–17; Governor General of Canada, 1921–26; commissioner of the London Metropolitan Police, 1928–31.

† Arthur Meighen (1874–1960), Canadian lawyer and politician; succeeded Sir Robert Borden as Leader of the Conservatives; Prime Minister briefly 1920–21, and, even more briefly, 1926; Minister Without Portfolio, 1932–35; resumed the leadership of the Conservatives, 1941–42, but failed to gain a seat in the House and retired.

During Winston's stay at Govt. House, he met both Meighen and King, separately. He invited each of them, in private conversation, to give his own view of the "Byng case", and of the procedure that should have been followed. From what Winston subsequently told me of these conversations, I understood that Meighen, in recounting his part in the proceedings, said that, when he found himself unable to carry on, he did actually recommend the G.G. to send again for King, believing this to be the correct constitutional procedure; he added that, in giving this advice to Lord B., he had said that, in his opinion, he was acting against the interest of his own Party, who strongly desired a dissolution; if the Party learnt that he had given such advice, he would forfeit his leadership of it.

Meighen went on to say that Lord B. refused to send again for King, and accordingly granted him (Meighen) a dissolution.

Meighen, therefore, agreed with Winston's view, as set down above.

King, in his conversation with Winston, stated that he had recommended a dissolution in the first instance: that he had advised Lord B. against sending for Meighen, because, in his opinion, M. could not form an Administration which would command the confidence of Parlt.: and that he considered that (in Winston's phrase) "the utility of Parlt. was already exhausted".

He went on to say, however, that he considered Lord B. to have acted entirely within his rights in refusing to accept his advice, but that he (Byng) was wrong in granting a dissolution to Meighen, having refused it to King so short a time previously. He held, too, that Lord B. should have sent for him (King) again, after Meighen's failure.

It appears, therefore, that King, no less than Meighen, agrees with Winston as to the correct constitutional procedure. There are, of course, no official records of what took place, but I have been given many different versions of the affair, and told many different stories about it.

So far as I am concerned, this is the first time I have heard an account of what actually took place between Meighen and Lord B., as described by Meighen to Winston.

* * *

By the time of Churchill's return to London, the National Government had introduced an immediate tariff on many imports. So far as the countries of the Commonwealth and Empire were concerned, its operation was deferred until the conference had met at Ottawa later that summer. The symbolic significance of this change was at least equal to the material; an issue which had divided British politics for much of the nineteenth century and the first thirty years of the twentieth largely disappeared from view. Many Liberals accepted, with varying degrees of enthusiasm, the abandonment of free trade; Churchill supported the new tariffs, and the inter-Imperial arrangements made at Ottawa that summer, in due course declaring that they had not been accompanied by the corruption or wire-pulling which free-traders had always feared from such a system.

The tour in North America, which had so nearly cost Churchill his life, had at least recruited his fortunes. Another serious illness scarcely interrupted the flow of articles and essays, some ephemeral, others weighty, all highly paid. The biography of Marlborough, Churchill's most substantial literary work of the decade, entailed intense research. He tramped over the battlefields and sought out the archives. For all the apparatus of scholarship, a good deal of the book is partisan. Determined to rescue Marlborough's reputation from the blight laid upon it by Macaulay, Churchill contrived to put a good complexion upon almost all the great Duke's transactions. The writing of these four volumes had a significance for the future which their author could not have apprehended. For years, he studied not only Marlborough's military strategy but also his management of a coalition which had to be kept together by a common purpose, an opportune suggestion, a timely concession, or sometimes by less avowable means. In this process, Marlborough had displayed endless patience, and his descendant, to whom patience did not come naturally, absorbed the lesson. Mrs. Churchill was to explain this to Mackenzie King at Quebec in 1943.

Meanwhile, the great question upon which Churchill had left the Conservative front bench reverberated. The bill to grant India a substantial measure of internal self-government was one of immense complexity and length. It aroused serious anxieties among many Conservatives, although in the event their numbers were never sufficient to threaten the government's immense majority. That this would prove the fact was not apparent at all stages, and Churchill waged a vigorous warfare outside as well as within Parliament. Indeed, he attempted something that recalled the tactics of his father; he tried to turn the party, at annual conferences and elsewhere, against its own leaders, than which there are few sins more heinous in party politics. This campaign separated Churchill not only from almost all the senior members of the Conservative Party, but from the Labour and Liberal Parties also. They argued that Dominion status for India had been promised, that only a substantial advance would keep India in a friendly association with the rest of the Commonwealth and that for so great a prize substantial risks must be run. For their part, Churchill and the opponents said that the steps proposed were too bold; Dominion status must imply the right to neutrality in international affairs and in the last resort to secede from the Empire. Moreover, the position of Muslim and smaller minorities and of the Untouchables would be imperilled and the high standard of British administration and justice in India compromised.

Many thought Churchill's attitude contrived or believed that he was merely old-fashioned and reactionary. Though Churchill had himself confessed to a steady movement rightwards in his thought, the springs of his attitude ran deeper than that. He understood that India was by far the most important country of the Empire; he knew the competence and valour of the Indian Army, of which the bulk came from the Muslim population; he regarded the work the British had done in India as wholly remarkable and the possibility of its early undoing as unthinkable. Beyond the merits of the question, there lay a vital fact which requires emphasis in justice to the government of the day and to Churchill: the campaign which he waged unremittingly against the Indian proposals would, if successful, have entailed the downfall of the administration. No government could react with anything other than hostility, part of which was bound to linger. Whether Churchill understood this aspect fully is open to doubt. He described Ramsay MacDonald as "the boneless wonder." This was hardly the language of a politician, however senior or distinguished, who sought an early recall to the Cabinet. It was not until the midsummer of 1935, when Baldwin replaced MacDonald as Prime Minister, that the Government of India Act finally became law, and Churchill thereupon made some attempt to mend his fences.

On the other great issue with which Churchill concerned himself in those years, that of German rearmament and the British response, the differences of policy between him and the National Government were less fundamental than over India. To be sure, Churchill would argue from time to time that the grievances of the vanquished must be assuaged before the disarmament of the victors took place. This doctrine sounded well, but lagged behind the facts since the victors (most prominently the Americans, with the British not far behind) had long since disarmed; and the prospects of assuaging the grievances of Hitler's Germany, which successive British governments attempted to meet, looked more remote year by year. Churchill was a good deal more sympathetic to France than were most British statesmen of the time, and did not recede from the position he had taken up in Canada in 1929 and 1932, that it would be foolish to press the French to disarm further on land. He always entertained a high opinion of the French Army. Churchill warned time and again of the rearmament of Germany and demanded that Britain's strength in the air should not lag behind Germany's. The government promised that it should not. Churchill said that the Luftwaffe was growing far faster than ministers realized. They denied it and were then obliged to recant, though we now know that Churchill's figures were exaggerated. In essence he was relying, as was the British government, upon the French Army to defend its own territory and perhaps the Low Countries; he did not advocate the creation of the large British Army which in the end proved necessary. He was looking to air power partly because he wished Britain to have the means to defend herself behind the moat of the Channel, and because air power, which had developed enormously since the First World War but the full effects of which could not yet be measured, must be sufficient to act as a deterrent and if necessary allow Britain to take the offensive against Germany.

None of this was in principle far removed from the thinking of the government; but British rearmament had begun too late, on too modest a scale. Churchill had grasped more fully than any other public figure the demonic character of Hitler's regime in Germany, its amorality, and its lust for revenge.

The problems confronting the British government of the 1930s were not simple, indeed by no means so simple as Churchill himself implies in *The Gathering Storm*. He underestimated, as he had done in the 1920s and was to do until 1941, the risk that Japan would engage in an open attack upon the British possessions in Asia. On grounds of prudence, despite all that he later said about collective security and the Covenant of the League, he was in essence at one with the National Government, which he supported heartily in the general election of 1935 – in avoiding war with Italy over the Abyssinian question. Nor did he have any sympathy with the belief, almost universal on the left, that Britain should intervene on the side of the government in the Spanish Civil War, still less with the notion that Fascism could be defeated on the plains of Spain.

In December 1936, there occurred the abdication of King Edward VIII. Churchill had imagined that the King's liaison with Mrs. Simpson would soon lose its fervour. He was by no means insensible to the charm and talents of the King, who in the last agonizing phases consulted Lord Beaverbrook a good deal and Churchill several times. Many believed that Churchill was moved by a desire to bring the government down. When he pleaded in the House of Commons that the King should be given time, the uproar was so great that he could not even be heard over the interruptions. It is likely enough that Beaverbrook's motives were far from pure, and not for the first or last time, Churchill suffered from association with a figure with whom he frequently disagreed but whom he found irresistible; as he once confessed, "Some people take drugs; I take Max."[17] The crisis is revealing of Churchill: his deep feeling of obligation to the King; his refusal to weigh other factors in a calculating manner; his unfitness for intrigue, for he always preferred straightforwardness and could never keep silent for long; his early recognition that the new King, George VI, was infinitely better suited to the throne than his brother could ever have been; the rather rueful recognition that the former monarch had outlived his promise. "Morning Glory," Churchill later said of him, thinking of those beautiful blooms which flower and wither in the first few hours of the day.

The abdication raised acute anxieties for the Dominions, which Baldwin consulted with care. Their general view was that they would not wish to have as Queen an American lady twice divorced, or to support an arrangement under which the King would marry Mrs. Simpson but she would not become Queen. Edward VIII was not only King of Canada but peculiarly identified with that country through his ownership of the ranch in Alberta. In Ottawa, Mackenzie King had won the election of 1935 and succeeded R.B. Bennett as Prime Minister, a position which he was to hold continuously until his retirement in 1948. It need hardly be said that while loyal to the sovereign he disapproved of the affair with Mrs. Simpson. The Governor General, Lord Tweedsmuir (who as John Buchan had been Churchill's colleague in the House of Commons), told Baldwin that Canadian opinion concerning the royal troubles had been "curiously hard, harder, I think, than at home. There is never much mercy for an idol whose feet have proved to be of clay. . . ." Baldwin's own prestige, and that of the government, stood high in Canada. However, "Winston has pretty well taken the place of Beaverbrook as Public Enemy No. 1, with Lloyd George a good second."[18]

In May 1937, at the time of the Coronation of the new King, Baldwin retired. He was succeeded by Neville Chamberlain, and Churchill had some hopes of a post in the new government. Despite all their disagreements, Churchill never felt as hostile to Chamberlain as to Baldwin. He knew that when the government eventually made up its mind to re-arm, Chamberlain had taken the leading part in the process; indeed, in the autumn of that year Churchill himself believed that the measures the British were now taking would prove sufficient, whereas he had himself only a short while before been "a loud alarmist." Chamberlain undoubtedly feared that Churchill would be a highly disruptive ministerial colleague, which was a generally held view; he mistrusted the impulses which had moved Churchill during the abdication crisis; and he feared that the arrival of Churchill in the Cabinet would be taken as a signal that Britain saw no alternative to war with Germany.

When Hitler seized Austria in March 1938, Churchill urged the formation of a Grand Alliance, whereas the government believed that the materials for such a coalition were not available and that Britain was in no state to fight Germany as yet. Chamberlain, in particular, had a much poorer view than Churchill of the French Army. In memorable language, Churchill condemned the Munich settlement of September 1938 as craven and futile; with a group of others, many of whom however were reluctant to accept his leadership, he voted against it. After the German invasion of the rump of Czechoslovakia in the spring of 1939, he supported the government's decision to give guarantees to Poland, Romania, Turkey and Greece, and believed that it might well be possible to make an effective military alliance with Soviet Russia.

There was by the summer of 1939 a strong demand for Churchill's inclusion in the Cabinet. He embodied toughness. No figure active in public life had a longer or more varied ministerial experience. His repeated warnings were vindicated by Hitler's aggressions and tearing up of the Munich Agreement. The general dread of unrestricted aerial warfare caused many to regret that the Royal Air Force had not been rebuilt more swiftly. In point of policy, little difference now remained between the government and Churchill. When Russia and Germany, hitherto sworn enemies, made a pact in late August 1939, Chamberlain told Hitler that the guarantee would nevertheless be honoured if Germany invaded Poland; and when war was declared by Britain and France on September 3, Churchill entered the War Cabinet as First Lord of the Admiralty. Thus he returned to the department he had been forced to quit, a prey to sorrow and frustration, nearly a quarter-century before.

One and all, the countries of the Commonwealth and Empire responded, although in South Africa it was a close-run thing. Mackenzie King and his colleagues had not doubted that if, after all efforts to meet Germany's grievances, conflict nonetheless came, their country would follow the call of the blood. Parliament met in Ottawa to make its own decision, and the Canadian declaration of war accordingly followed one week after that of Britain and France. The first Canadian volunteers reached Britain well before Christmas, in the lull in land warfare that followed the partition of Poland between Germany and Russia. For all that has been written about the "phoney war," the struggle at sea was waged unremittingly from the beginning. The British decided that in addition to front-rank naval and air forces they must build up a very large army, though it was not at all clear how they would finance it. Churchill and Chamberlain, despite their obvious differences of temperament, formed an effective alliance. The First Lord's tenure of the Admiralty was no peaceable affair. Some senior officers found him tiresome or worse, frictions with his fellow-ministers were intermittently acute, and he was by no means blameless for the ill-starred campaign in Norway, which brought about the fall of Chamberlain's government. But all that hardly mattered. He was free of responsibility for all the policies of the 1930s; he knew a great deal about warfare; the Labour and Liberal leaders were prepared to serve under him; he spoke on a level not attained by any other politician.

On May 10, 1940, as the German forces swept into the Low Countries, Churchill became Prime Minister. By an instinctive process, millions of people in Britain – including many who would never have dreamed of voting for him – and more millions abroad soon realized that he had a quality not easily defined; something beyond courage or resolution or stubbornness, what Stalin later called his "desperation." When pleading with Asquith that her husband should not be ejected from the Admiralty in 1915, Mrs. Churchill had put her finger on the point:

> Winston may in your eyes & in those with whom he has to work have faults but he has the supreme quality which I venture to say very few of your present or future Cabinet possess – the power, the imagination, the deadliness to fight Germany.[19]

4

The Atlantic Charter: August 1941

Long afterwards, Churchill reflected that his appointment as Prime Minister came as "an immense relief; I could discipline the bloody business at last. I had no feeling of personal inadequacy, or anything of that sort. I went to bed at 3 o'clock, and in the morning I said to Clemmie 'There is only one man who can turn me out, and that is Hitler.'"[1]

While Churchill had all the appurtenances – Blenheim, the ducal connections, a father who had been Chancellor of the Exchequer, his own long service in Parliaments and Cabinets – he did not conform to any recognizable type. English habits of reserve and understatement were wholly foreign to him. He lived by self-expression, not self-denial. He was given neither by taste nor talent to political intrigue. He valued his American as well as his British ancestry, always loved to be in America and believed with deepening fervour that the English-speaking peoples must draw more closely together, for the world's salvation as well as their own.

In a celebrated passage, Churchill wrote of the events of May 1940 that he felt he was walking with destiny and that all his past life had been but a preparation for this hour and for this trial. Astonishingly, given the circumstances of the hour, he was sure he would not fail.[2] To do justice to the implications, we have to remember that Churchill's "past life" embraced not only the ups and downs of politics but also his career as an historian and journalist, the life of an artist with words. Churchill had a genius for enlarging and simplifying great issues; he knew how to make men and women feel that they could, indeed must, play their part in a noble enterprise. Of course, his position within Britain was one of immense strength. There was never at any stage of the war serious Parliamentary opposition to the coalition and the trades unions in the emergency accepted many restrictions previously rejected.

He held from the beginning the office of Minister of Defence, though there was in Whitehall no such ministry. He worked directly with the Chiefs of Staff; General Ismay, head of the military side of the War Cabinet's secretariat, became the indispensable link and interpreter. The civilian and domestic aspects of the government's business were dealt with by the other part of the secretariat under Sir Edward Bridges, an arrangement which might in different hands have provoked back-biting and jealousies. That nothing of the kind happened owed a great deal to Bridges and Ismay, both of them inherited from Chamberlain's regime, and their senior colleagues; and for all Churchill's altercations with the Chiefs of Staff and senior commanders, relations between the politicians and the fighting men remained in the Second World War infinitely better than in the First.

Within a few weeks of taking office, Churchill and his colleagues had to face the collapse of the central assumption upon which Britain's European strategy had been built: that the French Army would be strong enough to hold Germany in the west. As each phase of the disaster unfolded, the new Prime Minister strove to rally the French ministers and then, when the case was clearly hopeless, to persuade them to carry on the war from one of their territories abroad, and above all to ensure that the fleet did not fall into German hands. When that could not be assured, he took the hateful decision early in July – which he likened to a father's killing of a child for the sake of the state[3] – to order the Royal Navy to attack and sink French warships. That step showed that in Britain there was a government determined to stop at nothing, or at any rate very little, to defeat Hitler.

Most of Europe lay by then in enemy hands. Italy had entered the war at a late stage, Mussolini assuming that since the whole affair would soon be over he had better join in while there was still the chance of spoils; whereas in Spain General Franco, whom Mussolini might have emulated with great profit to Italy and himself, preserved a somewhat partial neutrality, adjusting nimbly to the fortunes of war.

The rescue from Dunkirk in late May and early June of about 330,000 British and French troops, who left behind almost all their equipment, had seemed a miracle, almost a victory. But wars, as Churchill said, are not won by evacuations. It is commonly asserted but untrue that Britain stood alone after the fall of France, a fact witnessed by the presence in the island of a substantial Canadian force. All the same, the brunt fell upon her. Could she survive a prolonged period of warfare behind the moat? When Churchill expressed in the summer of 1940 his sober confidence that the position could be held, he was not indulging in mere talk for the sake of keeping everyone's spirits up. After all, the German navy had suffered substantial loss in Scandinavia; the Royal Navy was much the stronger, even after Italy's declaration of war altered the balance of power in the Mediterranean. Ill-equipped and ill-defended the British Isles might be; all the same, to land a sufficient force across the Channel would require command of the sea and, in all probability, command of the air. Hitler had neither. What none knew was whether Germany could gain mastery of the air. If that did happen, could air power be deployed in such a way as to dominate operations on land and at sea? The Polish and Scandinavian campaigns suggested that it might. This was not an issue which anyone in Britain wished to put to the test in the near future; and this was part of what Churchill meant when he proclaimed during the Battle of Britain, referring to the Royal Air Force, that never in the field of human conflict had so much been owed by so many to so few.

His speeches in that summer, couched in language which Gibbon or Macaulay or Pitt would not have disdained, expressed more than sober confidence: a loathing of Nazism and all its apparatus; a fine contempt for Mussolini ("There is a general curiosity in the British Fleet to find out whether the Italians are up to the level they were at in the last war, or whether they have fallen off at all")[4]; an unfeigned belief in the sturdiness, patriotism and fighting quality of the British. When a friend said that he had given the people courage, Churchill responded, "I never gave them courage; I was able to focus theirs."[5] He expressed the same conviction in other language on his eightieth birthday: "It was a nation and race dwelling all round the globe that had the lion's heart. I had the luck to be called upon to give the roar."[6]

Many had feared that Churchill's regime would be chaotic. In practice, it soon settled down, though his unconventional pattern of life imposed a strain upon all those around him; for he liked to work until 2 a.m. or later, then to begin again over a hearty breakfast. He would spend much of the morning in bed, dictating telegrams, memoranda and the Prime Minister's Personal Minutes, which, often accompanied by a tag reading ACTION THIS DAY, were eventually numbered in the thousands. Many of them dealt with high policy, others with more trifling matters. "Almost all the food faddists I have ever known," stated one, "nut-eaters and the like, have died young after a long period of senile decay." This had to do with his concern that the people's diet would be unduly restricted. "Have you done justice to rabbit production?" the Ministers of Food and Agriculture were asked. "Although rabbits are not by themselves nourishing, they are a pretty good mitigation of vegetarianism."[7]

Churchill had always attached the utmost importance to information derived from secret sources, and well understood the risks when undue filtering takes place; accordingly he laid it down that decrypted documents must be sent to 10 Downing Street in original. He prodded the staffs, often to their annoyance and discomfiture, and it is doubtless true that much time was expended to no great effect by harassed officials and fighting men. Nevertheless, the effect of this searchlight technique – where even in remote recesses of the bureaucracy nobody could tell when the beam might suddenly alight upon him and his department – was electrifying.

Mrs. Churchill once remarked, "It took me all my time and strength just to keep up with him. I never had anything left over" and again that he "never did anything he didn't want to do, and left someone else to clear up the mess afterwards."[8] That was not intended as a comment upon public business. Churchill could be unduly demanding, bullying, choleric, thoughtless. In that summer, knowing that a note was more likely than conversation to seize her husband's attention, she told him that she had noticed a deterioration in his manner:

> . . . you are not as kind as you used to be.
>
> It is for you to give the Orders & if they are bungled – except for the King, the Archbishop of Canterbury & the Speaker, you can sack anyone and everyone. Therefore with this terrific power you must combine urbanity, kindness and if possible Olympic calm. . . .
>
> Besides you won't get the best results by irascibility & rudeness. They will breed either dislike or a slave mentality.[9]

Mrs. Churchill had been astonished and upset because she was accustomed to Churchill's colleagues and subordinates loving him. That remained generally true of the staff at 10 Downing Street and the Cabinet War Rooms, not least among the ladies who placed the telephone calls, put the papers before the prime minister in the right order and took dictation in his bedroom, the Cabinet Room or the car. "I shall require you to stay late, my dear," he is reliably reported as saying to one of them. "I am feeling very fertile tonight." As people close to Churchill soon learned – they could hardly survive on other terms – his wrath endured but the twinkling of an eye. One night in August 1940, Churchill declared to one of his junior Private Secretaries, inherited from Chamberlain's regime, at first more than doubtful about the succession but soon converted and a lifelong friend thereafter, "My object is to preserve the maximum initiative energy. Every night I try myself by court-martial to see if I have done anything effective during the day. I don't just mean pawing the ground – anyone can go through the motions – but something really effective."[10]

Courage, Churchill liked to say, is the quality that guarantees all the others. Willingness to be unpopular, he understood, entails courage. Most of the men whom he esteemed most highly had displayed physical courage; that was true, for example, of Anthony Eden, Harold Macmillan, Oliver Lyttelton, Field Marshal Smuts, Lord Cherwell. By instinct he preferred Major Attlee, who had fought bravely at the Dardanelles, to Mr. Herbert Morrison, who had been a conscientious objector. He had no intimate circle, in the sense of a group meeting regularly; rather, there were people whose company he enjoyed even amidst the intense pressures of war. He did not seek out abstemious people, but would allow exceptions for particular merit; for example, Smuts, of whom he once said, "I imagine that Socrates might have been like that"[11] and Cherwell, exempted on account of his "beautiful brain." When the Archbishop of Canterbury passed away at the age of sixty-three, the Prime Minister remarked, "There's a total abstainer died of gout. How right we all are!"[12]

Churchill did not take readily to those whom he found "viewy," theoretical or donnish or Jesuitical. He looked for the exceptional man, the one with the courage to rise to – or better still, above – the level of events. On being told that a talented but underused general was too wild, Churchill asked the Chief of the Imperial General Staff to remember Wolfe, who had stood before the elder Pitt brandishing his sword: "You cannot expect to have the genius type with a conventional copy-book style."[13] This would not make a bad epitaph for the Prime Minister himself. With no strong Christian beliefs, he regarded the Sermon on the Mount as the last word in ethics. Although moved by familiar hymns and the beauties of the liturgy, he would go to church only for some great occasion; having been compelled to attend innumerable services at school, he felt he had built up so fine a surplus in the bank of observance that he could draw upon it with confidence.[14] This habit he followed for a good seventy years. Nevertheless, he would occasionally invoke a deity and regarded himself as a reverent agnostic – if not a pillar of the church at least a flying buttress.

Asked to define the art of public speaking, Churchill replied, "A strong pair of spectacles and a fountain pen."[15] For him, it was seldom a matter of spontaneous eloquence. He was not only an artist but an actor, with special glasses so that he could read his text with ease without appearing to do so. Another pair of spectacles with a shorter range helped him with quotations or figures, and he would take off the one pair and put on the other in mid-speech. In Parliament, his impromptu excursions from the script were sometimes more persuasive than grammatical, leaving his private secretaries to improve upon the text before it was printed in Hansard.[16] He was a practised master of the well-calculated pause and gesture, which would enable his audience to anticipate the next phrase. Before a big speech he would be edgy and apprehensive and to an inquiry whether he was not thrilled by a great audience waiting to hear him, retorted that if he were about to be executed, the attendance would be a lot larger.

His broadcast addresses in that summer of 1940 were relatively few – for he was conscious that their impact would be diminished by undue frequency – but profound in their impact. Churchill radiated energy, confidence, defiance. He had been a distinguished but turbulent minister in many departments of state; his performance as Prime Minister was raised to a higher plane. As Stanley Baldwin put it, "The furnace of war has smelted out all the base metal from him."[17]

* * *

The life of Canada was transformed. On the eve of war, her Armed Forces had numbered no more than a few thousand men. By the summer of 1945, a million had served. Her manufacturing capacity increased out of measure, and within a short time after 1945 she had become one of the main trading nations of the world. Her financial generosity had no parallel anywhere in the Commonwealth. Her strategic situation was, in round terms, the same as that of the United States. If such factors alone determine policy in crises, as "realists" sometimes claim, Canada would have remained neutral in 1939. As it was, Mackenzie King (whose government had been returned with an increased majority in the spring of 1940) did his utmost to persuade President Roosevelt and Secretary of State Hull to help the Allied cause. He believed they were both anxious to do so; but a Presidential election was due at the end of that year, the state of public and Congressional opinion was not favourable and the armed forces of the United States, in relation to the risks soon to be apparent, were distinctly small. In late May 1940, the President had suggested that if the British Isles were conquered but the Royal Navy remained intact, the British could carry on the war from Canada; however, perhaps the seat of government should be Bermuda because (as the British Ambassador in Washington rendered the President's thinking), "Canada might feel a difficulty about the transfer of Downing Street to Toronto and the American republics may be restless at monarchy being based on the American continent."[18] This message was received when the British forces seemed unlikely to escape catastrophe and capture in northern France.

Three days later, Churchill learned from Mackenzie King more of the President's private thoughts: it would be unwise to ignore the possibility that France would be overrun and Britain no longer able to repel mass attacks from the air; if the British Isles could withstand such bombardment, it was possible that a blockade of the Continent and the Mediterranean could be made so effective that Germany and Italy would be defeated; if successful resistance proved impossible, Britain might be called upon to make a hard choice, either to surrender the fleet and parts of the outlying Empire on terms which the Germans might or might not keep or to prolong the war against a merciless attitude on the part of Germany.

We may fairly say that Churchill and his colleagues had thought for themselves of these disagreeable contingencies. The telegram went on to remark that the United States could not give immediate help in war. However, if Britain and France could hold out for some months "aid could probably then be given." If resistance by the Royal Navy in British waters became impossible during that period (i.e., before aid could be given) the President believed that, since it would be disastrous to surrender the fleet, it should be sent to South Africa, Singapore, Australia, the Caribbean and Canada. Such vessels as could not be moved, especially ships under construction, should be destroyed. If all this were done, the United States would assist immediately by opening its ports to the British fleet "in so far as this could be done under the most liberal interpretation of International Law," for repair, outfitting and provisioning. The United States would do its best to help in the building up of bases at Simonstown, Singapore,

Halifax and elsewhere. It would extend the provisions for the defence of the Western Atlantic, while its fleet would hold the Pacific, and defend Australia and New Zealand against Japanese or other attacks. As soon as grounds could be found to justify "direct and active American participation (and neither Mr. Roosevelt nor Mr. Hull believes that this would be more than a very few weeks), the United States would participate in a stringent blockade of the continent of Europe. . . ." Both President and Secretary believed that if Germany threatened any unusual or vicious action against Britain as a punishment for allowing the fleet to escape, public opinion in the United States would demand active intervention. Should the Germans, for example, attempt to starve Great Britain into ordering the fleet to return, the United States would immediately send food ships under naval escort to the British Isles. "Any interference with such ships would mean instant war."

The Cabinet is unlikely to have derived much satisfaction from the assurance that "the President and Mr. Hull are quite certain that Hitlerism cannot last long if pressure – even remote pressure – is steadily applied. They have absolute confidence in ultimate victory so long as the United States is not faced with a hostile German (British and French) fleet in the Atlantic and hostile Japanese fleet in the Pacific." As for the Prime Minister of Canada, he had urged upon Roosevelt and Hull that aid given at once, if not as great as that which might be given later, would be decisive in maintaining Allied, and particularly French, morale and in deterring Italy. His American colleagues said that much as they would like to do this, they could not go beyond the steps already taken; these were mainly to do with filling up the gaps on the Atlantic coast, because Canada had already transferred some of her destroyers to United Kingdom waters and agreed to assist in the defence of naval stations in the North Atlantic and Caribbean.[19]

It need hardly be said that if the Royal Navy were dispersed to bases all over the world, it could not be effective against Germany or Italy. The United States' own preparations being so far in arrears, it was not at all clear how much help could be given from that source to the building up of, say, Simonstown or Singapore, and the thought that rescue might somehow come because the United States had sent food ships under a naval escort seemed less plausible than the prospect that once the fleet had disappeared and Britain had surrendered, Germany would take military possession of the United Kingdom.

Immediately after Dunkirk, Churchill replied crisply to Ottawa:

> We must be careful not to let Americans view too complacently prospect of a British collapse out of which they would get the British Fleet and the guardianship of the British Empire minus Great Britain. If United States were in the war and England conquered locally, it would be natural that events should follow line you describe. But if America continued neutral and we were over-powered I cannot tell what policy might be adopted by a pro-German administration such as would undoubtedly be set up.
>
> Although President is our best friend no practical help has been forthcoming from the United States as yet.[20]

The British government had to accept with regretful resignation the fact that Roosevelt did not even feel able to publish an encouraging message to the French Prime Minister immediately before France capitulated. After natural hesitations, the President made up his mind to run for a third term of office. The Prime Minister of Canada did his utmost with Roosevelt, whom he had known for many years. From London, Churchill continued to ask for some substantial demonstration of support, not because it was the duty of the United States to help from motives of altruism, but because her vital interests would be so plainly harmed by a British collapse. After all, American security in the North Atlantic had long depended on British control of the exits from Europe to the Atlantic – the North Sea, the English Channel, Gibraltar – and in the South Atlantic on the Royal Navy's ability to guard the passage round the Cape of Good Hope. Hence America's ability to concentrate in the Eastern Pacific.

It became evident that whatever Roosevelt's private wishes the United States would not enter the war, unless attacked, for a considerable while. The threatened German invasion of England failed to materialize, although the preparations were visible enough. Eventually with helpful interventions from Ottawa, Britain secured fifty American destroyers and the United States acquired the use of bases in the Caribbean and Newfoundland. By then, in September, British prospects looked less bleak than in June. It was not yet possible to tell, however, whether German bombing would disrupt the war effort heavily, or even make some of the great cities uninhabitable.

We cannot easily place in an order of significance the decisions that Churchill and the War Cabinet took in the five years from the formation of the government to the defeat of Germany. High on the list must stand the despatch of troops, tanks and guns to the Middle East in the late summer of 1940. Further large reinforcements followed in 1941. Without them, sent when the risks nearer home were palpable, the position in Egypt and the Middle East could not have been held. General Wavell, asked to conduct several campaigns with insufficient resources, succeeded well against the Italian forces in the deserts west of Egypt, and it is possible that the British decision to give military aid to Greece in the spring of 1941 prevented the completion of that campaign. In the event, the British and Commonwealth forces were defeated in Greece; Crete was lost; reverses in the Western Desert had already occurred.

In Britain, the bombing of London and other places caused devastation, some loss of production, but no collapse of morale. By the end of 1940 Churchill had ceased to use the Cabinet Room at No. 10 as his office, and transacted business at the Cabinet War Rooms, bomb-proof and well below ground, or in the flat above. On Chamberlain's resignation in the autumn, he had become Leader of the Conservative Party, against the inclinations of his wife. While the advantages of standing somewhat above party were obvious for the mainspring of a coalition, the Conservative majority in the House of Commons was so large that Churchill can scarcely be blamed for wishing to command it. "I have some misgiving – tho' this sounds egotistic – at leaving Winston! for there are not many of the colleagues who are prepared to stand up when the winds of fevered imaginings blow strongly." Thus Lord Halifax on the eve of his departure to become ambassador in Washington. "However when that really happens nobody can make much difference!"[21] His successor at the Foreign Office, Anthony Eden, was already close to Churchill and grew closer; in 1942, about to set off on another of his perilous journeys, Churchill recommended that, if he were killed, the King should send for Eden as the outstanding minister in the War Cabinet.

Churchill remarked in October 1940 that while sure the Allies were going to win the war, he did not see clearly how it was to be achieved.[22] Britain would be beleaguered for the foreseeable future and he placed, like almost everyone else, a heavy reliance upon Bomber Command. There were high hopes that the spirit of resistance might be fanned into flame across occupied Europe; in the upshot, this proved impossible on any large scale until Allied military power was close at hand. The Prime Minister correctly judged that Roosevelt would win the election with a large majority and said that while he quite understood the exasperation with which so many English people viewed the American attitude of criticism combined with ineffective assistance, "we must be patient and we must conceal our irritation." In between these observations, delivered to one of his private secretaries in the car, he sang snatches from "Under the Spreading Chestnut Tree" before remarking, "I should now like to have dinner – at Monte Carlo – and then to go and gamble!" Even at this stage of the war, he contemplated a reunited European family in which Germany would take a leading place. By January 1941, he was saying cheerfully that he did not see how a German invasion could succeed and now he woke up again in the mornings, as he nearly always had done, feeling as if he had a bottle of champagne inside him and glad that another day had come; it had been a different story six months before.[23] He continued to believe that Japan was unlikely to enter the war unless the Germans made a successful assault upon the British Isles.

Mackenzie King often pointed out, as he was to do throughout 1941, that American public opinion showed no appetite for entry into the war. "Give us the tools and we will finish the job," said Churchill to the United States. Whether he believed that this could be achieved without direct American participation is doubtful; certainly the task would be impossible without the tools. The effect of Lend-Lease, introduced in the spring of 1941 when the British had run out of gold and dollars to pay for munitions, was to enable the Allies – in the first phase mainly Britain and the Commonwealth countries, and, from the autumn of 1941, Russia – to wage war on a scale that would have been well beyond their individual strength. The program embraced the supply of ammunition, weapons, food, raw materials and a good deal else. Under Reverse Lend-Lease, Britain made a very large contribution of her own; and she was also contracting alarming debts to overseas governments – for instance, those of India and Egypt – on account of military expenditure there.

In Canada, a national appeal was made for a new loan, symbolized by a Torch of Victory which was flown from city to city across four thousand miles from Victoria to Halifax and thence taken over the sea to London. Mackenzie King said that the heart of Canada had been touched by what the British had been called upon to bear; the Houses of Parliament, Westminster Abbey, St. Paul's, the historic churches and homes of Britain, were part of Canada's heritage in the Commonwealth, and in their visit to Canada of 1939, King George and Queen Elizabeth had become

> very much a part of ourselves. To the love inspired by their presence we now add our highest admiration for the nobility of soul which we see revealed as their Majesties with smiling courage share amid scenes of cruel devastation the dangers and the sorrows of their people. With us, as with you, "God Save the King" has become the people's prayer.
>
> Regardless of fortune or circumstance you seem one and all to be endowed with the same fortitude and the same spirit. Do you wonder that you have made those of us who are of British stock increasingly proud of the race to which we belong?

Churchill in his broadcast reply remarked that the wicked men in Germany could not understand the deep currents of loyalty that flowed between the self-governing nations of the Empire. The people of Britain were proud of the fact that the liberty of thought and action they had won in the course of a long history should have taken root throughout Canada, and he did not fail to remark that Canadians were also the heirs of the true tradition of French valour which would in the end bring France back to life.[24] Not long after Lord Halifax went to America, Churchill offered the High Commissionership at Ottawa to Malcolm MacDonald, then Minister of Health, who had known Mackenzie King many years. The British High Commissioners in the capitals of the Dominions were men of ability and experience. None had closer relations with the government to which he was accredited than MacDonald. He had remarkable gifts of sympathy and a talent for finding the best in the people with whom he dealt. Ottawa soon provided opportunities to display those qualities.

With some difficulty the Allied forces suppressed a coup in Iraq in favour of the Axis; the battle in the desert swayed to and fro but came to no satisfactory conclusion; Churchill decided to move Wavell to another command, replacing him by General Auchinleck. Wavell, one of the people whom Churchill consistently undervalued, took his supersession with a resigned good humour which compels admiration.

Amidst so many reverses, Churchill remained resolute. He had to rally the people at home, and many abroad, never concealing that the war would be long and costly; stay at any cost on good terms with the United States; uphold the Middle Eastern theatre, at the price of depriving others; and somehow fight it out to a finish, or at least to the point when Germany acknowledged defeat. He would joke about this propensity. For some time, he had known from deciphered communications of the mounting German preparations against Russia, and had tried to warn Stalin. The Russian government seemed indifferent or oblivious. Churchill had made up his mind that when Germany invaded, immediate help should be given to Russia. Did this not create some problems for him, his Private Secretary asked as they paced the lawn at Chequers, since he had been so consistent an opponent of Communism and had done his best to strangle the Bolshevik revolution at birth? But Churchill merely replied that he had only one purpose, the destruction of Hitler; his life was much simplified thereby. "If Hitler invaded Hell, I would at least make a favourable reference to the Devil in the House of Commons."[25]

When news arrived of the German attack, on June 22, Churchill spent all day preparing his broadcast. Sometimes, he said to the Prime Minister of New Zealand (who chanced to be at Chequers), thoughts came only in a trickle; on this occasion, with a rush. The facts that Russia had made terms with Germany in 1939, supported Germany's conquests all over Europe and continued to the last to provide indispensable raw materials for the German war machine, no longer mattered. Churchill told the world that night that he saw the Russians fighting for hearth and home, and that Britain would give them all the help that could be sent.

At first, the German armies made progress so rapid that it seemed they might reach Moscow before Christmas. The general opinion among the military and intelligence people in London was that Russia could not hold out, whereas the Prime Minister, though sometimes tempted by that view, felt instinctively that Russia had at least a chance. It was manifestly in Britain's interest, and on a long view also in America's, that Germany should not capture the resources of Russia. In that event, Hitler might well turn on his remaining opponents with overmastering strength. Meanwhile, the threat from Japan had grown. The Japanese might simply be intending to expand with little risk in French Indochina or the Dutch East Indies, but by July the outlook had become so threatening that the American, British and Dutch governments announced serious sanctions against Japan. Urgent questions suggested themselves. What should America and Britain do if Japan decided to attack? Would America declare war if Japan attacked only British possessions? What would be the scale and nature of American aid to Russia? How rapidly could deliveries of ships, aircraft and munitions be made under the expanding Lend-Lease program? Would the United States assume more of the naval burden in the Atlantic?

To meet Churchill and the British Chiefs of Staff might by itself seem an un-neutral act, but Roosevelt, strengthened by his victory in the Presidential election, was willing to risk that; and Churchill, whose powers of persuasion were immense, longed to get on terms with him. It was quickly arranged that they should confer on board warships, south of a deserted coast in Newfoundland. Churchill had often hoped for early American entry into the war, an event which would to his mind make the outcome certain. If that could not be expected for some while, there was at least reason to believe, as his party set off for Placentia Bay, that the United States would take steps to make her neutrality even more benevolent toward Britain and her allies.

* * *

It is time to dwell upon the tremulous issues which arose that summer within the Commonwealth. The Prime Minister of Australia, Mr. Robert Menzies, had paid a prolonged visit to London. Like many of his countrymen, he felt deep fears about the situation in the Pacific. Judging the machinery for the higher direction of the war to be deficient, he believed he saw the remedy. Self-confident, decisive, a fine speaker and conversationalist, unabashed by his precarious political situation at home, making no secret of his convictions, he resembled Churchill in many particulars. The two men, though separated in age by twenty years, esteemed each other heartily. It is revealing of both that severe differences of opinion in the first part of the war caused no dilution of their friendship.

In mid-July, Mackenzie King read to Malcolm MacDonald a most secret telegram from Menzies, who had written similarly to Smuts in South Africa. It expressed grave concern about the state of affairs in London. What was wanted was a War Cabinet of a few men free from departmental responsibilities, able to think and plan under Churchill's leadership; the Dominions should have a representative, for their point of view was not taken sufficiently into account. Menzies wished to know whether his two fellow Prime Ministers thought an Imperial Conference might be held in August or September, and believed that a Dominion Prime Minister should always be present at the War Cabinet's discussions. King at once concluded that the main purpose of the message was to ensure that Menzies should be that representative. As it transpired, Lord Cranborne, the Dominions Secretary, already knew a good deal of this. Since it was clear that Menzies was going to start "a violent agitation in favour of a meeting of Dominion Prime Ministers, and that in doing so he was actuated to a considerable extent by personal motives, I felt it only right to warn Winston of what was in the wind, and did so."[26]

The British government found itself in an embarrassing position, because of strong criticism both at home and in the Dominions of the failure to call an Imperial Conference. The Prime Minister of Canada had wished Churchill to say that it was undesirable for the Prime Ministers of the Dominions to leave their own countries during the war. This Churchill could hardly do, because Menzies had recently been in London and Fraser of New Zealand was on his way there. Such an answer would have seemed absurd to the House of Commons, and would also have been in the nature of a snub to those two Prime Ministers. As Cranborne expressed it in his dry way, "The only way out seemed to be to tell the exact truth, and say frankly that in the case of two Dominions, Canada and South Africa, there were special circumstances which made it impossible for their Prime Ministers to come. We hoped that by coupling the name of Smuts with that of Mackenzie King, we would prevent unpleasantness for the latter. For obviously if Smuts could not come, the Conference could not in any case take place."[27]

Unpleasantness, however, was not so easily avoided. Mackenzie King, the British High Commissioner explained to Cranborne, had been "extremely upset" by Churchill's statement. The Prime Minister of Canada had already explained why he felt he must remain at home for the moment: the question of conscription had been raised and a serious split between the French and British communities in Canada might develop in his absence; America might come into the war, in which case he would need to confer immediately with Roosevelt; Far Eastern trouble was brewing up, with the possibility that Canada would have to take action against Japan; there were labour troubles in Canadian war factories. When Churchill said that "both General Smuts and Mr. Mackenzie King regret that the exigencies of their work in their respective countries make it impossible for them to come here in the near future," Opposition newspapers and politicians in Canada uttered insulting charges to the effect that by declining to go to a conference in London, King was hampering the full development of the Empire's war effort. By contrast, the Prime Minister expressed his views about Churchill's statement in "very strong language." The rest of the Cabinet and King's political friends had been keenly resentful, and even felt that Churchill's words had contained a veiled attack upon the Prime Minister of Canada.

"You will find it hard to understand all this," MacDonald wrote. "The statement made by Mr. Churchill was quite innocuous, though I cannot help feeling that if the political situation here, and Mr. King's sensitiveness, had been fully appreciated at home, the Prime Minister would not have mentioned individuals by name. . . . The evil consequences here of course spring from the intense bitterness of party politics which persists in the Dominion." Many sensitive Canadians believed that Britain had been trying to force Canada to do something contrary to her will, and that this was a mark of the inferior position which Canada would hold so long as she was tied to Great Britain.[28]

The crisis abated, at least for the moment. King planned to visit Britain after all, and Churchill sent him a message that did much to wipe out hard feelings: "You would be able to see for yourself the temper of the people and judge their ordeal. A great reception would await you, and you would of course take part in all our Cabinet proceedings. But I understand fully all your difficulties and do not suppose for a moment that I am pressing you against your better judgement."[29]

Realizing how much was at stake, Malcolm MacDonald offered an assessment of King upon which it would not be easy to improve:

> He admires Churchill enormously, but between you and me he does not like him much. But I am sure that Mr. Churchill will handle him extremely well if he sticks to the line of that last telegram, as well as being his own magnificent and inspiring self. Mackenzie King needs particularly careful handling. He is a deep and complex character. He is an experienced and wise statesman, who knows his Canada well, and (despite all the criticisms one can level against him) by his instinctive understanding and clever management of public opinion he has led and maintained a united Canada in the war. He can be extraordinarily charming and has a happy sense of humour and great tolerance and humanity. Yet he is full of vanities and inhibitions, and despite a political skin which has grown very thick is easily offended by some things. And often he hides his real feelings. . . .
>
> He is often suspected of being isolationist, anti-British Empire and pro-United States. All these charges are greatly exaggerated, but there is an element of all these factors in his complex make-up. But I am con-

> vinced that we have an opportunity now of strengthening immensely all the countering factors in his character and inclinations. He feels a tremendous admiration for Britain at present; he is absolutely whole-hearted in his support of the war and in his desire for Canada to give Britain every possible aid to the bitter or sweet end. We can win him over decisively, and make him a most powerful friend of ours in Canada, where his influence on young isolationist and nationalist opinion is very considerable.[30]

In strictest secrecy, King informed MacDonald that he had sent to Canberra a carefully composed thesis "upon the constitutional impropriety of Menzies' general conception"; – or so the High Commissioner surmised, because the Prime Minister had hidden the paper and "could not even find it himself in any of three or four locked boxes which he opened and searched. I will let you have," MacDonald wrote to Cranborne, "a précis of this State document, if the author can find it." In due course, the author did, and it is a measure of his confidence in MacDonald that he should have provided a copy of the text. Meanwhile, MacDonald gathered that Smuts had also telegraphed to Menzies turning down the latter's proposal.[31]

* * *

So elaborate were the precautions that many of those who accompanied Churchill to Newfoundland had simply been told to report with bags packed for a fortnight's absence; most imagined they were going to Russia. The special train left London on August 3, picking up Churchill at Wendover, near Chequers. At lunch, the Prime Minister remarked that for nearly fifty years he had averaged half a bottle of champagne a day. He set Lord Cherwell to make calculations with his slide rule, only to learn with deep disappointment that this impressive consumption would not even half-fill the dining car.[32]

The party sailed next day from Scapa Flow on the *Prince of Wales*. On board they found Harry Hopkins,* just arrived by air from conversations

* Harry Lloyd Hopkins (1890–1946), U.S. Secretary of Commerce, 1938–40; supervised much of the Lend-Lease program from 1941; probably Roosevelt's closest colleague until 1943, and much used for special missions; he and W.S.C. liked and admired each other. He had been sent to Moscow, immediately after the German attack, to assess the prospects and Russia's needs.

with Stalin in Moscow. The invaluable Captain Pim set up a war room, where the movements of ships and armies were plotted constantly. Thither Churchill would repair several times each day. For part of the voyage, the *Prince of Wales* ploughed forward alone because lesser vessels could not keep pace in the heavy seas, but a new escort, including two Canadian destroyers, soon arrived. Each evening, Churchill came to the wardroom, wearing the mess uniform of the Royal Yacht Squadron, bowed to the assembled officers and watched a film. When the recently released film about Lady Hamilton (which he was alleged to have seen five times already) was shown, he wept at the scene of Nelson's death. The lights went up; and Churchill, thinking of the part that the *Prince of Wales* had played in the sinking of the *Bismarck*, turned to the ship's company and said, "I thought this would be of especial interest to you gentlemen, who have been so recently engaged with the enemy in matters of equal historical importance."[33]

Rumour had it that the great German battleship *Tirpitz* might intercept Churchill's convoy. Warned of this possibility, he replied to London, "I fear there will be no such luck."[34]

After the miserable wartime rations of Britain, Churchill's entourage found themselves amply provided for. Grouse had been secured in Scotland, there was beef in abundance and plenty of butter and sugar. Hopkins produced a tub of caviar, given to him by Stalin. Churchill remarked that it was very good to have caviar, even though it meant fighting on the same side as the Russians to get it. He invited Hopkins, whose company he loved and whom he dubbed "Lord Root-of-the-Matter," to play backgammon. "Yes," said Hopkins, "but I play well." To which Churchill responded, "That's all right; I play low."[35]

Hopkins reported the Russians to be determined but in desperate need of help if they were to hold out. They had already asked for aid of a nature and on a scale wholly impossible; for example, the landing of twenty or twenty-five divisions on the continent of Europe, the supply of five thousand fighters and five thousand bombers and more to the same effect.

On August 6 a message reached London from Mackenzie King, saying that he would probably leave by air for Britain three days later. Rumours of a meeting between Churchill and Roosevelt were circulating in London, and telegrams informing the Dominion Prime Ministers of it, authorized for despatch on Sunday, August 10, had to be sent on August 6.[36]

This raised the possibility that Mackenzie King would wish to join in the conversations in Placentia Bay.

That evening, the British High Commissioner arrived at Kingsmere to announce that Roosevelt and Churchill were to foregather off Newfoundland. This caused the Prime Minister no surprise, for Roosevelt in a conversation at Hyde Park earlier that summer had said that he had in mind a meeting with Churchill. However, the news that Churchill and Roosevelt would be accompanied by their Chiefs of Staff, together with Cadogan and Sumner Welles, amazed King, who lamented that such great risks were to be run when German submarines were known to be operating within 150 miles of Newfoundland. What he did not say was confided to his diary:

> To me, it is the apotheosis of the craze for publicity and show. At the bottom, it is a matter of vanity. There is no need for any meeting of the kind. Everything essential can be done even better by cable communications, supplemented by conferences between officials themselves. Neither the Prime Minister of Britain nor the President of the United States should leave their respective countries at this present time. It makes me more satisfied than ever that I have held out against going to England to an Imperial Conference simply for the show that this might create.[37]

Churchill would have disagreed with every word of that, for no one was ever a more convinced believer in the value of conferences at the summit. He would have dismissed the notion that matters could be better handled by cable or officials. With Roosevelt in particular, Churchill soon found personal consultation much the best method of transacting business, particularly when large questions became enmeshed, for it was not always a simple matter to disentangle them at departmental level. The British Ambassador in Washington, until recently Foreign Secretary in London, compared the process with a disorderly day's rabbit shooting. "Nothing comes out where you expect and you are much discouraged. And then, suddenly, something emerges quite unexpectedly at the far end of the field."[38]

* * *

W.S.C. to C.R. Attlee [acting as Deputy Prime Minister], August 7, 1941[39]

TUDOR 6

HMS *Prince of Wales*

It would be a pity if anything happened to lead Mr Mackenzie King to join us in Newfoundland. Please make sure Dominions Office give no encouragement to any such a plan. I have no reason to suppose he has any idea of coming. Trust all arrangements will be made to receive him with most cordial welcome if he arrives England before I get back.*

[We need not ascribe to any petty motive Churchill's wish that the Canadian government should not be involved in the meetings. Roosevelt had shown no sign of desiring Canada's participation, and the British were anxious not to overplay a hand by no means strong; if only one Dominion were represented, difficulties would certainly arise with the others. Nor is it fanciful to imagine an apprehension on Churchill's side that if the party were joined by an enthusiastically belligerent Canada, the task with the Americans would become more difficult. Most of all, Churchill sought an unobstructed opportunity to make acquaintance, and as he hoped far more than acquaintance, with Roosevelt.]

Mackenzie King's diary, August 7, 1941

I told Malcolm MacDonald over the phone that I thought the public in Canada and certainly some of my colleagues and my own officials will think it extraordinary that Churchill should have brought his own staff to negotiate with the U.S. staff and ignore Canada altogether. While I had expected a personal visitation between Churchill and Roosevelt I had never thought of their bringing their own representatives on foreign affairs and chiefs of staff etc. for conferences on war plans, leaving Canada completely to one side – simply saying that we would be told what had been done, though having no voice in the arrangements. I said I did not propose

---

* Attlee replied reassuringly that King was now making preparations to come to London on or about August 13.

to make any difficulties about the matter but that it was on all fours with what has thus far been done between Britain and the States since they have been brought together, not wishing even a mission from Canada to Washington. I said to Malcolm it all bears out my view that the only real position for Canada to take is that of a nation wholly on her own vis a vis both Britain and the United States. That we can never expect to have any recognition of the Empire in any other way. In a way it is just what Hitler himself said to me* about nations conferring – that they will only seek to get in touch with others when they think the other is so strong that he will hit back unless he is recognized. I recognized Britain's problems in not wishing to bring Canada into a conference of the kind because of being unable also to bring Australia, New Zealand and South Africa and I recognized the difficulties of the U. S. in wishing to avoid difficulties with those parts of the Empire, but more particularly with Mexico and South American republics and where it is useless to even make a protest I do not attempt to make anything of the kind. I want, however, to register this time my own feeling and views in the matter.

I have no doubt at all that the Tory press of Canada will now begin to say that neither Churchill nor the President have any confidence in myself or feel it is necessary to take me into account. That will be the line of attack.

[On the morning of Saturday, August 9, land was sighted. American warships, smartly painted and polished, the Stars and Stripes fluttering from their mastheads, approached the *Prince of Wales*, camouflaged in dull grey. The band of the Royal Marines played the "Star-Spangled Banner" and from the American flagship the strains of "God Save the King" carried across the water. Churchill presented to Roosevelt on the *Augusta* a manuscript letter from King George VI, "to say how glad I am that you have an opportunity at last of getting to know my Prime Minister. I am sure that you will agree that he is a very remarkable man, and I have no doubt that your meeting will prove of great benefit to our two countries in the pursuit of our common goal."[40]

The conversations began at once; not only between President and Prime Minister, but among the senior representatives of the three armed

* When King visited him in 1937.

services (on the British side the Chief of the Imperial General Staff, the First Sea Lord and the Vice-Chief of the Air Staff) and their American counterparts. Churchill had devoted much thought to the entertainment of the President (turtle soup, grouse, a band) and equal care to the arrangements for divine service on board the *Prince of Wales*, which he ordered to be fully recorded on film for use at home and overseas. He chose the hymns and scrutinized all the prayers carefully.[41]]

Sir Alexander Cadogan's* diary, August 10, 1941[42]

HMS *Prince of Wales*

Drafted scheme of 'parallel' declarations by U.S., selves and Dutch, designed to restrain Japanese from further devilry and to provide mutual aid. Also, President last night said he might be prepared to make a joint general Declaration of principles, so started rough draft of that. P.M. approved both, with alterations.

11 [a.m.] combined Church service on quarter deck attended by President and his party and 250 U.S. seamen and marines, who were mingled in with our men. Very impressive. 3 good hymns – 'Onward Christian Soldiers', O God, our help in Ages Past' and 'Eternal Father'.

Sat about on deck. Talked to S[umner] W[elles].† Gave him some dope about Hess,** which I think interested him. Lunch President in Ward Room. I sat between Gen. Marshall†† and Harriman.*** Short speeches again by Pres. and P.M. Former awfully good – just like his fireside chats. Very hot by now and sun brilliant. Pres. left soon after lunch. I changed

---

* Sir Alexander George Montagu Cadogan (1884–1968), Permanent Under-Secretary of State, Foreign Office, 1938–46; Permanent British Representative to the United Nations Organisation, 1946–50.

† Sumner Welles (1892–1961), U.S. Assistant Secretary of State, 1933; Under-Secretary of State, 1937–43.

** Rudolph Walter Richard Hess (1894–1987), a member of the Nazi Party from 1920; Hitler's deputy from 1934; flew solo to Scotland on May 10, 1941, with vague proposals for a deal between Germany and Britain.

†† George Catlett Marshall (1880–1959), Chief of Staff of the U.S. Army, 1939–45; Secretary of State, 1947–49.

*** William Averell Harriman (1891–1986), a close friend of Roosevelt and W.S.C.; special representative of the President in London; chairman of a special mission to Russia, 1941, and Ambassador in Moscow, 1943–46; Secretary of Commerce, 1946–48.

and went ashore on a shingly bay with P.M. (in his Rompers!), Harriman, 'Prof', Martin and 'Tommy'.* We clambered over rocks, P.M. like a schoolboy and insisted on rolling boulders down a cliff. . . .

We gave a dinner on board, to Admirals and Generals and Sumner Welles. Sat and talked to S.W. after, and he stayed after others had gone. He improves on acquaintance, but it is a pity that he swallowed a ramrod in his youth. But I suppose that can happen in any family with sporting tastes.

[Roosevelt's original intention was to announce that the British and American staffs had discussed the grant of aid to democracies under the Lease and Lend Act and that the military and naval conversations had not been in any way concerned with future commitments other than as authorized by Act of Congress. Churchill pleaded earnestly against this emphasis on the fact of "no commitment," which he was confident would be exploited by Germany and a source of profound discouragement to the neutrals and the vanquished. Roosevelt agreed to confine the statement to the positive portion.

The U.S. government had suggested to the Japanese a period of standstill in the Far East, pending negotiations. Roosevelt recognized that it was unlikely the Japanese would hold back except on conditions unacceptable not only to the United States but to Britain. He told Churchill that he was disposed to negotiate and, if the negotiations failed, to issue a stiff warning to Japan. It was agreed between them that the full pressure of economic sanctions must be maintained.[43]]

W.S.C. to C.R. Attlee, August 11, 1941[44]

TUDOR 15
Most Secret

Have reached satisfactory settlement about Naval Plan No. 4,† as already reported to Admiralty.

Secondly, President is prepared to take very helpful action corresponding with, or consequent upon, operation 'Pilgrim.'**

---

* Respectively, Lord Cherwell; J.M. Martin, W.S.C.'s Principal Private Secretary; and Commander C.R. Thompson, W.S.C.'s Personal Assistant.

† By which the U.S. Navy would become responsible for naval operations in the Atlantic between North America and Iceland.

** Proposed operation to take the Canary Islands.

Thirdly, he intends to negotiate with Japan on the basis of a moratorium for, say, a month, during which no further military movements are to be made by Japan in Indo-China and no encroachment upon Siam. He has agreed to end his communication with a very severe warning, which I drafted, that further encroachments either in the South or North of the Pacific will be met by counter-measures which may lead to war between Japan and the United States. With this we should, of course, associate ourselves, and presumably the Dutch Government will do the same. The notification to Japan would be secret.

Fourthly, the President wishes to issue at the moment of general release of meeting story, probably 14th or 15th, a Joint Declaration signed by him and me, on behalf of His Majesty's Government, of the broad principles which animate the United States and Great Britain at this favourable time. I send you herewith his draft of the statement* (my immediately following telegram), which you will see is not free from the difficulties attaching to all such Declarations. The fourth condition would evidently have to be amended to safeguard our obligations contracted in Ottawa† and not prejudice the future of Imperial Preference. This might fall into its place after the war in a general economic settlement with decisive lowering of tariffs and trade barriers throughout the world. But we cannot settle it now. For the sake of speedy agreement I have little doubt he will accept the following amendments:

After the word 'endeavour' insert 'with due respect to their existing obligations'.

And after the word 'access' omit the words 'without discrimination and'.

Also, leave out the word 'markets' and insert the word 'trade'.

The seventh paragraph is most remarkable for its realism. The President undoubtedly contemplates the disarmament of the guilty nations, coupled with the maintenance of strong united British and American armaments both by sea and air for a long indefinite period.

Having regard to our views about the League of Nations or other International organization, I would suggest the following amendment after the word 'essential':

---

* The declaration drafted by Cadogan, amended by W.S.C. and further amended by Roosevelt.

† The agreements signed at the Ottawa Conference of 1932.

'pending the establishment of a wider and more permanent system of general security'.

He will not like this very much, but he attaches so much importance to the Joint Declaration, which he believes will affect the whole movement of United States' opinion, that I think he will agree.

It would be most imprudent on our part to raise unnecessary difficulties. We must regard this as an interim and partial statement of war aims designed to reassure all countries of our righteous purpose and not the complete structure which we should build after victory.

You should summon the full War Cabinet, with any others you may think necessary, to meet tonight, and please let me have your views without the slightest delay. Meanwhile, immediately full accounts are being sent you on the other points, together with Cadogan's report of the conversation. I fear President will be very much upset if no Joint Statement can be issued, and grave and vital interests might be affected.

I had purposed to leave afternoon 12th, but we have both now postponed departure twenty-four hours.

Please let me have your views about the Joint Declaration in advance of those on other points which I have mentioned to you in this skeleton form, and on which I am sending you separate telegram.

W.S.C. to C.R. Attlee, August 11, 1941

TUDOR 16
Most Secret

JOINT ANGLO-AMERICAN DECLARATION OF PRINCIPLES

The President of the United States of America and the Prime Minister, Mr Churchill, representing His Majesty's Government in the United Kingdom, being met together, deem it right to make known certain common principles in the national policies of their respective countries on which they base their hopes for a better future for the world.

First, their countries seek no aggrandisement, territorial or other.

Second, they desire to see no territorial changes that do not accord with the freely expressed wishes of the people concerned.

Third, they respect the right of all peoples to choose the form of government under which they will live; and they wish to see self-government restored to those from whom it has been forcibly removed.

Fourth, they will endeavour to further the enjoyment by all peoples of access, without discrimination and on equal terms, to the markets and to the raw materials of the world which are needed for their economic prosperity.

Fifth, they hope to see established a peace, after the final destruction of the Nazi tyranny, which will afford to all nations the means of dwelling in security within their own boundaries, and which will afford assurance to all peoples that they may live out their lives in freedom from fear.

Sixth, they desire such a peace to establish for all safety on the high seas and oceans.

Seventh, they believe that all of the nations of the world must be guided in spirit to the abandonment of the use of force. Because no future peace can be maintained if land, sea or air armaments continue to be employed by nations which threaten, or may threaten, to use force outside of their frontiers, they believe that the disarmament of such nations is essential. They will further the adoption of all the other practicable measures which will lighten for peace-loving peoples the crushing burden of armaments.

[The full War Cabinet met in the early hours of August 12, the Prime Minister of New Zealand being present. As Churchill's telegram of the next day to Attlee shows, the changes made to the draft declaration were comparatively few. The War Cabinet suggested the addition of a paragraph about improved labour standards and social security, which was accepted. On the face of it the Ottawa agreements and Imperial preference, not to mention many tariffs levied elsewhere, were safeguarded; "freedom from fear" became "freedom from fear and want."]

W.S.C. to C.R. Attlee, August 12, 1941

Most Secret

Please thank Cabinet for amazingly swift reply. I put your alternative clause 4 to the President, but he preferred to stick to the phrasing already agreed. I do not myself see any real difference. Phrase about 'respect for existing obligations' safeguards our relations with Dominions. We could not see how competition of cheap labour would come in as all countries preserve the right of retaining or imposing national tariffs as they think fit pending better solutions.

2. The President cordially accepted your new paragraph 5, but you will see that the reference to 'want' comes in where the President originally

wished it – at the end of paragraph 6. A few verbal flourishes not affecting substance have been added.

3. We have laid special stress on the warning to Japan which constitutes the teeth of the President's communication. One would always fear State Department trying to tone it down; but President has promised definitely to use the hard language.

4. Arrival Russia as a welcome guest at hungry table and need of large supplementary programmes both for ourselves and the United States forces make review and expansion of United States production imperative. President proposes shortly to ask Congress for another 5 billion dollars Loan-Lease Bill. President welcomes Beaverbrook's arrival at Washington,* and I am convinced this is the needful practical step. See also the Roosevelt-Churchill messages to dear old Joe.† I think they will send Harriman to represent them, and I should propose that Beaverbrook should go for us to Moscow or wherever Russian Government is.** We do not wish conference in Russia to start before latter part of September, by when it is hoped we shall know where the Russian front will lie for the winter.

5. They are sending us immediately 130,000 more rifles, and I look for improved allocations of heavy bombers and tanks. I hope they will take over whole ferry service and deliver both in England and in West Africa by American pilots, many of whom may stay for war training purposes with us.

6. Your promptness has enabled me to start home today, 12th. President is sending American destroyers with us, who are not considered escort but will chip in if any trouble occurs. Franklin Junior†† is serving on one of them and has been appointed Liaison Officer to me during my day in Iceland, where there will be a joint review of British and American forces.

7. Lord Beaverbrook is now proceeding with Harriman by air to United States. The joint telegram to Stalin comes out 48 hours after the main story.

---

* To discuss the expansion of American production of arms and determine priorities; Beaverbrook and Harriman negotiated in Moscow at the beginning of October a schedule for the delivery to Russia of tanks, aircraft, guns and ammunition.

† Stalin.

** This sentence reflects the possibility that the German onslaught might force the Russian government to leave Moscow; as it soon did, to Kuibyshev, some five hundred miles southeast of Moscow.

†† The President's son, who took the salute with W.S.C. at a parade of British and American troops in Iceland during the voyage back to Britain.

8. I trust my colleagues will feel that my mission has been fruitful. I am sure I have established warm and deep personal relations with our great friend.

W.S.C. and President Roosevelt to Premier Stalin, August 12, 1941

We have taken the opportunity afforded by the consideration of the report of Mr Harry Hopkins on his return from Moscow to consult together as to how best our two countries can help your country in the splendid defence that you are making against the Nazi attack. We are at the moment co-operating to provide you with the very maximum of supplies that you most urgently need. Already many shiploads have left our shores, and more will leave in the immediate future.

We must now turn our minds to the consideration of a more long-term policy, since there is still a long and hard path to be traversed before there can be won that complete victory without which our efforts and sacrifices would be wasted.

The war goes on upon many fronts, and before it is over there may be yet further fighting fronts that will be developed. Our resources, though immense, are limited, and it must become a question as to where and when those resources can best be used to further to the greatest extent our common effort. This applies equally to the manufactured war supplies and to raw materials.

The needs and demands of your and our armed services can only be determined in the light of the full knowledge of the many factors which must be taken into consideration in the decisions that we make. In order that all of us may be in a position to arrive at speedy decisions as to the apportionment of our joint resources, we suggest that we prepare for a meeting to be held at Moscow, to which we would send high representatives who could discuss these matters directly with you. If this conference appeals to you, we want you to know that, pending the decisions of that conference, we shall continue to send supplies and materials as rapidly as possible.

We realize fully how vitally important to the defeat of Hitlerism is the brave and steadfast resistance of the Soviet Union, and we feel therefore that we must not in any circumstances fail to act quickly and immediately in this matter of planning the programme for the future allocation of our joint resources.

W.S.C. to C.R. Attlee, August 12, 1941

Most Secret

President and I this morning agreed that following statement [the final text of the Atlantic Charter] should be broadcast on Thursday August 14 at three p.m. . . .

The President and Prime Minister have had several conferences. They have considered the dangers to world civilization arising from policy of military domination by conquest upon which Hitlerite Government of Germany and other governments associated therewith have embarked, and have made it clear the steps which their countries are respectively taking for their safety in facing those dangers.

[On that day, MacDonald brought to King a telegram saying that the declaration had been considered by the War Cabinet in London and would be given to the press shortly; whereupon the Prime Minister of Canada pointed out that "here again Canada was being ignored" and should have had the chance to consider the statement. He read out what he had told Menzies about the perfect means of communication within the Commonwealth. Yet the very opposite was happening, and over a matter which concerned all parts of the Empire directly, since the Atlantic Charter related to both military and economic co-operation. While he did not intend to make any difficulty, he could not prevent the effect which such events might produce on others. "It was the way in which the British lost their friends, wanting them in foul weather and ignoring them in fair. So long as they got their own way that was all they wanted. He [MacDonald] saw the point quite clearly and thought there should be more care exercised."[45]

It is not clear whether King spoke quite so sharply; if he did, MacDonald doubtless guessed that the mood would probably become a good deal more benign within a day or two. He reported to London King's warm approval of the meeting off Newfoundland, and believed him to be genuinely concerned at the possible consequences of failure to consult the Dominions about the draft Charter; these might prove "hurtful to the susceptibilities of the Canadian political public, who have been taught to take pride in the fact that Canada is a valuable as well as a vitally concerned third party in the United Kingdom–United States of America discussions."[46]

During the morning of August 13, Mackenzie King suggested that it might after all be of great advantage if the four Prime Ministers of the

Dominions could confer in London, for the talks between Churchill and Roosevelt had opened a new phase and touched on matters of special importance to the whole Commonwealth. This was unpractical, for the reasons revealed a few weeks earlier.

The Atlantic Charter, as the declaration was henceforth known, indicated that when Germany and Italy were defeated, they would be disarmed. It embodied the view that the world's interests would not be served by making Germany unprosperous. This was a point which attracted Churchill's particular attention and contrasts with the attitude which he adopted – though not for long – at Quebec in 1944. Most important of all, the President had agreed to a declaration which referred to the "final destruction of Nazi tyranny."[47]

It was obvious from the discussions that America was far from prepared for active operations of war. The British knew well that they were not the only claimants upon America's war production, since the demands of Russia, and to a lesser degree of China, must be taken into account. The American Chiefs of Staff had not formulated any joint strategy for the defeat of Germany should the United States enter the war; their British counterparts believed they had convinced them of the soundness of the policy being followed in the Middle East.[48]

Considering the frailty of the position at home – the House of Representatives passed by a single vote the bill extending the limited conscription without which even the existing American armies could not have remained in active being – the President had shown boldness of a remarkable kind. What he said in public was quite another matter. This delicate situation Churchill understood to the full. Small wonder that he always regarded Roosevelt, even after disappointing experiences in the last part of the war, as "the greatest American friend we have ever known." After Placentia Bay, they were to hold in a little over three years eight more conferences together, twice in company with Stalin, occupying a good four months in total.

Roosevelt sent two destroyers with the British party on the return journey, with orders to join in the fray if trouble occurred. The offer to escort the convoys to Iceland would release about fifty British and Canadian destroyers and corvettes, and the President ordered the escorts to attack any U-boat which showed itself, even if it were two or three hundred miles away from the convoy. More startling still, everything was to be done to force an "incident." The Germans would be presented with a dilemma which Churchill described as "acute and decisive." Either the convoys could be attacked, in which case U.S. naval forces would retaliate in kind, or the enemy could refrain from attack which, he hoped, would be "equivalent to giving us victory in the Battle of [the] Atlantic."

The Prime Minister had said at Placentia Bay that he would not answer for the consequences if Russia were compelled to sue for peace and, perhaps by the spring of 1942, hope died in Britain that the United States were coming into the war. Roosevelt took this very well. To other American colleagues, Churchill had remarked that he would rather have an American declaration of war at once and no supplies for six months than double the supplies and no declaration. He had been moved by Roosevelt's courage in mastering his physical disabilities and noticed how on one occasion the President had walked, every step causing him pain, a considerable distance in front of Marines drawn up on parade. On his return to London, Churchill told the War Cabinet that Roosevelt was determined that the Americans should come in but had been extremely anxious about the bill for further appropriations for Lend-Lease, which had passed by a very narrow majority; he was clearly skating on pretty thin ice in his relations with Congress, which, however, he did not regard as truly representative of the country. If he were to put the issue of peace and war to Congress, they would debate it for three months. The President had said that he would wage war, but not declare it, and that he would become more and more provocative. If the Germans did not like it, they could attack American forces.[49]

This was daring indeed, the more so because Roosevelt, upon his return to the United States, denied that there was any question of a new commitment. Mackenzie King warned the British that while there was no doubt of Roosevelt's attitude, much of American opinion was far from prepared for war.

If what the President and some of the senior American officers had said did not amount to a commitment in law, it exceeded the most genial form of neutrality. That situation was made possible only by the valiant struggle which Britain and the Commonwealth had put up for the fourteen months following the fall of France, and by Roosevelt's re-election for a third term. The supreme importance to Canada of the United States' approach to belligerent status needs no commentary.

Mackenzie King had now arrived in London, lodging in a splendid suite at the Dorchester Hotel. He went at once to meet Peter Fraser, Prime

Minister of New Zealand, who was about to leave for Washington. They agreed that the proper place for the Prime Minister of each Dominion was in his own country; no Prime Minister would hold office at home and simultaneously be a member of the War Cabinet in London. Nor did either approve of the notion that a Prime Minister could represent a Dominion other than his own. They thought that the arrangements for consultation and communication could not be improved upon. In short, Fraser did not agree with Menzies, whom he nevertheless liked. He had not found Menzies' criticism of the War Cabinet just, for Churchill was neither dictator nor the only member who spoke. Fraser had attended its meetings, where he found "the freest and frankest discussion and expression of view. He saw no need for an Imperial conference."[50]]

Mackenzie King's diary, August 21, 1941

[Mackenzie King attended the meeting of the War Cabinet on this morning. W.S.C. greeted him at the front door of 10 Downing Street.]

Churchill opened the proceedings by extending a very warm welcome to me and saying some exceedingly kind things in the presence of his colleagues. Among other things, he spoke of the great part which Canada was taking. Very much greater than anything done in the last war. He spoke not only of our contribution in the way of armed forces but also of the financial credit we had given the British Government, our help in the matter of finance. He spoke of the unity of Canada and attributed that to my leadership and long experience in public affairs. Hoped I would participate in the proceedings of the Cabinet and discuss any matter freely.

He also spoke of my friendship with the President and of what I have done in helping to bring the English speaking peoples together. At the door, when he received me, he spoke of me as a very old personal friend. When he had concluded, I expressed a few words of thanks saying the purpose of my visit was to find out in what way we could make our war effort more effective. But as he knew, Canada was of one mind in its determination to be in the war at the side of Britain till the end with all the resources, human and material, that we could effectively employ. As for troubles, we had not any to speak of with the British Government. That the relations had never been better between the governments of the two countries. I spoke also of the desire to see something of the situation in Britain, to study the British war effort and have the advantage of conferences with himself and his colleagues. Also to see something of our armed forces and as opportunity offered to express the admiration of Canada to the British people for their indomitable courage in the manner in which they were defending this citadel of freedom.

Throughout the morning, I listened to the discussion, which I found carried on in an admirable manner. Each Minister seemed well up on the subject with which he was expected to deal. . . .

I was particularly interested in hearing him [W.S.C.] say openly in the Cabinet that he felt it would be a great mistake to have any premature attempts at invasion of Europe. He felt quite sure that if the Russians were defeated, they would say that England had stood by and not given the help they should, but that it was very difficult for them to get help to Russia except by round-about ways which were difficult. The geography was very stubborn in her dictation. She, herself, had not allowed the assistance to be given; was unwilling to make arrangements when they could have been made, but that to endeavour to cross the channel and fight on the south [sic] of Europe unless they were absolutely certain to win, would be simply to incur another situation where they might have to evacuate, suffering vast losses and giving the enemy a change to restore his might. He was quite emphatic about not having expeditions of that kind.

He has a marvelous way of summing up situations in graphic phrases, a wonderful command of language and knowledge of history which he uses freely, and an ability to keep looking ahead making decisions in light of the long run rather than the short one. . . .

When the Cabinet broke up, Churchill took me downstairs to the basement of the house and showed me the concrete rooms which were constructed there like one large vault. A door on it like the door of a safe. What had been offices of stenographers but was now the dining room and sitting room. Quite an attractive spot, reinforced with steel beams, concrete, etc.

Before the proceedings of the conference had started, speaking of Chequers* and the week-end, he asked me something to the effect of enjoying a drink. I told him that I'd given up taking anything at all while the war was on. He asked me if it was for reasons of health. I said I felt better without it

* The country house in the Chilterns, some forty miles from London, given by Lord Lee in 1917 as a residence for the Prime Minister.

and found I suffered less from fatigue if I did not take stimulants at all. When he offered me sherry before luncheon, I declined and of course took nothing at luncheon. I was really surprised at the amount and variety of wines served.

As Churchill was sitting immediately opposite me at luncheon, I noticed he took several kinds of wine. His face got quite a different appearance – lost something of the intellectual look which it had had through the morning though it was clear that his brain became very stimulated and he talked very freely and most interestingly. . . .

Before anyone had come in, Churchill spoke about a communication I had sent as to [a] possible conference [of Dominion Prime Ministers] at this time but it was impossible, he said, for Smuts to leave Africa; also Fraser* to stay longer. He could not say whether Menzies† would be coming or not. He said he was against any Minister other than the P.M. from any of the Dominions attending the Cabinet. Also, if there was one there, there would have to be four and he did not see how one Minister could represent them all. I told him that was exactly my view and that I thought he and I were perhaps closer in our views than we imagined. He said he was sure of that.

Mackenzie King's diary, August 22, 1941

He [W.S.C.] said to me . . . that he would like to have had me at the conference with the President and himself, but that what he really wished it to be was a tete-a-tete where he could get to know the President without any third party. Told him I fully understood the situation and besides I could see the embarrassment I would have been to other parts of the Empire.

I told him about the talk at Hyde Park** and having been the first to whom the President had intimated his intentions of trying to see Churchill. Churchill said "I had really wanted to meet him. We had been writing each other love letters for some time. I wanted to talk with him. It was

---

* Peter Fraser (1884–1950), born in Scotland and emigrated to New Zealand; Prime Minister of New Zealand, 1940–49.

† Robert Gordon Menzies (1894–1978), Australian barrister and statesman; Attorney General, 1935–39; Prime Minister from 1939 to the end of August 1941; Prime Minister, 1949–66; succeeded W.S.C. as Lord Warden of the Cinque Ports, 1965–78; knighted, 1963.

** When King visited Roosevelt earlier that year.

of the utmost importance that we should talk together." He then went on to say that it is of the utmost importance that we keep very close to the U.S.; without the U.S. we cannot win this war. He then said that he would rather have the U.S. make a declaration of war tomorrow if they had to forego their help in other ways than to have the declaration delayed and to continue to receive the assistance we were getting. He believed the war would not end till the U.S. was in it. I said to him I thought the President, Stimson, Knox* and Mr. Hull were all anxious to have war declared feeling it was the quickest way to end everything. That the difficulties were with members of Congress who spoke for their constituencies. I said I felt that they should not count too much on the U.S. coming in quickly. That there was a real feeling among the people to stay out of the war altogether. . . .

He instructed Lord Cranborne† to let me have at once a full report of his conversations with the President. He then spoke of the President's great affection for me. Said in the presence of his colleagues there was no one who knew the President as well as I did or had the same influence upon America. . . . Churchill said he was pleased I had come immediately over for a conference with himself instead of going to Washington as he had understood from the President I would be doing after his return. . . .

Churchill in the course of his remarks said he did not want to make any more speeches than he could help, or broadcasts. That a man seldom opened his mouth without putting his foot into it.

[Churchill also said that he thought it well worthwhile to retain Pierre Dupuy, the Canadian representative, in France, even though that involved keeping a diplomat from the Vichy government in Ottawa; it was helpful to have the impressions and facts derived from Dupuy's reports. A day or two later, during the weekend at Chequers, Mackenzie King took care to raise this question again with Churchill, and noted the words of his reply: "I think it is most necessary to keep him, most necessary. By no means let him go." He had also told King, to the latter's considerable relief, that he saw no need whatever for conscription in Canada.[51]]

* William Frank Knox (1874–1944), Republican candidate for the Vice-Presidency in the election of 1936; U.S. Secretary of the Navy, 1940–44.

† Robert Arthur James Gascoyne-Cecil (1893–1972), later 5th Marquess of Salisbury; Dominions Secretary, 1940–42, 1943–45; Leader of the House of Lords, 1942–45, 1951–57; Lord President of the Council, 1952–57.

Mackenzie King's diary, August 23, 1941

Churchill talked very freely to me at dinner [at Chequers] about many topics and also fully with respect to any that I brought up. He took a good deal of wine to drink at dinner. It did not seem to affect him beyond quickening his intellect and intensifying his facility of expression. It is really a great delight to hear him converse. He is quite as eloquent in conversation and speech as in broadcasting. He ranges over such a field of knowledge and interest, always having something enlightening to say. What appeals to me most in him is his instinctive, innate love of truth and right and justice and his tremendous courage in asserting their claims. Also his great tenderness and gentleness and lovableness in his own home and with his own family. . . .

When it was time to go in to dinner, he appeared in the hall above and called down to me and one or two others: Now, children, dinner is ready. He came downstairs later and said: I suppose it is a long time since you have been addressed that way. It was characteristic of his whole outlook.

At dinner, conversation was very free altogether from any restraint. He was quite clearly enjoying relaxation from his work and entering completely into the spirit of the occasion with a real buoyancy. He really is a big boy at heart, untiring in energy and interest.

After dinner, we were shown the movie of [the] conference between himself and the President in Blanca Bay* – a fine series of pictures. I was terribly shocked, however, at the appearance of the President. He looked to me like a man who was near the end of his life. Indeed much as I appeared when I was suffering from arthritis. It was quite clear that in meeting the Prime Minister at the outset, he was conscious of participating in a momentous event, and feeling one might almost imagine, the kind of very consciousness of what his critics might be saying regarding it. Over and over again, Churchill referred to his great courage, his bravery in meeting physical pain. His fine spirit. This movie was followed by one showing some of the scenes from the Germans' attacks upon Russia. The pictures had come from Germany intended really to fill others with terror. They really gave one a revolting feeling, wanton destruction, the methods of it; arrogance of German soldiers; terrible poverty; striking almost ignorant look of the peasants; dead bodies; many of them seemingly decapitated.

---

* i.e., Placentia Bay.

Churchill felt very strongly and we all agreed with him, that these pictures should be shown in America and in England but shown first, the pictures regarding the conference between the Prime Minister and the President to follow later – to bring out the complete contrast.

I think the most moving of all the pictures were those of the service and the singing of hymns. After the movies, we adjourned to the long hall where the books are. Talked there for a while and I slipped off to my room about midnight.

Churchill had left, I thought, to work on his broadcast and I did not get to say goodnight but left shortly after the ladies did. . . . A little later, I heard a gramophone playing many numbers of songs. Churchill joined in the singing. Among other songs was "A Sailor's Wife, a Sailor's Star Shall Be Across the Sea." (Very significant). It was 1.30 before the singing ceased.

[On that day at Chequers, W.S.C. remarked, "I have no ambition beyond getting us through this mess. There is nothing that anyone could give me or that I could wish for. They cannot take away what I have done. . . . If I went on after the war what more could be added? What could I wish for?" Mackenzie King replied that there was a destiny about Churchill's life; he had been meant for these times. Churchill accepted that, but in a modest way. He also said, "I don't believe the Japanese will fight the U.S. and Great Britain." This was without question a grave misjudgment, in the light of which his broadcast of the next night must be read.]

Mackenzie King's diary, August 24, 1941

In speaking with Churchill at the table, I referred to my talk with the President and how the President had humorously remarked on the way in which Churchill had gone up in the air when the subject of tariffs had been discussed.

Churchill said he was leader of the Conservative Party. When the tariffs were discussed, while he, himself, was not sympathetic to the Conservative position, he nevertheless had felt it his duty to stand up for it. When Sumner Welles had brought up the subject of free trade, he had compared and he thought rightly, the different parts of the British Empire in this matter, as being similar to different States within the Union so far as other parts of the world were concerned. He had reminded the Americans that among others, they were the ones who had gone in for tariffs. . . .

Dinner was not until nine o'clock tonight, with Churchill going on the air at 8.30. I shall never forget the scene in the long library at Chequers, as we listened to the broadcast. Churchill made it from his own office. The radio was in the centre of the room between the fireplace and the sofa, which is in the bay window opposite. . . .

There was a profound silence throughout the whole of the speech. . . . There seemed to be unanimity of feeling that it was the best broadcast he had made, and I think it was the feeling of all that the part which related to the Service and the singing of hymns [on the *Prince of Wales*] was the most impressive of any. . . .

Later on, I spoke of the hymns being the most impressive part. Churchill himself said he felt that way. He knew that was the side which would appeal to the people, and America particularly. At the table, he told us that during the Service itself, he had felt overcome. He pretended it was the cold he had, but really found it impossible to keep back the tears. Churchill's nature is deeply religious. It would be strange if it were not, with his love of truth, love and justice, and his profound hatred of cruelty, barbarity and wrong. He quite frankly said there are things beyond which we do not yet begin to understand. I noticed, in his manuscript, that he had changed the word "one" to "Him",* in his last revise. He also added last of all his references to the parts of the meeting with the President which related to the after-war basis on which settlement would be made – no vengeance and disarming Germany, but allowing her to prosper in a material way. . . .

After dinner, Churchill turned on the radio for music, songs, and in the course of the evening, began to walk up and down and perform a sort of dance. He turned and said to me: could I not do the same, whereupon I joined him and the two of us took each other by the arm and performed a dance together. All present were almost in hysterics with laughter. Mrs. Churchill told me that he had felt very fresh on his return but had already begun to feel the complex of old routine returning and difficulties. How well I know what it is like.

It was after one before we noticed how the time was passing.

---

* On the quarter-deck of the *Prince of Wales*, W.S.C. said, "We sang the hymn founded on the psalm which John Hampden's soldiers sang when they bore his body to the grave, and in which the brief, precarious span of human life is contrasted with the immutability of Him to Whom a thousand ages are but as yesterday, and as a watch in the night."

[In his broadcast, Churchill said the meeting with Roosevelt symbolized the marshalling of the good forces of the world against the evil. He praised Russia's resistance and stated that one and a half million, perhaps two million, of Nazi cannon fodder had bitten the dust of her endless plains. It is still not clear why he made this wildly exaggerated claim; maybe to spread despondency among the enemy. As for the Japanese, they had carried carnage into China, snatched Indochina from the wretched Vichy French, menaced Siam, Singapore and the Philippines. "It is certain that this has got to stop. Every effort will be made to secure a peaceful settlement. . . . But this I must say: that if these hopes should fail we shall of course range ourselves unhesitatingly at the side of the United States."[52]

The substance of this had been agreed with all the Dominions. The Russians made a very stiff answer to a Japanese complaint about American supplies entering Vladivostok. Churchill told the Prime Minister of Australia at the end of August, "I cannot believe the Japanese will face the combination now developing around them. We may therefore regard the situation not only as more favourable, but as less tense."[53]

Mackenzie King attended the War Cabinet on five occasions between August 21 and September 4, as well as meetings of the Defence Committee. To the former, he remarked that Roosevelt's appeals to the American people had so far largely run along the lines that what he was doing would help the British, but would also keep America out of the war. The President had a large following for that reason, and the British should not bank upon the Americans' coming in too quickly. He pointed out that the President had not gone far in his warnings to the Japanese Ambassador.[54]

At a later meeting, King deprecated the notion that the Dominions had a collective opinion, as opposed to that of the Mother Country. Each Dominion had its own problems and its own point of view, and each was a separate state with its own access to the Crown. On that day, August 28, the dissensions within the Australian Cabinet became so acute that Menzies resigned. It was reported that he might come to London as a resident Minister for Australia. W.S.C. said at once that he was determined not to have any Minister other than a Prime Minister in the War Cabinet. Mackenzie King agreed that Canada would not wish anything of the kind and "that the less it appeared that all matters were being settled by [the] Cabinet sitting at Downing Street, the better it would be for the war effort of the several Dominions."[55]

Visiting Canadian troops in Britain, Mackenzie King was ill-received by some of them. Hostile organs of the Canadian press made something of this, while others pointed out that both Sir Robert Borden and Arthur Meighen had been booed by Canadian troops in the last war; Mackenzie King was therefore following a good Conservative tradition. His public statement that the government of Canada had long since agreed that the soldiers could be sent wherever they were wanted most, provided Canada was consulted first, did a good deal to restore the position.[56]]

W.S.C.'s speech at Mansion House, London, at the luncheon given by the City of London in honour of Mackenzie King, September 4, 1941[57]

In Mr Mackenzie King we have a Canadian statesman who has always preserved the most intimate relations with the great Republic of the United States, and whose name and voice are honoured there as they are on this side of the Atlantic. I had the opportunity of meeting the President of the United States a few weeks ago, and I know from him the great esteem in which Mr Mackenzie King is held and how much he has contributed to joining together in close sympathetic action the Republic of the United States and the Dominion of Canada.

I am grateful to Mr Mackenzie King today for having put in terms perhaps more pointed than I, as a British Minister, would use, that overpowering sense we have that the time is short, that the struggle is dire, and that all the free men of the world must stand together in one line if humanity is to be spared a deepening and darkening and widening tragedy which can lead only, as Mr Mackenzie King has said, to something in the nature of immediate world chaos.

I hope, Mr Mackenzie King, during your all too brief visit here, a visit which in a few weeks must draw to its close,* you have found yourself able to see with your own eyes what we have gone through, and also to feel that unconquerable uplift of energy and of resolve which will carry this old island through the storm and carry with it also much that is precious to mankind.

---

* King was due to fly home within a day or two, a fact that W.S.C. was here doing his best to obscure.

You have seen your gallant Canadian Corps and other troops who are here. We have felt very much for them that they have not yet had a chance of coming to close quarters with the enemy. It is not their fault, it is not our fault, but there they stand and there they have stood through the whole of the critical period of the last fifteen months at the very point where they would be the first to be hurled into a counter-stroke against an invader. No greater service can be rendered to this country, no more important military duty can be performed by any troops in all the Allied forces. It seems to me that although they may have felt envious that Australian, New Zealand and South African troops have been in action, the part they have played in bringing about the final result is second to none.

Mackenzie King's diary, September 5, 1941

We left [General Montgomery's headquarters at] Dover at 1.30 and were back in London a little after 3. On the way, I had lunch, a very pleasant talk with Mr. Churchill's brother.* We drove together from the station to Downing Street. Walked through the Cabinet offices and out to the garden where Churchill was seated. . . . He enquired about the visit and asked if they had fired one of the large guns. Had he been along, this certainly would have happened. He spoke about the strength of the fortress and its essential features.

Mr. C. then said he would show me the document which had caused him to forego the trip. He handed me the communication from Sir Stafford Cripps,† containing a letter** from Stalin to himself about the situation in Russia. The communication indicated a very critical state of affairs. Stalin was pointing out that Russia could not hold out much longer in some parts and was requesting that the British Government should arrange for a

---

* Jack, who had toured Canada with W.S.C. in 1929.

† Sir Richard Stafford Cripps (1889–1952), British Ambassador in Moscow, 1940–42; Minister of Aircraft Production, 1942–45; President of the Board of Trade, 1945–47; Chancellor of the Exchequer, 1947–50.

** This letter, of September 4, disclosed that the German forces had taken more than half the Ukraine, and also stood at the gates of Leningrad. In face of this "mortal menace," he saw only one possibility; the immediate opening of a second front in the Balkans or France, on a scale that would draw away thirty or forty German divisions. In addition, the U.S.S.R. required at once 30,000 tons of aluminium and a minimum of 400 aircraft and 500 tanks each month. Most of this lay in the realms of fantasy, as W.S.C. explained at once to the Russian Ambassador in London, the British Ambassador in Moscow and Stalin.

line of defence in the Near East, which would keep the Germans occupied there, if they were to be prevented from turning rapidly to the West in Europe. He was stressing the need for additional planes, equipment, etc, pointing out that if he could not get this assistance it might not be possible to hold out. Cripps was taking the position that England could not afford to take the view that the war was not hers, but rather the Russians', and asked the Prime Minister to try and meet Stalin's wishes about fresh assistance. Churchill showed me the reply which was being drafted, which indicated he could not possibly arrange for the additional assistance needed to keep the enemy occupied in the Near East. He promised to give some help in other directions. The whole communication indicated the possibility of a Russian collapse fairly soon. Minsky [I.M. Maisky, Russian Ambassador in London] had indicated something of the kind might happen. Churchill was prepared to part with large supplies, and hoped that the Americans would go one half and he would go one half. He said if the Americans did not, then he would try to go the whole way. It was clear, however, that England, from now on, has to figure on the possibility of the Russian situation becoming more rapidly deteriorated. Churchill said to me it certainly was not England's fault if Russia came to grief; they had tried to help her at the start; she could not fall in line, and they did not know until the last moment whether Russia was against them. It was not Russia herself who made the decision to fight the Germans. It was Hitler who made it for her. There is every truth in this. . . .

At the door at Downing Street, he said to me he really thought that they had passed the worst – that the war might go on for another two years. That there was always the possibility of something occasioning a sudden ending. Stalin, in his letter, had said that Russia did not want war with the Japanese, but that if the Japanese became aggressive, Russia would certainly fight them.

While in the Cabinet council chamber, Churchill said to me that my visit had been a great help and success from the point of view of the British Government. He hoped it had been pleasant and profitable to myself. I said it had been very much so indeed. I was particularly grateful to hear him say what he did.

5

In Defeat, Defiance: December 1941

On his return to Canada, Mackenzie King gave a ringing account of what he had seen in beleaguered Britain. All the resentments of that summer expunged, or anyhow submerged, he described the British martyrdom of daily anxiety and weariness and marvelled at the fidelity, ability and resilience with which Churchill and his colleagues carried on their duties. It would be difficult or impossible, he declared, to improve upon the system of Commonwealth consultation. Well might Churchill be impressed; he had the text of King's speech circulated to the whole Cabinet.[1] For his part, W.S.C. understood that the men of the Canadian Army, some of whom had already been in Britain for the better part of two years, were fed up with drill and discipline as a substitute for action. The war was turning out to be strangely different from the last; barely 100,000 people from Britain and the Commonwealth had so far been killed, of whom nearly half were civilians. It would be hard to argue in such circumstances the immediate necessity for conscription in Canada.[2]

In the Mediterranean theatre, the fortunes of battle fluctuated. Despite the substantial German effort diverted to the campaign in North Africa, the British and Commonwealth forces in Egypt and the desert were on the face of it stronger. Churchill longed for an unmistakable strategic success, as distinct from a tactical victory, though there were prolonged periods during which even the latter would have proved most welcome. He pressed Auchinleck to begin the next major offensive, Crusader, in mid-October, but it was postponed for a month. The Prime Minister fumed. Even his devoted admirer Oliver Lyttelton, then Minister of State in Cairo, admitted long afterwards, "I dreaded the appearance of irascible telegrams and exhortations."[3] Crusader succeeded, for the moment; by December 10, the German and Italian armies were in retreat, having lost (killed, wounded or captured) some 33,000 men and many tanks.

Given the reverses and disappointments of the past two years, hearty rejoicings might have been expected. But events in Asia and the Pacific dwarfed those nearer to home, for on the evening of Sunday, December 7, Churchill learned at Chequers that the Japanese had attacked the U.S. base at Pearl Harbor in the Hawaiian Islands, about two thousand miles southwest of California. Simultaneously, Japanese forces struck at Malaya, some five thousand miles to the west of Pearl Harbor, and at the Philippines and Hong Kong. Not for a day or two did the full scale of the damage at Pearl Harbor – where in a couple of hours the Japanese air attack had destroyed or damaged almost all the battleships of the Pacific Fleet – become known. The ship on which Churchill had travelled to and from Newfoundland a few weeks before, *Prince of Wales*, together with *Repulse*, had earlier been sent to Singapore. The decision to send only two capital ships, and without cover from an aircraft carrier, had been made by Churchill against the balance of naval advice. This marked one of the very few occasions when he acted thus in a matter of the first importance. Both ships were sunk by Japanese aircraft on December 10. "In all the war," he records, "I never received a more direct shock." It had seemed impossible that Japan would court destruction in war with Britain and the United States, and probably with Russia in the end. A declaration of war could not be reconciled with reason: "I have not hesitated to record repeatedly," he wrote in 1952, "my disbelief that Japan would go mad. However sincerely we try to put ourselves in another person's position, we cannot allow for processes of the human mind and imagination to which reason offers no key.

"Madness is however an affliction which in war carries with it the advantage of SURPRISE."[4]

By a melancholy coincidence, the naval position in the Mediterranean was also undermined. In November, *Ark Royal* and *Barham* had been sunk, and immediately after the disaster off Singapore, the battleships *Queen Elizabeth* and *Valiant* were both put out of action for months after an intrepid attack in Alexandria harbour. In a matter of a few weeks, seven great ships, more than a third of the Royal Navy's battleship and battle-cruiser strength, had been lost or disabled.

* * *

As soon as he heard of the catastrophes in the Pacific, Churchill determined to visit Washington. To him it seemed certain that now that the United States had gone to war with Japan, victory was only a matter of time and organization. "So we had won after all! . . . American blood flowed in my veins. . . . I went to bed and slept the sleep of the saved and thankful."[5]

Pausing only to issue a British declaration of war against Japan and give the House of Commons an account of the position, Churchill set off with his party in the brand-new *Duke of York*. The weather was so foul that the escorting destroyers could not keep up. As in August, Admiral Pound decided that the battleship should forge ahead on its own. Lord Beaverbrook said that it was like crossing the Atlantic in a submarine, and Churchill that it was like being in a prison, with the extra chance of being drowned.[6]

The Foreign Secretary, Anthony Eden, was meanwhile negotiating in Moscow. There, with the German forces so close that the thudding of their guns could be heard in the stillness of the Russian night, Stalin put forward large demands. In effect, Russia would retain the territories that she possessed before the German attack of June. This meant that she would take the Baltic States, part of Finland and a large portion of eastern Poland. From the *Duke of York*, the Prime Minister telegraphed immediately that these demands could not be accepted.[7] Britain had bound herself only a few months before, at Placentia Bay, to enter into no such secret arrangements during the war; and even on the most favourable interpretation, the demands themselves could not be reconciled with the Atlantic Charter.

* * *

C.R. Attlee to W.S.C. on board HMS *Duke of York*, December 16, 1941

TAUT 38

Following received from Lord Halifax*:

In view of the discussions I was having with them I felt obliged to tell the Canadian and Australian Ministers in the strictest confidence of the forthcoming visit. They have not (repeat not) reported this to their Governments but the Canadian Minister [Leighton McCarthy] has represented to me that failure to give advance information to the Canadian Prime Minister is likely to have unfortunate repercussions, especially since according to him, Mr. King was inclined to be hurt on the occasion of the last meeting [at Placentia Bay]. He thought that Mr. King would feel it imperative to be in a position to say he had been kept in the picture.

Lord Halifax to W.S.C., December 17, 1941

TAUT 39

I do not know whether you have told Mackenzie King of Arcadia.† If not would suggest it.

President spoke lately of great importance of strengthening King's domestic position and I imagine he would be much embarrassed if it transpired he had not been told.

Lord Halifax to W.S.C. and the Foreign Office, December 22, 1941

TAUT 103

Subject to your feelings President thought it would be a good thing to get Mackenzie King down on Friday [December 26]. I told him King knew about it but President will wait until he has spoken to you.

[In fact, it was already agreed that the Prime Minister of Canada should come to Washington, and Churchill promptly accepted King's invitation

---

* Edward Frederick Lindley Wood, previously Lord Irwin, later 1st Earl of Halifax (1881–1959); Viceroy of India, 1926–31; Foreign Secretary, 1938–40; British Ambassador in Washington, 1940–46.

† The code name for the forthcoming meetings in Washington.

to visit Ottawa as well. Roosevelt telephoned King with a highly significant message:

"We will be having an important discussion here. It will be to work out a long-range policy and also a short-range policy as regards the war. It will require very careful thought, and then will probably occasion much discussion. There will have to be a Supreme Council, and I am determined it shall have its headquarters in Washington."[8]

During the voyage, Churchill had composed three magisterial papers. In essence, they argued that the main purpose of the Anglo-American forces in Europe during 1942 should be the clearing of the Axis forces from North Africa, the effort to win control of French North Africa and the securing of that coastline; in the Pacific, the first task was to regain control of the sea; and in 1943, the British and American armies should invade Europe.

The Prime Minister knew from experience that the one who has written the documents under discussion, provided they are well-founded, holds no small advantage. He presented the President with all three memoranda as soon as the British party was established in Washington. Intense discussions, briefly interrupted by the festivities of Christmas, began at once.

On December 26, Churchill addressed both branches of Congress in the Senate Chamber at Washington, remarking to general amusement that if his father had been American and his mother British, instead of the other way round, he might have got there on his own. This was the speech in which, having observed that it was difficult to reconcile Japan's action with prudence or even with sanity, he asked to resounding cheers, "What kind of a people do they think we are? Is it possible they do not realize that we shall never cease to persevere against them until they have been taught a lesson which they and the world will never forget?"

That night, straining to open the window of his bedroom in the White House, Churchill suddenly found himself short of breath, with a dull pain over his heart and down his left arm. His doctor, Sir Charles Wilson (later Lord Moran), knew that the symptoms were those of angina, coronary insufficiency. In those days, the textbook treatment was six weeks in bed. We may imagine the doctor's dilemma; if it were announced that Churchill must take an immediate rest, the world would learn that he was an invalid with a crippled heart and a doubtful future "and this at a moment when America has just come into the war, and there is no one but Winston to take her by the hand." Moreover, if Churchill were told that his heart was affected, his work would suffer. Wilson took the risk and answered Churchill's question: "There is nothing serious. You have been overdoing things."

"Now, Charles, you're not going to tell me to rest," Churchill replied. "I can't. I won't. Nobody else can do this job. I must."[9]

These were exceptionally laborious days. Every word of the speeches for Washington and Ottawa had to be considered with care; there were endless conferences and telegrams; the issues at stake could hardly be more momentous, and over all hung the knowledge that horrible forfeits soon must be paid in the East. Even to those immediately surrounding him, Churchill seems to have shown no sign of concern about his health. The smallest suspicion that he had had an attack of angina would have undermined his own, and the Commonwealth's, position; and when Churchill said, "Nobody else can do this job," he was not uttering a conceit. We see why, a couple of days later in Ottawa, he bounded up the staircase of Laurier House, and why he found it prudent to move more sedately after he had reached the first landing.

Of all the conclusions reached in those few days at Washington, two stand out. To adopt a strategy of "Germany first" was not necessarily to be expected, since America was entering the war on account of an assault in the Pacific, and it followed that the war there must for some while be one of defence. That this should be established from the beginning was of the first importance to Britain, Europe and Russia. Doubtless the decision owed a good deal to the heedless declarations of war upon the United States just issued by Germany and Italy; all the same, Churchill's influence had counted for much.

No less significant was the decision that America and the Commonwealth would in effect fight the war together, with a co-ordination of effort and resources not previously paralleled. No machinery established in more than four years from August 1914 matched what was decided in principle at the end of 1941. The Combined Chiefs of Staff Committee would oversee the broad strategy of the war, subject to the decisions of the two governments. This was a revolutionary step, underpinned by the simultaneous agreement to set up boards which would oversee the allocation of shipping, munitions and food, the essentials without which war could not be waged.

The Japanese attack on Malaya presented an obvious threat to Burma, and by extension India. Churchill was adamant that nothing must be done to weaken India's war effort, which was formidable, and had no more taste in 1941 than ten years earlier for substantial concessions to Gandhi or the Congress Party. The publication of the Atlantic Charter, with its spacious promise to "respect the right of all peoples to choose the form of government under which they will live," raised potentially embarrassing questions. With the authority of the War Cabinet, he had stated in Parliament that the charter did not qualify in any way declarations already made about constitutional development in India or other countries of the Empire: "At the Atlantic meeting we had in mind, primarily, the restoration of the sovereignty, self-government and national life of the states and nations of Europe now under the Nazi yoke. . . ."[10]

Roosevelt discussed the Indian question with him "on the usual American lines" during this visit to Washington. W.S.C. reacted so vehemently and copiously that the President never raised the matter again in conversation.[11]

Just before Christmas, Free French forces took control bloodlessly of the small French islands of St. Pierre and Miquelon, south of the coast of Newfoundland. When such action had previously been proposed, the British had agreed; but then, learning that the United States would disapprove, told de Gaulle to desist. The Secretary of State in Washington, Cordell Hull, reacted violently and said that he wished Canada to order the Free French forces away from the islands and reinstate the Governor. He explained to Mackenzie King how serious it would be if anything happened to unsettle relations between Vichy France and the United States, for he had been doing everything in his power to prevent the French from turning over the remainder of their fleet to the Germans and to persuade them to be ready to help the British in Africa. King in return pointed out that it would not do to restore the Governor, who favoured the Axis and had a German wife. Strictly speaking, the matter was nothing to do with Canada; and her Prime Minister was determined to find out what, if anything, Churchill and Roosevelt intended.[12]

Agitated conversations took place in Washington in the next few days. Churchill and Roosevelt, it appeared, were anxious to close the incident. However, the State Department published a document referring to the "so-called Free French." De Gaulle telegraphed to Churchill: "It does not seem right to me that in war the prize should go to the apostles of dishonour. I am saying this to you because I know that you feel it and that you are the only one who can explain it in the right way."[13]

In London, de Gaulle admitted that he had intended to confront everyone with a *fait accompli*. A plebiscite in the islands showed a practically unanimous opinion in favour of the Free French. Churchill replied to de Gaulle that his action had raised a storm that "might have been serious had I not been on the spot to speak to the President. Undoubtedly, the result of your activities there has been to make things more difficult with the United States. . . ."[14]]

Mackenzie King's diary, December 27, 1941

At 2.30, arrived at the White House with McCarthy, Ralston, Power, Macdonald. . . .*

We were later taken on to the oval room in the White House and Mr. C. was there by himself for a few minutes. Mr. R. then took his seat behind the table. Said: Mackenzie, won't you introduce your Ministers. I presented each in turn. We sat around in a sort of semi-circle. The gas matter was mentioned at once, C. seeing the record for the first time.† He at once said that if that were the case, they had great supplies of gas in Britain and would give the Germans such a flooding of it, they would be destroyed. Use incendiaries to set houses on fire, and when they were putting out the fires, use the gas. He felt they could do more in Britain with gas against Germany than Germany could do against Britain, and that he would make this known at once. He immediately got off word to England to have gas masks brought out and kept in use.

Conversation was very general. Nothing was said about the unity of command or strategy. C tried to assure Casey** that Singapore would not be lost; that the Americans would send some troops to Australia if they were needed. Spoke of building a couple of large ships which would be ready by 1943. He said quite frankly that he never believed that the Japanese would attack U.S. or Britain. He based the argument on the production of iron and steel in both countries. Felt that the end was surer than ever seeing that it has brought in the U.S. with its great production. . . .

---

* Respectively, the Canadian Minister in Washington and the Canadian Ministers of National Defence, National Defence for Air and National Defence for Naval Services.

† This was a report from a source in Berne that Hitler was determined to use gas against Britain and elsewhere.

** Australian Minister in Washington.

The President looked to me pretty tired and it was clear they were both just filling in time, while behind the scenes the chiefs of the two staffs were working together. C is beginning to look rather flabby and tired. I could not help thinking of what a terrible thing it is that the fate of the world should rest so largely in the hands of two men to either of whom anything might happen at any moment.

C.R. Attlee to W.S.C., December 28, 1941

TAUT 246

While the King naturally does not want you to stay away a moment longer than is necessary, he entirely agrees that it would be a pity for you to come back before your task is completed. Moreover His Majesty thinks that the visit to Canada is most important and is glad that it is being fitted in. At the same time His Majesty appreciates that as a result of all this you cannot be back in time for the meeting of Parliament on January 8.

Mackenzie King's diary, December 28, 1941

When we got into the car together, Churchill sat to my right. We started to the station together [for the journey to Ottawa], a whole procession of several G-men following. Churchill said "What good were they? If a man took a shot they could only follow him up." The streets were pretty clear of people. The time of departure had been kept secret. However, little groups were assembling. Churchill responded immediately and in an enthusiastic way, giving them the V-sign. When we reached the station he fairly ran around in a semi-circle to show appreciation of the presence of those who were there and giving them a cheerful look and a V-sign.

We had only started from the White House when he said to me that he had succeeded that morning beyond all expectations in getting a solution to the problem of command. That the President himself had made the suggestion of giving the supreme command in the Pacific to General Wavell,* who was already familiar with conditions in the East and had great experi-

* To Churchill's considerable surprise. Archibald Percival Wavell, 1st Earl Wavell (1883–1950); Commander-in-Chief of British (and later Allied) forces in the Middle East, 1939–41; Commander-in-Chief, India, 1941, and South Pacific area, 1941–42; Field Marshal, 1943; Viceroy of India, 1943–47.

ence. Americans would appoint those next to him. That he and the President together would give the orders and direct the policy of the whole war. I asked him if he had arranged for a similar command on the Atlantic. He said no, and deliberately not, as he thought it best not to let things get into the shape of Americans looking after the Pacific and the British after the Atlantic. It was better to have both together in the whole world struggle.

[That evening the two Prime Ministers dined together on the train. King explained the pressure from some quarters in Canada for conscription, which, he feared, would mean a damaging split within the Dominion. They reached Ottawa next morning on a fine midwinter day, bright and sparkling, with a covering of snow.]

The *Globe and Mail*, Toronto, December 30, 1941

Ottawa, Dec. 29. – Puffing a big cigar and smiling broadly, Winston Churchill, the Empire's great war leader, arrived today in the capital of the senior Dominion to receive a welcome which he will remember to his dying day.

The cheers and the enthusiasm of the crowds which jammed the Union Station and lined the streets were without restraint, and the police of the city, augmented by the Royal Canadian Mounted force, were unable to control the thousands who crowded about Britain's incomparable Prime Minister as he emerged from the station.

The people surged so closely round him as he made his way to his automobile that all the carefully planned arrangements of the authorities were swept aside, and Mr. Churchill finally got to his motor car by himself and departed through lanes of cheering people, alternately puffing his cigar, smiling and giving the victory sign. . . .

The morning papers had been permitted to publish the news that Mr. Churchill was arriving at 10:10 a.m., and this little city of 160,000 turned out en masse to let the Empire leader know by their cheers what they think of him. If Hitler could have witnessed the demonstration, it would have given him some painful moments. . . .

Within an hour and a half Mr. Churchill was at work with the Canadian War Cabinet. . . . Later, one who was present, describing the effect of the British Prime Minister's personality, said: "He imparted to us something of his own unconquerable confidence and at the same time showed us how much has to be done. He was a real inspiration."

Mackenzie King's diary, December 29, 1941

I opened the conversation [at a meeting of the War Committee of the Canadian Cabinet] by enquiring as to the unity of command. He [Churchill] said little beyond that something of the kind had been arranged for the Pacific which would be disclosed later. . . .

I read the declaration [agreed between Churchill and Roosevelt, and accepted by Mackenzie King, at Washington]. Asked the specific question as to the pledge to give full resources, as to whether that meant conscription or whether it meant that each country would adopt what it believed was its own methods to have full war effort. Churchill was quite emphatic that it was for each country to decide for itself, to decide its own method, and that it did not signify any form of procedure to that end. Attention was drawn to the fact that Australia, South Africa, and Northern Ireland, if they signed it, would be clear that it could not mean Conscription. Churchill then gave us a most interesting talk about the whole war situation, describing what had been the most successful strokes of all. Referred to Hitler attacking Russia as some Cherub above watching over and directing affairs, meaning Providence. Said that from what Hess had told them, it was clear Hitler had expected to starve out the British by surrounding the islands and preventing food and munitions reaching them. He believed he could do that.

Had Hitler made a bargain for [with?] Russia, which she would have been willing to have him make, and gone through Turkey as he might have done, straight to the oil fields, he might have got his supplies there, and changed the whole situation in the Atlantic.

He said (at another time today) that things were 3 times better with Japan fighting America, thereby bringing her into the war unanimously, than the situation would have been if Japan had kept out of the war altogether and America not brought in. He said he literally danced when he learned that Japan had attacked America. Great as their losses were in their initial stages, he doubted – though he felt they [the British] might lose Malaya and different parts in the Far East, it being unwise to spread men too thin – if they [the Japanese] could take Singapore. They [in Singapore] could hold out 6 or 8 months. In the meantime, more ships would be around. He'd felt that perhaps the Japanese were pressing for one side of India and Hitler's troops for the other, but that India will keep supplying men for fighting, and they could hold their own there. That he was prepared to let the U.S. have all her ships off the Atlantic. The battle of the Atlantic had gone much better this year. The menace was from submarines. Great need was for construction of cargo ships and other ships particularly destroyers. . . .

As for attack upon Britain, he believed Hitler might mass divisions to the shores; assembling of boats and craft necessary to cross the Channel would give Britain time to do direct bombing and to bomb in the daylight. It would be extremely difficult for him to get many ships across with men; that at the narrow point – Dunkirk to Dieppe – Britain was now fortified as never before. They had, at the time of Dunkirk, been without anything to fight with worth speaking of. Were now in pretty good shape. Looked forward to '43 to roll tanks off ships at different points all around Europe in countries held by the Germans, getting rifles into the hands of the people themselves, making it impossible for Germany to defend different countries she has now overrun. He believed 1943 would be a year of liberation, rescuing the countries that were overrun. Thought Russia would hold out and inflict great damage. Believed the Libyan campaign would be wholly successful. Believed the U.S. would supply some troops to fight with in some parts of Europe.

He told me privately last night that the President was going to see that 3 or 4 divisions of men went to Northern Ireland which would enable him to get a couple of divisions elsewhere. . . .

He spoke feelingly of Hong Kong, saying that he was not sure at first about sending Canadians on the theory that if the war did not come, they would not be needed, and if it did come, it would be a difficult place to hold. It was thought that the extra Canadian battalions would supply just what was needed for defence. That the big ships, the *Prince of Wales* and the *Repulse*, had been sent at the right time to the right place. One of the ill fortunes of war had caused them to move out beyond the protection of their aircraft, and the ships were simply to show themselves and return to a secure place. That the people had not known the full story of the American losses which were much worse than had been told. He stressed strongly his great friendship with the President, and how ready the President was to give things. Said his coming to this side had enabled him to get much more and more favourable results than could have been acquired in any other way. He thinks Harry Hopkins is a wonderful fellow, has a living flame of a soul. Is invaluable. Most helpful.

Spoke about the Pacific Coast. Emphasized the need for having troops there in position to fight; thought ships should be carefully watched.

I spoke specifically about the Atlantic coast and the question of command between the Americans and ourselves in the Newfoundland area. Said quite openly to him the problem we face was that while we had been in during 2 and a ¼ years, things would be so arranged that the U.S. and Britain would settle everything between themselves, and that our service, Chiefs of Staff, etc. would not have any say in what was to be done. That in the last war, there had been a military mission in Washington. People thought in Canada there should be a military mission there now, watching Canada's interests. That he would understand our political problem in that regard.

I got the Chiefs of Staff later to explain the position. He said he thought we should be entitled to have representation there but expressed the hope that we would take a large view of the relationships of the large countries, to avoid anything in the way of antagonisms. He was quite strong and outspoken against the way in which Curtin,* of Australia, had spoken yesterday.

Minutes of a special meeting of the War Committee of the Canadian Cabinet held in the Privy Council Chamber, Ottawa, at noon, December 29, 1941[15]

VISIT OF THE PRIME MINISTER OF THE UNITED KINGDOM – WASHINGTON CONVERSATIONS – JOINT DECLARATION BY ALLIED GOVERNMENTS

The Prime Minister welcomed Mr. Churchill who, he suggested, might be willing to review, privately, for members of the War Committee, some of the points covered in recent conversations in Washington, possibly touching upon the question of unified commands and plans for co-operation in the prosecution of the war.

The Prime Minister of the United Kingdom said that, subject to the concurrence of the U.K. Cabinet, it had been agreed, in principle, to set up a unified command in the Southwestern Pacific. Details of the proposed arrangement would be communicated to Canada as soon as the U.K. Cabinet's concurrence had been obtained.

---

* John Curtin (1885–1945), Prime Minister of Australia, 1941–45, and Minister of Defence from 1942: he had just made a broadcast criticizing inadequate military preparations in Southeast Asia and the Pacific; and published a New Year message stating that Australia looked to the United States without inhibitions and "free of any pangs as to our traditional links or kinship with the United Kingdom."

The attitude of Mr. Roosevelt, throughout the discussions, had been altogether helpful and cooperative. The U.S. government had a wide conception of the requirements of the war and showed no disposition to confine their effort to the war against Japan.

A draft "joint declaration", to which all Allied governments would be asked to adhere, had been prepared in Washington. It was hoped that the U.S.S.R., as well as the other nations, would be willing to participate.

Mr. King read the draft declaration.

With regard to the pledge proposed in paragraph (1), namely, that each government employ its "full resources, military or economic" against the Axis powers, were these terms capable of being interpreted as implying an obligation to use any particular method of organising the national effort such as conscription?

Mr. Churchill said that, according to his understanding, no such implication should be read into the terms of the draft declaration. Each country was the best judge of the methods which it would employ to bring its full resources to bear against the enemy.

RELATIONS WITH FRANCE

The U.K. Prime Minister, in answer to a question by the Minister of National Defence* regarding the U.S. attitude toward the Free French, observed that Washington had been very angry about St. Pierre and Miquelon.

It should be remembered that France, even Vichy France, had much to give, or much to withhold. The maintenance of relations between Canada and France might turn out to be useful.

One could not tell when M. Dupuy's† contacts might again prove helpful; it was "good to have a window on that courtyard".

PROGRESS OF THE WAR – FUTURE STRATEGY

Mr. Churchill then reviewed the course of the war, the present position and prospective Allied strategy. It had been a great mistake for Hitler to attack Russia. The recent Russian victories were proving immensely helpful. Britain was giving every possible aid to the U.S.S.R., at serious sacrifice to the needs of her own forces; 250 tanks a month and 200 aircraft had been promised and were being delivered. A second great accession of strength had, of course, been the entry of the United States into the war.

---

* James Layton Ralston (1881–1948), Minister of National Defence, 1926–30, 1940–44.

† Canadian Minister to the Vichy government in France.

The position in the South Pacific was, however, full of danger. The Philippines were in serious case. Drastic measures were being taken to re-enforce Singapore and Southern Malaya, and to meet the threat to Burma, and in the Indian Ocean. It would be reasonable to hope that Singapore could hold out until the situation had been improved. It was essential not to divide our forces too much but to concentrate on strong points.

Mr. Churchill said that, while great plans were necessarily "subject to alteration", it might reasonably be predicted that 1942 would be a year of consolidation in which we would "strengthen our grip". 1943 would see the beginning of the "war of liberation" and the concerting of great forces against the enemy from the North Cape round to the Mediterranean. 1944 would, perhaps, prove to be the year of victory.

Of late the battle of the Atlantic had gone well. Gradually, largely increased troop movements would be possible. This improvement had been made despite the larger numbers of U-boats and aircraft operating against our shipping.

HONG KONG

Mr. Churchill expressed his sympathy for Canada in the loss of two gallant battalions at Hong Kong. Their heroic stand had served to gain valuable time. In spite of the tragic circumstances, there had been no "whimper" from Canada; none of the bitter and harmful criticism which had come from Australia. . . .

CANADIAN STAFF REPRESENTATION IN THE UNITED STATES

The Prime Minister referred to Canada's position in relation to U.S.–U.K. discussions of joint strategy. Canadian interests were, in many cases, directly concerned and it was felt that Canada should have a voice in making decisions. A Canadian Military Mission to Washington had been under consideration for some time prior to the United States' entry into the war.

Mr. Churchill expressed the view that, where Canadian interests were concerned, Canada should certainly be consulted, and should be represented on any body devised for the conduct of strategy in theatres of Canadian interest. At the same time, the U.K. government were anxious to keep the United States to the fore, and avoid anything in the nature of partisanship. As far as joint U.K.–Canadian matters were concerned, it was his own responsibility to see that the Canadian government were fully informed. . . .

CANADIAN ARMY PROGRAMME – 1942–43

The Minister of National Defence observed that the Army programme, for the next year, was now under consideration. Its recommendations included the conversion of an infantry division and its despatch to Britain as a second armoured division. The U.K. Secretary of State for War had, on an earlier occasion, expressed to him the view that a second armoured division would constitute, on the part of Canada, the most desirable form of additional army contribution. Had Mr. Churchill any comment to make?

Mr. Churchill said that armoured divisions were the highest form of army requirements. If Canada were to send another armoured division to Britain, it would certainly be most welcome and would constitute a most valuable addition to the forces now there.

SHIPBUILDING PROGRAMMES

The Minister of Munitions and Supply,* in connection with Mr. Churchill's reference to the vital importance of increased merchant tonnage, observed that the Canadian programme contemplated the construction of a total of one million tons over the next year. This was approximately the same figure as that for [the] British Isles. This was apart from naval construction.

Mr. Churchill, in answer to an enquiry by the Chief of the Naval Staff, felt that while both naval and merchant tonnage were urgently needed, the emphasis now should probably be placed upon the latter.

After the Prime Minister had expressed to Mr. Churchill the satisfaction felt by members of the War Committee at having had this opportunity of conferring with him, the meeting adjourned at 1.45 p.m.

[After the meeting of the War Committee on December 29, 1941, the Prime Ministers of Canada and Great Britain drove together to the Château Laurier, where great crowds had assembled. At a luncheon in the Quebec Suite with Canadian Ministers, the Chiefs of Staff, diplomatic representatives of the countries overrun by the Axis and the High Commissioners from the other Dominions, King spoke warmly of the leadership and courage displayed by Churchill and of Canada's determination to be at Britain's side to the end. In his turn, Churchill dwelt upon his friendship of many years with King, Canada's wonderful help, the assistance which the United States had also given before becoming a belligerent and his confidence that France would rise again.[16]]

---

* Clarence Decatur Howe (1886–1960), several ministerial posts, 1935–40; Minister of Munitions and Supply, 1940–45; Minister of Reconstruction and Supply, 1946–48; Minister of Trade and Commerce, 1948–57, and of Defence Production, 1951–57.

Lord Moran's diary, December 29, 1941[17]

On our arrival at Ottawa, the big fur-hatted Canadian Mounted Police kept back with difficulty the vast, enthusiastic crowds which pushed good-humouredly towards the P.M. and soon enveloped him. The atmosphere of Ottawa after Washington is like Belfast after Dublin. We drove to Government House through streets banked with snow. After a hot bath, Winston seemed his usual self, and we lunched with the Canadian Cabinet, a ceremony that lasted for two hours. There was still dinner at Government House to be got through, and then a reception. However, so far nothing untoward has happened. Whenever we are alone, he keeps asking me to take his pulse. I get out of it somehow, but once, when I found him lifting something heavy, I did expostulate. At this he broke out:

'Now, Charles, you are making me heart-minded. I shall soon think of nothing else. I couldn't do my work if I kept thinking of my heart.'

The next time he asked me to take his pulse I refused point-blank.

'You're all right. Forget your damned heart.'

He won't get through his speech tomorrow if this goes on.

Unsigned note addressed to W.S.C., December 29, 1941[18]

Mr. Mackenzie King rang up to say that the Government have this afternoon passed an Order in Council inviting you to become a Member of the Privy Council of Canada.

Mr. Mackenzie King very much hopes that you will accept this, and if you agree the Governor General has suggested that you should be sworn in at a short ceremony of about five minutes at Government House this evening at 8 pm before dinner.

I understand that the only other non-Canadian members of the Privy Council are Lord Baldwin* and the Governor of the Bahamas.†

[With Mackenzie King's knowledge, W.S.C. saw a number of the Conservative leaders. At dinner that night, he told King that he sensed a good deal of feeling that the Prime Minister ought to support conscription or

---

* Stanley Baldwin (1867–1947), 1st Earl Baldwin; British Prime Minister, 1923–24, 1924–29, 1935–37.

† The Duke of Windsor, formerly King Edward VIII.

form a national government with the addition of two or three of the Conservatives, who mainly wanted to be in the picture. King retorted that "it was financial interests that wanted control of Cabinet policy. Quite clearly the Conservatives had been urging him to try to persuade me on some of these matters." Moreover, he had offered them a chance in the previous year to join the government, and there were two other parties to consider. That was not the limit of the difficulties. Churchill said he would never press the point.[19]

No hint of Churchill's illness penetrated even to the British Ambassador in Washington, who wrote to his colleague MacDonald in Ottawa, "I am thinking of you in the thick of Winston. He is at the height of his energy."[20]]

W.S.C. to W.M. Hughes,* December 30, 1941

GREY 164

Speaking to you as a comrade of the last war and remembering how you faced the far worse shocks of the Dardanelles I cannot help expressing my wonder and sorrow at some of the things that are said. I am labouring for your interest night and day, and I feel sure that you will never fall out of the line.

W.S.C. to C.R. Attlee and Lord Cranborne, December 30, 1941

GREY 165

Curtin article in the Melbourne Herald has made a very bad impression in high American circles and of course excited lively scorn in Canada. I think you should call Earle Page† to account in Cabinet for it and ask him what is the meaning of this sort of language. By placing their relations with Britain after those with Russia, Dutch and China and by saying they rely

---

* William Morris Hughes (1864–1952), born in Wales; emigrated to Australia; Prime Minister, 1915–23; various ministerial offices from 1934, including External Affairs, 1937–39, the Navy, 1940–41; member of the War Advisory Council, 1941–44. He had been reported as saying that Brooke-Popham should have been removed sooner, but had also stated that it would be suicidal for Australia to regard Britain's support as less important than that of other countries.

† Sir Earle Christian Grafton Page (1880–1961), Australian doctor and politician; Deputy Prime Minister, 1934–39; Prime Minister briefly in 1939; represented Australia in the British War Cabinet, 1941–42.

on U.S.A. unhampered by any pangs of traditional friendship for Britain they must be taken as relieving us of part of our responsibility in pursuance of which we have sacrificed H.M. Ships PRINCE OF WALES and REPULSE. Once again to get better understanding you should take a firm stand against this misbehaviour which certainly does not represent the brave Australian nation. I hope therefore there will be no weakness or pandering to them at this juncture while at the same time we do all in human power to come to their aid.

In the same way a very firm attitude should be adopted in the House of Commons to snarlers and naggers who are trying to make trouble out of the Japanese attack on us in the Far East. I hope you will endeavour to let all issues stand over successively until I return so that I may face any opposition myself.

W.S.C. to Chiefs of Staff, London, December 30, 1941

GREY 166

Your TAUT 257. What was the point of doing ANKLET at all if not to try to interrupt north and south enemy coastal traffic. I understood ARCHERY was to be a baffle to cover real ANKLET.* But it is only baffling that seems to have come off. I cannot understand why on threat of dive bombers arriving Bodo the operation ANKLET should have been turned into "Raid of short duration". After all these elaborate preparations you have certainly made a very hasty departure. Pray let me have full explanation of what appears to be a complete abandonment of the original plans.

W.S.C. to C.R. Attlee, December 30, 1941

GREY 172

I do not think we ought to remove Brookepopham's† name from new year's honours list for Baronetcy. It was decided to remove him before war began, and the Baronetcy was awarded for his good service. It would be

---

* Anklet and Archery were code names for operations in Norway, the former to disrupt coastal traffic and the latter a raid near Vaagso.

† Air Chief Marshal Sir Henry Robert Moore Brooke-Popham (1878–1953) rejoined the Royal Air Force in 1939, having retired in 1937; Commander-in-Chief, Far East, 1940–41. It appears that he declined the baronetcy.

most unfair to make him a scapegoat. If Malay Peninsula has been starved for sake of Libya and Russia no one is more responsible than I and I would do exactly the same again. I hope, therefore, his name will be restored to the list, and Brendan Bracken* should be able to explain position to editors and place decision squarely upon me. Should any questions be asked in Parliament I should be glad if it could be stated that I particularly desire to answer it myself on my return.

W.S.C.'s address to the Members of the Senate and the House of Commons, Ottawa, December 30, 1941[21]

Canada, Sir, occupies a unique position in the British Empire because of its unbreakable ties with Britain and its ever-growing friendship and intimate association with the United States. Canada is a potent magnet, drawing together those in the new world and in the old whose fortunes are now united in a deadly struggle for life and honour against the common foe.

The contribution of Canada to the imperial war effort, in troops, in ships, in aircraft, in food and in finance has been magnificent. The Canadian army now stationed in England has chafed not to find itself in contact with the enemy, but I am here to tell you that it has stood and still stands in the key position to strike at the invader should he land upon our shores. In a few months, when the invasion season returns, the Canadian army may be engaged in one of the most frightful battles the world has ever seen. Upon the other hand their presence may help to deter the enemy from attempting to fight such a battle on British soil. Although, Sir, the long routine of training and preparation is undoubtedly trying to men who left prosperous farms and businesses or other responsible civil work, inspired by an eager and ardent desire to fight the enemy, although this is trying to high-mettled temperaments, the value of the service rendered is unquestionable, and the peculiar kind of self-sacrifice involved, will, I am sure, be cheerfully or at least patiently endured.

Sir, the Canadian government has imposed no limitation upon the use of the Canadian army whether upon the continent of Europe or elsewhere, and I think it extremely unlikely that this war will end without the Cana-

* Brendan Bracken (1901–58), later 1st Viscount Bracken; born in Ireland; entered Parliament at Westminster, 1929, and supported W.S.C. faithfully in 1930s; Minister of Information, 1941–45.

dian army coming to close quarters with the Germans as their fathers did at Ypres, on the Somme, or on the Vimy Ridge.

Already, at Hong Kong, that beautiful colony which the industry and mercantile enterprise of Britain has raised from a desert isle and made the greatest port of shipping in the whole world, at Hong Kong, that colony wrested from us for a time, until we reach the peace table, by the overwhelming power of the home forces of Japan to which it lay in proximity – at Hong Kong soldiers of the Royal Rifles of Canada and the Winnipeg Grenadiers, under a brave officer whose loss we mourn, have played a valuable part in gaining precious days and have crowned with military honour the reputation of their native land.

Another major contribution made by Canada to the imperial war effort is the wonderful and gigantic Empire Training Scheme* for pilots for the royal and imperial air forces. This has now been, as you know well, in full career for nearly two years under conditions free from all interference by the enemy.

The daring youth of Canada, Australia, New Zealand, together with many thousands from the homeland, are perfecting their training under the best conditions, and we have been assisted on a large scale by the United States, many of whose training facilities have been placed at our disposal. This scheme will provide us in 1942 and 1943 with the highest class of trained pilots, observers and air gunners, in the numbers necessary to man the enormous flow of aircraft which the factories of Britain, of the empire and of the United States are and will be producing. . . .

Sir, we did not make this war. We did not seek it. We did all we could to avoid it. We did too much to avoid it. We went so far in trying to avoid it as to be almost destroyed by it when it broke upon us. But that dangerous corner has been turned, and with every month and every year that passes we shall confront the evil-doers with weapons as plentiful, as sharp and as destructive as those with which they have sought to establish their hateful domination.

I should like to point out to you, Mr. Speaker, that we have not at any time asked for any mitigation in the fury or malice of the enemy. The peoples of the British Empire may love peace. They do not seek the lands or wealth of any country. But they are a tough and hardy lot. We have not

* Under which some 125,000 aircrew were trained in Canada during the war. This was a vital contribution to the Allied victory.

journeyed all this way across the centuries, across the oceans, across the mountains, across the prairies, because we are made of sugar candy.

Look at the Londoners, the cockneys. Look at what they stood up to, grim and gay, with their cry, "We can take it," and their wartime mood – "What is good enough for anybody is good enough for us."

We have not asked that the rules of the game should be modified. We shall never descend to the German and Japanese level; but if anybody likes to play rough we can play rough too. Hitler and his Nazi gang have sown the wind; let them reap the whirlwind. Neither the length of the struggle nor any form of severity which it may assume shall make us weary or shall make us quit. I have been all this week with the President of the United States, that great man whom destiny has marked for this climax of human fortune. We have been concerting the united pacts and resolves of more than thirty states and nations to fight on in unity together and in fidelity one to another, without any thought except the total and final extirpation of the Hitler tyranny, the Japanese frenzy and the Mussolini flop.

There shall be no halting or half measures, there shall be no compromise or parley. These gangs of bandits have sought to darken the light of the world, have sought to stand between the common people of all the lands and their march forward into their inheritance; they shall themselves be cast into the pit of death and shame. And only when the earth has been cleansed and purged of their crimes and their villainy will we turn from the task which they have forced upon us, a task which we were reluctant to undertake, but which we will now most faithfully and punctiliously discharge.

Mr. Speaker, according to my sense of proportion this is no time to speak of hopes of the future or of the broader world which lies beyond our struggles and our victory. We have to win that world for our children. We have to win it by our sacrifices. We have not won it yet. The crisis is upon us. The power of the enemy is immense. If we were in any way to underrate the strength, the resources or the ruthless savagery of that enemy we should jeopardize not only our lives – for they will be offered freely – but the cause of human freedom and progress to which we have vowed ourselves and all we have. We cannot for a moment, Sir, afford to relax. On the contrary, we must drive ourselves forward with unrelenting zeal. In this strange, terrible world war there is a place for everyone, man and woman, old and young, hale and halt. Service in a thousand forms is open. There is no room now for the dilettante, for the weakling, for the shirker or the sluggard. The mine, the factory, the dockyard, the salt sea waves, the fields to till, the home, the hospital, the chair of the scientist, the pulpit of the preacher – from the highest to the humblest, the tasks all are of equal honour. All have their part to play. The enemies ranged against us, coalesced and combined against us, have asked for total war. Let us make sure they get it.

That grand old minstrel, Harry Lauder – Sir Harry Lauder,* I should say, and no honour was better deserved – had a song in the last war which began:

> If we all look back o'er the history of the past,
> We can just see where we are.

Let us look back then. Sir, we plunged into this war unprepared because we had pledged our word to stand by the side of Poland, which Hitler had feloniously invaded and, in spite of a gallant resistance, had soon struck down. There followed that astonishing seven months which were called on this side of the Atlantic the "phoney" war. Suddenly the explosion of pent-up German strength and preparation burst upon Norway, Denmark, Holland and Belgium. All these absolutely blameless neutrals, to most of whom Germany up to the last moment was giving every kind of guarantee and assurance, were overrun and trampled down. The hideous massacre of Rotterdam, where thirty thousand people perished, showed the ferocious barbarism in which the German air force revels when, as in Warsaw and later Belgrade, it was able to bomb practically undefended cities.

On top of all this came the great French catastrophe. The French army collapsed and the French nation was dashed into utter and, as it has proved so far, irretrievable confusion. The French government had, at their own suggestion, solemnly bound themselves with us not to make a separate peace. It was their duty, and it was also their interest, to go to North Africa, where they would have been at the head of the French empire. In Africa with our aid they would have had overwhelming sea

---

* W.S.C. had written "comedian" but thought of "minstrel" on his way to deliver the speech, which Lauder heard with delight as he listened to the radio at home. This was the first time a broadcast had ever been made from Parliament in Ottawa. Nothing of the kind was allowed in Britain during the war, or for long afterwards.

power; they would have had the recognition of the United States, and the use of all the gold they have lodged beyond the seas. If they had done this, Italy might have been driven out of the war before the end of 1940, and France would have held her place as a nation in the councils of the allies and at the conference table of the victors.

But their generals misled them. When I warned them that Britain would fight alone, whatever they did, their generals told their Prime Minister and his divided cabinet, "In three weeks England will have her neck wrung like a chicken." Some chicken! Some neck!*

What a contrast, Sir, has been the behaviour of the valiant, stout-hearted Dutch, who still stand forth as a strong-living partner in the struggle. Their venerated Queen and their government are in England. Their princess and her children have found asylum and protection here in your midst. But the Dutch nation are defending their empire with dogged courage and tenacity by land, sea and in the air. Their submarines are inflicting a heavy daily toll upon the Japanese robbers who have come across the seas to steal the wealth of the East Indies, and to ravage and exploit its fertility and its civilization.

The British Empire and the United States are going to the aid of the Dutch. We are going to fight out this new war against Japan together. We have suffered together and we shall conquer together. But the men of Bordeaux, the men of Vichy – they would do nothing like this. They lie prostrate at the foot of the conqueror. They fawned upon him. And what have they got out of it? The fragment of France which was left to them is just as powerless, just as hungry as, and even more miserable because more divided than, the occupied regions themselves. Hitler plays from day to day a cat and mouse game with these tormented men. One day he will charge them a little less for holding their countrymen down. Another day he will let out a few thousand broken prisoners of war from the million and a half or million and three quarters he has collected. Or, again, he will shoot a hundred French hostages to give them a taste of the lash. On these blows and favours the Vichy government have been content to live from day to day. But even this will not go on indefinitely. At any moment it may suit Hitler's plans to brush them away. Their only guarantee is Hitler's good faith which, as everyone knows, biteth like the adder and stingeth like the asp. Some Frenchmen there were who would not bow

* W.S.C. was making a pun. "Neck" here means "cheek" or "nerve," as in "brass neck."

their knees and who under General de Gaulle have continued to fight at the side of the allies. They have been condemned to death by the men of Vichy, but their names will be held, and are being held, in increasing respect by nine Frenchmen out of every ten throughout the once happy, smiling land of France.

But now, Sir, strong forces are at hand. The tide has turned against the Hun. Britain, which the men of Bordeaux thought and then hoped would soon be finished, Britain with her empire around her carried the weight of the war alone for a whole long year through the darkest part of the valley. She is growing stronger every day. You can see it here in Canada. Anyone who has the slightest knowledge of our affairs is aware that very soon we shall be superior in every form of equipment to those who have taken us at the disadvantage of being but half armed.

The Russian armies under their warrior leader Joseph Stalin are waging furious war with increasing success along a thousand-mile front of their invaded country. General Auchinleck at the head of a British, South African, New Zealand and Indian army is striking down and mopping up the German and Italian forces who had attempted the invasion of Egypt. Not only, Sir, are they being mopped up in the desert but great numbers of them have been drowned on the way there by the British submarines and the Royal Air Force, in which Australian squadrons play their part. As I speak this afternoon an important battle is being fought around Agedabia. We must not attempt to prophesy its result, but I have good confidence. Sir, all this fighting in Libya proves that when our men have equal weapons in their hands and proper support from the air they are more than a match for the Nazi hordes.

In Libya as in Russia events of great importance and of most hopeful import have taken place. But, greatest of all, the mighty republic of the United States has entered the conflict and entered it in a manner which shows that for her there can be no withdrawal except by death or victory.

Et partout dans la France occupée et inoccupée, car leur sort est égal, les honnêtes gens, le grand peuple, la nation française, se redressent. L'espoir se rallume dans les cœurs d'une race guerrière, même désarmée, berceau des libertés révolutionnaires, et terrible aux vainqueurs. Partout on voit le point du jour et la lumière grandit, rougeâtre mais claire.

Nous ne perdrons jamais confiance que la France jouera le rôle des hommes libres et qu'elle reprendra, par des voies dures, sa place dans la grande compagnie des nations libératrices et victorieuses.

Ici, au Canada, où la langue française est honorée et parlée, nous nous tenons prêts et armés pour aider et saluer cette résurrection nationale. . . .

Now that the whole of the North American continent is becoming one gigantic armed camp; now that the immense reserve power of Russia is gradually becoming apparent; now that long-suffering unconquerable China sees help approaching; now that the outraged and subjugated nations can see daylight ahead, it is permissible to take a broad forward view of the war.

Sir, we may observe three main periods or phases in the struggle that lies before us. First, there is the period of consolidation, of combination, and of final preparation. In this period, which will certainly be marked by much heavy fighting, we shall still be gathering our strength, resisting the assaults of the enemy, and acquiring the necessary overwhelming air superiority and shipping tonnage to give our armies the power to traverse, in whatever numbers may be necessary, the seas and oceans which, except in the case of Russia, separate us all from our foe. It is only when the vast shipbuilding programme, on which the United States has already made so much progress, and which you are powerfully aiding, comes into full flood, that we shall be able to bring the whole force of our manhood and of our modern scientific equipment to bear upon the enemy. How long this period will take depends upon the vehemence of the effort put into production in all our war industries and shipyards.

The second phase, Sir, which will then open may be called the phase of liberation. During this phase we must look to the recovery of the territories which have been lost or which may yet be lost, and also we must look to the revolt of the conquered peoples from the moment that the rescuing and liberating armies and air forces appear in strength within their bounds. For this purpose it is imperative that no nation or region overrun, that no government or state which has been conquered, should relax its moral and physical efforts and preparations for the day of deliverance. The invaders, be they Germans or Japanese, must everywhere be regarded as infected persons, to be shunned and isolated as far as possible. Where active resistance is impossible, passive resistance must be maintained. The invaders and tyrants must be made to feel that their fleeting triumphs will have a terrible reckoning, and that they are hunted men and that their cause is doomed. Particular punishment will be reserved for the Quislings and traitors who make themselves the tools of the enemy. They will be handed over to the judgment of their fellow countrymen.

Sir, there is a third phase which must also be contemplated, namely, the assault upon the citadels and homelands of the guilty powers both in Europe and in Asia.

Thus I endeavour in a few words to cast some forward light upon the dark inscrutable mysteries of the future. But in thus forecasting the course along which we should seek to advance we must never forget that the power of the enemy and the action of the enemy may at every stage affect our fortunes. Moreover, Sir, you will notice that I have not attempted to assign any time limits of the various phases. These time limits depend upon our exertions, upon our achievements, and upon the hazardous and uncertain course of the war.

Nevertheless, I feel it is right at this moment to make it clear that, while an ever-increasing bombing offensive against Germany will remain one of the principal methods by which we hope to bring the war to an end, it is by no means the only method which our growing strength now enables us to take into account. Evidently the most strenuous exertions must be made by all. As to the form which those exertions take, that is for each partner in the Grand Alliance to judge for himself in consultation with others and in harmony with the general scheme.

Let us then, Sir, address ourselves to our task, not in any way underrating its tremendous difficulties and perils, but in good heart and sober confidence, resolved that, whatever the cost, whatever the suffering, we shall stand by one another, true and faithful comrades and do our duty, God helping us, to the end.

Mr. Speaker: We will close this historic meeting with the singing of the National Anthem.

The National Anthem having been sung, the gathering dispersed with three cheers for Mr. Churchill.

Saturday Night, Toronto, January 10, 1942

Mr. Churchill, who puts an immense amount of nervous energy into his speeches, and who had a very busy day in Ottawa, was reluctant to give even five minutes to being photographed. Here is Mr. Karsh's* description of the operation:

---

* Yousuf Karsh (1908–2002), celebrated photographer, who emigrated to Canada from Turkey; portrait photographer to the Canadian government from 1935. Despite the injunction, W.S.C. allowed Karsh to take two photographs of him alone on this occasion, and others in which the Canadian and British Prime Ministers posed together.

"I had observed him when speaking in the House and had made up my mind as to the attitude I wanted him to give me.

"He said that he would stand for one photograph only, and grudgingly stuck his cigar in his mouth and prepared to pose. But I had prepared an ashtray in advance and said: 'Sir, I have an ashtray all prepared for you.' I gave him no choice, and removed the cigar from his mouth. (I had no sooner placed it in the ashtray than it was immediately picked up and pocketed as a souvenir by one of those present.)

"After it was all over Mr. Churchill shook hands with me most amiably and said: 'Well, you can certainly make a roaring lion stand still and be photographed'."

Saturday Night, Toronto, January 10, 1942

GREATNESS AND HUMILITY IN WINSTON CHURCHILL

BY MARGARET LAWRENCE

A man has to be a very great man with his own personality carved sharply out of solid human material to stand today the mechanism of news gathering and presentation. For the machinery of the story we read in the press, and the instrument which picks up the voice and the manner and the meaning of what a man says over the radio, are overwhelming and only a man, or a woman, who is very strong in mind, in spirit and in nerves, and maybe also in convictions, can survive them.

Churchill in Ottawa survived. But watching it all I wondered how many could. Let me tell you about the detail first. The House of Commons is ordinarily a dim hall – dark green, dark brown, neutral grey, a little sombre old gold; what color it has is high placed and only tends to emphasise the sobriety of the place where men sit or rise to talk. The height of the hall itself dwarfs the human nature there; which is probably sound enough because the meaning of the place takes precedence therefore over the people in it. On Tuesday, December 30, 1941, there was a new scene in it. The microphone was there, to send the voices of men and words spoken there to the world. Press cameras and movie cameras were there in carefully selected and guarded positions. That meant powerful lights. From the lower end of the hall, and placed in the gallery where they would be most effective, these lights were trained upon the famous man as he entered and all through his speech. They were terrific blinding lights. I looked at them a moment, which was about all you could take, and thought of the phrase about the glare of publicity.

. . . The audience, for any other speech by almost any other person you can produce in your imagination to stand such a test, would not have been able to concentrate upon the speech. There was too much else around to take the attention.

But when Churchill entered the chamber, nobody noticed anything else, or anybody else. And there was nothing done to make this so. He just entered. A middle-aged man, in a dark business suit, with a short stocky figure and wispy thin grey hair. But his walk is not middle-aged. He walks like a young man going somewhere with his heavy shoulders getting him through the crowds and his head set down on a low full neck close to his shoulders. His eyes are not the tired, puzzled, inward-looking eyes of the middle-aged. They are bright, speculative and whimsical like the eyes of a man at the fullness of vital maturity. His voice is a gift from God. You can describe it no other way. You might refer momentarily to the possibility that it has come from generations upon generations of culture and sensitivity and authority. But you leave that soon; it is so full of human warmth it must have been a particular gift to him.

He is the darling of the camera folk. Churchill is human; the most human thing now in the limelight of the world. And that, I believe, is mostly the secret of his amazing grip on the imagination of the people. The camera folk love him because he knows that the world loves pictures; and that people like to see faces. When he stood up in the House of Commons to receive the homage of Canada he took care that the cameras had a chance and enough time. He let everybody have a good long look; and he himself had a thorough good look at the crowd.

In a less human man, the action might appear as a showman's bid for attention. That was said about Churchill in his earlier history. It took time and a terrific change in people to make them realize it was in him something infinitely more vital than zest for the limelight. It is sheer natural joy in human experience; it is unflagging concentrated interest in what is going on around him; and response to it. He is a man who goes to meet life as it is. . . .

When we shout for Churchill we shout for the human power to weather anything that comes. And because it is such a relief to us we shout very loud and very long. Here is something, we say to ourselves, that can take the glare and the click of life as it is now, that can take the machinery and use it instead of being used by it. . . .

Churchill's speeches are uttered rather than said. They are set down in a written text. Each sentence stands in a space by itself. On paper they look like verses; that is, it is the form familiar to us in the Scripture translations. One might guess that Winston Churchill had spent much time reading and re-reading the King James translation of the Bible. He uses English of that period; powerful, direct, richly intoned English. Yet it is simple. It is the English of poets trained to take the shortest route to an idea, and therefore using the most perfect word and the unforgettable, courageously emotional phrase. He strikes for the heart; because by the beats of their hearts men and women live.

The kinship of the old vigorous singing English of the sixteenth century to the twentieth century radio is a remarkable thing; and that we owe the discovery of that kinship to the British Prime Minister is another remarkable thing. Those who wish to be men, or women, of the hour, either in this hour or any future hour, will have to study Churchill's technique. The radio has utterly changed the art of making speeches. No longer can a man roll his sentences along, one after another, or wind them through involved thought to a great climax. Each sentence has to be delivered like a separate parcel; and while it has to be read following an exact text, it must sound as if spoken directly to one person; and that takes skill in language but most of all it takes knowledge of the human heart. . . .

There is another quality in Churchill which impresses the watcher and the listener. It is his humility. He knows that destiny in a terrific upheaval has made him for this time the crest on the wave of our human hope. He accepts it as such. It is a great quality, particularly on this continent where he receives adulation which might tempt even a saint. He said, you remember, in Washington words about the fact that had he been an American entering the House, he would not enter with an unanimous welcome. In Ottawa he included a sentence which had in it more than a shade of wistfulness about the fact that Mr. King had been Prime Minister for fifteen out of twenty years. In these delicate ways he paid tribute to the burden of leadership borne by Roosevelt, Mackenzie King and himself – the sorrows of which only they know in their souls; and he laid gently bare to our sight his awareness that destiny might be short, or might be long, but always was heavy with human pain. It was only in under-current that he touched upon this – that he had been tragically called to his destiny at the end of much suffering. The listeners heeded it a moment, and passed on to think about the gallantry of this man from Britain who can feel joy and mysteriously give joy as he carries the responsibility of the people's trust and their demanding love.

Record of W.S.C.'s conference with Canadian editors and publishers, Ottawa, December 30, 1941[22]

Following Mr. Churchill's speech in the House of Commons he held an informal and "off the record" Press Conference for about 100 Canadian editors and publishers. In introducing Mr. Churchill, Mr. King assured those present that they might ask any questions they wished. In reply to various questions raised Mr. Churchill's comments may be summarized as follows:

1. *Canadian diplomatic relations with Vichy:*

In reply to this question raised by Mr. King Mr. Churchill stated that the maintenance of relations between Canada and France was justified by the reports which Mr. Dupuy had given him following the latter's visits to Vichy. It was important to keep at least one window open, Mr. Churchill stated, and while Mr. Dupuy's reports were obviously not the only ones on which he depended, they were of considerable value, particularly in the early days following the French collapse. On the reverse side of the picture was the fact that the Vichy representatives in Canada could do little harm. If the situation changed, as it might still change, suddenly, it would not be difficult to arrange for the withdrawal of the Vichy representatives here. This was the situation as Mr. Churchill and Mr. King had discussed it during the latter's recent visit to London.

2. *Occupation of St. Pierre et Miquelon by the Free French:*

Mr. Churchill stated that some time ago he had personally been favourable to the proposal to occupy St. Pierre et Miquelon advanced by General de Gaulle. The Service Departments and the Foreign Office were consulted, and while the advice from the Service Departments was favourable to de Gaulle's plan, the Foreign Office urged the necessity of checking at Washington and Ottawa. It was subsequently learned through the State department that the United States had entered into an agreement with Admiral Robert at Martinique and were, therefore, opposed to any occupation of French territory adjacent to this continent by the Free French. In view of the importance of the broad question of Anglo-American relations, and the comparative insignificance of St. Pierre et Miquelon, Mr. Churchill had informed General de Gaulle that he was not to carry out his plan. General de Gaulle then proceeded to occupy the Islands without further consultation. Mr. Churchill suggested to the editors present that the question might well be played down, and said that it was likely that a solution satisfactory to the United States, Canada, and the Free French would probably be worked out.

3. *The French fleet:*

Mr. Churchill's information was that while Admiral Darlan* might be prepared to hand over the French fleet to the Germans, officers and men in charge of the fleet would prefer to scuttle the ships rather than to turn

---

*Jean Louis Xavier Francois Darlan (1881–1942), French admiral and politician; Commander-in-Chief of the French Navy, 1939–40; Minister of Marine, 1940–42; assassinated in North Africa, December 1942.

them over. The British authorities would be prepared to take any steps necessary to stiffen their resolution, even to the point of participating in the scuttling of the vessels.

4. *The shipping situation in the Atlantic:*

There was cause for optimism on the general position in the Atlantic on the basis of recent communications. The situation in February had been extremely acute, but progress had been made both in ship building and in ship repairs, which had greatly eased the situation.

5. *The Pacific:*

Mr. Churchill did not under estimate the difficulties in the Pacific situation. It was impossible to defend all points simultaneously and the Japanese were now in the position where they had both air and naval superiority, and thus were able to land troops and reinforcements at many points in the Pacific virtually without opposition. It would be many months before the Allies would be strong enough to take the offensive against Japan.

6. *Italy:*

In reply to a question as to whether there was any chance of negotiating a separate Peace with Italy Mr. Churchill said: "The organ grinder still has hold of the monkey's collar".

7. *Russia:*

Mr. Churchill was full of praise of the achievements of the Russians under Stalin. He stated that the Germans had lost roughly 4,000 aircraft, several thousand tanks and not less than 3,000,000 men. The wound which the Russians had inflicted on the Germans was "grievous and possibly mortal". The situation for the Germans this winter would be extremely difficult in view of their losses, the difficulties of winter operations, and the typhus conditions which were developing in various parts of German-occupied Russia. Referring briefly to Mr. Eden's recent visit to Moscow Mr. Churchill implied that the negotiations had been extremely successful.*

---

* Eden had explained to Stalin that his territorial demands could not be met there and then; but the talks had ended amicably enough.

8. _Bombing offensive against Germany:_

It was unfortunate that this past year when the Allies were rapidly gaining air superiority, weather conditions had been unfavourable to mass bombing attacks. Mr. Churchill's advice to the Air authorities was that they were not to ask pilots to fight both the Germans and the weather at the same time. In cheerful mood, he stated that good weather would be coming along shortly and that there would be many opportunities to deal Germany a powerful blow from the air. Mr. Churchill pointed out that while the Royal Air Force restricted its operations to military objectives, it was understood that civilian morale in Germany was a military factor which the Air Force would have to take into account.

9. _Case of Rudolph Hess:_

He said that Hess was on the verge of insanity, but that from the British point of view in view of his long and close association with Hitler, he occasionally and unwittingly provided information which was extremely useful. Hess' flight had been based on a misconception. He had met the Duke of Hamilton* at a sporting event in Germany and having heard that the Duke had the title of Lord Steward of Scotland assumed that the latter was on extremely close and intimate terms with the King. Mr. Churchill pointed out that the Duke of Hamilton was an honourable and loyal member of the British Forces. Hess' objective was to return to his fuehrer after his flight with the assurance that England would not continue the war. Churchill stated that it was unfortunate that the Germans were not as naive and unrealistic in military matters as in political matters.

10. _Ireland:_

Churchill stated that Ireland's position at the present time† was tragic and that if Irish leaders persisted in their present attitude, Ireland at the close of hostilities would be a country without a name. Churchill reminded those present that he had strenuously opposed the return of the British bases in

* Having been the first man to fly over Mount Everest, he served throughout the war in the Royal Air Force; he had met Hess at the Olympic Games in Berlin, 1936. Hess on landing in Scotland had immediately asked to see the Duke, who was Lord Steward of His Majesty's Household from 1940.

† Of studious neutrality, and sometimes (from a British point of view) worse.

Ireland many years ago,* which he said the Irish had requested but had never expected to obtain. Ireland had always been a country to fight for great causes and for the rights of small nations, which made their present position all the more tragic. He, however, did not give up hope that the Irish Government would come to see their true interests and with assistance from the United States the position might well be changed in the future.

[W.S.C.'s guesses about German losses of aircraft and vehicles may not have been far wide of the mark, though they were probably optimistic. The estimate of German losses of men, though not out of line with other figures cited at the time, indicates either a serious failure of information or an effort to damage enemy morale, for three million represented the total strength of the German force invading Russia. The actual losses by Christmas amounted perhaps to eight hundred thousand men.[23]]

Mackenzie King's diary, December 30, 1941

I was glad to see at both the govt. luncheon and last night, that C. himself took tomato juice and apparently did not take cocktails at all or sherry. He is accustomed to other things but clearly watches himself carefully. . . .

I met Churchill under the arch-way on his arrival. Waited on the landing while he inspected the guard of honour: the navy, the army and the air force. There were great crowds on the hill and in fact all along the route. . . .

I entered with Mr. Churchill on the government's side. There was tremendous applause, all present standing as well as applauding. The arrangement of spotlights blinded one with respect to those in the distance. Churchill asked if it was necessary to keep the lights on all the time. I spoke of this to someone near the door, and it was apparent nothing could be done to turn them off.

When the applause ceased, I was about to go forward when the Speaker in a few words called on me to introduce Mr. Churchill. He had said nothing previously of that intention but evidently was anxious to take some part as was quite natural. I had intended following the strict parliamentary procedure. Had he mentioned calling on me, I would have approved the idea.

---

* By the Treaty of 1938. The fact that the Royal Navy could not use the ports cost many Allied lives.

When I went forward to speak, I received a tremendous reception. Indeed in a way quite equal to that which was given Churchill. I was rather embarrassed by it and taken completely by surprise. It was a welcome tribute and particularly so paid in the presence of Churchill, and is something which was heard over the radio in all parts of the world. It could leave no doubt as to the feeling toward myself.

I found the reading of my little introduction quite easy, and I think succeeded in giving it the right emphasis. Its sentiments were roundly applauded.

When I concluded, I took my seat with Dandurand* to my right. It gave me great pleasure to have him there as the leader of the govt. in the other House, and also as the representative of the French. Churchill was given another great ovation. He made a kindly and I felt just the right reference to myself all circumstances considered referring to me on the personal side as an old friend, and on the public side, as having been P.M. 15 years out of 20 which helped to bring that fact anew to the public mind, and to help to make clear a special note of authority and of service and confidence which spoke for itself. The press have completely recorded the incidents of interest in connection with his speech.

Personally I felt that it was not as good as the address at Washington. That he showed evidences of fatigue in its delivery and, in part, its matter was less clear-cut than that of some of his other addresses. But it had been prepared with the greatest care so as to say nothing which would possibly offend any party.† He had been meticulously careful in that.

As we walked down the Hall of Fame together, he said to me: what I am going to say will be all right, and it was. All political aspects had been exceptionally closely watched. At different times, he referred to what a job it was to prepare a speech, this one in particular. He found it hard to get time for it; worked late at night and was at it again in the morning. When he had concluded the address and the national anthem was sung, I walked over and shook hands heartily with him, congratulated him and thanked him for what he had said. As we stood together shaking hands, there was again very great applause. There was something very spontaneous about

---

* Raoul Dandurand (1861–1942), a Montreal lawyer; colleague of Mackenzie King from 1921 as Leader of the government in the Senate and Minister Without Portfolio, 1921–30, 1935–42.

† i.e., in Canada.

the applause with respect to each of us. I felt that the atmosphere had wonderfully cleared, and that his visit had served to put the facts into their right place. . . .

I had earlier had the Country Club prepare me some cocktails. The only time I have had them at L[aurier] H[ouse].* Felt that because of Churchill's guests as well as the Ministers, it might be better to make an exception for this dinner. In a way I am rather sorry that I did, making a difference. C. himself and several of the others, like myself, took the tomato juice.

Those present were members of the War Committee; Sir Charles Wilson,† Sir Charles Portal,** Brigadier Hollis,†† and Commander Thompson, in addition to Mr. C. The table looked very pretty. Indeed the whole house was most attractive. C. was relieved after having completed his speeches, and could not have been happier than he was in conversation with us all at the table. He told a good many stories back and forth; amusing incidents, etc. Much serious talk first.

After dinner, we came to the library. C. sat in the big chair, facing my mother's picture. When I showed it to him, he spoke of how very beautiful her face was, kept repeating: a lovely face; a lovely face. . . .

There were great crowds gathered in front of the house when Mr. C. arrived and there were still large crowds in front of the house when he left. They gave him a great reception. It was the King and Queen all over again, only at night instead of by day and in the winter instead of by spring.

At dinner, after proposing the King's health, I rose and proposed the health of our latest Privy Councillor; thanked him [W.S.C.] for the honour he had done myself and colleagues in coming to dine with us; the honour he had done L.H. in coming for the evening. I wished him all that was best. He made a nice little response speaking in a very feeling way about the great honour which he felt it to be to him to be admitted to the Canadian Privy Council.

Mary served an excellent dinner which I think all really enjoyed. Oysters on half shell, soup, broiled trout, prairie chicken, lamb and green peas,

---

* Mackenzie King's home in Ottawa.

† Later Lord Moran.

** Air Chief Marshal Sir Charles Frederick Algernon Portal (1893–1971), later Marshal of the Royal Air Force and 1st Viscount Portal; Air Officer Commanding-in-Chief, Bomber Command, 1940; Chief of the Air Staff, 1940–45.

†† Leslie Chasemore Hollis (1897–1963), Assistant Secretary, Office of the War Cabinet, 1939–46; Deputy Secretary (Military) to the Cabinet, 1947–49.

and a baked Alaska the top of which was brought in like a Christmas plum pudding with flaming brandy, still later fruit.

We spent only a little time in the morning room before coming up to the library.

After dinner, to show how frisky he was, C. would not come up in the elevator, but ran upstairs fairly fast to the first floor. He found after that it was as well to go easy. All present came up by the stairs. I felt very happy and proud to have War Committee, C.'s new friends with him. Only wish we might have had the entire Cabinet. As we went downstairs together, C. told me that he was feeling very anxious about a situation near Singapore. That a large convoy of troops were on their way to Singapore, and that they were not sufficiently protected. That there just had to be a chance to save the situation but that the lot might be destroyed. He spoke very feelingly of it.

The morning paper had something about our financial proposal. At dinner, when I told him what we had in mind,* he asked me how we could possibly do it; what we had done in a financial way was very great. He spoke really with amazement of what was contemplated.

I felt a great peace through the day and a quiet joy, sense of confidence, particularly happy that all had gone so well and grateful to God for His mercy. It was exactly 5 past 1 when I turned out the lights, both hands together when I went to bed.

[In his speech, Churchill had paid tribute to de Gaulle and the Free French, notwithstanding all the troubles over St. Pierre and Miquelon. To the Canadian Ministers he spoke at dinner that night of the ultimate liberation of the European countries; tanks would land with troops and place firearms in the hands of the population all the way round from Norway to Greece.[24] This conception fitted with the instruction he had given when establishing the Special Operations Executive in the summer of the previous year: "Set Europe ablaze." In practice, the idea proved too romantic. The strength of the resistance movements in Europe varied greatly from one place to another, and their full value was felt only when the Allied armies got back into the continent from 1944.]

* An outright gift of one thousand million Canadian dollars. When Mackenzie King first mentioned this figure, W.S.C. thought he had misheard.

Lord Moran's diary, December 31, 1941[25]

Winston's speech, particularly his attack on Vichy, roused the Canadians, though it was not up to the Washington standard. At one point he talked in his variation of the French tongue. And then he told them how he had warned the French Government that Britain would fight on alone whatever France did, and how Weygand had gone to the French Cabinet and said:

'In three weeks England will have her neck wrung like a chicken.'

The P.M. paused.

'Some chicken. Some neck!' He spat out his contempt.

Gust after gust of delighted laughter ended in applause, which went on for a long time.

At night we dined with Mackenzie King. I got there early. He had been my patient in London, and did not hesitate to speak his mind. I found him restive about the P.M. He said that there were many men winning the war and confessed that he was 'rather put off by a strain of violence in the Prime Minister.' I argued that it is no more than a certain lack of restraint, but it was plain that this was no passing mood.

Wilson [Moran]: 'You have known Winston for a long time?'

Mackenzie King: 'Yes; I have. I first met him when he was going round Canada on a lecture tour.'

Wilson: 'That can't have been long after the Boer War.'

Mackenzie King: 'No. I found him at his hotel drinking champagne at eleven o'clock in the morning.'

'The great thing in politics,' said our host later, 'is to avoid mistakes.' I could almost see the P.M. sniffing as Mackenzie King, looking at us through his pince-nez, which were tethered to a button-hole by a long black ribbon, made this pronouncement. King had never been a man to take risks, and this prudent outlook no doubt accounts for some lack of fervour on the P.M.'s part. The two men are, of course, quite friendly, but the P.M. is not really interested in Mackenzie King. He takes him for granted.

I cannot help noticing Winston's indifference to him after the wooing of the President at the White House. There the P.M. and the President seemed to talk for most of the day, and for the first time I have seen Winston content to listen. You could almost feel the importance he attaches to bringing the President along with him, and in that good cause he has

Churchill (third from left) with hosts at Government House in Victoria, 1929.
Son, Randolph, is at the far left, and Churchill's brother, Jack,
and Jack's son, Johnnie, stand at the right.

Churchill in Edmonton, 1929. (Glenbow Archives NC-6-12603a)

Churchill and William Lyon Mackenzie King at Moorside, Kingsmere, Quebec, 1929.
(Library and Archives Canada/PA-126203)

LEFT: Viscount Byng of Vimy and Lady Byng. (Rice Studios/ Library and Archives Canada/c-033995)

BELOW: William Lyon Mackenzie King at home. The portrait of his mother, which so entranced Churchill, is in the background. (Hands Studio/Library and Archives Canada/c-009063)

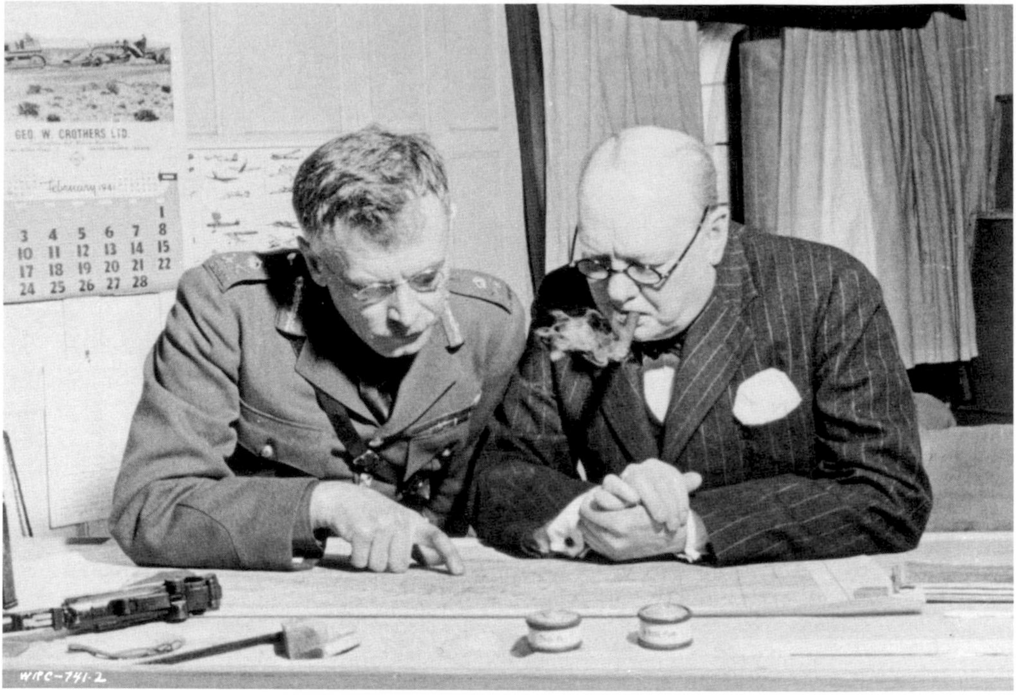

Churchill with Gen. A.G.L. McNaughton at Canadian Military Headquarters in England, 1941. (Canada Dept. of National Defence/Library and Archives Canada/PA-119399)

Churchill welcomes Mackenzie King to London, August 1941.
(National Film Board of Canada. Photothèque/Library and Archives Canada/C-047565)

ABOVE: Churchill arrives at Union Station, Ottawa, December 1941. (Left to right) Detective, Churchill, Commander Thompson, Mackenzie King, Sir Charles Wilson (later Lord Moran; on step behind King). (Library and Archives Canada/PA-148541)

LEFT: Churchill waves to the crowd. (Library and Archives Canada/C-000129)

Churchill addresses the combined Houses of Parliament, December 30, 1941.
(Library and Archives Canada/c-022140)

Churchill and Mackenzie King leave the Parliament Buildings after Churchill's speech.
(Library and Archives Canada/c-015132)

Taken at the same time as the more famous scowling shot, this Karsh portrait shows Churchill in a more relaxed mood. (Yousuf Karsh)

ABOVE: Churchill gives his familiar V-for-Victory sign as he arrives for the first Quebec Conference (Quadrant), August 1943. (*Globe and Mail*, neg. 43224-07)

LEFT: Mackenzie King greets Churchill, Mrs. Churchill and their daughter Mary during the Quadrant Conference, 1943. (National Film Board of Canada. Phototheque/Library and Archives Canada/c-007478)

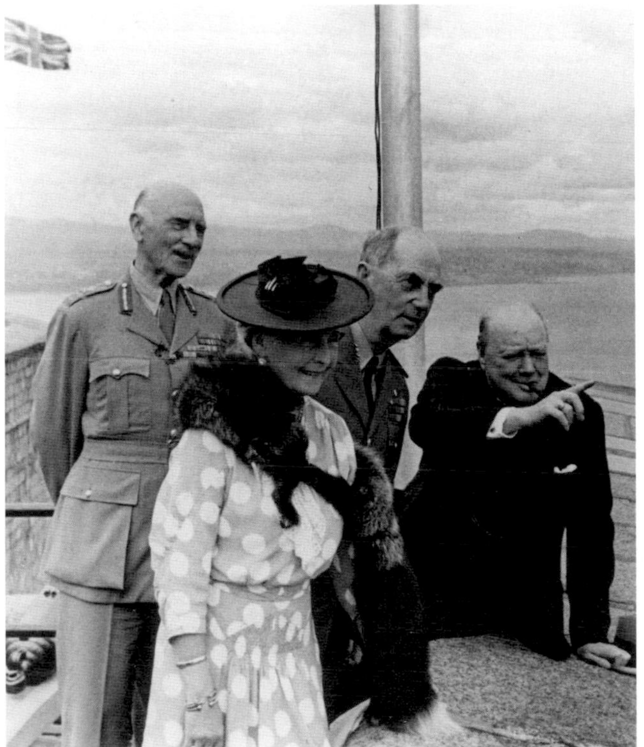

ABOVE: Mackenzie King, President Roosevelt and Churchill with the British and American Chiefs of Staff, 1943. Standing at rear (left to right) are Gen. Henry Arnold, Air Chief Marshal Sir Charles Portal, Gen. Sir Alan Brooke, Adm. Ernest King, Gen. Sir John Dill, Gen. George Marshall, Adm. Sir Dudley Pound, Admiral Leahy. (Harry Rowed/National Film Board of Canada. Photothèque/Library and Archives Canada/PA-183423

LEFT: Churchill joins (left to right) the Governor General, The Earl of Athlone, his wife, Princess Alice, and Admiral Leahy, as they look over the St. Lawrence at Quebec, August 1943. (Franklin D. Roosevelt Library, #48223868 (508))

ABOVE: Churchill and Mackenzie King greet enthusiastic crowds during the Quadrant Conference, 1943. (Franklin D. Roosevelt Library, #48223868(530))

LEFT: Churchill descends from his train after being welcomed by Mackenzie King at the second Quebec Conference (Octagon), September 1944. Behind him are Mrs. Churchill and King. (National Film Board of Canada. Phototheque/Library and Archives Canada/c-026942)

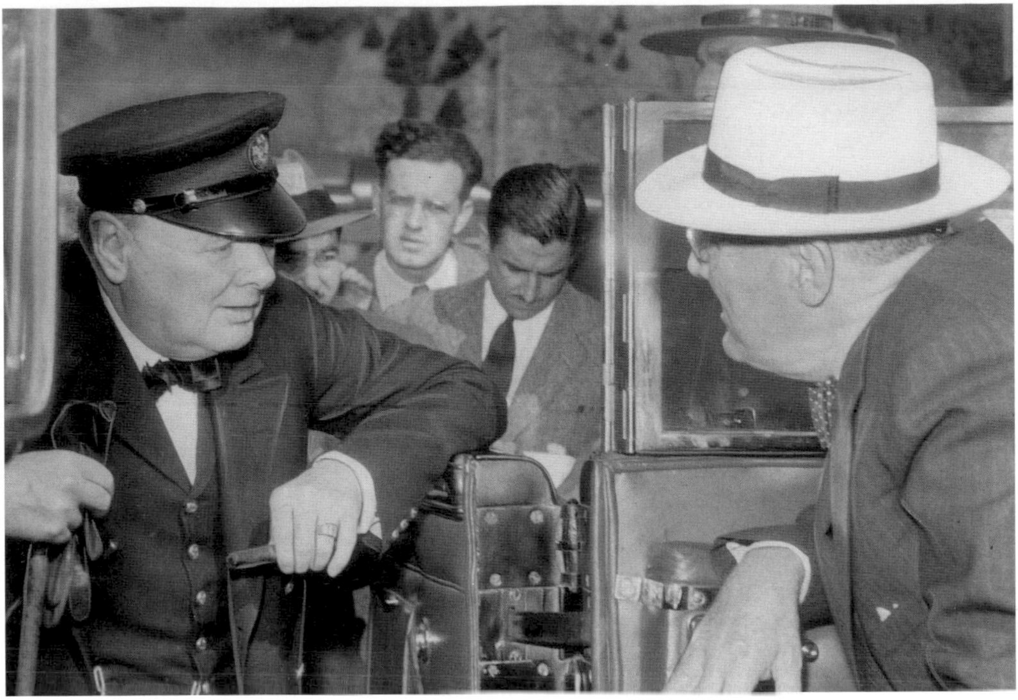

Churchill and Roosevelt exchange greetings as they meet at Wolfe's Cove, Quebec, for the Octagon Conference of 1944. (John Boyd/*Globe and Mail*)

Churchill draws the usual media attention, Quebec, 1944.
(Franklin D. Roosevelt Library, #48223916(31))

LEFT: Churchill waves from the steps of the Château Frontenac during the Octagon Conference. Accompanying him are (left to right) Canadian Cabinet ministers C.G. Power and C.D. Howe, along with Prime Minister King. (National Film Board of Canada. Photothèque/Library and Archives Canada/c-071095)

BELOW: Churchill and Roosevelt receive honourary degrees from McGill University during the Octagon Conference. (National Film Board of Canada. Photothèque/Library and Archives Canada/c-026931)

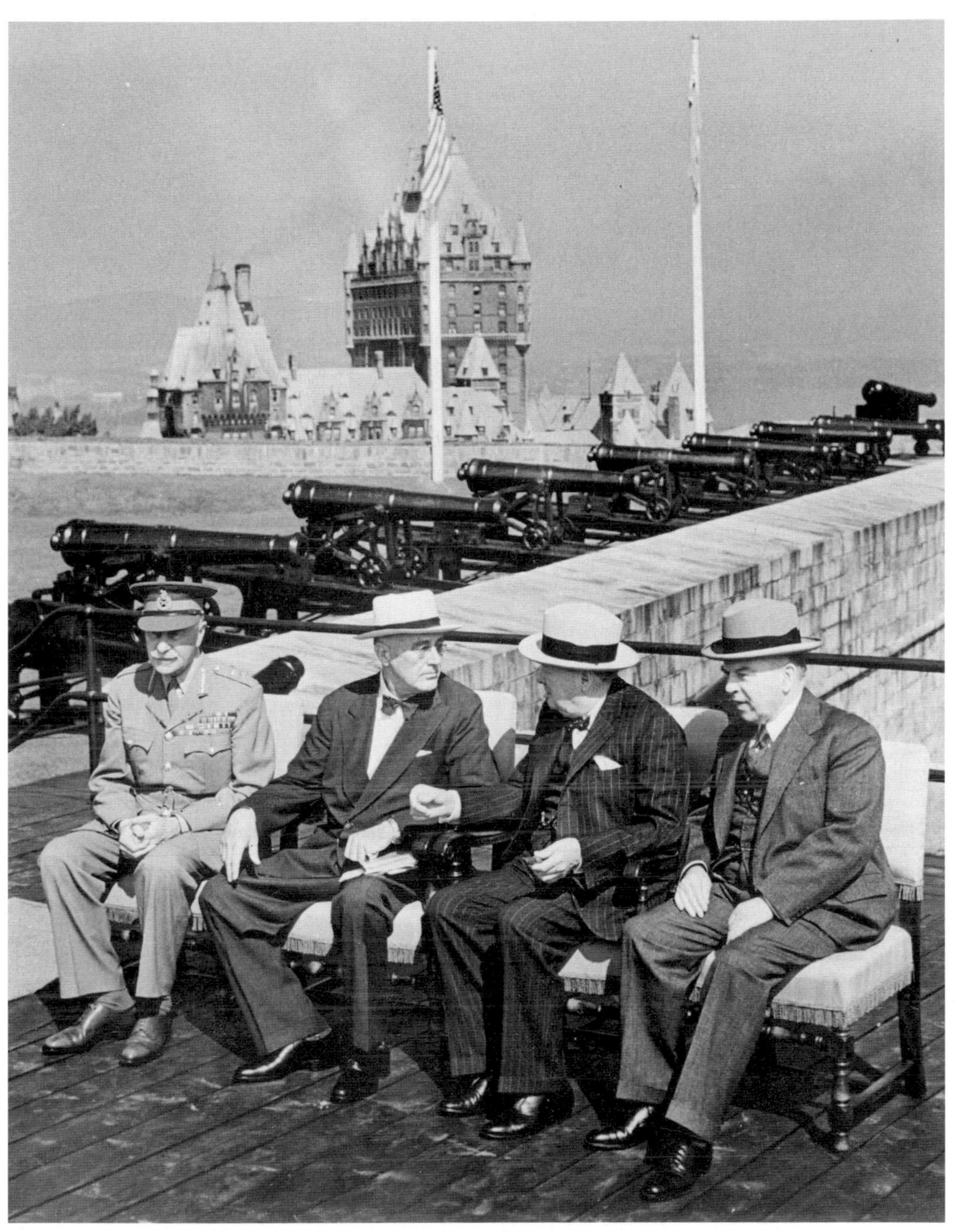

The Earl of Athlone, Roosevelt, Churchill and Mackenzie King during the Octagon Conference. The Château Frontenac rises in the background.
(National Film Board of Canada. Photothèque/ Library and Archives Canada/c-021525)

LEFT: Clement Attlee walks with Mackenzie King through the corridors of the Parliament Buildings, November 1945. (George Hunter/National Film Board of Canada. Photothèque/Library and Archives Canada/C-047582)

BELOW: Mackenzie King and colleagues attend the Paris Peace Conference, August 1946. (Left to right) Norman Robertson, King, Brooke Claxton and Arnold Heeney. (Library and Archives Canada/C-031312)

Churchill and Anthony Eden on Canadian visit, 1952. (left to right) Eden, Lord Ismay, Churchill, Lord Cherwell, C.D. Howe and Prime Minister Louis St. Laurent. (*Toronto Star*)

(Front, left to right) Viscount Alexander of Tunis, Churchill, and St. Laurent attend dinner at the Château Laurier, January 1952. (W.M. Noice/*Ottawa Journal*/W. Howard Measures Collection/Library and Archives Canada /PA-148521)

ABOVE: Prime Minister St. Laurent (left) and Lester B. Pearson (right) pose with Churchill and Eden on their arrival in Ottawa, June 1954. (National Film Board of Canada. Phototheèque/Library and Archives Canada/c-004047)

LEFT: Churchill waves to workers in the East Block of the Parliament Buildings as he and Anthony Eden arrive for a meeting with the Canadian Cabinet. (Harold Robinson/ *Globe and Mail*)

become a very model of restraint and self-discipline; it is surely a new Winston who is sitting there quite silent. And when he does say anything it is always something likely to fall pleasantly on the President's ear. But here, in Ottawa, he does not seem to bother.

We go back to Washington tomorrow.

The *Globe and Mail*, Toronto, December 31, 1941

Winston Churchill spoke today to the Parliament and the people of Canada from Parliament Hill in Ottawa. In prose which had the splendor of poetry at its best, and in phrases which had a Shakespearian glow and the fervor of the Bible, Britain's "man of destiny" electrified a joint session of the Senate and the House of Commons as he had thrilled the Congress in Washington.

With his instinct for the dramatic, the Old Master poured out phrases that rang like a bell and sallies that were filled with impish humor. . . .

The Commons Chamber, in which this distinguished statesman and warrior delivered his speech from the head of the table, was packed as it has never been packed before. On the floor of the House were seated Senators and members of the House of Commons from every corner of the Dominion. In the wide centre aisle were the judges of the Supreme Court and the Exchequer Court, the Ministers from other countries, the High Commissioners from Britain and the sister Dominions, dignitaries of the Church, high officers of the fighting forces and others of the official set.

In the second row of seats, as part of the vast audience which was partly composed of French-speaking Canadians, the French Minister, René Ristelhueber,* and his chief secretary were prominent among the diplomatic corps listening closely to Mr. Churchill's vehement and biting references to the men of Vichy and Bordeaux. . . .

Canadians who have seen and heard Mr. Churchill find it difficult to understand how only ten years ago the Manchester Guardian could call him a mountebank, or Lord Asquith and Oxford, who had Mr. Churchill in several of his Cabinets, could conclude that "Winston has genius without judgment."

Certainly, Mr. Churchill has taken Ottawa by storm, and will recross the Atlantic with the complete confidence of the people of Canada in his genius, his judgment and his leadership, and in the ultimate triumph of British and Allied arms.

---

* Representative in Canada of the Vichy government.

The *Spectator*, Hamilton, December 31, 1941

There is about the man a deadly seriousness of purpose that makes his utterances against freedom's foes sound not like maledictions but the most solemn of judgements.

His voice gains strength as he warms to his topic, his round, almost cherubic face, which in repose, with its tortoise shell rim glasses perched on the end of his nose, is suggestive of Mr. Pickwick, hardens into the John Bull contours his followers associate with him.

If the man's phrases and clear diction fire the imagination, his appearance no less stirs the heart. Watching him on Wednesday was as though one were watching a matchless orator giving to his vocal art the consummate skill of the great actor. . . .

The Prime Minister began in a low voice whose tone might have conveyed weariness unless one realised this restrained method of speech was a deliberate device to command listening attention to the straining point.

As a hush fell over the House of Commons, the voice gained power. Winston Churchill was getting into his stride. There is nothing he does, down to the slightest shrug of the shoulders or tilt of the head, that hasn't a definite connection with the thought he is expressing.

Nothing illustrates this more than his wonderful pair of hands. For the writer, who was seated some ten yards from him, these hands held a fascination. They belong to a strong man who knows how to use them. They are as eloquent as his voice.

Sometimes they rested on his hips as he stood surveying the crowded benches and galleries. When he spoke of "Hitler tyranny, Japanese frenzy and Mussolini flop," his hands grasped the lapels of his coat as he turned and stared full into the faces of his listeners in the gallery directly above his head. On his face was written contempt and scorn. Magically, an impish smile spread over his countenance as he paused during the roar of laughter and shout of approval which came in response to this latest Churchillian blast. At other times, the left hand rose and fell in perfect time with his voice. . . .

Once when he was bitingly describing the weak men of Vichy and their hopeless and pathetic subservience to Hitler, and remarked that Hitler, when he was through with them, would "brush them away," he used his left hand as though he were ruthlessly forcing from any contact with him some object of detestation.

His words addressed in French to the French-Canadians present had an electrifying effect. Over the faces of French-Canadian members and senators swept delighted expressions.

Occasionally the hands made deprecating gestures, sometimes they were locked together.

This much is certain – the real Churchill must be seen in the flesh to be really known. The voice which comes through the ether with its ringing assurances, its growling, menacing promises to the axis war lords of the fate in store for them does not fully indicate the powerful personality of the man. The voice does make one say, as Clemence Dane puts it in one of his poems, "I say, I could follow that voice and, whatever order it chose to give, I'd be glad to obey," but one must gaze upon the owner of the voice to get the proper estimate of Churchill's true stature. The face and the hands have their story to tell, and they tell it well.

The *Ottawa Morning Citizen*, December 31, 1941

As the people dispersed and left the Chamber to go their various ways, all realized that somehow a strange, indefinable transformation had been worked within their hearts. They weren't quite the same people.

They had listened to an Englishman talk. But they had heard more than words. They had heard the waves beating on the coasts of England, listened to the guns of British ships, felt the scorching heat of African deserts, heard the roar of Spitfires in the skies. They had listened to Churchill. They had heard the voice of England.

The *Globe and Mail*, Toronto, December 31, 1941

It is impossible to overestimate the contribution which Mr. Churchill's leadership is making to the successful prosecution of the war. He has the qualities which a leader must have in times of great crisis; he is forthright and uncompromising; he does not pander to men's weakness or prejudices; he does not attempt to reconcile conflicting factions by throwing sops to each. His method is rather to offer every man an ideal larger than any of the petty impulses by which he has been motivated, and challenge each to live up to it.

It is Mr. Churchill's ability to transmit his own bright vision, his own passionate conviction, his own devotion and courage to his listeners that has earned him the gratitude and affection, as well as the unquestioning loyalty, of all who fight for freedom. His visit to Washington was like a tonic to the whole American people.

. . . He has done the same for us. . . . Mr. Churchill has renewed in us an eagerness to do our duty, and our Government will be better able after these conferences to tell us where our duty lies.

W.S.C.'s press conference at Government House, Ottawa, December 31, 1941[26]

[A British Columbia seal wedge cap was presented to Mr. Churchill at the beginning of the interview.]

Ladies and Gentlemen: –
A very odd thing that when I woke up very early this morning, I thought what a pity I haven't got one of those lovely Canadian hats, and wondered if it would be possible to get one; I am only sorry that I am not staying longer. There is nothing that I shall value more than this. There is one thing I will say, that people often think I am hot-headed. It fits beautifully, and is large enough to allow for any swelling which may take place. . . .

QUESTION: What progress do you find in the battle of the Atlantic?

ANSWER: It is very good. February losses were very heavy and exacting, as the result of Focke-Wulf aeroplanes being able to fly from Brest to Norway and back in one day. In this way they had been able to report on the movement of our convoys. Hitler thought he had got a very great advantage. He made a boastful speech that we would be crushed by this blockade last summer. However, we managed to drive them further abroad and break the link and shoot down a great many aeroplanes by very heavy armaments, both on the merchant ships and by a number of other methods which I won't go into, as they are very technical. We have had in the last 5½ or 6 months losses by sinking which, when you make allowances for British new building, and not Canadian, places our losses for the last 5½ or 6 months at one-fifth of those in the preceding 5 months. These losses are not such as to be a decisive danger. I feel quite sure now we are going to be able to carry on all our convoys till we get into the great flow of U.S. building, which as you know will make a very important addition, and I thus feel that we may see our way through the year 1942 and, of course, in 1943, I hope we shall be very much more mobile than we are now across the sea.

QUESTION: Do you feel we can still handle the Atlantic in spite of the number of ships required in the Pacific?

ANSWER: As you know, we are building Corvettes, which are so valuable. We haven't got nearly as much as we would like to have.

QUESTION: What about the occupation of St. Pierre and the Miquelon Islands?

ANSWER: I think I would not say anything about this now. Of course, they were taken by the Free French without the knowledge of the British, Canadian or United States Governments. No doubt things will be settled in a satisfactory way. I regard it as a very minor matter in comparison with the other things which were going on.

QUESTION: Do you think Singapore can hold on?

ANSWER: I sure do.

QUESTION: Are you satisfied that Hong Kong was worth the sacrifice it has cost us?

ANSWER: I think the Canadian reinforcements enabled the defence of Hong Kong to be an effective defence. Resistance in any case was difficult. . . .

QUESTION: What about an Imperial War Cabinet?

ANSWER: We went into all that last year. There are a great many difficulties. It is difficult for the Prime Ministers of the Dominions to leave their own Dominions, where they have their own Governments to conduct, and their Parliaments to lead. General Smuts is unable to leave his Dominion and, as you know, your Prime Minister paid a "flying visit" to us. Mr. Menzies and Mr. Fraser have been over. It would be extremely difficult to get them all together at any one time. A conference of three or four of them could be arranged and would be very pleasant. There are so many matters which only the Prime Minister can deal with himself. There has been an immense flow of despatches all the time. It is very difficult when we are all scattered over the globe. . . .

QUESTION: In view of the extreme measures to which Britain has gone in regard to the use of their manpower, what about Conscription in Canada?

ANSWER: I do not interfere in matters of this kind in the Dominions. You have got to settle your own problems. Canada has given assistance in a great many ways. They are greatly delighted in England at all Canada has done. I have a feeling that we are all more united in this war than in the last. That is true of all classes in Great Britain. After all the working people in the English-speaking countries, the British Isles and the United States have gained a great many things in these centuries, and there is a strong feeling that a victory for the Nazis would take us back to the Middle Ages. . . .

QUESTION: Have we a better chance of holding Malta than we did Crete?

ANSWER: I haven't the slightest fear that Malta can be taken. It is a fortress of first class order, and is probably unsurpassed in the whole war. They have a very strong fortress there. The anti-aircraft defences are the best in the world.

QUESTION: Do you think Hitler will march into Spain?

ANSWER: I really don't know. He did not tell me. If you happen to hear, tell me.

QUESTION: Yugo-Slavia?

ANSWER: They are fighting with the greatest vigour and on quite a large scale and we don't hear very much of what is going on there. It is all very terrible. Guerilla warfare and most frightful atrocities by the Germans and Italians, and every kind of torture. The people manage to keep the flag of freedom flying.

QUESTION: What about Hess, the greatest mystery of 1941?

ANSWER: I don't want to add anything to what has been said.

QUESTION: Have you had any peace feelers from the Axis?

ANSWER: We have had none at all, but then I really think they must be hard pressed for materials of all kinds, and would not want to waste the paper and ink.

The *Ottawa Journal*, January 1, 1942

Mr. Churchill came striding into the room as though there were nothing in the world he would rather do that last morning of the year than face the questions of some scores of reporters and blink into the dazzling flashlights of twenty cameras. Mr. Mackenzie King was just behind him, and some members of his staff, and everybody was in excellent humor.

The Prime Minister of Great Britain, strength in every line of his face and confidence and resolution in his walk, smiled as the waiting lines of correspondents from Britain, the United States and Canada parted to let him through. Then he stepped upon a low platform and to his chair behind a covered table. . . .

Before Mr. Churchill came in a secretary mounted the platform and said the Prime Minister was not to be quoted directly. Later, when Mr. Churchill said something especially quotable, somebody asked him if his direct words might be used, and he said Yes, anything might be quoted. There was, as a matter of fact, nothing said by him which could have done the enemy the least good. The conversation ranged from Norway to Singapore and from Malta to India, touched many angles of the war, but for the most part it was a thoughtful and ironic Churchill the reporters saw, rather than the savage Churchill speaking the voice of Hitler's doom.

The *Ottawa Citizen*, January 1, 1942

Mr. Churchill informed the [press] conference that he had had a telephone conversation from Government House Tuesday morning with Mrs. Churchill in London. She had told him about the success of her fund* to provide medical supplies for Russia. He explained that the fund was still growing and that it was encouraging how many small contributions were coming in. He praised the efforts being made in Canada to raise funds by the Canadian Red Cross for the same purpose. It was a most important undertaking to help the Russian people who had suffered so grievously in the fighting there.

The *Ottawa Citizen*, January 1, 1942

When Mr. Churchill had to brave the wintry weather Tuesday on his trip to Parliament Hill, the correspondents of the Parliamentary Press Gallery decided it would be a nice gesture to present him with a fur cap. Accordingly, an order was given to an Ottawa furrier whose staff labored all night to complete the fuzzy headgear of shining black seal fashioned in a rakish wedge. . . .

At the end of the conference, Mr. Churchill left the Government House badminton court accompanied by Prime Minister King. Puffing on his huge cigar, his hands in his pockets and tossing an occasional glance at the paintings in the hallways, the Happy Warrior presented a strange sight as he strolled through the storied corridors of Rideau Hall with his new sealskin skimmer enveloped in a fragrant smokescreen.

Incidentally, when Mr. Churchill visited Uplands† later in the day, the time-honored black hat with the turn-up brim had gone the way of all flesh. The British Columbia seal was having its innings! As the train carrying Mr. Churchill left, the great man stood on the observation car still wearing his new fur cap.

---

* The appeal had in a few weeks raised more than £1,000,000.

† The aerodrome just outside Ottawa, then being used, like others in Canada, for the British Commonwealth Air Training Plan.

Lord Beaverbrook to C.R. Attlee, December 31, 1941

GREY 176

Washington

I am sure you would like me to tell you what is going on here. The Prime Minister has established his authority with Government and has secured a measure of popularity with public exceeding anything I had expected.

It appeared to be impossible that he would win bigger triumph in Canada, but in fact this is just what he has done and it is a triumph not only with the public but with the Government and opposition as well.

He had a difficult role to play in Canada because of Government's trial over conscription issue and belief of opposition that he should do something to help their viewpoint. He surpassed himself in holding the balance between the two.

I think the War Cabinet might like to send him a message.

C.R. Attlee to W.S.C., January 1, 1942

TAUT 329

War Cabinet at this morning's meeting asked me to send you their warmest good wishes for 1942 and their felicitations on the outstanding success of your speech in Canada, which delighted us all.

General de Gaulle to W.S.C., January 1, 1942

TAUT 327

Veuillez agréer mes voeux profondément sincères de nouvelle année. Ce que vous avez dit hier sur la France au parlement du Canada a touché toute la nation française. Du fond de son malheur la vielle France espère d'abord en la vielle Angleterre.

Saturday Night, Toronto, January 10, 1942

The almost magic power wielded in this emergency by Mr. Churchill is by no means all due to his mastery of words, great as that is. Much more is it due to the compelling influence of his personality. It has been well explained by the editor of the Winnipeg *Free Press* in his comment on last week's utterance: "He can be cheerful as to performance and prospects without inviting complacency; he can tell of dangers and demand sacrifices in bold and uncompromising language without inducing despondency." It is not what he says alone that produces this effect; it is what he says and what he is. No leader since Lincoln has had the same genius for inspiring men and women to faith and to devotion.

The *Toronto Star*, January 2, 1942

BY FREDERICK GRIFFIN

All over the Anglo-Saxon world men and women, wherever they were together at midnight, joined hands to sing Auld Lang Syne but we – a group of newspaper writers, railroad men, secret service men, Negro porters, servants, clerks and high officials – sang Auld Lang Syne with Winston Churchill.

And here was the New Year's toast he gave us in that voice which you know so well and love so much:

"Here's to 1942. Here's to a year of toil – a year of struggle and peril – and a long step forward – to victory."

Here was the New Year's wish that he gave to us: "God bless you all" and we cried out with one voice: "And God bless you, sir."

He said: "May we all come through safe – and with honor." And he cracked out "honor" with that rising Churchill inflection that has a sound as of rapiers clashing.

It was a brief five minutes of such a fellowship with such a man in such a setting as we who were given the privilege of it will never forget. Nothing will ever efface it from our memories or our souls. He showed us the steel and the fire in him last night in those five minutes when he gave us blessing. . . .

There were no cameras, and so there is no photographic record of a unique scene. Perhaps some day an artist will construct that midnight gathering in Vermont as the train thundered through the still New England night out of 1941 and into 1942.

[No unpleasantness had marred the visit to Ottawa. The Prime Minister of Canada, whatever he may have said to Sir Charles Wilson, recorded that he had found Churchill's nature wonderfully kind, sympathetic and understanding. As they parted on New Year's Eve, Churchill said, "You can count on me." There were other satisfactions; King reflected that the powerful demonstration of support by his friends in Parliament would let the Tories and also the members of his own Cabinet see "where the people are in relation to myself. I shall fight on with a view of [to?] the war being won without resort to conscription, without, I hope, a referendum, and without a General Election."[27]

Churchill recognized afterwards that he had been lucky in the timing of his two speeches; they came at the moment when everyone could rejoice at the creation of the Grand Alliance and before worse blows were felt at the hands of the Japanese. He had never doubted that the supreme object of British and Commonwealth policy must be to bring the United States into the war, preferably a war in which Japan had the good sense to remain neutral. What had happened was different. The drastic alteration in the balance of power caused by the Japanese assaults on Pearl Harbor and Malaya, the naval losses in the Mediterranean, the inability of the Allied forces in North Africa to secure a decisive victory, all meant that further blows must fall, and fall soon. Vast as the industrial, financial and human resources of the United States might be, they would take a long time to bring into full play; in the meanwhile, the armed forces of the United States that were available for combat would remain far less substantial than those of the Commonwealth. As Sir Charles Wilson put it on New Year's Day 1942, "It is as if Winston has a family of twelve children and there is not enough food for all of them – some of them must starve to death. He has to decide which."[28]

On their return to Washington, the British party found the arguments over St. Pierre and Miquelon still raging. At one stage, Hull's resignation seemed likely. In the upshot, the Secretary of State was partially pacified. The Free French were not displaced from the islands and the radio station there no longer broadcast Vichy propaganda; there had always been the risk that it would send out signals or disguised messages to the German submarines which had already taken a dreadful toll of allied shipping and were soon to take a worse.

The United Nations, as the Allied powers were henceforward known, pledged themselves publicly to employ their full resources against Germany, Italy and Japan and not to make a separate armistice or peace. Plans for a vast expansion of American production of aircraft, tanks, ammunition, shipping were agreed. The new arrangements for command in the Pacific were put in train; and the Combined Chiefs of Staff Committee was formally established. Field Marshal Dill had just been superseded as Chief of the Imperial General Staff by Gen. Sir Alan Brooke. Churchill's intention had been to appoint Dill as Governor of Bombay. During the meetings in Washington, however, it became clear that the American military leaders had a profound respect for Dill. The idea of Bombay was abandoned and Dill remained in Washington as the principal British representative on the Combined Chiefs of Staff Committee. There he rendered priceless service and the Committee itself generated a combination of effort, a cohesion of planning, production and thought, never equalled in the history of coalition warfare.

At the beginning of 1942, the Royal Navy did not have a single capital ship operational east of Suez. The Mediterranean position was precarious indeed. Needless to say, every precaution had been taken to keep secret the scale of the damage. In Churchill's absence, Attlee decided that the Dominions must be told, though only by word of mouth and directly to each Prime Minister. Churchill regretted this, pointing out by telegram on January 11, "We do not give our most secret information to the Dominions or, indeed, even to the whole of our own Cabinet." The U.S. government had not been told the full facts about the Mediterranean; what was the point of telling Canada and South Africa? Neither they nor any of the other Dominions could do anything immediate about the position disclosed. "It is not a question of trusting people, but of not spreading the secrets over a needlessly large area when no action is required from parties informed."[29]

General Wavell had now to confront in the Pacific a series of tasks even more unpromising than those with which he had grappled in the Middle East. Before he knew of his latest assignment, he had written to a friend in London, "1941 has on the whole been a better year than we had any right to expect. I hope that whatever happens the PM's position will remain untouched, his courage and drive and leadership are indispensable. A very great man, if he had a better balanced judgement and chose men with his head rather than his heart he would be almost superhuman, and how unpleasant people approaching the superhuman are!"[30]

After a few days of partial rest in the sunshine of Palm Beach, W.S.C. returned once more to Washington. He gave another carefully written memorandum to Roosevelt, dealing with the prospects in each main theatre of war. It pointed out that the defeat of Germany, entailing a collapse, would leave Japan exposed to overwhelming force; whereas the defeat of Japan would not bring the world war to an end. Between the American and British military staffs, as between President and Prime Minister, a large degree of harmony prevailed. Having intended to sail home in the *Duke of York*, Churchill elected to fly from Bermuda.]

W.S.C.'s speech asking the House of Commons for a Vote of Confidence,* January 27, 1942[31]

Having crossed the Atlantic, it was plainly my duty to visit the great Dominion of Canada. The House will have read with admiration and deep interest the speech made by the Prime Minister of Canada yesterday on Canada's great and growing contribution to the common cause in men, in money, and in materials. A notable part of that contribution is the financial offer which the Canadian government have made to this country. The sum involved is one billion Canadian dollars, about £225,000,000. I know the House will wish me to convey to the Government of Canada our lively appreciation of their timely and most generous offer. It is unequalled in its scale in the whole history of the British Empire, and it is a convincing proof of the determination of Canada to make her maximum contribution towards the successful prosecution of the war.

During those three weeks which I spent in Mr. Roosevelt's home and family, I established with him relations not only of comradeship, but, I think I may say, of friendship. We can say anything to each other, however painful. When we parted he wrung my hand, saying, "We will fight this through to the bitter end, whatever the cost may be."

---

* Accorded by 464 votes to 1.

6

Quadrant: Quebec, 1943

TROUBLES DID NOT CEASE, even at home, with the House's emphatic vote of confidence. Mr. Menzies of Australia was by no means alone, though few dared voice such opinions so openly, in his view of Churchill's methods of government. The Prime Minister, said the critics, towered over colleagues of lesser talents than those who had formed the War Cabinet a generation earlier:

"I am afraid it would be in vain for any voice to be lifted in protest or criticism as long as Winston has the unchallenged control of war direction," lamented the Prime Minister of those days, Lloyd George. "He is displaying all the qualities of brilliant, but erratic judgement, pursued with blind stubbornness which characterised his actions in the last war. Were he subject to control by a War Cabinet of experienced and mature minds, like that which helped me to guide the nation through in 1917–18, there would be some hope. But alas! he persistently refuses to accept any such restraint."[1]

The crucial questions were two: should there be a War Cabinet composed of ministers who were not heads of the great departments of state; and should Churchill continue to combine the posts of Prime Minister and Minister of Defence? On the latter point, he was adamant. He knew that within the War Cabinet and the machinery of government, with Roosevelt, the Dominions and the wider world, his strength derived essentially from this concentration of offices, whereas his position outside the political circle sprang from a popular support, constant despite all the reverses suffered since 1940. So long as he remained Minister of Defence, Churchill could dominate the three civilian ministers responsible for the armed services. He remembered 1915.

On February 15, 1942, Singapore fell to the Japanese. This event was characterized by Churchill as "the worst disaster and largest capitulation in British history,"[2] for some 85,000 men had surrendered. Not by coincidence the government in London was now reshaped. Attlee, who had for some while acted as Deputy Prime Minister, formally assumed that title, and became Secretary of State for the Dominions; Beaverbrook was replaced by Oliver Lyttelton. Sir Stafford Cripps, recently returned from the Embassy in Moscow with an immensely high reputation – it was even hinted that he had by some mysterious means brought Russia into the war on the Allied side, whereas a more realistic view reserved that honour for Hitler – became Lord Privy Seal and Leader of the House of Commons. Cripps had intelligence of a high order, and integrity. Admittedly, as his and Churchill's close friend Lady Violet Bonham-Carter (the former Violet Asquith) had to concede, Cripps fed "on raw turnips & other unpalatable cattle-fodder"[3]; but he had at least the merit of savouring a good cigar.

With an unselfishness which Churchill readily acknowledged, Cripps soon set off to see whether a settlement could be reached in India. The situation there was a peculiarly difficult one, for the Commonwealth's war effort relied heavily upon Indian forces, all volunteers, and a powerful movement led by Gandhi took the view that if only the British would quit India, Japan would have no incentive to invade. With the Japanese forces at the borders of India and soon to cross them, Churchill could be forgiven for dissenting. From Washington, the President tendered suggestions which in London seemed detached from reality. This is one of the few subjects upon which Churchill in his own account permits himself a sharp criticism of the President. He records his thankfulness that events in India had already made it impossible to adopt Roosevelt's solution, which would have been "an act of madness" and, further, that "I would not have hesitated to lay down my burden, which at times seemed more than a man could bear" if his colleagues had not been of like mind.[4]

Cripps did his utmost and used his considerable influence with the Congress Party, a section of which supported India's vigorous participation in the war. The mission failed in its immediate purpose. The Indian war effort was sustained, however. While always answering Roosevelt courteously – at one stage in this dismal spring Churchill telegraphed to him about India "Anything like a serious division between you and me would break my heart and would surely harm the Allied cause"[5] – he refused to permit any serious American intervention. As he once explained it to Mackenzie King, he had an agreement with the president: "You leave my Indians alone and I'll leave your Chinese alone."

The regular membership of the War Cabinet now stood at seven. Despite the Conservatives' enormous preponderance in the House of Commons, that party provided only three ministers (Churchill, Eden, Lyttelton); Labour had three (Attlee, Bevin, Cripps); and, presiding over much of the domestic business of the government, Sir John Anderson as a former civil servant remained resolutely unattached to any party. All except Cripps bore heavy departmental duties, on top of which each member, if he were to deal conscientiously with the memoranda and telegrams reaching him in that capacity, had to read the equivalent of a full-length novel every day.[6]

Many accounts suggest that Churchill in this spring of 1942 lacked a good deal of his old buoyancy. He did the work of two or three men; he had not enjoyed so much as a week's holiday since the war began, and was apt to be scandalized when others suggested that they needed rest and recuperation; he took no exercise to speak of; he was in his sixty-eighth year. He had not at any stage of his life been careful of himself. The President wrote that once a month he went to his country home at Hyde Park for four days, crawled into a hole and pulled the hole in after him; he was called to the telephone only if something of vital importance occurred. "I wish you would try it, and I wish you would lay a few bricks or paint another picture."[7] Churchill was so constituted that there was little chance of his doing anything of the kind.

Perhaps he knew in his heart of hearts that the attack of angina in Washington could not be entirely ignored. "Papa is at a very low ebb," his youngest daughter recorded at the end of February 1942. "He is not too well physically – and he is worn down by the continuous crushing pressure of events."[8] Churchill was fond of animals and especially of cats. He had a favourite among them all, the marmalade cat at Chartwell. On one of the few visits that he paid there in the war, accompanied only by a Private Secretary, the cat was given a seat of honour in a chair at the Prime Minister's side; Churchill provided titbits from his plate, cleaned the cat's mouth and deeply regretted his inability, thanks to the restrictions of wartime, to offer cream, all the while rehearsing under his breath an answer to Beaverbrook, criticism of dispositions in the Middle East and a speech. When the marmalade cat died in a week of black tidings, Mrs. Churchill insisted that her husband not be told until the news became brighter.[9]

As if the disasters in Southeast Asia and the Pacific were not enough, the enemies' submarines levied a terrible toll on Allied shipping, especially in the Atlantic. The sinkings there amounted to 3,295,000 tons in 1941, not to mention another million tons elsewhere; in 1942 those figures were almost doubled, to 6,150,000 and 1,638,000 tons. Leaving aside the loss of warlike supplies, the British Isles came within measurable distance of being starved out. This position was not reversed until 1943, by which time the number and tonnage of new ships being completed exceeded the sinkings.

In the spring of 1942, Churchill felt mounting dissatisfaction with the Middle Eastern situation and pressed the Commander-in-Chief, General Auchinleck, to resume the attack. The new Chief of the Imperial General Staff, General Brooke, explained to Auchinleck that "Some of the telegrams which you did not like were the results of saving you from more unpleasant ones." To the same correspondent General Ismay, the indispensable hinge between Churchill and the Chiefs of Staff, confessed that he himself had been called every name under the sun during the previous six months, except perhaps a coward; but he knew perfectly well that these storms meant nothing. He also understood how wounding Churchill's language could be:

"You cannot judge the P.M. by ordinary standards: he is not in the least like anyone that you or I have ever met. He is a mass of contradictions. He is either on the crest of the wave, or in the trough: either highly laudatory, or bitterly condemnatory: either in an angelic temper, or a hell of a rage: when he isn't fast asleep he's a volcano. There are no half-measures in his make-up. He is a child of nature with moods as variable as an April day, and he apparently sees no difference between harsh words spoken to a friend, and forgotten within the hour under the influence of a friendly argument, and the same harsh words telegraphed to a friend thousands of miles away – with no opportunity for 'making it up.'"[10]

At the price of postponing the matter of Russia's demands over Poland and the Baltic States, an Anglo-Soviet Treaty was signed in May 1942. The Russians demanded the opening of a second front, and could not be persuaded that it lay outside British power to put sufficient land forces across the seas into Western or Northern Europe. Roosevelt and the American

Chiefs of Staff were at first a good deal more sanguine on that subject. When Churchill visited Washington in June for their third conference in ten months, they examined again the plans for a landing in France. Churchill pointed out the immense difficulties. While he was in Washington, news came that Tobruk, on the North African coast, had fallen. More than thirty thousand troops had surrendered to a force inferior in numbers. At first, Churchill could not believe it. He felt the event, like the fall of Singapore, to be a disgrace. Roosevelt, Hopkins and Marshall responded with sympathy, which meant much at such a moment, and Sherman tanks for the Middle East, which soon meant even more.

In sum, there was little cheering news for the British in the middle of 1942, except that the U.S. Navy showed its mettle and strength against the Japanese in the Coral Sea (alarmingly close to the shores of Australia) and then more decisively at the battle of Midway Island, in which Japan lost no less than four aircraft carriers. In London, the government survived comfortably a vote of censure. The Royal Air Force mounted massive attacks on Germany at a heavy cost but with less effect than the exponents of area bombing had predicted. Convoys to Russia by the northern route had been severely mauled. Above all, the Middle Eastern situation remained precarious. Churchill understood well that, without some solid military successes, his capacity to argue with the Russian and American governments was compromised. With some difficulty, the British persuaded their American colleagues that the alliance could not possess, at least until 1943, the troops, the command of the air, the armour, the landing ships or indeed any of the indispensable ingredients of the huge amphibious operation which would eventually take place in June 1944, and even then succeeded only by a narrow margin. Torch, the Allied invasion of French North-West Africa, was decided upon.

Churchill determined to see for himself in Cairo. He consulted Attlee and Bevin, who agreed or anyhow did not say they disagreed. Eden argued for two hours against this plan. At last Churchill said, "I see what you mean – you think I would be like a fat old bluebottle on a cowpat!"[11] Nevertheless he soon went to the Middle East, and then on to Moscow, where he met Stalin for the first time, endured for a while his taunts about British cowardice, and burst out that he had come all this way at some peril hoping to find the hand of friendship. He had not found it, and was grievously disappointed. For five minutes or more Churchill spoke with such eloquence that even the interpreters forgot to take notes. Before they could retrieve the situation, Stalin commented, "I don't understand what you say, but by God I like your spirit." Churchill and the high military authorities who accompanied him to Moscow explained why an invasion across the English Channel was impossible in 1942. Instead, Torch would constitute the second front; in view of the campaigns being waged in the Middle East and Atlantic, not to mention the Pacific, it might have been termed the third, fourth or fifth front.

In August 1942, Churchill replaced Auchinleck, who was later to render fine service as Commander-in-Chief in India, with General Alexander, and Montgomery took over the Eighth Army. It was not yet clear that Rommel's advance, bringing him perilously close to Cairo, had been finally halted in the last days of Auchinleck's command at the first battle of Alamein. Wavell, who knew the complexities of that theatre, wrote in mordant style: "The P.M. is in his most Marlburian mood, and sees himself in the periwig and red coat of his great ancestor, directing Eugene (for which part Alexander is now cast) to begin the Battle of Blenheim. Heads are falling so fast that the supply of chargers to put them on must run short soon, and the 1st Reinforcements Camp of Superior Commanders must be almost empty."[12] The new men declined to take the offensive immediately; but once the battles began in earnest, British and Commonwealth arms were crowned by their first consistent successes on land in three years of warfare. At the other end of the Mediterranean, Torch began early in November 1942. At last, though the process took some six months to complete, the Allies were converging to seize from east and west all the territories of North Africa. The Germans moved into the hitherto unoccupied southern portion of France; a large portion of the remaining French fleet was scuttled by its own sailors at Toulon; and the Allies had now to consider more seriously the future of France and the French overseas possessions. By intellectual capacity and sheer persistence, de Gaulle outdid all his rivals. Roosevelt, Hull and other members of the American administration continued to dislike and mistrust him heartily. Even Churchill, conscious that de Gaulle had genius, resented his intermittent but bitter hostility to the British, and more than once reproached him for it. Almost worse, British support for de Gaulle often threatened to embroil the Prime Minister with the President. "I brought him up from a pup, but I never got him properly trained to the house," said Churchill sorrowfully.[13]

When Roosevelt and Churchill met at Casablanca in January 1943, an attempt was made to patch up relations between de Gaulle and another prominent French leader, Gen. Henri Giraud. President and Prime Minister announced there the doctrine of unconditional surrender, for which both have been much blamed. For a long time, it was imagined that this was more or less a whim of Roosevelt's, to which Churchill assented. It was in truth a more considered business than that; the issue was put to the War Cabinet in London, which not only endorsed the doctrine of unconditional surrender for Germany and Japan but asked that Italy should be added to the list. Though no decision had been taken to abandon a cross-channel invasion in 1943, the prospect even then looked remote, for large armies were still battling in North Africa. It was agreed that Sicily should be the next step. The conference over, Churchill said to the President, "You cannot come all this way without seeing Marrakesh. Let us spend two days there. I must be with you when you see the sunset on the snows of the Atlas Mountains."[14] Off they bowled across the desert. At Marrakesh Churchill painted the only picture which he essayed during the war. He gave it to Roosevelt.

* * *

For the obvious political reasons, the British government accorded a high degree of prominence to the role which the Australian, New Zealand and Indian troops played in the Middle East, and the Americans in Torch. What was to the British the Far East was to the Australians the Near North, and after pained exchanges Churchill had to agree in 1942 that a good portion of the Australian forces should be withdrawn from the Middle East. The earlier loss and capture of many Australians at Singapore had done nothing to reduce the frictions between the two governments. Since the main Canadian land forces were still confined to the British Isles, less attention was then paid to Canada's fighting role than to the exploits of the other Dominions. Britain's own effort, inevitably on a grander scale than that of any Dominion and much larger than that of the United States at this stage, received smaller notice than it warranted. This state of affairs has persisted in many accounts ever since.

Canada contributed numerous airmen to the Royal Air Force, in addition to those who served in the RCAF. The Royal Canadian Navy had by now some five hundred ships in commission, mainly used in the Atlantic, and Canadian forces had suffered severely in the abortive raid at Dieppe, which did at least serve to illustrate in a grievous fashion the difficulties of an opposed landing across the seas. In the other three Dominions, elections held in 1943 strengthened the position of Smuts and Curtin and confirmed that of Fraser in Wellington. Mackenzie King, with his ample majority from 1940, looked secure. All the same, he had felt obliged to call a plebiscite in the spring of 1942, asking that the government might be released from its promise that conscription for service overseas would not be imposed. The province of Quebec provided more than a quarter of all MPs at Ottawa, and the divisive power of this issue, which had rent the country a generation earlier, became evident when the bill authorizing the introduction of conscription if necessary was passed only with the help of the Conservatives.

In the early part of the war, Britain's purchases of Canadian munitions and food were largely financed by the sale of gold and securities. British exports to Canada had inevitably fallen away to very modest levels. Soon the British had no hope of paying in cash; but they continued to receive the supplies and in the spring of 1942, Canada converted sterling balances to the tune of $700 million into an interest-free loan; this was in addition to the outright gift of $1,000 million. The British then expected that their adverse balance of payments with Canada would thus be covered until well into 1943. In fact, expenditure on munitions and foodstuffs and other necessaries of war rose so rapidly that the gift had been exhausted by the end of 1942. The Canadian government then said it would buy from Britain at a cost of some $200 million the munition factories originally built at British expense in Canada. Canada also assumed financial responsibility for thirty-five squadrons of the Royal Canadian Air Force formed or forming in the United Kingdom. That meant a further relief of some $185 million, and at least equivalent sums for the years to come. As if that were not enough, the Canadian government said it would transfer to the United Nations – in practice chiefly to Britain – war supplies to a value of a further $1,000 million. Apart from the immediate effect on the war-making capacity of the Alliance, these processes prevented the creation of the mountainous war debts that had bedevilled international relations for so long after 1918.

It helps to place such huge figures in context if we recall that, while the population of the United States (rather more than 130 million) was eleven or twelve times as great as that of Canada, Canadian gifts were equal to more than a quarter of the aid coming to Britain from the United States under Lend-Lease. In other words, the Canadian contribution per head of population had been more than three times as great.

"She is giving away goods to the value of nearly one quarter of her budget expenditure," the Chancellor of the Exchequer and the Deputy Prime Minister explained to their colleagues in London,

> whereas lend-lease assistance by the United States to all countries has been running recently at about one-eighth of *her* budget expenditure. We should have to give away goods and services to the value of something like £1,300 million a year in order to be giving away as high a proportion of our budget expenditure as Canada is doing. The new proposals will place a tremendous burden upon the Canadian taxpayer. Direct taxation in Canada is now, generally speaking, as high as in this country: it may have to go higher. The broad position is that Canada is not only devoting as large a proportion of her national income to defence expenditure as any other country, but that the proportion of the defence expenditure which is given away in the form of free supplies is higher in Canada than in any other country.[15]

Needless to say, the purpose of the comparison with Lend-Lease was not to display ingratitude to the United States. It is right to record, nevertheless, Canada's unmatched generosity, which continued throughout the war and into the peace.

Churchill had warned that success in North Africa must not be taken as the end, or even as the beginning of the end; rather, the end of the beginning. When the campaign ceased in May 1943, with some half-million German and Italian troops captured, the fortunes of the war had at last taken a decisive turn. Conferring again with the President at Washington in that month, Churchill took care to see all the Commonwealth representatives and give them a candid account. There, in the presence of Roosevelt, Mackenzie King said pointedly that the fact that all the Dominions had with one accord fought from the beginning was something which none would forget.[16]

It was clear, though accepted by the U.S. Chiefs of Staff with reluctance and by the Russians with disappointment and suspicion, that a full-scale invasion of France could not be attempted in 1943. The Canadian Chiefs of Staff, Minister of National Defence and Prime Minister shared the British view. To the latter Churchill explained that "he did not want to see the beaches of Europe covered with slain bodies of Canadians and Americans. That there might easily be many Dieppes in a few days."[17] The invasion of Sicily was confirmed; after that the task would be to knock Italy out of the war. This, Churchill argued with vigour, was the best way of taking some of the weight off the Russian front in 1943; the large forces in the Mediterranean must not be allowed to stand idle between the conquest of Sicily and the Overlord operation.

The war had progressed so favourably that the three heads of government began to discuss at Washington the possible shape of the postwar world, Churchill proposing that, beneath a Supreme World Council of the major powers, there should be three regional councils, one for Europe, one for the American hemisphere and one for the Pacific. He suggested that, in the regional council for the Americas, Canada would represent the British Commonwealth. In private, Mackenzie King had no enthusiasm for anything of the kind; nor, it must be added, had most of Churchill's colleagues in London. The President and Churchill remained in a state of high indignation with de Gaulle. All the same, Churchill pointed out the importance of a revived France, for the prospect of having no strong country on the map between England and Russia was not attractive.

When Roosevelt observed that Canada was the only country in the American continent that had a Legation, rather than an Embassy, in Washington, Mackenzie King replied that he was thinking of making this change. The President asked if the consent of the King of England would be needed. The two Prime Ministers explained the reality. Churchill said, "No, he is the King of Canada just as much as he is the King of England. Canada has complete control of her own affairs." Mackenzie King put the point neatly and clearly: "We have a perfect equality of status, not stature but status, in all that pertains to our domestic and external affairs."[18]

On the rising tide of military success, most domestic criticism of Churchill was borne away. Talk of Sir Stafford Cripps as an alternative had faded, not least because his tenure as Leader of the House of Commons proved so disappointing that within nine months he had been replaced by Anthony Eden; who thus found himself Foreign Secretary, a member of the Defence Committee, a member of the War Cabinet and Leader of the House. No other minister, except Churchill himself, carried such a load.

The Prime Minister continued to concentrate upon the tactics and strategy of the war. Not that he was indifferent to proposals for better pensions, a national health service, a great housing program; but he could no more foresee than the next man when the war might end, or in what conditions. He did know that Britain would be by any normal standard bankrupt. It was also clear, since there had not been an election since 1935, that the life of the House of Commons could not be indefinitely prolonged. In other words, he believed it would be wrong in all senses for a wartime prime minister to make large and expensive promises which a peacetime administration might not be able to fulfill. Meanwhile, his verbal felicity did not diminish. An example may give the flavour. To a friend he remarked memorably that the duty of a democracy in wartime is not to conceal but to confuse, "not the silence of the oyster serene in its grotto – but the smudge and blur of the cuttlefish."[19] He made time to entertain a former colleague, old and lonely: "I lunched alone Monday last week," wrote Stanley Baldwin early in 1943, "with the P.M. who kept me till 20 past 4!"[20]

* * *

Despite their genial conversations in Washington, Mackenzie King went back to Ottawa believing that Churchill was determined both to make no adequate mention of the Commonwealth's military effort and to centralize, if possible, the direction of the Empire's affairs. Both fears were exaggerated, if not entirely unfounded. An unhappy sequel ensued. The invasion of Sicily, the largest operation of its kind ever attempted though soon to be overshadowed by Overlord, began on July 10. The 1st Canadian Division, entering a major battle for the first time, had come from Britain. Other parts of the armada, involving nearly three thousand ships, gathered from the Levant, Alexandria and North Africa. When the draft announcements reached Ottawa, they contained references only to the "British-American" troops, but none to the Canadian forces. The Canadian government naturally asked London and Washington for amendment. Both agreed promptly; but in the tangle of telegrams this fact was not immediately apparent to Mackenzie King. He made a statement in Parliament, which plainly implied that the British had turned down the request, whereas Roosevelt had immediately met Ottawa's wishes. This speech caused a sensation in Canada and was loudly cheered in every part of the House.

Malcolm MacDonald recorded that almost everyone in Canada had understood that, when at last the Canadian troops were going into battle on a considerable scale, the authorities in London had tried to prevent the facts from reaching the public:

> Although this wrong impression can no doubt be corrected sooner or later amongst Canadians of good will, those groups in Canada who wish to see the connection with Britain broken will always use Mackenzie King's statement to further their ends. I fear the evil effects of this deplorable incident will last for many years.

Against this paragraph Churchill wrote pithily, "rubbish."[21] He had already expressed his sorrow that Mackenzie King should have been vexed, pointing out that the papers in London had been full of the exploits of the Canadian Division in Sicily:

> Indeed they have been featured far more than any single one of the British divisions engaged. The form of your remarks . . . seemed rather to suggest that Canada got better treatment from the United States authorities than from us. This was painful reading.
>
> As a matter of fact we have felt somewhat at a disadvantage through the great prominence given to the United States direction and contribution. You know I suppose that we have by far the larger share in this venture. . . . The main thing however is to win the battles and then there will be credit enough for all. . . .
>
> I am sure you will realise how difficult it is to keep all these things straight especially when so much else is going forward, and I know you will believe that my most earnest desire is to give the utmost satisfaction to you and to your troops on whose dramatic entry into this successful battle I offer you and your colleagues my sincere congratulations.
>
> Please always if possible let me know if anything causes trouble, as I am always most desirous of meeting your wishes and making all go well.[22]

By the next day, however, Churchill had received the full text of King's statement and notice of a Parliamentary Question due for answer in the following week. He telegraphed at once "Obviously I cannot accept the position created. Equally obviously I wish to say what causes the least friction" and invited King to suggest the terms of the reply to be given to Parliament in London. He also disclosed that he and Roosevelt wished to hold another meeting in August; would Canada welcome them "at Quebec in the historic setting of the Heights of Abraham"?[23]

What, King now asked MacDonald, did Churchill mean by saying that he could not accept the position? The High Commissioner made the obvious reply. Thereupon King became angry. If Churchill gave an answer in Parliament which reflected on the truth of his, King's, statement, he would seek a dissolution of Parliament. Nor would he fight the election on this single incident. Rather, he would appeal against the treatment of Canada by the British government, which had frequently forgotten that Canada was a Dominion. Though Canadian ministers had gladly accorded supreme leadership to Churchill and Roosevelt, their colleagues in London had gone much further than the emergency warranted. On matters of importance to Canada, they had ignored Canada's rights as a free member of the Commonwealth. He gave instances. He had sometimes permitted himself, said King, to be ignored as no Canadian Prime Minister should be, and had been criticized for that by friends as well as critics. He was not however prepared to remain quiet when Canadian soldiers were put in a position of inferiority to those of Britain and America. The time had come for him to speak out, and the vast majority of Canadians would support him.

He strode up and down. MacDonald interrupted to point out that with King's own permission, he had read all the relevant papers. Expecting to tell London that somebody there had blundered, he found instead that London's attitude had been as unexceptionable as Washington's. The two governments had actually co-operated in sending instructions to Allied Headquarters in North Africa to carry out the Canadian requests. Mackenzie King, surprised, argued vigorously against this view. He vowed that he would suggest no part of a helpful reply for Churchill to make in Parliament. The next morning, King was rather less incensed but the two went over all the ground again. By that afternoon, he had agreed to a draft answer. When MacDonald asked whether King still wished him to inform Churchill that, if an unsatisfactory statement were made at Westminster there would be a general election in Canada, the Prime Minister replied "No."

Churchill found the draft too long, but made an emollient statement, saying that no one was to blame for the misunderstanding. Officially, the incident was closed.

MacDonald was convinced King would never have carried out the threat of a general election; that had been an unconsidered explosion of pent-up feelings. But it did indicate how serious the situation was, and he begged his colleagues at home to realize the true position. The feeling of irritation at the treatment of Canada, extending steadily through the Dominion, was widespread among ministers, other public servants and informed citizens:

> United Kingdom ministers who visit Canada get an incomplete impression of Canada's sentiments towards Britain. You all exert a hypnotic influence upon your Canadian hosts. The magnificent genius of the Prime Minister and the prestige surrounding you, Sir [Attlee], and the Foreign Secretary over-awe Canadian ministers when they find themselves momentarily in your presence. This is one of the last survivals of that period of Colonial tutelage to Britain out of which Canada has passed and which these ministers themselves are amongst the first to relegate to the irrevocable past. They appreciate your visits, and treat you with a respect which makes them incapable of expressions about British policy couched in other than impeccably polite terms. They do not feel the same respect for a High Commissioner. When you have left Ottawa, believing all is for the best in the best of all possible Canadas, they turn round and tell me exactly what they feel about Britain. Their sentiments are a mixture of affection, admiration, gratitude and annoyance.

Not for the first time, MacDonald set out the issues over which Canada felt she had not been properly consulted, or not consulted at all. Some were more serious than others. He had pointed out the innumerable preoccupations of ministers directing the war in London, which made occasional mistakes inevitable, and the countless instances in which the British government had informed the Dominions upon the war's strategy and diplomacy. Canadian ministers, while impressed, were not convinced. They had pursued a conciliatory policy in order to reduce difficulties to a minimum and, even when they had a grievance, had sought to make as little fuss as possible. "They have supported us magnificently and unswervingly," MacDonald remarked. "Let us treat them in the same comradely spirit. . . . Their feelings have reached a point where they rankle badly. I urge again that we should give most careful heed to this situation."[24]

However dismissive he may earlier have been of MacDonald's views, Churchill exerted himself to meet Canadian wishes and susceptibilities at Quebec and to take Mackenzie King into his confidence. By stages the relationship changed; a long-established but not especially cordial friendship developed into something deeper. The frictions did not survive their meetings, for King was susceptible, as few were not, to Churchill's blend of boyishness, high spirits and solemnity. Disagreements by their nature generate urgent messages, intemperate or dismissive remarks; cordiality occupies less space in archives.

The essential fact is that in circumstances of unrelenting pressure a remarkable degree of cohesion was maintained between the governments and armed forces of the two countries. King realized that the President and Prime Minister would wish to have at the forthcoming conference a good deal of talk between themselves and their staffs, and that he could not participate in all the discussions without creating prickly problems about the position of other Dominion Prime Ministers. At the same time, it would be extremely embarrassing to the government in Ottawa if its Prime Minister seemed to be less than a fairly full partner in the meeting. Churchill at first anticipated that King and the Canadian Chiefs of Staff would attend the plenary meetings. Such arrangements would not prevent him from having private discussions alone with the President; nor would they prevent Anglo-Canadian discussions. But Roosevelt objected that to include the Canadian staff would almost certainly result in an immediate demand from Brazil and China, and probably from Mexico, for membership of the Combined Chiefs of Staff Committee in Washington, which had been prevented from degenerating into a debating society by refusing membership to other countries. If Canada were brought into the Quadrant discussions, it would be extremely difficult, if not impossible, to exclude representatives of the Dominions and other allied nations. He sent the Canadian Minister in Washington to explain the matter to Mackenzie King, and left Churchill no room for argument by telegraphing: "Rather than face the difficulties that would follow admitting Canadian Staff to Quadrant, I would prefer to have the meeting elsewhere, say Bermuda."

Churchill therefore suggested that, while the Canadian and British staffs should confer together, the British alone should be represented at meetings with the Americans. Mackenzie King made no difficulties and wisely took the view that the meeting would be an incomparable event in Canadian history; he expected Roosevelt and Churchill to realize the situation and play fair.[25]

* * *

The campaign in Sicily progressed so rapidly that the arguments for a frontal assault against Italy were strengthened. This had been a subject of sharp dispute, the American military authorities fearing a prolonged campaign in the Mediterranean, the British arguing that the conquest of Italy would be of the highest value in the general struggle; for example, many of the German factories could be attacked effectively only from Italian airfields. The fall of Mussolini on the evening of July 25, followed by the swift crumbling of the Fascist regime, made an invasion of the mainland a still more attractive proposition. The British Chiefs of Staff, and especially the CIGS, believed that the needs of Overlord and the Mediterranean must be related to each other and articulated. The Allies should take as much of Italy as they could, and thus draw off German forces from Russia, the Balkans, and France. As Brooke put it, "If we pin Germany in Italy, she cannot find enough forces to meet all her commitments."[26]

* * *

Churchill dined on August 4 with Brig. Orde Wingate, fresh from Burma. Thrilled by Wingate's account of jungle warfare behind the Japanese lines, the Prime Minister felt himself "in the presence of a man of the highest quality," whose account should be heard by the Chiefs of Staff and the Americans. Wingate accordingly joined the party leaving for Quebec an hour later. Churchill arranged that their train should also pick up Mrs. Wingate, who had not known of her husband's arrival in Britain, at Edinburgh.

To preserve secrecy, the *Queen Mary* sailed from a remote port on the west coast of Scotland. The British party numbered some 250. For the first time in the war, Mrs. Churchill accompanied her husband on a transatlantic crossing, as did their daughter Mary.

On the ship, at Quebec and then in Washington, nearly a thousand telegrams were received in the CONCRETE series from London and 777 were sent back in the WELFARE series. Some additional signals went to and from the United States, and those dealing with most secret subjects were transmitted unnumbered by special channels. This chapter prints a selection, showing something of the range of subjects with which Churchill dealt. Among those for which there is not space, we find his observations to the Secretary of State for War about the importance of preserving the characteristics of the cavalry regiments and the issue by Canada of its own Service Medal and Ribbon. He despatched a long message to Generalissimo Chiang Kai-Shek, promising to exert strong pressure on Japan and establish contact with the Chinese forces through northern Burma. To colleagues in London he expressed concern about the size and cost of the Indian native army. Other telegrams concerned parliamentary business; an alleged lack of energy in the Middle Eastern command; the appointment of the Governor of Bermuda; a determination to retaliate if the Germans should use gas in Italy; provision of landing craft for Overlord; the position of King George II of Greece; the tangled affairs of the French Committee of National Liberation; and, probably most important of all, the confusing and tortuous negotiations for the surrender of Italy.[27]

* * *

W.S.C. to General Ismay, August 8, 1943[28]

I have crossed out on the attached paper many unsuitable names. Operations in which large numbers of men may lose their lives ought not to be described by code-words which imply a boastful and over-confident sentiment, such as "Triumphant", or, conversely, which are calculated to invest the plan with an air of despondency, such as "Woebetide", "Massacre", "Jumble", "Trouble", "Fidget", "Flimsy", "Pathetic", and "Jaundice". They ought not to be names of a frivolous character, such as "Bunnyhug", "Billingsgate", "Aperitif", and "Ballyhoo". They should not be ordinary words often used in other connections, such as "Flood", "Smooth", "Sudden", "Supreme", "Fullforce", and "Fullspeed". Names of living people – Ministers or commanders – should be avoided; e.g. "Bracken".

After all, the world is wide and intelligent thought will readily supply an unlimited number of well-sounding names which do not suggest the character of the operation or disparage it in any way and do not enable some widow or mother to say that her son was killed in an operation called "Bunnyhug" or "Ballyhoo".

Proper names are good in this field. The heroes of antiquity, figures from Greek and Roman mythology, the constellations and stars, famous racehorses, names of British and American war heroes, could be used, provided they fall within the rules above. There are no doubt many other themes that could be suggested.

Care should be taken in all this process. An efficient and successful administration manifests itself equally in small as in great matters.

W.S.C. to C.R. Attlee, August 8, 1943

WELFARE 9

I am still pondering about the supreme [command?] south east Asia Front. Some time ago Amery suggested Mount Batten.* My mind has come back to this, after thinking of various other alternatives. Will you consult with Eden and Amery and let me know your impressions. All would depend upon whether the Americans liked the idea. Personally I think he might well be acceptable to the President. He knows the whole story from the top; he is young, enthusiastic and triphibious.

I am so glad Mackenzie King became reasonable. It would have made a breach between him and the President.

All well here and working hard.

[On board, Churchill watched films every evening. He found that they absorbed his attention and distracted him completely. Others did not always share his taste. However, all agreed that four films made by a unit of the U.S. Army were of high quality. W.S.C. had a lively appreciation of the importance of the cinema. The fact that these films had been made by Americans redoubled their value to the British. "There is no finer statement of our case," Churchill said. He prodded the Ministry of Information, and took the time at Quebec to record an introduction to the films.[29]]

W.S.C. to A. Eden, August 8, 1943

WELFARE 10

We agree with course you have taken. Badoglio† admits he is going to double cross some one, but his interests and the mood of the Italian people make it more likely Hitler will be the one to be tricked. Allowance should be made for the difficulties of his position.

Meanwhile the war should be carried forward against Italy in every way

* Louis Francis Victor Albert Nicholas Mountbatten (1900–1979), 1st Earl Mountbatten, naval commander; great-grandson of Queen Victoria; Chief of Combined Operations, 1941–43; Supreme Allied Commander, Southeast Asia, 1943–45; Viceroy of India, 1947; First Sea Lord, 1955–59; Chief of Defence Staff, 1959–65.

† Pietro Badoglio (1871–1906), Italian soldier; appointed Marshal, 1926; commanded Italian forces in Abyssinia, 1936; Commander-in-Chief, 1940–41; formed a non-Fascist government on the fall of Mussolini in late July 1943; resigned, 1944.

that Americans will allow. We do not have to ask their permission about bombing the towns of Northern Italy and Harris* should be limited only by weather. No answer seems to have come from the President about open cities so I suppose he has accepted my proposal to wait till we can talk it over.

Premier Stalin to President Roosevelt, August 8, 1943

WELFARE 209

Only now, having come back from the front, I can answer your message of 16th July. I have no doubt that you take into account our military position and will understand the delay of answering. Contrary to our expectations, the Germans launched their offensive not in June but in July, and now battles are in full swing.

As it is known, the Soviet Armies repelled the July offensive, recaptured Cape Orel and Byelgorod and now are putting the further pressure on the enemy.

It is easy to understand that under present acute situation at Soviet-German front, a great strain and utmost vigilance against enemy actions are required from the Command of Soviet troops.

In connection with the above I have at present time to put aside other questions and my other duty for the primary duty – the direction of action at the front. I have frequently to go to the different parts of the front and to submit all the rest to interest of the front. I hope that under such circumstances you will fully understand that at present time I cannot go on a long journey. . . .

I regret it very much but as you know circumstances are sometimes more powerful than people who are compelled to submit to themselves.

I consider that a meeting of the responsible representatives of the two countries would positively be expedient. Under present military situation it could be arranged either in Astrakhan or Archangel.

Should this proposal be inconvenient for you personally, in that case you may send to one of the above mentioned points your responsible and fully trusted personages. If this proposal is accepted by you, then we shall have to determine a number of questions which are to be discussed and

* Arthur Travers Harris (1892–1984), Air Officer Commanding-in-Chief, Bomber Command, 1942–45.

the draft of proposals which are to be accepted at meeting. . . . I do not have any objections to presence of Mr Churchill at this meeting, in order that meeting of representatives of the two countries would become the meeting of representatives of the three countries. I still follow this point of view on the condition that you will not have any objections to this.

I use this opportunity to congratulate you and Anglo-America on the occasion of the outstanding successes in Sicily which are resulting in the collapse of Mussolini and his gang.

Thank you for your congratulations sent to the Red Army and Soviet people on the occasion of successes at Orel.

From W.S.C.'s *The Second World War*[30]

Halifax was reached on August 9. The great ship drew in to the landing jetty and we went straight to our train. In spite of all precautions about secrecy, large crowds were assembled. As my wife and I sat in our saloon at the end of the train the people gathered round and gave us welcome. Before we started I made them sing *The Maple Leaf* and *O Canada!* I feared they did not know *Rule, Britannia*, though I am sure they would have enjoyed it if we had had a band. After about twenty minutes of hand-shakings, photographs and autographs we left for Quebec.

[The journey took twenty-four hours. Along the route, crowds or knots of people had gathered, often from great distances, to see Churchill pass by.

During the voyage, W.S.C. had acquainted himself with all the plans for Overlord. He had for years taken a keen interest in the artificial harbours without which the operation could not succeed. The higher authorities were bidden to his bathroom. An Admiral agitated the water at one end of the bath to represent a rough sea, while a Brigadier stretched a lilo, or inflatable mat, across the other end to show how it broke up the waves. "The stranger would have found it hard to believe," says Ismay, "that this was the British High Command studying the most stupendous and spectacular amphibious operation in the history of war."[31]]

Admiral Sir Dudley Pound* to the Admiralty, August 10, 1943

WELFARE 14

Prime Minister has made comments and asked questions as follows: –

On (i) BUBBLE BREAKWATER

a) When are trials taking place? It is important that these should be 12 inches to the foot, and that arrangements be made for a film to be taken of results.
b) What is the diameter and spacing of the holes?
c) What is the size and H.P. of compressors together with their weights?
d) What pressure is maintained in pipes?
e) What is the length and diameter of pipe in trial?
f) At what depths can it be operated?
g) What is the limit of length of pipe for operational use?
h) The requirement is dealing with waves which might be expected to occur at the time and place of the action. A good margin should be allowed but task should not be made too difficult by catering for conditions which are extremely unlikely.

(ii) LILO

a) Is rubber necessary at all, or is there any other means of making canvas watertight?
b) Is it really necessary to sink barge?
c) When are 12 inch to the foot trials taking place?

W.S.C. to A. Eden, August 10, 1943

WELFARE 22

The wording I should prefer would be: Begins: Badoglio must state that he is prepared to place himself unreservedly in the hands of the Allied

* Alfred Dudley Pickman Rogers Pound (1877–1943); Commander-in-Chief, Mediterranean, 1936–39; First Sea Lord, 1939–43. He informed W.S.C. in Washington that he had suffered a stroke, and resigned his office. He died a few weeks later, on Trafalgar Day, 1943.

Governments who have already made it plain that they desire Italy to have a respectable place in the new Europe. Ends.

Reference should also be made to General Eisenhower's offer of the return of Italian prisoners of war taken in Tunisia and Sicily, providing allied prisoners are speedily set free.

The object of the above is to convey to the Italian Government the feeling that, while they have to make surrender formal act of submission, our desire is to treat them with consideration so far as military exigencies allow. Mere harping on "unconditional surrender" with no prospects of mercy held out even as act of grace may well lead to no surrender at all. The expression "honourable capitulation" has also been officially used by the President and I do not think it should be omitted from the language [we are?] now to use.

[W.S.C. was anxious to encourage Italy's participation against the Germans; as for the latter, there was no need continually to utter the slogan "Unconditional Surrender." He remarked to the Foreign Secretary, "We certainly do not want, if we can help it, to get them all fused together in a solid desperate block for whom there is no hope."[32]]

A. Eden to W.S.C., August 10, 1943

CONCRETE 85

This* is better than I had dared to hope for and a great relief.

Should we not now at once agree a meeting in principle, time, place, personnel and agenda to be decided later? . . .

Joe is unaccountable.

[The Co-operative Commonwealth Federation (CCF), the nearest Canadian equivalent to the Labour Party in Britain, gained strength rapidly in these years. At the beginning of August, it did remarkably well in the election for the Ontario Legislature. A few days later, the results of four by-elections for the Federal Parliament were announced. The Liberals had lost all four; two in the prairies to the CCF and the other two there in Quebec, one to a French-Canadian nationalist and the other to a Communist. The

* A message from Stalin dated August 9, in essence similar to his telegram to Roosevelt of August 8.

Minister of Finance in Ottawa told MacDonald that if a general election were held at once, the CCF would win more seats than either the Liberals or the Conservatives, though not enough to gain a clear majority.[33]]

Mackenzie King's diary, August 10, 1943

As Churchill stepped off the platform of the last car, I greeted him very warmly and then Mrs. Churchill and Mary.* Introduced them to the Lieutenant-Governor and to Premier [of Quebec] Godbout.† Churchill wished to walk along the road a short way so as to greet the people assembled on either side. They were mostly young persons but they applauded enthusiastically. He and I drove together to the Citadel across the bridge and around later by the Plains of Abraham, past Wolfe's monument, and then into the Citadel grounds.

Churchill kept commenting on the beauty of the country and magnificent expanse of the river. . . .

We had just started out [for the Citadel] when almost the first thing he said to me was: I hope you won't want us to hurry away. I would like to make a good stay, mentioning a period of a month. Indicated that if he could be at the Citadel, he could readily keep in touch with the President, and go back and forth, if need be, from there. He said: you and I would carry on the war from this side.

He spoke of the conditions in Italy being in a fluid state. Everything unsettled. Said I am not going to be too insistent on unconditional surrender. What they must do is yield, and when they yield, they will be given such reasonable terms as those who have them yield are prepared to give.

They will not get back their empire, but they will have their own country to live in.

When Churchill spoke of the stay, I said I was glad to hear him speak of not hurrying away. That the country would welcome his having a complete change here. That I had been hoping he might plan to stay a while. He rather indicated that the Citadel was where he would make his headquarters.

He then said to me, I would like to go up to Toronto and drive through the streets there, as I have done in London. He said you and I will go

* Mary Churchill was then serving in the Auxiliary Territorial Service.

† Adélard Godbout (1892–1956), Premier of Quebec, 1939–44.

together, if that would be agreeable to you. I spoke of the pleasure that would be. I suggested to him that it might be well to do the same in Montreal. He said I would be glad to do that; anything that you suggest.

At a later stage, I said to him I thought it might be pleasant were he to take a journey right across Canada; go out to the Rocky mountains. He said: yes, I remember Lake Louise and what a lovely place it was. He thought it would be very pleasant for Mrs. Churchill and his daughter. He kept explaining what a great joy it was to them to see Canada.

As we went along, he brought up different matters in a quiet way. He said: we have got them beaten, but it may take some time. I asked him how long. He said: one, possibly two years. On the other hand, no one knows what might happen in Germany. It might be six months. But there is also Japan.

In speaking about not hurrying back, Churchill said: much more can be done by giving time for things to develop. I can do more with the President by not pressing too hard at once. He is a fine fellow. Very strong in his views, but he comes around.

I said I understood his difficulty would be to persuade the President not to be too quick about fighting from the North instead of from the South [of Europe]. He replied: yes. That there would have to be much careful work done there. That the trouble was the Americans did not realise how long it took to accomplish some things. He felt it would be very hard to get into Germany. He was entirely for going on with the war in Italy.

I had taken the latest despatches to show him, including one which referred to Badoglio's readiness to make terms, though appearing to still be with the Germans. Churchill said: a man who is ready to betray another is apt to betray you, if it suits his purpose. I would not trust him.

He said that our men had done well in Sicily. Remarked upon them being the hinge, with the Americans to one side, and the British to the other.

[Among the other subjects Mackenzie King and Churchill discussed that afternoon were recognition of the French National Committee; the prospect of a conference of the Commonwealth Prime Ministers in London; and a request that the Chiefs of Staff and others might have a little holiday in Canada after the conference, to which Mackenzie King agreed at once. They spoke also of Tube Alloys, the code name for the development of atomic energy. In the early stages, co-operation between Britain and the United States had been intimate and the British contribution large. Matters had then gone amiss. The costs were enormous and American resources vast. Moreover, to place the main effort in America had another priceless advantage; whereas every corner of the United Kingdom was open to bombing, the United States was invulnerable. There were, in theory, alternatives: Britain could set about building an atomic bomb on her own, or in collaboration with Canada. Several times W.S.C. intervened with Hopkins or Roosevelt. In this as in other matters he was convinced of the supreme importance of collaboration with the Americans, and the more so when it transpired that they had secured the entire output of the Canadian uranium mines and heavy-water plants, essential to the process of manufacture. At Washington in May 1943, President and Prime Minister agreed that Tube Alloys should be a joint endeavour; even the code name, let alone the substance, was so secret that it was omitted from telegrams circulated to the War Cabinet. Little happened until W.S.C. intervened again two months later, and a tangle of misunderstandings came to light. To unravel them, the Lord President of the Council, soon to be Chancellor of the Exchequer, was sent from London. Sir John Anderson was reputed to know something about everything, and much about most things; as a young scientist, he had actually undertaken research on the chemistry of uranium. Within a day or two it was agreed that a Combined Policy Committee should be formed in Washington, with a full interchange of information. This Committee would allocate the materials and plant. Churchill was by now on his way to Canada. Meanwhile, Anderson arrived in Ottawa and explained to Mackenzie King that the atomic experiments would probably require another two years before they reached the stage of practical application; this was a remarkably accurate forecast. They would "give control of the world to whatever country obtains them first." The British knew that both Germany and Russia were pursuing similar experiments, and he thought that Russia might perfect the discovery first of all.[34]

Thus, after many months of bickering, agreement had been reached. That Canada should have a seat on the Combined Policy Committee in Washington was evidently right. Churchill said so on August 10 to Mackenzie King, who immediately nominated C.D. Howe. Churchill took the proposal a day or two later to Hyde Park, where it was agreed.

At dinner on that evening, King broached a sensitive subject, the problems of the previous month concerning the announcement of the Canadian Forces' role in the invasion of Sicily. Churchill replied sympathetically. The

Canadian people, King explained, needed to feel that their government had a real voice in matters pertaining to the war. There were two kinds of pressure: from the Opposition in Parliament continually drawing attention to the fact that Canada was not represented in the higher direction of the war, with the implication that, if Canada's position went by default, she would have no real voice when the time came for peace-making; and from ministerial colleagues and members of the civil service, who urged him to assert Canada's position more strongly. King's diary records that he found Churchill "very understanding in matters of this kind." In his experience, Churchill added consolingly, by-elections resembled a fire started on ice; it blazed up at the beginning, but did not necessarily spread over the whole, and went out after a while.

Since Mackenzie King had special reason for paying attention to the opinions of French Canada, it is perhaps worthwhile to record that Churchill emphasized how keenly Roosevelt felt against de Gaulle. For himself, he thoroughly disliked the man, despite his many qualities; he was one of those Frenchmen who hated Britain "and might even be prepared to join with the Germans in attacking Britain some time. His ambition to control France was very great." We need not take the possibility of de Gaulle's joining with the Germans as a considered judgment, but Churchill had ample reason for saying that de Gaulle's ambition to control France was great, and there was at least occasional evidence that he was one of those Frenchmen who hated Britain.

W.S.C. believed the Canadians were intensely pleased that Quebec had been chosen for the conference, and felt "pretty sure" that he would be able to smooth down many ruffled plumes.[35]]

W.S.C. to Premier Stalin, August 11, 1943

WELFARE 44

Your telegram of August 9 gives me the opportunity to offer you my heartfelt congratulations on the recent most important victories gained by the Russian Armies at Orel and Byelgorod opening the way to your further advances towards Bryansk and Kharkov. The defeats of the German Army on this front are milestones to our final victory.

I have arrived at the Citadel, Quebec, and start this afternoon to meet the President at his private home. Meanwhile the Staffs will be in conference here and the President and I will join them at the end of the week.

I will show the President your telegram about a meeting of our responsible representatives in the near future which certainly seems to be most desirable. I quite understand you cannot leave the front at this critical period when you are actually directing the victorious movement of your armies.

Thank you for your congratulations on our Sicilian success, which we shall endeavour to exploit to the full without prejudice to OVERLORD.* Certainly our affairs are much better in every quarter than when we met at Moscow exactly a year ago.

I am sending you a small stereoscopic machine with a large number of photograph slides of the damage done by our bombing to German cities. They give one a much more vivid impression than anything that can be gained from photographs. I hope you will find half an hour in which to look at them. This we know for certain, eighty percent of the houses in Hamburg are down. It is only now a question of a short time before the nights lengthen and even greater destruction will be laid upon Berlin. This subject only to weather. This will be continued for several nights and days and will be the heaviest ever known.

Finally in the U-boat war we have in the months of May, June and July destroyed U-boats at the rate of almost one a day, while our losses have been far less than we planned for. Our nett gain in new tonnage is very great. All this will facilitate the establishment of the large scale Anglo-American fronts against the Germans which I agree with you are indispensable to the shortening of the war.

W.S.C. to C.R. Attlee, August 11, 1943

WELFARE 64

I do not think Cunningham† would be a good appointment.** He has telegraphed to Pound, who sounded him, that it is not his line of country. I am, however, grateful to you for your opinion and will reflect upon the matter before taking my decision. I will find out tentatively how the President reacts to suggestion. Personally I should feel more confidence in

---

* The Allied invasion of northern France, launched June 6, 1944.

† Andrew Browne Cunningham (1883–1963), 1st Viscount Cunningham; Commander-in-Chief, Mediterranean, 1939–42, and Naval Commander-in-Chief, Expeditionary Force, North Africa, 1942–43; First Sea Lord in succession to Pound, 1943–46.

** For the command in Southeast Asia.

Mountbatten than in any other. The question is whether his health will stand it and also he would be a loss here. He is the Master [of] Combined Operations and his appointment would I think command public interest and approval and show that youth is no barrier to merit. Brigadier Wingate* is a remarkable man and he also in his Jungle sphere would fit in with my ideas of vigour and inventiveness in this decayed Indian scene. The above is only for you and Eden.

W.S.C. to King George VI, August 11, 1943

WELFARE 54

With humble duty.
The Citadel is in every way delightful and ideally suited to the purpose. Arrangements for the President are perfect. He has the upper floor and ramps are fitted everywhere for his convenience. I am most grateful to Your Majesty for arranging this. I have telegraphed to the Governor-General thanking him for the trouble he has taken and for his kindly welcome.

The holding of this conference in Canada and especially at Quebec is most timely as there is a lot of fretfulness here which I believe will soon be removed. I meet the Canadian Cabinet this morning and the Quebec Cabinet this afternoon, and start thereafter for H[yde] P[ark]. . . .

Your Majesty will also have noticed that I have heard from the Great Bear† and that we are on speaking or at least growling terms again.

[Roosevelt, Churchill and King occupied the Governor General's quarters at the Citadel. Under the hospitable roof of the Château Frontenac, which one of the British reporters described loftily as resembling "a cross between a medieval castle and a railway station," the British and American delegations lived and worked together. This proved an important factor in the running of the conference, as it would again in 1944. The British, accustomed to stringency at home, marvelled at the food and drink. Fresh orange juice appeared each morning at breakfast. Not until they had returned to London was it realized that the manager of the hotel had caused

---

* Orde Charles Wingate (1903–44); service in the Sudan, Palestine, Transjordan, Abyssinia, Burma; appointed to command the Long Range Penetration Group in Burma, August 1943; killed on active service, 1944.

† Stalin.

the oranges to be flown from the United States, at no mean cost. After the conference dispersed, orange juice disappeared from the menu.[36]

By contrast with the hotel, the Citadel had a classical austerity of line. From its walls Churchill could observe the Plains of Abraham. Around him were many reminders of the Duke of Kent, Queen Victoria's father, who had made himself heartily disliked in Quebec a century and a half earlier. Mackenzie King reflected with justifiable pride that while he as Prime Minister of Canada was receiving the President of the United States and the Prime Minister of Great Britain, Queen Victoria's granddaughter (wife of the Governor General) was spending a holiday on the farm at Kingsmere.

The Canadian government insisted on bearing the entire cost of the conference, even down to the provision of special furniture and a large fleet of cars available day and night.]

Extracts from the minutes of a joint meeting of the War Cabinet of the United Kingdom and the War Committee of the Canadian Cabinet, held at the Château Frontenac, August 11, 1943, at 11:30 a.m.[37]

[At the outset of the meeting, Churchill remarked that this joint session of the British War Cabinet, represented by Sir John Anderson and himself, and the Canadian Cabinet's War Committee marked a unique occasion of major importance; two of His Majesty's Governments were sitting together in a formal conference for the first time.

Mr. Heeney's* record of the meeting runs to nine printed pages. The more important items are reproduced below.]

CANADA'S POSITION IN RELATION TO CONFERENCE; BRITISH – CANADIAN CHIEFS OF STAFF DISCUSSIONS

The Canadian Prime Minister referred to the position of the Canadian government and Canadian Chiefs of Staff in relation to the forthcoming discussions with the President and the conference of the Combined Chiefs of Staff.

The Canadian government had accepted the position that the higher strategic direction of the war was exercised by the British Prime Minister and the President

---

* A.D.P. Heeney, Secretary of the Canadian Cabinet.

of the United States, with the Combined Chiefs of Staff. It was recognized that the participation of the Canadian military heads, in meetings of the Combined Chiefs of Staff, might give rise to difficulties with other United Nations. It had been agreed that suitable opportunities would be made for consultation between the British and Canadian Chiefs of Staff.

The United Kingdom Prime Minister observed that arrangements had already been made for a meeting, that afternoon, between the British and Canadian Chiefs of Staff. Further meetings could be held, subsequently, as required, and conclusions reached during these meetings could be reviewed later on by the Canadian Prime Minister and himself.

It was agreed that the position as described by Mr. King and Mr. Churchill was satisfactory.

EMPLOYMENT OF CANADIAN ARMY OVERSEAS

The Minister of National Defence [Mr. Ralston] pointed out that it had been, and continued to be, the policy of the Canadian government that the Canadian Army overseas should be employed, in whole or in part, wherever, in the judgment of those charged with the strategic direction of the war, it could make the most effective contribution.

Canada did not demand an equal voice in determining the high strategy of the war, but the military advisers of the Canadian government should, in all cases, have the opportunity of passing [an opinion] upon operations which involved Canadian troops, reserving the right of reference to the Canadian government for final decision.

In view of the long period which most of the Canadian Army had spent in Britain, in a defensive role, and the prospect of further delay before operations would be launched from the British Isles, it was, in Mr. Ralston's own opinion, desirable that additional Canadian formations should be given an opportunity of participating in the Mediterranean area, possibly with the establishment of a Canadian Corps Headquarters there.

Mr. Churchill expressed his appreciation of the desirability of employing further Canadian forces in active operations at the earliest possible date. Decisions in this respect, however, could not be made until the Combined Chiefs of Staff had, at their coming conference, reached definitive conclusions regarding future strategy. Thereafter, full and sympathetic consideration would be given to the questions raised by the Minister.

It was agreed that further consideration would be given to these matters, following the conference of the Combined Chiefs of Staff.

CANADA'S POSITION IN RELATION TO DIRECTION OF THE WAR

The Canadian Prime Minister observed that the Canadian government had recognized fully that the higher direction of the war could be not exercised by all of the United Nations, and was satisfied, in this respect, that authority should rest with Mr. Churchill and President Roosevelt, and their Combined Staffs. While this was so, the Canadian public were increasingly concerned that there should be adequate recognition of the substantial contribution which Canada was making to the total war effort of the United Nations.

It was widely felt that, while Canada had been at war two years before the United States, she was not being accorded, in the council of the United Nations, a role proportionate to her contribution. It was felt that in certain fields in which Canada was playing a major role her right to a more decisive voice might well be recognized.

Mr. King stated that the Canadian government appreciated the full information provided from day to day through the Dominions Office, the U.K. High Commissioner, and in personal messages from Mr. Churchill to himself. In most cases an opportunity was given for consideration, in advance, by the Canadian government, where Canadian interests were affected.

Nevertheless, in some instances, decisions taken jointly by the United Kingdom and the United States, affecting Canada, had been taken and announced without opportunity for Canadian comment. Such occasioned serious difficulties for the Canadian government. It was recognized that the necessity for rapid action might compel certain decisions to be taken without there being time for consultation.

He felt sure that the Canadian position in this respect would be appreciated and that Canada would be fully consulted in advance, wherever Canadian interests were affected.

The United Kingdom Prime Minister expressed appreciation of the points brought forward by Mr. King. . . .

[The joint meeting then discussed the relations between the RCAF and the RAF, which were generally excellent, and the need to give suitable recognition in public announcements to the role played by Canadian aircrew; the difficulties which had arisen over prompt announcement of the participation by Canadian Forces in the landings in Sicily; the issue of monthly communiqués, suggested by President Roosevelt, which would review anti-submarine warfare in all theatres of action; and the conditions attaching to the award of the 1939–43 Star. In all these instances, W.S.C. did his best to meet the position of the Canadian government.]

INTERNATIONAL CIVIL AVIATION

The United Kingdom Prime Minister referred to the difference of opinion between the U.K. and Canadian governments with regard to the advisability of special Commonwealth discussions, in advance of a meeting with the United States and other countries.

It was difficult to see how the U.S. government could reasonably take exception to such prior Commonwealth discussions. It would be a natural and proper thing for the nations of the Commonwealth to hold a "family council" in such circumstances.

The Minister of Munitions and Supply [Mr. Howe] referred to the position of the United States air lines who were laying plans for a large expansion after the war, including extensive developments northward, over Canadian territory.

Under these conditions it would be unwise for Canada to embark upon any formulation of policy with other nations, without some prior opportunity for obtaining the views of the U.S. government.

The Canadian Prime Minister said that it was the view of the Canadian government that the institution of prior Commonwealth discussions, on these important questions, would create, in the United States, the impression that the members of the Commonwealth were seeking to achieve a common policy before consulting the U.S. government, and would thereby prejudice the course of any subsequent international conference and the hope of achieving a satisfactory result.

This was true in other fields of post-war policy, as well as in civil aviation.

Mr. Churchill said that he had recently made international air transport his own special concern. It was his intention to hold preliminary discussions, on the subject, with the President. During the coming week Mr. King would participate with him in discussing the subject with Mr. Roosevelt.

The U.K. government and other members of the Commonwealth were, however, anxious to have exploratory discussions among themselves. For that reason it was intended to proceed on this basis, whether or not Canada felt able to participate.

At the same time, Canada's position vis-à-vis the United States would be strengthened if members of the Commonwealth could reach common agreement.

The Minister of Mines and Resources [Mr. Crerar*] pointed out that Canada's reluctance to participate in Commonwealth discussions arose not so much from fear that the U.S. government itself would misunderstand the purpose of such discussions, but rather from apprehension as to the influence upon American opinion

* Thomas Alexander Crerar (1876–1975), Canadian businessman and politician; Minister of Mines and Resources, 1935–45.

and policy of the powerful private companies which controlled air transport in that country.

Discussions on general postwar air policy, from which the United States were excluded, would present the private air lines with an opportunity to exert powerful pressure which would prejudice satisfactory international negotiations on a wider basis.

Mr. Churchill said that this was an element in the Canadian position which had not, perhaps, been appreciated by the U.K. government. The Lord President of the Council would bring it to the attention of their colleagues in the War Cabinet, upon his return.

It was understood that the general question would be raised by Mr. Churchill, at Hyde Park, and be discussed further in subsequent conversations between the President, Mr. Churchill and Mr. King.

FRENCH COMMITTEE OF NATIONAL LIBERATION

The United Kingdom Prime Minister explained the difficulties that had been experienced in finding a common basis for agreement in regard to recognition of the Committee.

Despite the difficulties encountered in regard to de Gaulle, there was no gainsaying his identification with the forces of French resistance. In the circumstances, there was no object in delaying the clarification of our relations with the Committee, and he intended to urge the President to agree to prompt action. If agreeable to the Canadian government, he would tell Mr. Roosevelt that Canada was anxious for early settlement of the French position. If definitive agreement was not reached at Hyde Park, the question would be taken up during the coming week, with Mr. Roosevelt and Mr. King at Quebec.

Mr. Churchill said that he had thought of suggesting to the President that de Gaulle be invited to join them at Quebec. Would this be helpful from the Canadian point of view?

It was hoped that Canada would take no action with regard to recognition of the Committee until agreement on common policy had been clinched with the United States, and that recognition would then be simultaneous and couched in similar terms.

The Canadian War Committee were of the opinion that a visit by General de Gaulle, at this time, might have a disturbing effect.

It was agreed that no action be taken with regard to recognition of the Committee, pending discussions between Mr. Churchill, Mr. Roosevelt and Mr. King, and that recognition, when agreed upon, should be simultaneous and on similar terms.

Memorandum by Mackenzie King, attached to his diary, August 11, 1943

At the close of the discussion [at the War Committee of the Canadian Cabinet] Churchill was asked about Russia. He made quite an impassioned speech to the Cabinet in which he spoke of how marvellous Russia had been; how at the outset she would of course have been prepared to leave Britain to be swallowed up by Germany (There was the other side that Britain would have allowed Russia to be swallowed up by Germany.)

He spoke of the millions of people in Russia. Thought that after the lives she had lost, she would not be anxious to spread communism in other countries but would give her time to restoring her own country. We must not forget that she was very advanced in her scientific developments and industries and would soon become all powerful. But her doctrines were certain to influence all parts of the world and that she might someday become a nation that would be powerful enough to more than control the rest of the world unless, in the interval, some new system of world control were instituted which would prevent anything of the kind on the part of any country. . . .

I said to him when we were talking that I believed he was the one man who had saved the British Empire. He said no, if I had not been here someone else would have done it. I said I did not believe that was so. I could not think of any other man who could have done what he did at the time. It was so necessary. He then said he had had very exceptional training, having been through a previous war and having had large experience in government. I said yes, it almost confirmed the old Presbyterian idea of predestination or pre-ordination; of his having been the man selected for this task. I truly believe that but for his bold stand and vision Britain would never have been able to meet the situation as she has.

Mackenzie King's diary, August 11, 1943

I think my colleagues felt that I had not in any way failed [at the meeting of the War Committee] to bring out all the points of possible difference and those things which had given rise to feelings of Canada being ignored.

Churchill was obviously greatly pleased with the meeting, as indeed were all the members of the War Committee of the Cabinet. . . .

He told us a very good story in Council about continuing the meeting until we had completed the discussions. He said it was like bride and the groom at the altar when the clergyman asked would he take this woman to be his lawful wedded wife. His reply was: we came here on purpose. In other words, that was our purpose to settle all these matters.

Mackenzie King's diary, August 11, 1943

We were met at the door [of the Legislative Buildings, Quebec] by Godbout, who led us through the buildings, different chambers, into the Cabinet Council where his colleagues were seated on either side of a long table. He introduced them all in turn to Mr. Churchill. . . .

To help along conversation at the beginning, I spoke to Mr. Churchill of the government [of Quebec] having been very helpful to our govt. in our war effort. They had many problems here but dealt with them in a co-operative way. Spoke a little about Mr. Churchill's desire to do some fishing, and said perhaps someone present could let him know the best places.

On the way, I had suggested to Churchill to say a few words in French. He, himself, said he would like to say a word or two to the Quebec Cabinet. He began speaking in French, rather slowly but choosing his words carefully. He became quite emotional toward the end as he referred to Quebec and the historic significance of the meeting here, and what it might mean to the world to have decisions made in this old city which would help to relieve the situation in France.

He spoke about his great desire to see France restored, given a worthy role and place in the world, etc. There was quite a silence after he had completed speaking. I, myself, broke it by beginning applause in which others joined heartily.

The *Daily Telegraph*, London, August 12, 1943

The people of Quebec got their first real glimpse of the British Prime Minister shortly after noon, when he drove up with Mr. Mackenzie King to the courtyard of the Château Frontenac. The grey stone courtyard rang with cheers as Mr. Churchill, smoking a cigar, stepped from the car, smiling and with two fingers of his hand raised in the "V" sign. He wore a black jacket and waistcoat, with grey, striped trousers and a black Homburg hat. He posed for photographers on the steps of the chateau, repeatedly giving the "V" sign. "Wait a minute," he called. "We will take one with Mr. Mackenzie King shaking hands."

Mr. Churchill was described by those close to him as being in "fine form" and excellent spirits. "We want Churchill," cried the Quebec crowds, as the word spread that he was about to leave the War Cabinet meeting. He stopped to sign autographs and appeared in gay and confident mood. . . .

Evacuation orders were issued to hotel residents [at the Château Frontenac] by letter a week ago, and only one ordinary hotel guest now remains. She is a woman with heart trouble. Her doctor has certified that it would be dangerous for her to move.* She remains in the room which she has occupied for the past few years with her maid. . . .

Mr. Churchill's arrival is front-page news in all the newspapers, French as well as English language. Editorial comment, since official statements on the purpose of the Conference have been few, ranges over a wide field, but it is in unison in expressing gratification that the conference is taking place on Canadian soil. As one put it, a new chapter is being added to the history of the ancient city of Quebec which may rival in importance any event in its past.

The *Montreal Gazette* states: "As Casablanca saw the charting of the strategy of the war, which is now fulfilling itself before our eyes, Quebec may be remembered as the charting ground of peace.

"No thinking person believes the war is already won or that our fighting men have not many hard tasks still before them. But enough has happened to show that when peace does come it may come suddenly and it will require a unified strategy as urgently as the war does."

L'Evénement, a journal in the French language, says: "This remarkable occasion recalls many moving memories, not the least among them being the proved friendship of Mr. Churchill for France.

"Canadians of French origin are vividly impressed by the presence among them of this dynamic personality, from whom they have learned to expect both wise guidance and unshakeable confidence, which will lead us with our Allies to that heroic victory of which, under Providence, Mr. Churchill has been the herald."

[W.S.C. and Mary now left for a brief visit to Hyde Park. Mrs. Churchill, fatigued, remained at Quebec.]

---

* It was said that she might not live two weeks. When the second Quebec Conference met more than a year later, this lady was still in occupation of her room.

Mackenzie King's diary, August 12, 1943

Had tea with Mrs. Churchill in her own sitting room, and we talked together from about 5 till a quarter to 7. Very interesting conversation.

In the course of it, she spoke about how much Churchill relied upon me and spoke of how glad he was to be with me and to share days together....

She told me many things about Winston. One thing was his being out of office for a number of years and writing the life of Marlborough,* had had a real effect upon his character. He had discovered that Marlborough possessed great patience. That patience became the secret of his achievements. He would have to listen for hours to the Dutch telling him how he should carry out operations, etc., but he would bear all patiently. That Winston would ask her whether she thought he would ever be back in government again. That she had told him he might not. She then told me that when Neville Chamberlain took over and succeeded Baldwin [in 1937], and did not invite him into the Cabinet, she said then she did not think he would be in any future government....

He, himself, in driving with me told me that he was quite different than he had been in earlier years. Had learned a great deal. He had made many mistakes in the first war. He was making fewer mistakes in this war because of those he had made earlier.... Above all, he had learned to consider very carefully many matters and to be cautious.

Mrs. Churchill said Winston is fond of attractive, interesting people.

W.S.C. to Mackenzie King, August 14, 1943[38]

The attached† is a very mischievous message and I do not know what Canadian source in England has inspired it. The President spoke to me about it this morning and seemed concerned.

As you know, the First Canadian Division has only been withdrawn from the line [in Sicily], after having achieved remarkable things, in order to rest for a further stroke. This message gives the impression of a disagreement between the Allies, and it would be a very serious thing if such messages were encouraged. After all, the Canadian Divisions when they

---

* Published in four volumes between 1933 and 1938.

†A despatch from A. Randal, a Canadian Press journalist, sent from London on August 13 and appearing in the *New York Herald Tribune* and other newspapers on the next day.

come into the line must take their chance and do the same as others. They cannot always be kept on fighting irrespective of the exertions and losses. The Commander-in-Chief on the spot must have reasonable latitude to rest some Divisions and use others as circumstances may require without it being suggested that there is friction between the Dominion and the Mother country.

I wonder who started this hare? I think you will agree with me it is a hare which should have its ears pulled.

Memorandum by Mackenzie King, attached to his diary, August 15, 1943

Almost the first word Churchill said was that he was so glad to be back in his own headquarters. He then spoke of what an ideal place Quebec was for a conference meeting.

He then began outlining his talks with the President. Spoke of the business known as "Tubal" [Tube Alloys]. Said that the President had agreed to Howe being on the committee. Asked me if I had seen the text of the agreement. I told him I had not. He said he would see that I did see it. It contained references to not using this against each other, etc. It was important to get under way. He did not want the Russians particularly to get ahead with the process.

He then spoke of the question of recognition of the French National Committee in Africa. Said that the President and Mr. Hull were quite determined not to use the word "recognition". He, Churchill, had sought to persuade them that if they were going to do anything, to do it generously. The President was to see Mr. Hull today.

If they won't agree to recognition in the same terms that we wish to make it, then we will have to make our own statement separately, and we will go full length on our own.

He then spoke to me about the meeting to be arranged with Stalin. I said while he was away that I had thought a good plan would be for the President and himself to go out and see the developments of the Alaska Highway and to get the other gentleman to meet them out there. He said I will have to be here about 2 months. I won't be on your back all the time. The President has invited Mrs. Churchill and myself and Mary to go down and spend a little time with them at Hyde Park after the conference. We can then arrange for something else.

Referring to Stalin, he said: we will send the "blighter" an invitation to try and have him meet us. If he does not accept it, we can't help it. We must try to arrange something now if we can.

W.S.C. to F.D. Roosevelt, August 15, 1943[39]

For you alone.

1. After pondering this morning I feel pretty sure that we ought to make a renewed final offer to U. J. [Stalin] to go to meet him at Fairbanks [Alaska] or at the farther point you had in mind [the Bering Strait] as soon as this Military Conference is over. If he accepts it will be a very great advantage: if not, we shall be on very strong ground. We must mind the Japanese do not get us (!).

2. I am having a fair copy made of the Tube Alloy Memorandum ready for our respective initials. I am assuming that you would be agreeable to Howe being the Canadian representative on the General Policy Committee. Our two men would be Dill* and Llewellin.†

3. I will now take up with my Staffs the most important question of the Commands as we outlined them. I am sure the plan you have in mind is the best.

4. I was very favourably impressed with Gray's** Irish message. The only amendment I suggest is to leave out any suggestion that we shall continue being nice to de Valera†† even if he won't play. The Irish are very practical people and if they don't have to do a thing they don't like, they don't do it. I should be glad if you could let me have a copy of the message

---

* John Greer Dill (1881–1944), British soldier; Commander, 1 Corps in France, 1939–40; Chief of the Imperial General Staff, 1940–41; head of the British Service Mission, Washington, 1941–44, where he rendered outstanding service to the Allied cause; accorded the honour, unique for a British citizen, of burial in Arlington Cemetery.

† John Jestyn Llewellin, 1st Baron Llewellin (1893–1957), British politician; President of the Board of Trade, 1942; Minister Resident in Washington for Supply, 1942–43; Minister of Food, 1943–45.

** David Gray (1870–1968), U.S. Minister to the Irish Free State, 1940–47; he suggested that the U.S. government should put a request directly to the government of Eire for the use of airfields and ports.

†† Eamon de Valera (1882–1975), Irish politician born in the United States; reprieved after a sentence of death for his part in the Easter Rising of 1916; leader of opposition to the Anglo-Irish Treaty of 1921; President of the Executive Council (later Taoiseach) of the Irish Free State, 1932–48, 1951–54, 1957–59; President of the Irish Republic, 1959–73.

when the State Department have seen it in order that I may put it before my Cabinet. I feel it is very important to try to get this additional security for the troops before the concentrations for OVERLORD become very large. It really is not fair that all your Divisions should be ticked off as they come.

5. You said we had dealt with half-a-dozen out of the dozen big points we were to talk over. Here is the fifth: the French Committee. I beg you to go as far as you can in your formula because however justly founded one's misgivings may be there is no use making a gesture of this kind in a grudging form. If you do not like our wording of the formula there seems to me no reason why we should not have separate documents conveying our different shades of meaning, provided they are both issued at the same time. Mackenzie King will have his own variant.

I did so enjoy my visit and my only regret is that Clemmie was not there to share it. This however perhaps you will allow us to repair.

Brigadier Jacob* to Brigadier Hollis, Office of the War Cabinet, London, August 15, 1943

WELFARE 139

Conference has now started. Yesterday was spent in agreeing on the Agenda, which follows the lines of our proposals, and on a general discussion of the war. Today they are down to the European theatre – here it appears that the Americans want us to do even more far reaching operations in Italy and southern France than we have contemplated, but without allowing us the resources which would make them possible. They demand an overriding priority in all cases for "OVERLORD". They have it firmly fixed in their minds that "OVERLORD" is like the western front in the last war, i.e. the main theatre, and that the Mediterranean is a side show.

[Earlier in 1943, it had been understood that a British soldier would command the forces for Overlord. President and Prime Minister had agreed that General Brooke should be appointed, and he had been told, more than once. The vast scale of the invasion was now clearer, after all the planning by General Morgan and his staff; more to the point, it was apparent that

---

* Edward Ian Claud Jacob (1899–1993), British soldier; Assistant Secretary (Military) to the War Cabinet, 1939–46; Director General of the British Broadcasting Corporation, 1952–59.

while at the outset of Overlord the Commonwealth and American forces would be more or less equal in strength, the American armies would soon predominate. Churchill therefore proposed to Roosevelt at Hyde Park that the commander should be an American, and broke the news to the CIGS at Quebec on August 15. "Not for one moment did he realize what this meant to me. He offered no sympathy, no regrets at having had to change his mind, and dealt with the matter as if it were one of minor importance!" Thus the distressed Brooke in his diary for that day.[40]]

Lord Alanbrooke's diary, August 15, 1943

Quebec

The whole COS [British Chiefs of Staff] lunched with PM and then went hurriedly back for our 2.30 conference with the American Chiefs of Staff. It was a most painful meeting and we settled nothing. I entirely failed to get Marshall to realize the relation between cross Channel and Italian operations, and the repercussions which the one exercises on the other. It is quite impossible to argue with him as he does not even begin to understand a strategic problem! He had not even read the plans worked out by Morgan* for the cross Channel operation and consequently was not even in a position to begin to appreciate its difficulties and requirements. The only real argument he produced was a threat to the effect that if we pressed our point the build up in England would be reduced to that of a small Corps and the whole war reoriented towards Japan. We parted at 5.30, having sat for 3 very unpleasant hours.

[That evening, Dill had to report to the CIGS that he had found Marshall most unmanageable and irreconcilable, even threatening to resign if the British pressed their point. Next day, all but the most senior officers having been asked to leave the room, Brooke said candidly that neither side was trusting the other; the Americans doubted that the British would put their full hearts into Overlord and the British did not feel full confidence that the Americans would not insist on carrying out previous agreements irrespective of changed conditions. He produced what even his

---

* Lt.-Gen. F.E. Morgan, Chief of Staff, Supreme Allied Commander, had been engaged on detailed preparations for Overlord for the previous six months.

own account calls "countless arguments" to prove the close relationship between the Italian operations and Overlord.[41]

It was at this stage that the Italian negotiations took a more definite turn; Badoglio, who had formed a government after the fall of Mussolini, was now suggesting not only an armistice, but that Italy should help to drive the Germans out of Italy. Meanwhile, German reinforcements were rapidly transferred to Italy, and the Allies were not in a position to mount an immediate invasion of the mainland.

Churchill, on learning that the Australian government had requested consultation about the postwar settlement in Europe, at first judged that to accede would "have the effect of paralysing foreign policy"; and since the British lived within twenty miles of Europe and were bearing perhaps nine-tenths of the whole Commonwealth's war burden, they "must be accorded reasonable latitude." But all this had a bearing upon the recent fretfulness in Canada, as Attlee immediately pointed out:

> You will have heard at first hand in Canada the importance which the Canadian Government attach to full and early consultation about post-war arrangements. The Australian Government's attitude is the same. Even if Dominion contributions to the war are small in comparison with ours, they are very great in proportion to Dominion resources. In my view the whole future of co-operation within the Commonwealth and Empire depends on the Dominions being given an opportunity to pull their full weight with us in considering the post-war settlement.[42]

A more immediate Australian issue also arose. Arthur Fadden, briefly Prime Minister in 1941, had referred in public to a message in which Churchill had reported his conversations with Roosevelt at Placentia Bay. Curtin wished to publish this telegram, which would certainly have caused a considerable uproar in the United States. Attlee recommended refusal.]

W.S.C. to J. Curtin, Canberra, August 15, 1943

WELFARE 141

I cannot give my sanction to the partial publication of Most Secret and Personal telegrams interchanged with Dominion Governments about the conduct of the war. Such a practice would render impossible the full and free transmission of opinion between the Mother Country and the Dominions. If anything said in these Secret messages is liable to be brought out at elections the whole character of our correspondence would be affected.

W.S.C. to A. Eden, August 16, 1943

WELFARE 147

Present line I am taking with President and United States authorities is that we pay no attention to unilateral [Italian] declaration about Rome being an open city but continue to bomb remorselessly. Combined Chiefs of Staff take this view strongly and I understand that orders have now been given to resume Rome bombing. If later on we should be forced off this position, your conditions seem well chosen.

W.S.C. to General Eisenhower, August 16, 1943

WELFARE 146

My personal and secret telegram to Mr. Hopkins* was not written for your eye and was couched in unceremonious style.

I hope you will realise that I am liable to be cross-examined in the House on the exact wording of every Declaration to the Italian people that carries or purports to carry your high authority. I cannot therefore disinterest myself in communiques which, at moments when public opinion is so sensitive, profess to explain the attitude of our joint Governments to Italy. Still more is this the case when your name is used by subordinates about pronouncements which you have not even seen. It would be no help to the common cause if I were to say publicly that H.M.G. take no responsibility for the Algiers Radio. Therefore I hope you will consider my difficulties as well as your own, which I fully understand and will always endeavour to mitigate.

* This telegram, marked "Personal and Secret," reflected dissatisfaction with a statement issued in Eisenhower's name by his propaganda branch and sought the President's agreement that such pronouncements should be approved in advance by the two governments.

Memorandum by Mackenzie King, attached to his diary, August 17, 1943

En route to Wolfe's Cove Station [to greet Roosevelt] I spoke to Churchill about the memorandum re gin and whiskey and the memorandum I had sent to him. He said he did not care about the memorandum, as long as he got the whiskey. I then told him what the facts were and the kind of things that had been put into the memorandum were the sort of things that were circulated to political opponents. He said he thought the memorandum was an impertinent one and that he would send a note to the quartermaster general telling him that he thought so.

I took advantage of this to show Churchill the little prayer pamphlet issued* on "Our Leaders" and spoke of the billboard and of the detraction that had followed. He said to me not to be concerned about that. He knew all about that sort of thing. He said, after all what can you expect. You kept your opponents out of office for 20 years and you cannot expect any love from them or anything but bitterness just because you have defeated them.

He then said to me: did I not think it might be necessary to join with the Conservatives to keep the C.C.F. from getting control of things? I said that the Conservative Party was going down and down. They were at the bottom of everything. I could not see what strength they would bring to the government and I felt certain that were I to join with them, a very large part of my own party would leave me and join with the C.C.F. That I felt the Liberal Party was the only one that could hold the country. That the way things were now, I felt it was better for our own party to proceed on lines as they had begun.

As we drove together past the bushes near Wolfe's Cove, Churchill mentioned how easy it would be for anyone to take a shot from there. I asked him if he cared to have any security men about him. He said: no. That he liked to be on his own. In London, he walked through the streets by himself.

Tonight at dinner, he said the British people liked work but did not like drill. The Americans were much the same way. Our people don't mind fighting but do not want to be regimented.

---

* By a church in Winnipeg; the "Leaders" were Roosevelt and W.S.C.

[By a happy augury, the conquest of Sicily was completed on this day.

Roosevelt was enchanted by Quebec. "Look, Winston, what the French did for La Nouvelle France. Did the British do anything like this for the Thirteen Colonies?"[43]]

W.S.C. to C.R. Attlee, August 18, 1943

WELFARE 209

The President and I have agreed together that he should send following from both of us to Stalin. If he accepts it will be good. If he does not accept we at any rate cannot be reproached with not having done everything in human power. . . .

BEGINS.

We have both arrived here with our staffs and will probably remain in conference for about 10 days. We fully understand strong reasons which lead you to remain on battle-fronts where your presence has been so fruitful of victory. Nevertheless we wish to emphasize once more importance of a meeting between all 3 of us. We do not feel that either Archangel or Astrakhan are suitable but we are prepared ourselves, accompanied by suitable officers to proceed Fairbanks in order survey whole scene in common with you. The present seems to be a unique opportunity for making a rendezvous and also a crucial point in War. We earnestly hope that you will give this matter once more your consideration. Prime Minister will remain on this side of Atlantic for as long as may be necessary.

Should it prove impossible to arrange the much needed meeting of 3 heads of Governments we agree with you that a meeting on the Foreign Office level should take place in near future. This meeting would be exploratory in character as, of course, final decisions must be reserved to our respective Governments.

Generals Eisenhower and Alexander* have now completed the conquest of Sicily in 38 days. It was defended by 315,000 Italians and 90,000 Germans, totalling 405,000 soldiers. These were attacked by 13 British and United States Divisions and with a loss to us of about 18,000 killed

---

* Harold Rupert Leofric George Alexander (1891–1969), later 1st Earl Alexander; Commander-in-Chief, Middle East, 1942–43; commanded the invasions of Sicily and Italy; Field Marshal, 1944; Supreme Allied Commander, Mediterranean, 1944–45; Governor General of Canada, 1946–52; Minister of Defence, 1952–54.

and wounded, 23,000 German and 7,000 Italians dead and wounded were collected and 130,000 prisoners besides those Italians who have dispersed in country side in plain clothes. It can be assumed that all Italian forces in Sicily have been destroyed. Mass of guns and munitions are lying scattered about all over the island. Over 1,000 enemy aircraft have been taken on airfields. We are as you know soon to attack the Italian mainland in heavy strength.

Lord Moran's diary, August 18, 1943[44]

Quebec

The Canadian Prime Minister was our host at a Citadel dinner. There was apparently a proposal that Canada should take part in the Conference, but this came to nothing. As it is, Mackenzie King seems rather like a man who has lent his house for a party.* The guests take hardly any notice of him, but just before leaving they remember he is their host and say pleasant things. I wonder if he is as enamoured of his role at this Conference as the P.M. imagines.

W.S.C. to C.R. Attlee and Foreign Office, August 18, 1943

WELFARE 195
Most Secret and Personal.

The President and I are deeply impressed with the advantages of inducing Italy to change sides which would save much time and blood in the struggle with the Germans. The two chief dangers are –

a) the Germans occupying Rome and setting up a Quisling administration, or,
b) the whole country sliding into hopeless anarchy.

Either or both of these evils may still come upon us, but we think the course we have adopted gives us the best chance of averting them. The Combined Staffs were unanimous in their advice, the Foreign Sec-

* Long afterwards, King observed in a self-deprecating fashion that he had been not so much a participant in the discussions at the two Quebec conferences as "a sort of general host, whose task at the Citadel was similar to that of the General Manager of the Château Frontenac."

retary was stormbound* and the nature of the case required immediate decision†. . . .

There seems to me to be no need to inform the Russians at this stage** as the whole design will either come to nothing or be productive of important Military advantage. No bargain of any kind has been made with the Italians or their Government. After unconditional surrender they will have to work their passage.

Combined Chiefs of the Staff are unanimous against our hampering ourselves in any way by the unilateral declaration of the Italian Government that Rome is an open city and I have very little doubt that the President will be in accord with his Military advisors, but I will speak to him this morning on the subject.

Memorandum by Mackenzie King, attached to his diary, August 18, 1943

I said [in a speech at a dinner given by the government of Canada in honour of Roosevelt and Churchill] I, too, had had my dreams, and one that I had cherished through life was that the British Empire and the U.S. might be drawn closer together, and that in some small way, immediate or remote, Canada might be an instrument toward that end and toward furthering the friendship between the two.

[During his brief visit to Hyde Park, Churchill had reached agreement in principle with Roosevelt about Tube Alloys. They signed at Quebec on August 19. The United States and Great Britain pledged that atomic weapons would never be used against each other, nor against third parties without each other's consent. Neither would communicate any information to third parties except by mutual consent. The British recognized that as by far the greater part of the financial burden had fallen on the United States, "any post-war advantages of an industrial or commercial character shall be dealt with as between the United States and Great Britain on terms to be specified by the President of the United States to the Prime Minister of Great Britain. The Prime Minister expressly disclaims

* On his way to Quebec.

† To negotiate with an emissary of Badoglio.

** In the event, W.S.C. did inform Stalin by a telegram of August 19.

any interest in these industrial and commercial aspects beyond what may be considered by the President of the United States to be fair and just and in harmony with the economic welfare of the world."[45]

Within the tiny circle that knew about Tube Alloys, Churchill was sharply criticized for giving away so great a prize. The probability is that, once he had understood the damaging suspicions that had arisen on the American side, he determined to allay them in a handsome manner. He could hardly foresee that for a prolonged period after the war the United States would refuse collaboration and withhold information on atomic and nuclear matters. These were subjects that were to loom large in Churchill's visits to Canada of 1952 and 1954.

His warmest admirer would not have called Roosevelt a tidy administrator. Even when so much time had been lost, nothing had been done by the beginning of September to resume co-operation. It turned out that Mr. Stimson did not know that he was to preside over the Combined Policy Committee or Dr. Conant of Harvard that he had been appointed a member. However, harmony reigned at last from the autumn of 1943. At least there could be no complaint of failure to consult Canada in this most momentous of matters. King and Howe knew henceforth what was imparted to no more than a handful of people; not even the Deputy Prime Minister in London was given the information. Neither Roosevelt nor W.S.C. had the least inclination to share such information with Russia, nor, it appears, any inkling that excellent secret intelligence enabled Stalin to know in considerable detail what was going forward. The fact that such information was withheld by his British and American allies doubtless increased his deep suspicion of them, just as the devastating atomic power demonstrated against Japan in August 1945, showed Russia how potent a weapon the West had acquired.]

Lord Alanbrooke's diary, August 19, 1943[46]

Another poisonous day! I had a rushed time going through papers from 9 to 10.30. Then a difficult COS till 12 noon when we went to Citadel to see the PM to discuss South East Asia operations. I had another row with him. He is insisting on capturing the tip of Sumatra Island irrespective of what our general plan for the war against Japan may be! He refused to accept that any general plan was necessary, recommended a purely opportunistic policy and behaved like a spoilt child that wants a toy in a shop irrespective of the fact that its parents tell it that it is no good! Got nowhere with him, and settled nothing. This makes my arguments with the Americans practically impossible!

[The opportunity was taken that afternoon to demonstrate a wonderful new material called pykrete, which consisted of wood pulp mixed with ice. It seemed possible that a floating aerodrome, estimated to weigh two million tons, could be created, which under its own power would take up a position just offshore and enable aircraft to be rearmed and refuelled. W.S.C. was much attracted. Upon this project, somewhat infelicitously named Habbakuk, a good deal of effort and money was expended, chiefly in Canada; the practical difficulties proved too great in the end.]

J.M. Martin to Sir Alan Lascelles,* August 19, 1943[47]

I do not know if it was shrewd instinct or just a happy accident that made the President suggest a meeting in Canada. Anyhow it was most timely. The Canadians seem to have become thoroughly ruffled and fretful for various reasons; but direct contact and Winston's handling of the situation are, I think, smoothing out all the difficulties. Anyhow there is a much closer understanding.

The President is in very good form. He made one of the most charming and graceful little speeches of the kind I have ever heard in proposing the King's health at the dinner given by H. E. [the Governor General] on his arrival.

General Alexander to W.S.C., August 20, 1943

CONCRETE 401

Many thanks for your kind message, . . . which I value very highly. Everything possible is being done to put on Avalanche† at the earliest possible date. We realise here very clearly that every hour gives enemy more time to prepare and organise against us.

---

* Alan Frederick Lascelles (1889–1981), Secretary to the Governor General of Canada, 1931–35; Assistant Private Secretary, 1936–43, and Private Secretary, 1943–45, to King George VI.

† The amphibious attack at Salerno.

[The dangers of an open split between the United States and Britain over the French question were as apparent to Mackenzie King as to Churchill, and to both Prime Ministers the formation of the French Committee of National Liberation in June 1943 was heartily welcome. On paper at least, de Gaulle would be subject to the restraining influence of his colleagues in the Committee. In mid-July, General Giraud had been warmly received in Ottawa. The Canadian government would have liked to recognize the French Committee at once, but had held back in deference to British views. The British still hoped to persuade the United States, so that all three powers could recognize together. Churchill in his imaginative way particularly wished this to be announced from Quebec.

On August 20, Eden pointed out to Hull that the British had to live twenty miles from France and "I wanted to rebuild her so far as I could." Recognition of the French Committee would be a first, though small, step. Hull said that the British had financed de Gaulle, which was true enough; he implied that the money had been used to attack him, the Secretary of State. The argument resumed with vigour on the next day, but to no greater effect.[48]]

Lord Alanbrooke's diary, August 21, 1943[49]

Another difficult day! We started our COS by considering the paper Portal, Dill and I, aided by Planners, had produced yesterday evening. We altered it slightly and accepted it. We then had to meet Winston at 12 noon to discuss it with him. He was more reasonable, and did accept the fact that an overall plan for the defeat of Japan was required, but still shouted for the Sumatra operation like a spoilt child! However, he accepted our paper. At 2.30 pm we met the Americans and presented the paper to them, suggesting that we should withdraw to let them discuss it between themselves. For this they took a full hour and when we returned we found that they wished to amend those points which would have made the paper entirely unacceptable to Winston! More discussions ensued in getting them to agree to a form which should be acceptable to Winston and to ourselves. This was a relief as it broke the final difficulties of this conference and practically finished our work.

W.S.C. to C.R. Attlee, August 22, 1943

WELFARE 326

The President and General Marshall are very keen on Mountbatten's appointment, which it is certain the United States Government will cordially accept. Our Chiefs of Staff concur. There is no doubt of the need of a young and vigorous mind in this lethargic and stagnant Indian scene. I have no doubts whatsoever that it is my duty to make this proposal formally and to submit Mountbatten's name to The King. Mountbatten and Wingate working together have thrown a great deal of new light upon future plans. It is essential that following upon this conference an announcement should be made in a few days. I hope my colleagues will feel this is the best course to take.

We have also cleared up to our satisfaction the difficulties about the south-east Asia Command. Broad strategic plans and major assignments of forces and supplies will be decided by the Combined Chiefs of Staff subject to the approval of their respective Governments. But all operational control will be vested in the British Chiefs of Staff acting under His Majesty's Government, and all orders will go through them. . . .

Eden and Hull are locked in lengthy discussions. Hull remains completely obdurate about not using the word "recognition" in respect of the French Committee. We have therefore agreed that they shall publish their document, and we ours and the Canadians theirs, after communicating with Russia and others concerned. Eden has this matter in hand. I have pointed out in the plainest terms to the President that they will certainly have a bad press, but he says he would rather have a sheet anchor out against the machinations of de Gaulle. Our position is of course different, for we are doing no more for the Committee by our formula than we did for de Gaulle when he was alone and quite uncontrolled by others.

[Mountbatten's command in Southeast Asia was largely modelled upon the structure of American Gen. Douglas MacArthur's in the Pacific. Churchill had in effect exchanged British command of Overlord for British command in Southeast Asia. Reasoning that, despite the promises made earlier to Brooke, American command of Overlord was inevitable, he was insistent that the British and Commonwealth forces must be seen to play a large part in the defeat of Japan. He feared that American critics would otherwise say, "England, having taken all she could from us to help her beat Hitler, stands out of the war against Japan and will leave us in the lurch."[50] He appointed a personal representative to the government of Chiang Kai-Shek and another to the headquarters of General MacArthur. Both officers were well chosen and rendered notable service.]

Lord Alanbrooke's diary, August 23, 1943[51]

Last day but one of our conference – and thank God for it! I do not think that I could possibly stand another day of these meetings. The strain of arguing difficult problems with the Americans who try to run the war on a series of lawyer's agreements which, when once signed, can never be departed from, is trying enough. But when you add to it all the background of a peevish temperamental prima donna of a Prime Minister, suspicious to the very limits of imagination, always fearing a military combination of effort against political dominance, the whole matter becomes quite unbearable! He has been more unreasonable and trying than ever this time. He had during the sea voyage in a few idle moments become married to the idea that success against Japan can only be secured through the capture of the north tip of Sumatra! He has become like a peevish child asking for a forbidden toy. We have had no real opportunity of even studying the operation for its merits and possibilities and yet he wants us to press the Americans for its execution! We have struggled all day with a series of COS, Combined COS, and Plenipotentiary meetings with PM and President. As a result we have practically broken the back of all the work and have had our proposals accepted and approved by the Almighty! I am not really satisfied with the results, we have not really arrived at the best strategy, but I suppose that when working with allies, compromises, with all their evils, become inevitable.

Mackenzie King's diary, August 23, 1943

At noon, Churchill and I drove together through the streets of Quebec. It was a triumphal procession from the time we reached the Garrison Club at the foot of the Citadel until the time of our return. There was a great demonstration in front of the City Hall. Churchill was visibly pleased. He remarked on the happy expression of the people. Indeed, as we looked at the people from the car, it was like a vast throng hailing a deliverer. Churchill was dressed in a white linen suit. At times, he sat up at the back of the car. I had a grey suit and was careful to remain seated except for a moment at the City Hall. As we talked together en route, he told me that he had sent word to ease up on the bombing in Italy. That Sinclair* had sent him a telegram advising this on account of the terrific damage which had been [done] in Milan and Turin. He told him to keep bombing the Germans instead.

I could see that Brendan Bracken [then in Quebec] had told him of my conversation about coming to England this autumn. I said to Churchill that he could see how great the necessity was for me to begin the mending of my fences – getting my party properly organized and seeing to it that I did not lose any members through the C.C.F. That Curtin's victory in Australia† was certain to be of assistance to the C.C.F. I thought, too, that it might of assistance to Fraser. Churchill's reply was that Smuts would be coming to England for a short visit. That he would then be coming on to America, and that we would have him here. He recognized that I had a big problem and said: you may be sure that I will do all I can in return to help you.

[In the end, the intractable difficulties had been worn down by argument and goodwill. The British, who had feared that the United States would wish to restrict the Mediterranean operations too severely in order to concentrate upon Overlord, found that the differences were surmountable by compromise. They conceded that, by the end of 1943, seven divisions should be removed from Alexander's command to strengthen the invading force in northern France, and that a separate attack should also be launched upon the south. Meanwhile, operations against enemy submarines, about ninety of which had been destroyed in the three months before Quadrant, were to be co-ordinated and extended; the dislocation of the German economic and military system was planned, and an intensified bombing offensive approved. The hope of establishing air bases around Rome or even farther north was rapidly belied by the swiftness of Germany's response to Italy's defection. Operations in the Balkans were restricted to improve supply to guerrillas, minor commando operations, and bombardment of strategic objectives. For Asia and the Pacific, it was

---

* Archibald Henry MacDonald Sinclair (1890–1970), later 1st Viscount Thurso; Liberal MP and close friend of W.S.C. for many years; Secretary of State for Air, 1940–45.

† At the recent election in Australia; Curtin was leader of the Labour Party.

agreed to do all that could be done to help China; islands would be prised out of the Japanese grasp one by one; land communications with China would be re-established through Burma.

Almost all these decisions turned on shipping. The British liked and trusted Lewis Douglas, head of the American war-shipping administration. His opposite number, Lord Leathers,* Minister for War Transport, was said to carry in his head the whereabouts of every important ship in the world, naval and merchant. The two of them worked day and night at Quebec.]

Press conference held by President Roosevelt, Mackenzie King and W.S.C. on the terrace at the Citadel, Quebec, August 24, 1943[52]

PRIME MINISTER CHURCHILL: . . . This is the sixth conference I have had with the President; and I know that there are some people who say, "Why is it necessary to have all these conferences?" But I think a much more reasonable way of looking at it would be to say, "How is it they are able to get on with such long intervals between the conferences?"

When you think that our armies are linked together as no two armies have ever been – our fleets, air forces and armies linked together as never before in history, not only side by side but intermingled very often – and that the operations which they are conducting are being achieved with unexampled rapidity ahead of schedule and ahead of program . . . then I feel sure that you will agree with me, and with the President, that we are right to come together, and to bring our staffs together, to bring not only the head staffs but all the very large staffs together indispensable to the working of modern operations.

A great advantage is achieved by personal contact. I assure you it would not be possible to carry on the complicated warfare we are waging without close, intimate, friendly, personal contacts, and they have been established at every level in the very large organizations which have been brought together here at Quebec.

I certainly must tell you that I have found the work very hard here. I have hardly had a minute to spare, from the continued flow of telegrams

* Frederick James Leathers (1883–1965), later 1st Viscount Leathers; British shipowner and businessman; Minister of War Transport, 1941–45; held office also in Churchill's Cabinet, 1951–53.

from London to the necessity of dealing with a number of great questions which cannot be hurried in their consideration; and a great many minor decisions, some of which take just as much time and trouble. . . .

I never felt more sure about anything than I do about the fact that these conferences are an indispensable part of the successful conduct of the war, and of a shortening of the struggle, and of the saving of bloodshed to the troops. The least we can do for them is to make sure that they go into action under the best conditions and the best planning, that our foresight and deliberations have played their part in all those plans.

W.S.C. to C.R. Attlee, August 25, 1943

WELFARE 404

Following is paraphrased message despatched to Marshal Stalin through United States channels on August 24 on behalf of Governments of United States and United Kingdom.

BEGINS.

The following is the decision as to military operations to be carried out during 1943 and 1944 which we have arrived at in our conference at Quebec just concluded. We shall continue the bomber offensive against Germany from bases in the United Kingdom and Italy on a rapidly increasing scale. The objectives of this air attack will be to destroy the air combat strength of Germany, to dislocate her military, economic and industrial system and to prepare the way for an invasion across the channel. A large scale build-up of American forces in the United Kingdom is now under way. It will provide an initial assault force of American and British Divisions for operations across the channel. Once a bridgehead on the continent has been secured it will be reinforced steadily by additional American troops at the rate of from three to five divisions per month. This operation will be the primary American and British air and ground effort against the Axis. The war in the Mediterranean is to be pressed vigorously. In that area our objectives will be the elimination of Italy from the Axis alliance and the occupation of Italy as well as of Corsica and Sardinia as bases for operations against Germany. In the Balkans our operations will be limited to the supply by air and sea transport of the Balkan guerrillas, to minor commando raids and to the bombing of strategic objectives. In the Pacific and in South East Asia we shall accelerate our operations against Japan.

Our purposes are to exhaust the air, naval and shipping resources of Japan, to cut her communications and to secure bases from which Japan proper may be bombed.

ENDS.

[In a message of August 22, Stalin complained vigorously that Russia had not been given timely information about the Italian armistice negotiations and said that a military-political commission, with representatives of Russia, the United States, and Britain, must be established to take up the questions arising from negotiations with powers dissociating themselves from Germany. Another message, of August 25, stated that Stalin could not leave the front for so distant a point as Fairbanks but would welcome a meeting of Foreign Secretaries, which should be more than "purely exploratory." He also wished a Russian representative to take part in the Italian armistice negotiations.[53]]

W.S.C. to C.R. Attlee and War Cabinet, August 25, 1943

WELFARE 421

Everything here has gone off well. We have secured a settlement of a number of hitherto intractable questions, e.g. the South East Asia Command, tube alloys and French Committee recognition. On this last we all had an awful time with Hull, who has at last gone off in a pretty sulky mood especially with the Foreign Secretary who bore the brunt. Unanimous agreement is expressed in a masterly report by the Combined Chiefs of Staff which the President and I have both approved. All differences have been smoothed away except that the question of the exact form of our amphibious activities in the Bay of Bengal has been left over for further study. I think, however, it is settling itself as I wished. There is no doubt that Mackenzie King and the Canadian Government are delighted and feel themselves thoroughly "on the map".

The black spot at the present time is the increasing bearishness of Soviet Russia. You will have seen the telegram received from Stalin about the Italian overtures. He has absolutely no ground for complaint as we have done no more than to hand the Italian representative the severe directions expressing unconditional surrender which had already received the cordial approval of the Soviet Government and have immediately reported all these matters to him.

The President was very much offended at the tone of this message. He gave directions to the effect that the new Soviet Charge d'Affaires [in Washington] was to be told he was away in the country and would not be back for some days. So far I have not received a similar communication but Eden and I will naturally leave the matter in suspense till the President is more inclined to take it up. Stalin has, of course, studiously ignored our offer to make a further long and hazardous journey in order to bring about a tripartite meeting. In spite of all this I do not think his manifestations of ill temper and bad manners are preparatory to a separate peace with Germany as the hatreds between the two races have now become a sanitary cordon in themselves. It is disheartening to make so little progress with these people, but I am sure my colleagues will not feel that I myself or our Government as a whole have been wanting in any way in patience and in loyalty.

I am feeling rather tired as the work at the Conference has been very heavy and many large and difficult questions have weighed upon us. I hope my colleagues will think it proper for me to take two or three days' rest at one of these mountain camps before I broadcast on Sunday and proceed to Washington. I am also planning to broadcast when taking a degree at Harvard University on September 3rd and to return home immediately thereafter. It is only in the event of some unexpected development in Italy or elsewhere which would make it desirable for me and the President to be close together that I should prolong my stay. In any case, I shall be back in good time before the meeting of Parliament. The Foreign Secretary returns by air on Saturday and is sending Cadogan with me to Washington.

C.R. Attlee to W.S.C., August 25, 1943

CONCRETE 572

Congratulations on the success of the Quebec Conference. I am so glad to hear that you will take some rest before returning.

I think Stalin's attitude is largely due to a misapprehension as to full information not having been given to him which has now been cleared up. His latest message about the proposed meeting shows better spirit.

Everything all right here.

W.S.C. to H. Macmillan,* August 25, 1943

WELFARE 424

This is a moment when a friendly attitude towards the United States would be singularly helpful to the interests of France. If on the other hand newspapers or radio polemics and reproaches are indulged in, the only effect will be arouse new flames of resentment in the State Department.

[The British government on August 26 recognized the French Committee of National Liberation as responsible for the administration of those French overseas territories which acknowledged its authority and as the body "qualified to ensure the conduct of the French effort in the war within the framework of inter-allied co-operation." The desire of the Committee to be regarded as "the body qualified to ensure the administration and defence of all French interests" was noted with sympathy. All this was conditional upon the French Committee's acceptance of the principle of collective responsibility, and of its own temporary character. The American announcement was couched in less forthcoming terms.]

King George VI to W.S.C., August 27, 1943

CONCRETE 610

I am so glad to hear that you are going to have a few days rest which will set you up again after the strenuous time you have had in Quebec. I send you my hearty congratulations on the outstanding success of the conference in all its aspects.

President Roosevelt to Colonel Warden [W.S.C.], August 26, 1943

WELFARE 445

I hope that Lady Warden is getting a real rest and that you are too. Also I hope that you have gone to One Lake.† Be sure to have big ones weighed and verified by Mackenzie King.

---

* Maurice Harold Macmillan, (1894–1986), later 1st Earl of Stockton, British publisher and politician; Minister Resident in North Africa, and then in the Mediterranean, 1942–45; Prime Minister, 1957–63.

† So called because on a previous expedition W.S.C. had caught only one small fish there.

[W.S.C. enjoyed himself enormously in these few days of comparative leisure, instructing Lord Moran in the arts of fishing and singing music-hall songs of forty years before. However, when summoned to dinner at the Lake of the Snows, Eden found him fussed about the risks to the party that would shortly be returning to England in a single aircraft. "I don't know what I should do if I lost you all. I'd have to cut my throat. It isn't just love, though there is much of that in it, but that you are my war machine. Brookie, Portal, you and Dickie. I simply couldn't replace you."[54]]

Colonel Warden to President Roosevelt, August 27, 1943[55]

Starting from Quebec Tuesday 31st. Will reach you for dinner Wednesday. Subaltern* and I have caught a few, and the change and air are doing us all good. Portal and Brooke have won great victories on the same front. Cabinet have cabled expressing pleasure at the satisfactory result of our Conference and urging me to take a holiday as all is quiet in England.

U.J.'s last two telegrams have been distinctly more civil. I think we should agree both to the secondary meeting and to the setting up of the Commission, though not in Sicily. This is certainly the view of my Cabinet subject to settlement of details. Anthony is coming here to-night, and I shall be ready to settle the whole thing with you in detail when we meet.

If you think an interim message is required I suggest something on these lines.

BEGINS.

We are considering your proposals and have little doubt that plans satisfactory to all of us can be made both for the meeting on the Foreign Office level and for the Tripartite Commission. Prime Minister and I will be meeting again early next week and will telegraph you further.

ENDS.

It may well be however that you will think no interim reply need be made.

Mountbatten's appointment seems to have gone well.

---

* Mary Churchill's code name.

President Roosevelt to W.S.C., August 28, 1943[56]

It is a coincidence that I was on the point of sending you a suggestion for an interim message to U. J., when yours came this morning. Therefore I am sending one you suggest to Russian Embassy in Washington.

I am delighted, as Quebec newspapers say, you are teasing the trout, but I do not believe, nevertheless, newspaper accounts that you have landed a five pounder. I shall require sworn verification.

The Earl of Athlone* to W.S.C., August 29, 1943[57]

Government House,
Ottawa

Dear Winston,

My wife and I are on the point of leaving for the week and in the first place we thank you for so kindly sending us the trout from the Lac des Neiges which were quite delicious and which we ate for dinner. Then we hope that you have enjoyed your very short rest in Canada which, had the situation allowed, we trusted would have given you a chance of a little more leisure here.

You have made Mackenzie King a very happy man and I must say that he deserves far more confidence than his fellow Canadians place in him but it was ever so in Politics as you yourself know! He has done extraordinarily well in this war.

We were delighted to hear about Dickie Mountbatten and I am certain he will "deliver the goods".

We wish you all "Bon voyage" and to you personally all success in your undertakings.

Yours very sincerely,
Athlone.

---

* Alexander Augustus Frederick William Alfred George Cambridge (1874–1957), 1st and last Earl of Athlone; soldier; uncle of King George VI and married to Princess Alice, a granddaughter of Queen Victoria; Governor General of South Africa, 1923–1931; Governor General of Canada, 1940–46.

Lord Alanbrooke's diary, August 30, 1943[58]

I wonder whether any historian of the future will ever be able to paint Winston in his true colours. It is a wonderful character – the most marvellous qualities and superhuman genius mixed with an astonishing lack of vision at times, and an impetuosity which if not guided must inevitably bring him into trouble again and again. Perhaps the most remarkable failing of his is that he can never see a whole strategical problem at once. His gaze always settles on some definite part of the canvas and the rest of the picture is lost. It is difficult to make him realize the influence of one theatre on another. The general handling of the German reserves in Europe can never be fully grasped by him. This failing is accentuated by the fact that often he does not want to see the whole picture, especially if this wider vision should in any way interfere with the operation he may have temporarily set his heart on. He is quite the most difficult man to work with that I have ever struck, but I should not have missed the chance of working with him for anything on earth!

Extracts from the minutes of a special meeting of the War Committee of the Canadian Cabinet, held at the Citadel, Quebec, August 31, 1943, at 3 p.m.[59]

[Canada was represented by the same nine ministers and three civil servants who had been present at the joint meeting of the British War Cabinet and the Canadian War Committee held almost three weeks before. They were joined by the three Canadian Chiefs of Staff (Vice-Admiral Nelles, Air Marshal Breadner and Lieutenant-General Stuart) and by the Secretary of the Canadian Chiefs of Staff Committee (Wing Commander Morrow).

The United Kingdom was represented by Churchill; the First Sea Lord (Adm. Sir Dudley Pound); the Permanent Under-Secretary for Foreign Affairs (Sir Alexander Cadogan); and the Chief Staff Officer to the Minister of Defence (Lieut.-Gen. Sir Hastings Ismay).

The Canadian record is detailed but discreet. It notes, for example, that Churchill read out and commented upon a summary of the operational decisions taken at the Quebec Conference. He gave information to his Canadian colleagues about the prospects of a capitulation by Italy, and referred to "the situation created by the presence of German forces." In both instances the Canadian ministers therefore had immediate access to information of the highest secrecy. The minutes printed below record some of the weighty subjects considered. The meeting examined proposals for an increase in the already substantial Canadian assistance to the Royal Navy, and then the postwar development of civil aviation.]

The War Committee, after further discussion, noted that Mr. Churchill would, in the near future, discuss with President Roosevelt the subject of postwar international air transport and would communicate the result of these discussions to the Canadian government, and agreed:

1) that Canada consent to be represented at a preliminary Commonwealth meeting on the subject, in London, in the near future, on the understanding that the meeting be informal and exploratory and involve no commitment on the part of the government, and that the nature of the meeting be fully understood, in advance, by the U.S. government; and
2) that the questions of the basis and locale of any subsequent international conference stand over for subsequent consideration.

POSTWAR INTERNATIONAL ORGANIZATION

The United Kingdom Prime Minister said that discussions of postwar organization with President Roosevelt had been of a tentative, exploratory character.

The U.S. government were thinking along the lines of a central agency consisting of the four Great Powers – the United Kingdom, United States, China and the U.S.S.R., and a broader committee on which all nations would be represented, but in which voting would be limited to regional or other groupings of the smaller countries with, for example, one vote for Europe and one for the Dominions.

These proposals were being given to the United Kingdom, unofficially, for study and comment, in the form of a memorandum. The Dominions would be given full opportunity to comment on this U.S. paper and on any other proposals for postwar organization which might be put forward.

Mr. Churchill observed that these tentative proposals did not accord with his own approach to the problem of postwar machinery. He would prefer a system of regional councils, a Council of Europe, a Council of Asia, and a Council in the Western Hemisphere upon which Canada would represent the Commonwealth.

The restoration of a strong France was essential to the security of Europe and adequate provision would have to be made for French representation.

The only firm basis for the postwar world lay in the continued close co-operation and association of the British Commonwealth and Empire, with the United

States, and the establishment of a strong and satisfactory understanding between both and Soviet Russia.

The Prime Minister observed that, in the Canadian view, the establishment of machinery which created even the impression of domination by the Great Powers would inevitably have grave results. After the war each nation would be looking to its own place in international organization. Clearly, each could not be given an equal voice in the councils of the nations, but some method should be sought which would enable an equitable apportionment of rights, functions and responsibilities to be made. It had been possible to leave the supreme direction of the war largely in the hands of the U.K. and U.S. governments, but the same conditions would not obtain in time of peace.

The War Committee noted the statements of Mr. Churchill and Mr. King.

EMPLOYMENT OF THE CANADIAN ARMY OVERSEAS

The Minister of National Defence [Mr. Ralston] enquired as to the prospect of employing additional Canadian forces in the Mediterranean. This question had been discussed at the joint meeting held on August 11th when he had mentioned the desirability of having a second Canadian Division and a Canadian Corps Headquarters sent to that theatre.

The United Kingdom Prime Minister explained this question had to be considered in relation to plans for operations against Europe. In the immediate future the U.K. government were under obligation to bring back certain forces from the Mediterranean to the British Isles. If further Canadian troops were to be sent out, additional British troops would have to be withdrawn. An exchange of this kind might well be feasible.

The question would be taken up at once with the War Cabinet and the Chiefs of Staff in London and, if possible, arrangements made accordingly.* If the movement were acceptable a request would be presented to the Canadian government, through the usual channels.

The War Committee noted Mr. Churchill's statement. . . .

RELATIONS WITH THE U.S.S.R.

The United Kingdom Prime Minister described the course of recent relations with Soviet Russia.

---

* In the event this proved impossible, despite W.S.C.'s efforts.

The U.S.S.R. had suggested to the U.K. government the establishment of a commission in the Mediterranean, on which Britain, the United States and the Soviet Union would be represented, to deal with problems in that area and, in particular, with immediate questions relating to the position of Italy. In addition, the Soviet government had proposed a meeting between the countries, at the Foreign Secretary "level," for the discussion of postwar questions.

These developments should be taken as further evidence of the determination of Soviet Russia to co-operate with the United Nations in carrying the war to a successful conclusion and settling the problems of the postwar world.

The War Committee noted Mr. Churchill's report.

Mackenzie King's diary, August 31, 1943

I pointed out [at the meeting of the War Committee] the unwisdom of talking too much about the Big Four governing in the post-war world. That, unhappily, we could not count on having the President and himself at the head of affairs for all time. That any post-war order would have to take account of the persons who might take their places, and that each nation would want its say and that the Dominions would wish their individuality respected. He [Churchill] spoke of different nations and said something would have to be worked out. It was clear, however, from what Churchill said that nothing was too definite even in his own mind.

Mackenzie King's diary, August 31, 1943

I asked if he [Churchill] thought Stalin would make peace with Hitler. He said he was positive he would not. That they had come to hate each other with an animal hate. He would never make peace with him. Later he said it was just possible that if Stalin went on winning, and got near to the borders of Germany, the Germans might prefer opening their Western front to British and American armies and have them conquer Germany rather than Stalin.

[W.S.C. told King, but not for repetition even to ministers, that almost immediately a force including a Canadian division would cross the Straits of Messina into Italy; a larger army would strike farther north.]

W.S.C.'s broadcast from the Citadel, Quebec, August 31, 1943[60]

Here at the gateway of Canada, in mighty lands which have never known the totalitarian tyrannies of Hitler and Mussolini, the spirit of freedom has found a safe and abiding home. Here that spirit is no wandering phantom. It is enshrined in Parliamentary institutions based on universal suffrage and evolved through the centuries by the English-speaking peoples. It is inspired by the Magna Carta and the Declaration of Independence. It is guarded by resolute and vigilant millions, never so strong or so well armed as to-day.

Quebec was the very place for the two great Powers of the sea and of the air to resolve and shape plans to bring their large and growing armies into closer contact and fiercer grips with the common foe. Here above all, in the capital and heart of French Canada, was it right to think of the French people in their agony, to set on foot new measures for their deliverance, and to send them a message across the ocean that we have not forgotten them, nor all the services that France has rendered to culture and civilisation, to the march of the human intellect and to the rights of man. For forty years or more I have believed in the greatness and virtue of France, often in dark and baffling days I have not wavered, and since the Anglo-French Agreement of 1904 I have always served and worked actively with the French in the defence of good causes.

It was therefore to me a deep satisfaction that words of hope, of comfort and recognition should be spoken, not only to those Frenchmen who, outside Hitler's clutches, march in arms with us, but also to the broad masses of the French nation who await the day when they can free and cleanse their land from the torment and shame of German subjugation. We may be sure that all will come right. We may be sure that France will rise again free, united, and independent, to stand on guard with others over the generous tolerances and brightening opportunities of the human society we mean to rescue and rebuild.

I have also had the advantage of conferring with the Prime Minister of Canada, Mr. Mackenzie King, that experienced statesmen who led the Dominion instantly and unitedly into the war, and of sitting on several occasions with his Cabinet, and the British and Canadian Staffs have been over the whole ground of the war together. The contribution which Canada has made to the combined effort of the British Commonwealth and Empire in these tremendous times has deeply touched the heart of the Mother Country and of all the other members of our widespread family of States and races. . . .

All this, of course, was dictated by no law. It came from no treaty or formal obligation. It sprang in perfect freedom from sentiment and tradition and a generous resolve to serve the future of mankind. I am glad to pay my tribute on behalf of the people of Great Britain to the great Dominion, and to pay it from Canadian soil. I only wish indeed that my other duties, which are exacting, allowed me to travel still farther afield and tell Australians, New Zealanders, and South Africans to their faces how we feel towards them for all they have done, and are resolved to do.

I mentioned just now the agreement Britain made with France almost forty years ago, and how we have stood by it, and will stand by it, with unswerving faithfulness. But there is another great nation with whom we have made a solemn treaty. We have made a twenty-years' treaty* of good will and mutual aid with Soviet Russia. You may be sure that we British are resolved to do our utmost to make that good with all our strength and national steadiness.

It would not have been suitable for Russia to be represented at this Anglo-American conference, which, apart from dealing with the immediate operations of our intermingled and interwoven armed forces in the Mediterranean and elsewhere, was largely, if not mainly, concerned with heating and inflaming the war against Japan, with whom the Soviet Government have a five-years' treaty of non-aggression.

It would have been an embarrassing invitation for us to send. But nothing is nearer to the wishes of President Roosevelt and myself than to have a threefold meeting with Marshal Stalin. If that has not yet taken place, it is certainly not because we have not tried our best. . . .

Let us then all go forward together, making the best of ourselves and the best of each other; resolved to apply the maximum forces at our command without regard to any other single thought than the attack and destruction of those monstrous and evil dominations which have so nearly cost each and all of us our national lives and mankind its future.

Of course, as I told you, a large part of the Quebec discussions was devoted to the vehement prosecution of the war against Japan. The main forces of the United States and the manhood of Australia and New Zealand are engaged in successful grapple with the Japanese in the Pacific.

---

* In May 1942.

The principal responsibility of Great Britain against Japan at present lies on the Indian front and in the Indian Ocean. The creation of a Combined Anglo-American Command over all the forces – land, sea, and air – of both countries in that theatre, similar to what has proved so successful in North-West Africa, has now been brought into effect. . . .

I have been asked several times since I crossed the Atlantic whether I think the Germans will give in this year or whether they will hold out through another – which will certainly be worse for them. There are those who take an over-sanguine view. Certainly we see all Europe rising under Hitler's tyranny. What is now happening in Denmark is only another example. Certainly we see the Germans hated as no race has ever been hated in human history, or with such good reason. We see them sprawled over a dozen once free and happy countries, with their talons making festering wounds, the scars of which will never be effaced. Nazi tyranny and Prussian militarism, those two loathsome dominations, may well foresee and dread their approaching doom. . . .

For myself, I regard all such speculation as to when the war will end as at this moment vain and unprofitable. We did not undertake this task because we had carefully counted the cost, or because we had carefully measured the duration. We took it on because duty and honour called us to it, and we are content to drive on until we have finished the job.

W.S.C. to Mrs. F.W. Clarke,* August 31, 1943[61]

I have just returned from five most delightful days spent at La Cabane de Montmorency and at the camp on the Lac des Neiges. It is the first real holiday I have had since the war began, and I can imagine no more pleasant place in which I could have spent it. Your husband has told me how largely you were responsible for the making of these two camps, and I do want you to know how very much my wife, my daughter and myself benefitted from our stay there and how sorry we all were that you could not be with us.

It was a great pleasure to me to get to know your husband. I sympathize with you both in your anxieties about your gallant son who is a prisoner of war.

---

* Wife of Col. F.W. Clarke, President of the Gulf Pulp and Paper Company and a director of numerous others.

[W.S.C. reached Washington on the evening of September 1, and remained there for ten days. He attended conferences with the American Chiefs of Staff and, in accepting an honorary degree at Harvard on September 6, spoke with feeling about the supreme significance of the English-speaking peoples' association, lauding the work of the Combined Chiefs of Staff; so fine a machine should be kept running after the war. On September 3, four years to the day from the outbreak of war, Allied troops crossed from Sicily and landed in the toe of Italy. The armistice terms were at last signed with Italy, and the news was broadcast on September 8; most of the Italian battle fleet made its way to Malta, having been attacked by the Germans. The Allied landings at Salerno, near Naples, began on September 9. They were fiercely contested by the German forces, and for some days it seemed possible or even likely that the invading forces would be thrown back into the sea. Churchill had told Attlee and Eden a week earlier that this amphibious assault constituted "the biggest risk we have yet run though I am fully in favour of running it."[62]]

W.S.C. to A. Eden, September 5, 1943

WELFARE 628

Surely we should say to the Russians "As soon as our special operation in the far North has been completed, we are willing, if you desire it, to withdraw all our personnel from North Russia. This of course will mean that no more convoys will come by the Arctic route.* We should be sorry for this, as it is the best route, and if the aforesaid operation succeeds it may become much easier. Nevertheless we will certainly withdraw our personnel if that is your wish. There is no question of their remaining under present conditions."

Let me know what objections there are to this course from the Admiralty or Air viewpoint. I think myself it is the only way to get consideration.

What has happened to the two British merchant seamen who have been sentenced to long terms of penal servitude by the Russian Courts for trifling offences? They must not be forgotten.†

---

* The convoys had been suspended since February; each one placed a heavy strain on Allied naval resources. They resumed in November.

† They were pardoned in late October.

W.S.C. to C.R. Attlee, A. Eden and the Chiefs of Staff Committee, His Majesty the King to see, September 7, 1943

WELFARE 650

The Italians have surrendered unconditionally and that is very good. But it will be far better if they will fight against the Germans and help to drive them out of Italy. One does not win a war in order simply to pay off old scores but rather to make beneficial arrangements for the future. It is our interest to have a friendly Italy whose people know they have been mercifully treated by the British and American conquerors.

It seems to me that Italy has much to give. We shall need at least a dozen or a score of Italian divisions to help us hold the Italian front against the Germans. We also want Italian manpower in England for many purposes.

At the present time apparently we are to repatriate all the Italian troops in the Balkans. But it may be that some of these troops would join with the patriots and help drive the Germans out or destroy them. This would be very good considering how few troops we have for all our needs. We must not be more nice than wise.

These views are warmly shared by the President and Admiral King whom I have seen this morning on my return. There is no need to make any great pronouncement at the present time. The Italians have got to work their passage but if they make good we ought to treat them certainly in everything but name, as Allies. It may be they will fight much better with us than they ever did for Hitler. We must not underrate the deadly character of the struggle against the German army, enjoying interior lines.

Of course I am immediately thinking of forming a powerful fleet against Japan. It is not much use keeping such a fleet loafing about in the Indian Ocean until our amphibious operations in 1944 are due. It would have a great moral effect both upon the Japanese enemy and upon all our friends in America if we sent a strong squadron round Australia to do a spell of say four months in the Pacific. Alternatively they could come through the Panama Canal, which would be an eye opener for the American public and make so many other things easier. I have asked Admiral King to think out what he really wants and in what way we can best help. His reaction to Cunningham's telegram No. 061246 was that he thought the Littorios ought to fight under the Italian Flag and with Italian crews.

I pointed out that such valuable ships must have resolute crews, but that perhaps some Italian eye-wash might be added.

The fact is we are probably about to inherit two new Fleets, the Italian and our own that was watching it. This is a very great event. The First Sea Lord is coming down here to-morrow and we will look into all possibilities.

I saw the President in his bedroom on return, and he is entirely satisfied with what I said in my speech yesterday [at Harvard]. I am now trying to set on foot preliminary studies to put the Combined Chiefs of Staff machinery on say a ten-year footing. He liked the idea at first sight. It involves no treaty and can be represented simply as a war-time measure. An organism of this kind once set up and maintained for some years in peace, would have such great advantages to both sides that it might well become permanent.* Of course I contemplate interchange of Officers at the Colleges, similarity of training and weapons, continued sharing of research and inventions, mutual accommodation at bases – all this springing up under the guise of military needs but in fact weaving the two countries together as the one ultimate bulwark against another war. There is no need for any decision at the moment, but I am anxious that you should know how my mind and the minds of others here are moving.

There is no doubt that Americans have a high respect for us now and have become deeply conscious of our military efficiency and strength. This is a great change from pre-Pearl Harbour and even from pre-Alamein days. I hope our countries will be pleased at the brilliant fruition of our plans and efforts. However, our chickens are not yet hatched though one can hear them pecking at their shells.

* * *

The Allies had gained the Italian fleet, and the use of their own ships which had been doing battle with Italy. Moreover, a large Italian army was scattered in the Balkans and the Germans might well be forced to retire, Churchill hoped, a considerable distance. For Overlord, every transport capable of carrying the armies, apart from those needed by the Americans in the Pacific campaign, was being used. Yet there were so far only two

---

* These hopes were eventually disappointed; the machinery of the Combined Chiefs of Staff was dismantled after the war.

U.S. divisions in Britain. After the initial assault, the build-up would have to be entirely American, Churchill explained to Smuts,

> as I am completely at the end of manpower resources and even now have to ask the Americans to interrupt the movement of field troops in order to send over some thousands of engineers to help make the installations and establishments required for the gathering of their trans-Atlantic army.
>
> These projects in Europe, together with the air offensive and the sea war, completely absorb all our resources of manpower and of ship-power. . . .
>
> I think it inevitable that Russia will be the greatest land power in the world after this war which will have rid her of the two military powers, Japan and Germany, who in our lifetime have inflicted upon her such heavy defeats. I hope, however, that the "fraternal association" of the British Commonwealth and the United States, together with sea and air power, may put us on good terms and in a friendly balance with Russia at least for the period of re-building. Further than that I cannot see with mortal eye and I am not as yet fully informed about the celestial telescopes.[63]

Retreating for a few days' rest, the President brushed aside the suggestion that his guest should move to the British Embassy and invited him to convene meetings as he wished. W.S.C. accordingly presided over the Combined Chiefs of Staff and other high military authorities on September 11 in the Council Room of the White House. That evening he travelled with his wife to spend a day with the President. The Sunday, September 12, marked their thirty-fifth wedding anniversary; he told Clementine that he "loved her more and more every year."[64] They moved onwards by train for a day and a half to remote Halifax, he brooding anxiously about Salerno and remembering the Dardanelles.

The Churchills sailed on the battleship *Renown*, and reached London on September 20 after an absence of nearly seven weeks. The "war machine" of the British government had in effect been transplanted for a while to Canada, as happened again in the following year – or rather, that part of the machine which determined high strategy and foreign policy. The domestic part of the machine, coping with innumerable problems, ran well then and throughout the war. But for that fact Churchill could not have spent so many months abroad.

It was settled that the Foreign Ministers should meet in Moscow, after much discussion of alternatives, including London. Roosevelt gave no more than lukewarm support to the idea, and Stalin as usual had his way. The same pattern was repeated in respect of the first meeting of the three heads of government; Stalin insisted on Tehran. Churchill would have preferred Cyprus or Khartoum. However, as he telegraphed to Stalin, "I have for months past informed you that I will come anywhere, at any time, at any risk, for such a meeting." Roosevelt understandably blenched at the notion of Tehran, but acquiesced.

W.S.C. said he must pay for his wife's passage to and from Canada. The bill has recently come to light; it amounted to £76.

7

Octagon: Quebec, 1944

At the Kremlin in August 1942, Churchill had drawn a sketch of a crocodile. When the purposes of Torch, instantly understood by his interlocutor, had been explained, Stalin said, "May God prosper this undertaking!" By rights, the crocodile should have possessed a soft underbelly, ready for the slitting. Matters turned out differently in 1943 and 1944, for the German armies in Italy resisted so tenaciously that hopes of a rapid advance up the peninsula had to be abandoned. Worse, from Churchill's point of view, was the fact that the Allied armies there had progressively to be weakened, in men and material, to provide additional strength for Overlord and the landings in southern France.

Subjects left open at Quebec between Britain and Canada – for example, those relating to the organization of international air routes after the war, and proposals regarding the 1939–1943 Star for those who had served in the Armed Services during the first four years of war – were taken up and generally resolved with goodwill. The possibility that a meeting of the Commonwealth countries to consider civil aviation might have to be held without Canadian participation was removed, because President Roosevelt said genially that he would put no unfavourable construction upon such a meeting; whereas the Canadian Cabinet, as they had explained to Churchill, had been troubled not so much by the President's attitude as by the fear that "well-organized special interests in the United States might succeed in presenting to the United States people a mischievous picture of the purpose of the Commonwealth meeting."

All had agreed at Quebec that the three great men must foregather. To the general surprise, the elderly and frail Cordell Hull made the pilgrimage to the Foreign Ministers' meeting in Moscow, which prepared the ground in an atmosphere of apparent cordiality. This was the more welcome because Stalin had recently sent a message so intolerable that Churchill refused to receive it and handed the document back to the Russian Ambassador in London. The British and Americans, on a longer view, urgently needed to co-ordinate their policies before encountering so implacable a negotiator as Stalin. For all the harmony manifested at Quebec, substantial issues still remained; for example, though Churchill had been given to believe that General Marshall would command the Allied armies for Overlord, the appointment had still not been decided. Like the British Chiefs of Staff, Churchill believed that opportunities in the Mediterranean were being lost. It was beyond dispute that Russia had now paid for more than two years the blood-tax on land, suffering losses and devastation on a scale scarcely imaginable. To the argument that a date for Overlord must be irrevocably settled, because by mounting that operation the western Allies would best draw German forces away from Russia, Churchill retorted that to take considerable strength from Italy, the only front where the Allies were doing substantial land battle with the Germans, seemed to be an odd way of helping the Russians.

Roosevelt and Stalin met for the first time at Tehran. With a candour which tells us much about his close relationship with Churchill, and reveals not a little about himself, the President had written in March of the previous year: "I think I can personally handle Stalin better than either your Foreign Office or my State Department. Stalin hates the guts of all your top people. He thinks he likes me better, and I hope he will continue to do so."[1] Since then, Russia's relationship with Britain and America alike had sustained some sharp shocks. Nevertheless, admiration for Russia's heroic resistance; the rapid advance of the Red Army; recognition that it was Russia which, as Churchill liked to put it, had torn the guts out of the foul Hun; fear that a serious breach with Russia would have unthinkable consequences; Stalin's steel as a negotiator; the confidence of both western leaders in their own powers of persuasion and their eagerness to believe that they had found a genuine response in Stalin – all strengthened the Russian hand.

At Tehran, arrangements for Overlord (to be an assault by thirty-five divisions with strengthened air and naval support) were confirmed, the date to be May 1944, if humanly possible – or, failing that, June. It was clear that Stalin would claim eastern Poland for Russia. This the British had no particular desire to resist, since they had long been convinced that Poland's former frontiers could not – indeed should not – be regained. What was less clear was the degree of control which Russia would exert in the crescent of states running round her borders from the Baltic to the Balkans and Black Sea.

The plans for the invasion of the south of France were also approved. They meant that a considerable number of landing craft would have to be kept in the Mediterranean, rather than sent to the Bay of Bengal. For the moment, the Allied armies in Italy were mired in dreadful weather. Nevertheless, it was hoped soon to mount another amphibious operation, near Rome. Churchill argued vigorously, but without success, for bold action in the eastern Mediterranean. His efforts to induce Turkey to enter the war, or at least to display a more favourable neutrality, failed.

Stalin made the vital statement that Russia would declare war on Japan once Germany was defeated. It is easy to forget now how important this factor was, and how long it continued to influence British and American attitudes, for none could know until the summer of 1945 whether the atomic bomb would work, and all the plans for the war to bring down Japan envisaged a prolonged and bloody campaign. Small wonder that a Russian undertaking to enter the war against Japan was valued at a very high price.

Roosevelt avoided seeing Churchill alone at Tehran, presumably on the theory that the Russians must not be left with any impression that the British and Americans were colluding against their Russian ally. Once the President and Prime Minister were back in Cairo, it became clear that the scale of help to China which Roosevelt had envisaged could not be provided. The plans were modified substantially. It was now also decided that Eisenhower, not Marshall, would be Supreme Allied Commander for Overlord. After Tehran, Churchill confessed that he realized for the first time what a small nation Britain was: on the one side sat the great Russian bear, with paws outstretched; on the other the great American buffalo; and between the two the poor little English donkey, the only one of the three that knew the right way home. He was to say something similar, but in much grimmer circumstances, fifteen months later after the conference at Yalta.[2]

Hardly had the President departed than Churchill fell seriously ill at Carthage with pneumonia. The situation was deemed so grave that Mrs.

Churchill flew there from London. In the early hours of December 18, her husband had a slight attack of "auricular fibrilation," about which, she confided to their daughter, he was "very upset . . . as he is beginning to see that he cannot get well in a few days and that he will have to lead what to him is a dreary monotonous life with no emotions or excitements." And again two days later, "Papa very refractory and naughty this morning. . . ." Churchill was accustomed to shrugging off illnesses which would have defeated most younger men. On this occasion, he made the supreme sacrifice and gave up cigars for a few days; his daughter Sarah read to him large parts of *Pride and Prejudice*, after which he completed that work before tackling *Northanger Abbey*, which he did not like nearly so much. On Christmas Day he took a meal for the first time outside his bedroom and presided over a conference with the senior military commanders.[3]

Convalescing at his beloved Marrakesh, Churchill received de Gaulle, to whom Mrs. Churchill said, "Mon Général, you must take care not to hate your allies more than your enemies." The General spoke English throughout, most unusually for him; and Churchill, to even matters up, insisted on speaking French.[4] Everything passed off agreeably, which is more than be said of some other encounters between the two. (On a previous occasion, when Churchill explained that restrictions had to be placed upon the General's travel, de Gaulle broke out, "Enfin, je suis prisonnier. Bientôt vous m'enverrez à l'iloman." When, at the third attempt by the interpreter, it transpired that this meant "the Isle of Man," Churchill beamed and replied, "Non, mon général, pour vous, très distingué, toujours la Tower of London."[5])

Churchill returned to London at the end of January, having been away some ten weeks. Meanwhile, the British Ambassador in Washington, Lord Halifax, had made a speech in Toronto that said in essence that the countries of the Commonwealth should fortify their partnership and leave nothing undone in the fields of foreign policy, defence, economic affairs, and other spheres to bring their peoples into closer unity of thought and action. Mackenzie King reacted with what the Canadian High Commissioner in London afterwards called "paranoiac fury," mistakenly believing that what Halifax had said "was all part of a plan which had been worked out with Churchill to take advantage of the war to try and bring about this development of centralisation, of makings of policies in London, etc."[6] Halifax had no notion that his oration would arouse such a tumult.

Mackenzie King's political opponents applauded its message; the Conservative Premier of Ontario had attended the lecture. Malcolm MacDonald had known nothing of it in advance, and once more had to weather the storm. He did his best to dismiss the notion that the British government and others were trying to revive an Imperialism which would leave the Dominions with something less than full sovereignty. Mackenzie King was perhaps making the most of the opportunity. He talked once again of going to the country and fighting a general election; he had, reported the High Commissioner, been put quite unwarrantably into one of his worst moods. "He is, of course, looking for a slogan which will win him the next Election and one which resisted 'reactionary Imperialism' would undoubtedly help to do the trick." All the same, King spoke warmly of the existing methods of consultation.

Lord Cranborne, by now back at the Dominions Office, judged that a serious political crisis had been averted by MacDonald's influence with King, who informed Parliament in Ottawa that he did not approve the suggestion of Smuts that Britain and the smaller democracies in western Europe should gather more closely together, or of Halifax, who thought of the Commonwealth as forming a fourth great power. Rather, Canada favoured collaboration with all nations seeking peace. "Behind the ideas of Lord Halifax and General Smuts there lurks an inevitable rivalry between the Empire and other countries."[7]

MacDonald himself told a Canadian audience later that spring that competition between great states must be replaced by co-operation, and confidence established. The goodwill of all the less-powerful nations would be required, and could not be gained unless they had their say in the settlement of international questions: "If we frame our post-war policy on the basis of the balance of power between Britain, America, and Russia we shall be heading for a disaster worse than anything which has yet happened to humanity." Not by accident, this address was delivered at Montreal. When it first came to Churchill's attention, he noted dismissively: "It seems to be suitably vague & recalls the boneless wonder." As controversy grew, he wished to send a sharp rebuke. Cranborne, although of one mind with Churchill in thinking that such musings went far beyond the normal functions of a High Commissioner, asked that a message from himself should be substituted, for MacDonald had "done great work while he has been in Canada. Mr. Mackenzie King told me yesterday that he thought of him as one of his own colleagues, and had no secrets from him, and this is the result of unremitting and devoted labours. . . . He remains in his present post merely from a sense of public duty. If he now receives a crushing reprimand from you, he will feel that he has not your confidence, and it will take the heart out of him." As on many other occasions, Churchill decided not to send his tart message. "As you wish," he minuted to Cranborne, though he could not resist an addition: "I do not mind his coming back to tease the Govt."[8]

King was then in London for the much-delayed conference of Dominion Prime Ministers, the first held in nearly five years of war. Churchill had prefaced it by reflecting in Parliament upon a wonderful fact: that despite all the disillusionments and privations of the two decades between the wars, the inner life of the Commonwealth and Empire had grown and intensified so that when the signal came in 1939, all had responded, from the poorest colony to the most powerful Dominion:

> What is this miracle, for it is nothing less, that called men from the uttermost ends of the earth, some riding twenty days before they could reach their recruiting centres, some armies having to sail 14,000 miles across the seas before they reached the battlefield? What is this force, this miracle which makes Governments, as proud and sovereign as any that have ever existed, immediately cast aside all their fears, and immediately set themselves to aid a good cause and beat the common foe? You must look very deep into the heart of man, and then you will not find the answer unless you look with the eye of the spirit. Then it is that you learn that human beings are not dominated by material things, but by ideas for which they are willing to give their lives or their life's work. . . . It is our union in freedom and for the sake of our way of living which is the great fact, reinforced by tradition and sentiment, and it does not depend upon anything that could ever be written down in any account kept in some large volume.[9]

At the meetings of Prime Ministers, Mackenzie King spoke as if the turbulences of recent years had never occurred, paying warm tribute to the thoroughness with which Canada had been kept informed about all the great questions. Every Canadian decision about the war had been made by the government in Ottawa. He had good hopes of improving relations with Russia, though conceding that no one could say how the future might shape. He had been glad to hear Churchill and Eden speak of the need for a strong France. The Prime Ministers ranged widely over the affairs of the world and discussed in a preliminary way the proposals for an organization to ensure the security in peacetime. King was satisfied that these discussions showed that the Commonwealth could not be treated as a unit possessing a single foreign policy. He took care to pay tribute to Malcolm MacDonald, who "had proved exceptionally helpful, and whom he consulted on many occasions almost as if he were a member of the Canadian Cabinet."[10] Proposals for a closer co-ordination of military policy were remitted for consideration by each government.

There was a general optimism about the outcome of the war, coupled with a degree of apprehension about Russia, but Churchill expressed his confidence that the spirit of freedom in the world would face up to the brutish regimentation of Communism, and refused to consider the possibility of a confrontation between Russia and the English-speaking peoples.

Everyone acknowledged that the methods of consultation within the Commonwealth had improved markedly. The Prime Minister of Canada argued, with much force, that any attempt at a formal unity of policy might bind the Commonwealth countries together in such a way that differences would be magnified; whereas the prestige of the Commonwealth, which had never stood higher than in 1944, was based upon a belief that it constituted a unique alliance of a particularly enduring kind, the members of which acted together not because they were compelled to do so but because they had the will. This gathering of Prime Ministers also demonstrated an extraordinary fact: that the foreign policy conducted during the war from London had in effect if not in name become a policy for the whole Commonwealth. Smuts and the Indian representative spoke strongly in that sense. King "felt that situation after situation had been met marvellously and the way in which they had been handled commanded the strongest possible admiration. In saying that, he felt that he spoke from the heart of the people of Canada."[11] Addressing both Houses of Parliament in Westminster Hall, he foretold that the security and welfare of the Commonwealth, and in large measure of all peace-loving nations, would depend on its capacity to give leadership in the pursuit of inclusive policies. This represented his profound belief: "So long as Britain continues to maintain the spirit of freedom, and to defend the freedom of other nations, she need never doubt her pre-eminence in the world; so long as we all share that spirit we need never fear for the strength or unity of the Commonwealth."[12]

We may pause here, on the eve of Overlord, to notice that the British Commonwealth Air Training Plan had by now achieved its original purpose, to create air forces equal in size and superior in quality to those of the enemy. Yet more squadrons of the Royal Canadian Air Force were to be sent to Britain, making a total of forty-four serving abroad. Canadian shipyards had by this stage built no less than one hundred warships for the Royal Navy, with more under construction. Of that year's Canadian budget of over $6 billion, more than a half was to be found by borrowing. The Co-operative Commonwealth Federation won almost all the seats in Saskatchewan, displacing a Liberal administration; this was the first victory ever recorded in a provincial election by a Socialist or Labour party. A little later, the Social Credit government was re-elected in Alberta by an enormous majority; the Liberal administration in Quebec was defeated by Maurice Duplessis, of the Union Nationale party; whereas the Liberals held New Brunswick with an increased majority. To Churchill's satisfaction, the American government had in effect asked that Ireland should close the Axis missions in Dublin, for it was widely believed that valuable information on military and naval matters went out from them, and the point mattered more than ever now that Overlord was close. When the Irish government sought Canada's good offices to secure the withdrawal of these American requests, King refused. Canada's contribution to the very large supplies going to Russia was also remarkable; for example, of rather more than 5,000 tanks sent since October 1941, 1,223 had been built in Canada, and since the beginning of July 1943, munitions had also been despatched directly from Canada to the U.S.S.R., in addition to those sent through the United Kingdom.[13]

Rome was at last captured on June 4, 1944. Two days later, Overlord was launched. The plans had been altered over the months to increase the strength of the initial assault, which meant more landing craft and warships. It is even now hard to visualize the scale of the enterprise, which could not possibly have been matched in 1942 or 1943. It involved more than 4,000 ships and numerous smaller vessels; 11,000 aircraft; and the landing of about 250,000 men in the first two days. Churchill and the British had to bear at the time – and have had to bear ever since – much criticism over their supposed lack of enthusiasm for Overlord. In fact, no belligerent had a more obvious interest in a swift ending of the war. Often Churchill is thought of as impetuous or rash; the expedition to Dakar in 1940, or the decision to intervene in Greece in 1941, or the attempt to secure Kos and Leros in 1943, may be taken as examples. His insistence that Overlord should be attempted only when it had at least a sporting chance of success – for nothing more than that was assured even in June 1944 – ought to be regarded as one of his chief contributions to Allied strategy. Mackenzie King had always supported this policy. The artificial floating harbours, an early version of which had attracted Churchill's attention during the First World War, which he had written about immediately after Dunkirk, and then pressed insistently from 1942 ("Don't argue the matter. The difficulties will argue for themselves."[14]), worked admirably and enabled thousands of tons of indispensable stores to be landed each day on the beaches of Normandy. On the eastern front a fresh Russian attack, synchronized with Overlord, pushed back the German forces.

Ottawa received in rapid succession the Prime Ministers of Australia and New Zealand, each of whom addressed Parliament, and before long General de Gaulle himself, who spoke to a large crowd on Parliament Hill. The time of the visit could not have been better chosen, said Mackenzie King pointedly, since French and Canadian soldiers were now fighting side by side.

By mid-July, Churchill was anxious that the three leaders should meet again; if that were impossible for the moment, he and Roosevelt must foregather. At first, the President was attracted to the notion of a conference in Scotland, but Stalin turned down the idea, on the grounds that he could not leave Russia. Thereupon Roosevelt made it clear that he would not come to Britain for an Anglo-American meeting. However, Mackenzie King had long since said that the hospitality of Quebec would be gladly offered, and so it was settled. Quite apart from his preoccupations at home, Stalin could scarcely fail to see the advantages of delaying a meeting of the three. The Red Army was advancing inexorably on several fronts; by the end of July it had almost reached Warsaw. Moreover, he had the Far Eastern factor to consider. With the Allies' mounting success in France and Italy, and the steady tightening of the tourniquet upon Japan, any summit meeting was bound to concentrate heavily on the Pacific; but Russia and Japan had throughout maintained diplomatic relations and a strict neutrality. Until Germany was defeated, Russia had no intention of fighting Japan, and for the best of reasons. In short, there was everything to be said for staying away. The rising in Warsaw, which took place with some Russian encouragement at the end of July, was during the next two months suppressed with brutality by the German forces. Whatever the reasons, upon which it was not difficult to put a sinister complexion, Russia did nothing of substance to help and refused requests that British and American aircraft refuel behind the Russian lines after dropping supplies and munitions over Warsaw. Stalin replied curtly to British and American messages on the subject.

The landings in the south of France, Dragoon, began on August 15. Churchill watched the proceedings from a warship at a safe distance, safer than he would have wished. For these landings, originally intended to coincide with Overlord, it was necessary to take away a good deal from the armies in Italy. Churchill deplored the process but had been obliged to give way. In Italy for much of August, he determined that the campaign there must be a main subject of discussion at Quebec. Numerous urgent questions were arising in Greece, Bulgaria, Hungary, Romania, Yugoslavia. The campaign in Burma demanded attention.

General de Gaulle entered Paris on August 25. A week later, Canadian Forces took Dieppe. In the first few days of September, Lille, Ostend and Brussels were liberated.

By then Churchill, again accompanied by his wife, had embarked on the *Queen Mary*. He had returned from Italy so unwell, with a high temperature and incipient pneumonia, that for a day or two arrangements for the conference were thrown into doubt. The "war machine" was on its way to Canada again – all three Chiefs of Staff, Ismay and two ministers (Leathers and Cherwell), with a third to follow by air in the person of Eden.

Rumours of a German capitulation circulated widely in the first part of September. Occasionally Churchill was tempted to believe, as he certainly hoped, that the European war would end quickly; more often, he judged that it would last well into 1945.

* * *

W.S.C. to President Roosevelt, September 1, 1944[15]

I look forward so much to seeing you again and to making good plans with you for the future in these days of glory.

J.R. Colville's diary, September 5, 1944[16]

I found a large and spacious cabin and devoured an even larger and more spacious dinner (oysters, champagne, etc.) in the P.M.'s dining-room. There were just eight of us, the P.M., Mrs C., their immediate entourage, Lord Moran, Lord Leathers and Lord Cherwell. Talking about a coming election the P.M. said that probably the Labour Party would try to stay in the Government (though the rank and file might not let them) until a year or so after the armistice so that they might profit from inevitable disillusionment at the non-appearance of an immediate millennium and might give time for the glamour to fade from a Government which had won the war. But if after that there was a great left-wing majority, let it be so: "What is good enough for the English people, is good enough for me."

After dinner I played three games of bezique with the P.M.

Lord Alanbrooke's diary, September 5, 1944[17]

I am not looking forward to this journey and conference. Winston is still always set on capturing the tip of Sumatra,* he has agreed to our airborne campaign on lower Burma, but limits his sanction to the capture of Rangoon alone without the clearing of the rest of Burma. This makes the expedition practically useless and what is worse converts it into one which cannot appeal to the Americans since it fails to affect upper Burma where their air route [to China] is situated. I should have a difficult enough task to get the Americans to agree to the Burma plans, but with the PM in the background it becomes relatively impossible. Added to all that I am feeling frightfully mentally tired and disinclined for a difficult conference!

[As usual, each side had said that its delegation would be kept small; and as before, each numbered some 250. The British party included a large cyphering staff. The incoming messages numbered 422 in the CORDITE series; 326 were sent to London (GUNFIRE).[18] Churchill was directly responsible for 112 of these; he received 114, including a daily summary of information, from home. In addition, he exchanged

---

* Largely because its possession would enable the Allies to harass Japan's sea communications between Burma and Singapore, and provide a jumping-off ground for an assault on the latter.

messages with Washington and used special channels for business of particular secrecy. Among the subjects in the main series we find meat contracts with Argentina; the uprising in Warsaw; the publication of a report about an explosion which had occurred in Bombay in April 1944; the future use of the New Zealand divisions; the prospects of putting a British force into southern Greece; demobilization plans; the scale of Lend-Lease after the defeat of Germany; the Prime Minister's wish that the Minister of Information should refer to "Aix-la-Chapelle," not to "Aachen"; Russian insistence that the four great powers with permanent seats on the proposed Security Council of the UN must agree even when one was party to a dispute; and the reported desire of the State Department to threaten or impose sanctions against Sweden, which the British opposed.]

Prime Minister's Private Office, London, to J.M. Martin,* September 6, 1944

CORDITE 10

Following received personal for Prime Minister from President Roosevelt. No. 619 dated 5th September, 1944.

BEGINS.

Replying to your 779, 780 and 781, I am informed by my Office of Military Intelligence that the fighting Poles have departed from Warsaw and that the Germans are now in full control.

The problem of relief for the Poles in Warsaw has therefore unfortunately been solved by delay and by German action and there now appears to be nothing we can do to assist them.

I have long been deeply distressed by our inability to give adequate assistance to the heroic defenders of Warsaw, and I hope that we may together still be able to help Poland be among the victors in this war with the Nazis.

ENDS.

Foreign Secretary has no comments except to say that our information so far does not confirm the President's.†

---

* W.S.C.'s Principal Private Secretary.

† Roosevelt's information was indeed incorrect. The Warsaw rising was not finally suppressed until the beginning of October.

J.M. Martin to Prime Minister's Private Office, London, transmitting the text of a telegram from W.S.C. to Roosevelt, September 7, 1944

GUNFIRE 4

There are a number of U. S. Service personnel returning home in this ship for leave I am told beginning from their date of embarkation. The sailing of the ship was delayed on account of OCTAGON and they may therefore lose in some cases as many as 7 days leave.

May I indicate through your good offices this will be made up to them? It would be pleasure to me if this could be announced before end of voyage and their anxiety relieved.

President Roosevelt to W.S.C., September 7, 1944

CORDITE 30

Your thoughtfulness greatly appreciated. Necessary adjustments will be made in all cases that do not interfere with war effort, which I hope may include all.

J.R. Colville's diary, September 6, 1944[19]

The P.M. says that after all he will not "beat up" the Americans about DRAGOON.* He will suggest that the controversy be left to history and add that he intends to be one of the historians. More talk about a coming election. If the Opposition tried to sling mud about the past, they would be warned that the other side, though preferring a truce to recrimination, had a full armoury of mud to sling back. The P.M. would not regret the loss of any of his Labour colleagues except Bevin,† the only one for whose character and capacity he had any real esteem. The others were mediocrities.

On another subject, he said that of all the paper and the theories one reads it was wise to pick out certain firm principles (e.g. milk for babies!)

---

* The landings in the south of France, August 1944, which W.S.C. had accepted chiefly out of deference to the U.S. government.

† Ernest Bevin (1871–1951), English trade-union leader and politician; Minister of Labour and National Service, 1940–45; Foreign Secretary, 1945–51. This remark did not express a settled conviction; on other occasions W.S.C. expressed his high regard for Attlee.

and pursue them actively. One of his major tenets was this: we did not enter this war for any gain, but neither did we propose to lose anything through it.

J.R. Colville's diary, September 7, 1944[20]

Lords Cherwell and Moran were invited to dine. The P.M. produced many sombre verdicts about the future, saying that old England was in for dark days ahead, that he no longer felt he had a "message" to deliver, and that all that he could now do was to finish the war, to get the soldiers home and to see that they had houses to which to return. But materially and financially the prospects were black and "the idea that you can vote yourself into prosperity is one of the most ludicrous that ever was entertained".

The menu for dinner was: Oysters, consommé, turbot, roast turkey, ice with canteloupe melon, Stilton cheese and a great variety of fruit, petit fours, etc.; the whole washed down by champagne (Mumm 1929) and a very remarkable Liebfraumilch, followed by some 1870 brandy: all of which made the conversation about a shortage of consumers' goods a shade unreal.

Lord Alanbrooke's diary, September 8, 1944[21]

Queen Mary

We have been travelling in the Gulf Stream all day and consequently living in a Turkish bath of hot clamminess. We began with a short COS and at 12 noon had a meeting lasting till 1.30 with the PM. He looked old, unwell and depressed.* Evidently found it hard to concentrate and kept holding his head between his hands. He was quite impossible to work with, began by accusing us of framing up against him and of opposing him in his wishes.

J.R. Colville's diary, September 9, 1944[22]

The P.M. had a slight temperature again and was highly irascible. Lord Moran does not think seriously of it – probably it is the heat – but he told

---

* Lord Moran said, "He glared at me as if I had invented the Gulf Stream."

me that he does not give him a long life and he thinks that when he goes it will be either a stroke or the heart trouble which first showed itself at Carthage last winter. May he at least live to see victory, complete and absolute, in both hemispheres and to receive his great share of the acclamations. Perhaps it would be as well that he should escape the aftermath. . . .

Perhaps foolishly, I took the P.M. a telegram from Attlee about the proposals for increasing service pay in the Japanese war.* The P.M. thinks these proposals inadequate and ill-conceived and has said so. This telegram announced the War Cabinet's intention, notwithstanding, of publishing them before his return. He was livid, said Attlee was a rat and maintained there was an intrigue afoot. He dictated a violent reply (which was never sent) full of dire threats.

W.S.C. to C.R. Attlee and A. Eden, September 10, 1944

GUNFIRE 34

You will by now have received my GUNFIRE 26. It would be utterly impossible for me to commit myself to a scheme of this kind for the war against Japan which I have not even heard discussed and with which so far as I have studied it I am not in agreement. Moreover as I have pointed out nothing can be settled about inducement until scale of our contribution has been settled in accordance with war plan.

I must pray you to use some consideration to me when I am absent on public duty of highest consequence. Naturally I will take full responsibility to House of Commons for any delay which arises on grounds of policy. I shall be back in fortnight and we can then go into the whole matter together.

W.S.C. to A. Eden, September 10, 1944

GUNFIRE 37

I am sure I may rely on you not to try to hustle me without discussion into approving pay inducements for Japanese war. This need only entail a delay of a fortnight or 3 weeks and Parliament will be quite content if a date is given within such limits when statement will be made. I will take full responsibility for this.

---

* Which, it was then expected, might well last for eighteen months after the end of the war in Europe.

My colleagues have really no right to make me responsible for so deadly a matter as inducements for war against Japan without giving me an opportunity of full discussion. The whole future of the war against Japan may be affected. I rely on your aid and friendship in this matter.

["The War Cabinet," Attlee telegraphed on September 11, "are greatly distressed that you should feel that we have shown any lack of consideration to you in asking you to authorize the announcement about conditions of service during your absence from the country." Detailed explanations followed. Should not one of Churchill's colleagues, conversant with all the facts, go out to Quebec?[23] It was partly with this purpose that Eden flew there a few days later.]

W.S.C. to Field Marshal Sir Alan Brooke,* September 10, 1944[24]

I should be glad if this [table of divisions deployed in Europe, dated September 1, 1944] could be brought up to date. . . .

It would seem that, taking Italy and France together, the British Empire has 34 divisions and the United States 30 divisions. This figure may have been altered by new arrivals, but in any case it shows the strong basis on which we approach this Conference.

Lord Alanbrooke's diary, September 10, 1944[25]

We had another meeting with Winston at 12 noon. He was again in a most unpleasant mood. Produced the most ridiculous arguments to prove that operations could be speeded up so as to leave us an option till December before having to withdraw any forces [for operations in Burma] from Europe! He knows no details, has only got half the picture in his mind, talks absurdities and makes my blood boil to listen to his nonsense. I find it hard to remain civil. And the wonderful thing is that ¾ of the population of the world imagine that Winston Churchill is one of the Strategists of History, a second Marlborough, and the other ¼ have no conception what a public menace he is and has been throughout this war! It is far better that the world should never know, and never suspect the feet of clay of that otherwise superhuman being. Without him England was lost for a

---

* He had been promoted to that rank on January 1, 1944.

certainty, with him England has been on the verge of disaster time and again.

[Commenting on this entry after the war, Alanbrooke remarked: "My criticism of Winston's wrath on that day was obviously unnecessarily hard, it should however be remembered that they were written at a moment of exasperation due to his attitude during the meetings we had held, and desperation as to how I was to handle the conference in front of me with his continuous obstruction."]

From Joan Bright Astley's *The Inner Circle*[26]

General Ismay was not happy when he arrived. Mr. Churchill had not been at all well and there had been serious disagreements between him and his three Chiefs of Staff. . . .

A tremendous reception at Halifax had added to the Prime Minister's fatigue, though he had not shown any sign of it. As soon as the *Queen Mary* had come into the harbour, she had been greeted by ships dressed overall, sirens in full voice, fire-boats playing their hoses, and, on the quay, hundreds of red-coated Canadian Mounties and dense crowds all around, on roof tops, everywhere they could find a vantage point. When he had come ashore, Mr. Churchill had walked straight up to the crowd, who were being kept back from the two special trains, and had given the 'V' sign. He had then called them around his observation car at the back of the train, and after a short speech, had led community singing, beating time with his cigar as he sat on the steps of his coach. As the train left, the crowd spontaneously broke into the National Anthem; it had been an impressive and moving moment as the train drew away from the sound of 'God Save the King'. As before, along the whole route to Quebec there were groups waving, crowds at the different stations and the many motor-cars which had been driven from outlying parts of the country to be there when Winston passed by.

Lord Moran had taken the precaution of bringing a specialist in antibiotics, Brigadier Whitby, and a nurse. Such was Mr. Churchill's resilience, however, that after a short period of private anxiety among those close to him, he recovered from the threatened pneumonia and once more confounded his doctors.

The *Globe and Mail*, Toronto, September 11, 1944

The announcement of Mr. Churchill's arrival on Canadian soil stilled a series of rumors that ranged from the barely plausible to the utterly fantastic. Highly imaginative speculation, fostered with a professional touch in the Hotel Clarendon headquarters of Canadian and international press representatives, paled into insignificance – was a puny thing – compared with rumors available from amateurs for the picking on the street.

The gilded palm, or any other suitable award, goes undoubtedly to the burgher who, on the authority of his wife's sister Françoise, who has a cousin at (the name is deleted for security reasons) said Mr. Churchill actually did come over with Air Marshal L. S. Breadner on Friday's record-breaking London-to-Ottawa flight, and was dumped by parachute at a censored locality to join Governor-General Athlone in a spot of fishing before the conference opened.

From Lord Ismay's *Memoirs*[27]

I was shocked to see the great change that had taken place in the President's appearance since the Cairo Conference. He seemed to have shrunk: his coat sagged over his broad shoulders, and his collar looked several sizes too big. What a difference from the first time that I had set eyes on him less than two and a half years ago! Seated at the desk of his study, on what I shall always remember as 'Tobruk morning',* he had looked the picture of health and vitality. His instinctive and instantaneous reaction to the shattering telegram had won my heart for ever. No formal expression of sympathy, no useless regrets: only transparent friendship, and an unshakable determination to stand by his allies. 'Winston, what can we do to help?' Thereafter I had seen him in action in many different parts of the world, and had never ceased to marvel at the fortitude which enabled him not merely to defy, but to ignore, his physical affliction. He had much in common with my beloved chief. Both were unspoiled by success; both had the exuberance of youth; both were incurable optimists. To see them together, whether at work or play, was a joy; and to read their telegrams to each other was a revelation of their mutual understanding and friendship. Above all, the President had proved, by all that he had done for us in the days when we seemed alone, that he was a friend who would never fail. It

---

*June 21, 1942.

was grievous to think that the shadows were closing in. There had been a marked change, too, in Field Marshal Dill. He looked frail and almost at the end of his tether. He would work till he dropped, but it was only too clear that his days were numbered. Within seven weeks he was dead; and the President within seven months.

Mackenzie King's diary, September 11, 1944

[During luncheon at the Citadel] The conversation at the table turned largely on discussion of personalities. It was clear that Churchill feels as strong as ever against De Gaulle. The President mentioned that he and De Gaulle were now friends. Princess Alice [wife of the Governor General, Lord Athlone] and I also stood up for De Gaulle and spoke of the favourable impression he made here. Finally Mrs. Churchill, I think it was, said we are all against you. It was mentioned that De Gaulle had two strains in him and he was quite a different man at times. The President having in mind the uncertainties of the times felt he would either be President or in the Bastille a year from now.

Similarly with regard to Madame Chiang Kai-Shek.* There was criticism of her pretentions and extravagances. Churchill not anxious to have her in England. Mrs. Roosevelt felt she found it difficult to distinguish between being at one time the head of the State, and at another, just a natural person. They all seemed to feel she had theoretically democratic ideas but really was unpractical. Churchill remarked to the President that he was the head of the strongest military power today, speaking of air, sea and land. The President said it was hard for him to realize that, as he did not like it himself. He could not feel that way. Asked me if I could feel that I was the head of a strong military power. I told him no. It did not enter into my feelings. Churchill said quite frankly he was sure if Britain had not fought as she did at the start, while others were getting under way, that America would have had to fight for her existence. If Hitler had got into Britain and some Quisling govt. had given them possession of the British navy, along with what they had of the French fleet, nothing would have saved this continent and with Japan ready to strike,

* Wife of the Chinese leader, née Mayling Soong; educated in the United States. She had accompanied her husband at the talks with Roosevelt and W.S.C. at Cairo in November 1943.

the President was inclined to agree with him they could not have got ready in time.

The President again spoke about his chances of re-election.* Said there was nothing they did not stop at. Referred to the story about Fala† having been left at Kiska and sending a destroyer back a thousand miles for him. All pure fabrication. What is most serious is that the vote regarding the army depends on the action of individual States. Several States will not allow their soldiers to vote. They [the soldiers] are favourable to the President.

I can see that he is really concerned; also that he is genuinely tired and weary. He has lost much weight – 30 pounds, I should think. He looks much thinner in the face and is quite drawn and his eyes quite weary. Churchill, on the other hand, who was sitting opposite to me, looked as fresh as a baby. He seemed to enjoy having a chance again to take some Scotch as well as a couple of brandies. It is a delight to listen to him talk. He does so in such a distinguished way, not affected but genuine. . . .

. . . In talking with Mrs. Churchill she told me she was very anxious about Winston. That he must really stop flying. That it was while flying that various temperatures were felt and the danger of pneumonia asserted itself. She said he was really very sick on the way over. Had felt the heat of the gulf stream very much. Had been in bed most of the time. It was only on the day of arrival at Halifax that he began to feel like himself again.

Mrs. Churchill said we must all try to prevent him going fishing whilst he was here. She realizes that this means sitting up late at night, etc. She told me that they were planning to go back on the Queen Mary which would mean that the conference must be over by the 20th.

[On the morning of September 12, W.S.C. presented his wife with a bowl of Quebec roses to mark the anniversary of their wedding in 1908. In that span of thirty-six years, he had been a member of the Cabinet for about twenty-two years and Prime Minister for rather more than four.]

The *Globe and Mail*, Toronto, September 12, 1944

Shining out of this early contact between Mr. Churchill and Mr. Roosevelt and their

---

* Roosevelt was standing for an unprecedented fourth term as President.

† The President's dog. Roosevelt remarked in one of his speeches that although he did not mind libellous attack, the dog resented it.

aides – and this impression stands out like a tank in a pasture – is the spirit of optimism and confidence that is shown by all, down to the last secretary accompanying the parties. The Prime Minister and his British party have just come from a London [that is] freed from the death and destruction of robot bombing* and is going to show her lights again and relieve her people of depressing blackout.

The British party, on two C.N.R.† specials (the Washington delegation came by C.P.R.**), rode through sun-bathed landscapes of New Brunswick and Eastern Quebec. Every station platform – and this includes a greater part of the night journey – held its cheering crowds. For the Prime Minister it was in the nature of a triumphant tour rather than a business trip of grim implications.

During that journey, in the hours of light, he was continually either on the observation platform or at a window. Persons in close contact with him said they reached the inescapable conclusion that Mr. Churchill was more buoyant than on any previous conference mission. They said that buoyancy was reflected among his staff. . . .

He came, dressed in dark blue of navy cut, brass buttons reflecting stabs of sunshine, chin a shade more aggressive in its upward slant [than on previous visits], cigar stabbing forward and upwards like the bowsprit of an old ship of the line. The smile was a bit broader and the eyes had a deeper twinkle.

A. Eden to W.S.C., September 12, 1944

CORDITE 147

Following sent to [British Ambassador in] Moscow. . . .

Please inform Molotov that we are glad to note that Soviet Government are prepared to agree to supply weapons and food to insurgents in Warsaw and to the arrangement of a plan for carrying out of this supply in the most efficient manner.

Proposals for carrying this out have been put to Soviet authorities by Allied Military Mission and we hope clearance will be given so that operation can take place tomorrow September 13th.††

---

* The attacks on southern England by flying bombs (V-1s, known to Londoners as "doodlebugs") began on June 13 and had just ended; but the attack by long-range rockets, V-2s, was beginning.

† Canadian National Railway.

** Canadian Pacific Railway.

†† In practice, the Russians did little to help the insurgents, and hampered British and American efforts to drop supplies.

W.S.C. to C.R. Attlee and A. Eden, September 12, 1944

GUNFIRE 86

If the question of the revised pay was so urgent and vital I might have hoped I could have seen it before I left so as to have some chance of talking it over with my colleagues. I am most anxious that the increased pay scheme should not be a flop. If so it would result in a great loss of prestige and of the initiative in these matters, and our hand might well be forced into much higher expenditures. From this point of view the comparatively low total cost of the scheme, i.e. one hundred million pounds per annum, caused me misgivings. . . .

I am in full discussion with the C. O. S. about the movement of troops to the East involved in Dracula,* etc. I am not in agreement with the excessive scale of the staff demands for Dracula nor with the length of time required. On this detailed discussions are proceeding here. Moreover the general military situation in Europe governs the date at which the first of the Indian divisions can be released from Italy. . . .

I have arranged to leave by the Q.[ueen] M.[ary] on 20th and hope to be back early on 26th. I will at once go into the whole scheme with you and the moment I am satisfied that it will achieve its purpose, namely, the contentment of the troops ordered to begin what will seem to them a new war, an announcement can be made. . . . It is really worth while avoiding precipitancy in so delicate and far-reaching a matter and I cannot believe that the British Public are likely to attribute hesitancy or lack of foresight to His Majesty's government in view of our admittedly successful conduct of the most complicated operations of war.

The *Globe and Mail*, Toronto, September 12, 1944

Electric bells have been installed at two hotels to inform newspaper-men of press conferences. Last year a dinner-bell was used to summon them but lost its popularity when a practical joker paraded hotel corridors ringing it in the early morning. . . . Mr. Churchill is an artist and his eye for color was satisfied yesterday as he saw the flaming trees of the Maritimes. He was assured that within a week or two all Eastern Canada will be gay with bright maple and other leaves and he indicated he would like to see it.

---

* Proposed amphibious operation across the Bay of Bengal to capture Rangoon.

Lord Alanbrooke's diary, September 12, 1944[28]

Today we started work and after a COS at 10 am we had our first [Combined] COS at 12 noon till lunch and again from 2.30 pm to 4.30 pm. It went off most satisfactorily and we found ourselves in complete agreement with American Chiefs of Staff. They were prepared to leave American divisions in Italy till Alex* had finished his offensive. They were also prepared to leave LSTs† for Istrian venture if required. At 4.30 pm we had an ordinary COS to discuss latest minute by PM on Pacific strategy. He is gradually coming round to sane strategy, but by heaven what labour we have had for it. He now accepts a naval contingent to the Pacific, a Dominion Task Force under MacArthur,** etc, etc. At 6.30 pm we had to go up to the Citadel for a meeting with him. He was all smiles and friendliness for a change. How quickly he changes. An April day's moods would be put to shame by him!

W.S.C. to A. Eden, September 12, 1944

GUNFIRE 93

I see no point in precipitancy. I will show your telegram to the President and we will discuss it together. Our present intention is that the [French] Government and its foundations should be definitely widened before we give recognition to it beyond what is already agreed. . . . I do not consider that grounds are established for so serious a change. On the contrary we should withhold our recognition as a means of leverage to make them broaden their base. . . . Why cannot you leave it alone for a while and let things develop? At any rate as at present advised I am quite unable to agree. The whole matter must be carefully considered here.

The President would be very glad to see you and would no doubt send for Hull or Stettinius.†† I suggest that if weather permits you start

---

* General Alexander.

† Landing ships (tanks).

** Douglas MacArthur (1880–1964), American soldier; Commander of the U.S. armed forces in the Far East, 1941; later Supreme Commander, South-West Pacific; formally accepted the Japanese surrender, 1945; dismissed by President Truman, 1951.

†† Edward Reilly Stettinius (1900–1949), Special Assistant to Roosevelt, 1941–43; Under-Secretary of State, 1943–44; succeeded Hull as Secretary of State later in 1944; U.S. Ambassador to the United Nations Organisation, 1945–46.

tomorrow, Wednesday, arriving here Thursday or Friday. Thus you will see him for a day or two before he leaves for Hyde Park. Do not on any account attempt to come if the weather conditions are adverse. You will also be able to tell me about the pay problem.

I will ring you up tomorrow about the same time and tell you it is my intention to come back by air. You may deprecate this but I will insist. This is of course cover plan as we talked over the open telephone. My intentions remain to leave on September 20th on the Queen Mary.

Mackenzie King's diary, September 12, 1944

Churchill took me into the map room and went over the different battle areas. What he is particularly interested in is the movement of British and other troops across the Adriatic over to the mainland and up the route that Napoleon took with a view to making a drive in through the Balkan States during the winter months and the spring, should the war continue beyond the end of the year. He said of course if the war should end in a couple of months, all this would go up in smoke but we have to be prepared with our plans in advance in case the war should run through the winter on into the next year.

W.S.C. to A. Eden, September 13, 1944

GUNFIRE 101

I am in general agreement* and am putting it to COS and President here. I think this has already occurred to the President. There is a general feeling among the Staffs that we ought to have a showdown with the Bear pretty soon, and we are in a much better position to do this than we were two months ago. But these are profound matters.

W.S.C. to C.R. Attlee and War Cabinet, September 13, 1944

GUNFIRE 112

The Conference has opened in a blaze of friendship. The Staffs are in almost complete agreement already. There is to be no weakening of

---

* Eden wished to warn Moscow that a British force would shortly move into Greece, not least as a counterbalance to the rapid advance of Russian troops in Bulgaria.

Alexander's army till Kesselring* has bolted beyond the Alps or been destroyed. We are to have all the L. S. T.'s in the Mediterranean to work up in the Northern Adriatic in any amphibious plan which can be made for Istria, Trieste, etc.

The idea of our going to Vienna, if the war lasts long enough and if other people do not get there first, is fully accepted here.

After their work in the Adriatic, the L. S. T.'s will of course be free to go on to the Bay of Bengal or farther as circumstances may require.

The President shares my view that U. N. R. R. A.† should be open to the Italians. Law** is coming here tonight and we will explain it to him. We are also preparing a friendly gesture to the Italians on the lines of my telegrams from Rome.

Lord Moran's diary, September 13, 1944[29]

There was a men's dinner at the Citadel tonight; the President, the P.M., Morgenthau,†† the Prof.,*** Admiral Leahy,††† Leathers, Ross McIntire**** and I were all seated at a round table. How to prevent another war with Germany was the only subject of conversation. The Americans were all for drastic action, maintaining that Germany should not be allowed ships or the yards in which to build them; what they needed could be carried in our ships. Morgenthau wanted to close down the Ruhr to help British exports, especially steel. The P.M. was against this. He did not seem happy about all this toughness.

'I'm all for disarming Germany,' he said, 'but we ought not to prevent her living decently. There are bonds between the working classes of all

---

* Commanding the German forces in Italy.

† United Nations Relief and Rehabilitation Administration.

** Richard Kidston Law (1901–1980), later 1st Baron Coleraine; British politician; son of Prime Minister Bonar Law; Parliamentary Under-Secretary, 1941–43, and Minister of State, 1943–45, at the Foreign Office.

†† Henry Morgenthau (1891–1967), U.S. Secretary of the Treasury, 1934–45.

*** Prof. Frederick Alexander Lindemann (1886–1957), British scientist, head of Churchill's statistical office from 1939 and Paymaster General from 1942; 1st Baron (later Viscount) Cherwell, 1941; an intimate friend of W.S.C. since 1921, valued highly for his "beautiful brain."

††† William Daniel Leahy (1875–1959), U.S. Admiral; Ambassador to France, 1940–42; Chief of Staff to the Commander-in-Chief, U.S. Army and Navy, 1942–49.

**** President Roosevelt's physician.

countries, and the English people will not stand for the policy you are advocating.'

I thought he had done when he growled:

'I agree with Burke. You cannot indict a whole nation.'

If the P.M. was vague about what ought to be done with Germany, he was at least quite clear what should *not* be done. He kept saying:

'At any rate, what is to be done should be done quickly. Kill the criminals, but don't carry on the business for years.'

Morgenthau asked the P.M. how he could prevent Britain starving when her exports had fallen so low that she would be unable to pay for imports. The P.M. had no satisfactory answer. His thoughts seemed to go back to the House of Commons and what he knew of the English people. In five years' time, when passions would have died down, people, he said, would not stand for repressive measures. He harped on the necessity for disarmament. At that point one of the Americans intervened: he thought that Germany should be made to return to a pastoral state, she ought to have a lower standard of living. During all this wild talk only the P.M. seemed to have his feet on the ground. The President mostly listened; once he remarked that a factory which made steel furniture could be turned overnight to war production.

After three hours' discussion there seemed to be an absolute cleavage between the American point of view and that of the Prime Minister. The Prof., however, sided with the Americans. At last Roosevelt said: 'Let the Prof. go into our plans with Morgenthau.'

Lord Alanbrooke's diary, September 13, 1944[30]

At 11.30 we had a Plenary meeting, which consisted of a long statement by the PM giving his views as to how the war should be run. According to him we had two main objectives, first an advance on Vienna, secondly the capture of Singapore! However he did support the employment of naval forces in the Pacific.

[After the war, Field Marshal Alanbrooke commented upon this day's entry:

"It is worth noting that the two objectives he had named in the Plenary Meeting were neither of them in our plans. We had no plans for Vienna, nor did I ever look at this operation as becoming possible. Nor had we any plans for the capture of Singapore. However, by mentioning these objectives he was not assisting in our discussions with the American Chiefs."

Churchill's opening statement contained a good deal more than Brooke's diary suggests. Having congratulated the U.S. Chiefs of Staff on the success of Dragoon, he pointed out that the Commonwealth had now entered its sixth year of war. Its effort in Europe, counted in terms of divisions fighting, was about equal to that of the United States, but had now reached its peak; whereas the strength of the American forces was ever increasing. The Italian theatre held the most representative British Empire army in existence: eight British, two Canadian, one New Zealand, one South African and four British Indian divisions. He understood that the Combined Chiefs of Staff had agreed that there should be no withdrawals from General Alexander's army until the German forces had been destroyed or pushed out of Italy. Marshall confirmed this statement.

In that event, it would never do for the armies to remain idle. He had "always been attracted by a right-handed movement, with the purpose of giving Germany a stab in the Adriatic armpit. Our objective should be Vienna." If the German resistance collapsed, the Allies would reach Vienna the more quickly; if not, Churchill had given "considerable thought to an operation for the capture of Istria, which would include the occupation of Trieste and Fiume," and was relieved to learn that the U.S. Chiefs of Staff would leave in the Mediterranean landing ships to provide an amphibious lift for the Adriatic operation if it were found desirable and necessary. An added reason for this right-handed movement was the "rapid encroachment of the Russians into the Balkans and the consequent dangerous spread of Russian influence in this area."

Churchill pointed out that 250,000 men had already been engaged in the Burmese campaign. It was estimated that the Japanese had lost 100,000; the campaign "represented the largest land engagement of Japanese forces so far." However, it would be most undesirable to go on fighting in the jungles of Burma indefinitely, not least because of the dreadful rate of sickness among the troops; hence Dracula, the proposed operation across the Bay of Bengal to take Rangoon. The question was whether the necessary forces could be moved from Europe to the east in time, before the monsoon of 1945, and the situation in Europe was not yet sufficiently favourable to enable a decision to be made at Quebec.

As for the war in the Pacific, Churchill pointed out that Japan was as much the bitter enemy of the British Empire as of the United States.

British territory had been captured and grievous losses suffered. He proposed that the British main fleet should take part in major operations against Japan under American command.

At this Roosevelt intervened to say, "No sooner offered than accepted."

Churchill also volunteered a large bomber force for the assault on Japan. Once Germany was defeated, perhaps six divisions might be moved from Europe to the east, to be followed by another six at a later date; and there were already sixteen divisions in Burma. He had always favoured operations to recover Singapore, "the loss of which had been a grievous and shameful blow to British prestige which must be avenged. It would not be good enough for Singapore to be returned to us at the peace table. We should recover it in battle."

However, all that was for the future and, as it then seemed, a somewhat remote future. There was nothing cast iron in these ideas, Churchill remarked; the first step was to undertake Dracula and then survey the situation. If a better plan could be evolved, it should certainly not be ruled out in advance. The essence must be to engage the largest number of our own forces against the largest number of the enemy at the earliest possible moment.

Having thanked Churchill for this "lucid and comprehensive review," Roosevelt said that it was a matter of profound satisfaction that, at succeeding conferences between the American and British representatives, there had been a growing solidarity of outlook and identity of basic thought, to which there had always been added an atmosphere of cordiality and friendship. He agreed that all forces in Italy should be engaged with the greatest vigour. In the west of Europe, one more great battle would have to be fought, since the Germans could not yet be counted out. He also confessed that, while he had not been greatly attracted thus far to an operation in Sumatra, this prospect had now "acquired greater merit." Would it be possible to bypass Singapore by seizing an area to the north or east of it, perhaps Bangkok? Churchill replied that there would undoubtedly be a large Japanese force in Malaya, and it would help American operations in the Pacific if it could be destroyed, in addition to achieving the great prize of the recapture of Singapore. Admiral Leahy then supported Churchill's view that the engaging of as many Japanese as possible in Malaya would be a most valuable contribution. It should not be overlooked, Churchill remarked, that at Tehran Stalin had volunteered a solemn undertaking that Russia would enter the war against Japan as soon as Hitler was beaten and "There was no reason to doubt that Stalin would be as good as his word. The Russians undoubtedly had great ambitions in the east. If Hitler was beaten, say, by January, and Japan was confronted with the three most powerful nations in the world they [the Japanese] would undoubtedly have cause for reflection as to whether they could continue the fight."[31]]

General Hollis to Major-General Jacob [London], September 14, 1944

GUNFIRE 126

There has been much manoeuvring over our offer of the British Fleet for main operations in the Pacific. At the Plenary yesterday President said "No sooner offered than accepted", but it was clear from a paper put in by U. S. Chiefs of Staff, and by Admiral King's attitude at today's C[ombined] C[hiefs of] S[taff] meeting, that while accepting in principle, they intended to use our Fleet only in the S. W. Pacific. They have now been committed in theory to our Naval participation in the Central Pacific and we have agreed to drop our second choice, i.e. the formation of a British Empire Task Force in the S. W. Pacific.

It was agreed to recommend that the planning date for the end of the war against Japan should be eighteen months after the defeat of Germany; this date to be adjusted according to course of the war.

We have agreed to the American version of a directive which, in effect, places the control of strategic bomber forces where we want it. In fact the situation <u>at the moment</u> seems nice and tidy bar the complex problem on scraping the pot for DRACULA which is not, I fear, more than an even money pre-monsoon starter.

[On September 6, the full Canadian Cabinet had agreed that, once the war in Europe was ended, Canadian military forces should take part in the war against Japan in "operational theatres of direct interest to Canada as a north-American nation." A week later, its War Committee met, knowing that a general election could not be long delayed. King held strongly that no Canadian government could send its men to India, Burma and Singapore and hope to win an election. The latest requests from Britain would, if conceded in full, have meant such an addition to Canadian expenditure that the Prime Minister and Minister of Finance agreed they could never get a budget of such size through Parliament. While the War Committee sat, word came that the British and Americans had agreed to let their navies fight together in the Pacific. That opened the way for a Canadian contribution, which Mackenzie King believed must be confined to the North Pacific. He felt the point so deeply that he would have to consider resignation if the other ministers felt differently – or so he remarked to his trusted confidant and eventual successor, Louis St. Laurent.[32]

The War Committee now gathered again, this time with W.S.C. present.]

Mackenzie King's diary, September 14, 1944

I returned to the Citadel and at 3 o'clock members of the War Committee met first with Mr. Churchill alone. I had asked for this. When we were assembled I said to Churchill the reason I had asked for this meeting was that we were contemplating a general election and that he would understand that all our policies would have to be considered in the light of the issues that might be fought out on the platform and we wanted to be perfectly sure of our position. I then said the main question is that of extent of participation in the war with Japan and read to him the statement which Heeney had prepared as embodying the decision reached both yesterday and at a meeting of the full Cabinet as to our preference for fighting in the northern Pacific rather than in the southern Pacific. Churchill instantly said that the problem really was one of whether the Americans were going to take over the whole business themselves. He said that has been their attitude. That so far as the British were concerned they had said to the Americans that they had to regain some of the territories which they themselves had lost in Burma, Singapore, etc. That they could not do other than insist on taking this in hand themselves. He said that only this morning the British had agreed to place their navy under the command of an American commander. They had agreed to fight along with the American navy as one. How far the agreement could be reached and what part Canada would play he said he would have to speak with the President about. He asked me to let him have the memo* which I had read and which he would take up with the President at once.

He then made quite clear that he did not expect the Canadians to fight in any tropical region. In fact he used those very words either at that

---

* The record of the Cabinet's decision of September 6.

time or later when the chiefs of staff were present that our men should not be expected to go into the Southeast Pacific. . . .

When the Chiefs of Staff came in the question was reopened without mention of a general election. Churchill stated what our preference was and repeated what he had said that the Americans would have to be consulted.

Minutes of a special meeting of the War Committee of the Canadian Cabinet held at the Citadel, Quebec, September 14, 1944[33]

[In addition to Mackenzie King, all eight members of the War Committee attended, together with the Canadian Chiefs of Staff, the Secretary of their Committee and four senior officials. On the British side were present W.S.C., the Minister of War Transport (Lord Leathers) and Malcolm MacDonald, together with the three Chiefs of Staff, Ismay and Field Marshal Dill.]

WAR AGAINST JAPAN: PARTICIPATION BY CANADIAN FORCES

The Prime Minister expressed appreciation of the opportunity of having the War Committee and the Chiefs of Staff confer with Mr. Churchill, the other United Kingdom representatives present and the United Kingdom Chiefs of Staff.

Mr. King explained that the question of the nature and extent of Canadian participation in the Japanese war had been receiving the consideration of the government and their military advisers.

In recent discussions, it has been generally agreed that, at the end of the war in Europe, Canadian military forces should participate in the war against Japan, in operational theatres of direct interest to Canada as a North American nation, for example, in the North or Central Pacific, rather than in more remote areas, such as Southeast Asia, that government policy with respect to the employment of Canadian forces should be based on this principle and that the form and extent of participation should be determined following the present Quebec meeting.

This represented a statement of preference in the matter of operational theatres. The government would be prepared to have Canadian forces employed in the Northern Pacific or in the Central Pacific area, the latter to include operations from as far south as Hawaii, and against, for example, Formosa or the Philippines.

The government could not take firm decisions nor could plans be made for appropriate Canadian participation until the general strategic plan for accomplishing the defeat of Japan had been settled. The roles to be allotted to U. K. forces –

Navy, Army and Air, in the execution of the overall plan would affect the form of Canadian participation.

In general, the government felt that the Canadian military effort should be in the main areas of assault through the North or Central Pacific and not in remote tropical theatres.

The Prime Minister of the United Kingdom emphasized the difficulty which the United Kingdom itself was experiencing in having the United States agree to participation by British forces in the Pacific. He would discuss with the President what might be possible in the matter of Canadian participation in the light of the statement made by Mr. King. The difficulty was that there were only a limited number of "front seats" for the Japanese war.

Detailed plans for operations against the Japanese and as to the part to be played by the British forces had not yet been settled. Only that morning it had been agreed that a full strength British Battle Fleet would operate, under United States command, in the main Pacific theatre. This would offer an opportunity for employment of units of the Canadian Navy in accordance with Canadian policy. It had also been agreed, in principle, that a substantial long range bomber force would be provided by the Commonwealth for the bombing of the Japanese Islands.

Solely for purposes of planning and subject to regular review, it had now been agreed to assume that the war against Japan would terminate eighteen months after the end of European hostilities.

[The meeting then discussed in greater detail the contributions that Canada might make to the forthcoming campaigns in the Pacific; arrangements for the acceptance by Eisenhower, on behalf of all the United Nations, of the eventual German surrender; other issues ranging from the occupation of Germany to the role of the 1st Canadian Corps in the Mediterranean campaigns; and then Canada's co-operation with Great Britain.]

THE CANADIAN WAR EFFORT; CO-OPERATION WITH THE UNITED KINGDOM

The U.K. Prime Minister expressed the deep appreciation and gratitude of the British government and people for the part played by Canada in the extent and quality of her military effort, in the provision of great quantities of supplies and in the generous extension of large measures of financial assistance.

The problems which had confronted the U.K. and Canadian governments in the course of the war had been solved through close and ready co-operation. The success of our joint efforts might be attributed not only to these factors but to the fact that our actions had been hallowed by a righteous cause.

The financial position of the United Kingdom, after the war, would be one of the greatest difficulty. She would emerge the world's greatest debtor, the world's only debtor. Assurances had already been received that the United States would continue those measures of material assistance which would enable the United Kingdom to play her full part in the war against Japan and to re-establish herself following the final victory. It was hoped that it would be possible for the Canadian government to pursue a similar policy.

The Prime Minister expressed appreciation of Mr. Churchill's remarks. This eloquent tribute belonged properly to the Canadian people themselves. The government had merely interpreted in action the will of the people. From the outset Canada based her policy on a total effort for total war. Canada would continue to do her part until final victory had been won.

The Canadian government and people were fully aware of the vital nature of the issues involved in the conflict and appreciated the unique role which was being played by Mr. Churchill in accomplishing the final victory.

Mackenzie King's diary, September 14, 1944

On the way to and from the Citadel I had a good chance for an intimate talk with Churchill. I asked him when he expected to have a general election. Said not to answer if it would embarrass him. He said he would tell me what was in his mind though he had not said a word of it to his own colleagues. He did not think that it was in accordance with democratic principles of government that he should try to carry on with a Parliament that was ten years old. Some of them would like to justify continuing for another year, but he did not feel that would be right. He said of course something depended on what might happen with the labour members in the present administration. Their party might call them out. He would be just as glad if that were the case, as it would be easier to line up and have a straight election. He thought the people should have freedom to express their views. He said of course, the election would come after the war. It might be that the war would string out. For instance, there might have to be fighting in the Alps with no real end. In that event he would come out and say frankly he thought the real war was over, that this was only mopping up and that he thought the time for an election had come. This would be three months before the election itself. He spoke as if it might be February when he would make that statement, which would bring an election about in May. . . . He believed that the people would return him again. He would then seek to form a new kind of coalition – one to deal with the domestic problems, the need for food, housing, etc. But what he would like to do would be to stay on in office until at least the troops had all returned to their homes and were demobilized. That would take at least a year. He said of course, there is the Japanese war. That he would like to see that through. He believed the people would give him the chance to see the Army demobilized and a start made on these problems.

I said I hoped he would not try to carry on long after the war. He had knowledge of so many things it was important the world should have the record from himself. He replied that all of this was practically in his papers already; except to give it a certain turn, there was nothing he could tell that would not be known in that way. I could see that his feeling at present is more than it was some time ago for a continuance in parliament. . . .

He said he thought the President would be returned. Said it would be ingratitude itself were he not, so far as he was concerned. He said he would be prepared to come and help by making speeches on my behalf to ensure my election if I thought that would help. I said he had already said things which were more helpful than speeches. That the tributes he had paid me were greater I believed than any man could have received from another. He said they were all meant. He also said they wanted me in public life for all that it meant to the British Empire for the problems that lie ahead.

Earlier in the afternoon when we were concluding the meeting with the ministers and chiefs of staff he spoke very feelingly of what Canada had done in the war and wished on behalf of Britain to thank us for all that we had done, the government, the ministers and he mentioned myself particularly by name.

[As in 1943, Churchill found time to go to the Legislative Buildings for a meeting with the Premier of Quebec, now M. Duplessis, and his Cabinet.]

From J.R. Colville's *Footprints in Time*[34]

Certainly the British left Quebec with a favourable answer to every one of the questions on which they had expected the Americans to prove difficult. It was to be a different story five months later at Yalta.

There was, of course, the occasional crisis. One, which affected me, arose when it was discovered that Churchill had failed to read the papers about the vexed 'Zones of Occupation' problem. The British having, to their entire satisfaction, been allocated the south of Germany had now changed their minds and wanted to occupy the north so as to control Hamburg and the other German ports. It was believed that the Americans would quite reasonably object to this capricious change of plan. However that might be, Churchill had not read his brief and the discussion with the President on this issue was to take place after dinner. The Prime Minister said he did not need to read his brief: he knew all about the matter. The Foreign Secretary and the Chiefs of Staff, disbelieving him, enjoined me with severe mien to make absolutely sure that he read it. Like Uriah the Hittite I was flung into the forefront of the battle by men who themselves seldom succeeded in persuading Churchill to do anything against his will.

I waited till he went up to dress for dinner and volunteered to read the brief aloud. He vanished into the bathroom. I followed, sat on a chair and started to read. Every now and then he submerged completely under the bath-water and it was necessary to pause in mid-sentence until he reappeared. I finished the document just before he went downstairs and was subsequently reprimanded for being late for dinner myself. The time-factor was something which Churchill never understood.

Roosevelt agreed to a zone-swap immediately the subject was raised. The arguments carefully martialled in the brief were not required; and had they been, Churchill would probably have used totally different ones with equal or greater effect.

J.R. Colville's diary, September 14, 1944[35]

While going to bed the P.M. told me some of the financial advantages the Americans had promised us. "Beyond the dreams of avarice," I said. "Beyond the dreams of justice," he replied.

W.S.C. to C.R. Attlee, Sir J. Anderson and War Cabinet, September 15, 1944

GUNFIRE 166

In very agreeable conversations yesterday between me and the President and Cherwell and Morgenthau all our desires were met both on munition and non-munition supplies. . . .

In addition to the above the President and Morgenthau opened out their plan for expanding the British Export Trade to meet the loss of Foreign Investments. It is proposed that the Ruhr and the Saar steel industries shall be completely dismantled. The Russians will claim the bulk of machinery to repair their own plants. In addition some International Trusteeship and form of control would keep these potential centres of rearmament completely out of action for many years to come. The consequences of this will be to emphasise the pastoral character of German life and the goods hitherto supplied from these German centres must to a large extent be provided by Great Britain. This may amount to 300 or 400 million pounds a year. I was at first taken aback at this but I consider that the disarmament argument is decisive and the beneficial consequences to us follow naturally.

Lord Alanbrooke's diary, September 14, 1944[36]

I hurried with breakfast and some office work and then saw Ismay. Found him very upset, having had a ghastly time on previous evening with Winston! PM had, on his own, wired to Dickie Mountbatten to find out how it was he was now wanting 6 divisions to capture Burma having originally said he only wanted 2 from outside. Dickie had wired back giving full details of the series of changes in plans that had occurred. As a result Winston had accused us all to Ismay of purposely concealing changes of plan from him to keep him in the dark. That we were all against him, and heaven knows what not! As a result Ismay had written out a letter handing in his resignation to him, and asked for my advice as to whether he should send it in!! I told him this decision must rest with him, but that I agreed it would probably bring Winston to his senses.

I then started off to see Winston at 9 am, wondering what awful row I should find myself mixed up in. To my surprise I found him in his bed and in a very good mood. Another wire from Dickie had arrived with new suggestions. He had now got over all his bad humour, he was now prepared to move 2nd Indian Div from Alexander, which he would not look at before! . . .

I then dashed back for a COS at 9.30 am which was followed by a Combined meeting at 10 am lasting till 12 noon. A very successful meeting at which we got the Americans to accept the British fleet in Central

Pacific, and also the Burma operation. We had great trouble with King* who lost his temper entirely and was opposed by the whole of his own committee! He was determined if he could not to admit British naval forces into [Admiral] Nimitz's command in the Central Pacific. At 12.15 we had another short COS to decide how to deal with King's evident animosity towards the conclusions we had arrived at. We decided to get the PM at the final Plenary Meeting to 'cross the T's and dot the I's' in this respect. . . .

My mind is now much more at rest. We have nearly finished this meeting and they are the most awful strain. Things have gone well on the whole in spite of Winston's unbearable moods.

[Reading this entry years later, Alanbrooke wrote:

'The fact that dear old patient Pug† had at last reached the end of his tether and could stand Winston's moods no longer is some indication of what we had been through. Of course, poor old Pug always got the worst of it, but he was always so patient, and made so many allowances for all Winston's whims, that I felt it would take a climax to make him hand in his papers. I believe he did hand in his resignation and that Winston refused to take any notice of it. But for all that it relieved the tension.']

W.S.C. to C.R. Attlee, Sir J. Anderson and War Cabinet, September 15, 1944

GUNFIRE 168

Following is agreed record of conversation between the President and Prime Minister at Quebec on September 14th, 1944.

BEGINS.

The Prime Minister said that when Germany was overcome there would be a measure of redistribution of effort in both countries. He hoped that the President would agree that during the war with Japan we should

---

* Ernest Joseph King (1878–1956), American naval officer; born in Ohio of British parents; Commander-in-Chief, Atlantic Fleet, 1941, and of U.S. Fleet, December 1941; Chief of Naval Operations, 1942–45.

† General Ismay.

continue to get food, shipping etc. from the United States to cover our reasonable needs. The President indicated assent.

He hoped also that the President would agree that it would be proper for Lend/Lease munitions to continue on a proportional basis even though this would enable the United Kingdom to set free labour for re-building exports, etc., e.g. if British munitions production were cut to three-fifths, U. S. assistance should also fall to three-fifths. The President indicated assent. Mr. Morgenthau however suggested that it would be better to have definite figures. He understood that munitions assistance required had been calculated by the British at about 3 and a half billion dollars in the first year on the basis of the strategy envisaged before the Octagon Conference. The exact needs would have to be recalculated in the light of decisions on military matters reached at the conference. The non-munitions requirements had been put at 3 billion dollars gross against which a considerable amount would be set off for reverse Lend/Lease. The President agreed that it would be better to work on figures like these than on a proportional basis. The Prime Minister emphasised that all these supplies should be on Lease/Lend. The President said this would naturally be so.

The Prime Minister pointed out that if the United Kingdom was once more to pay its way it was essential that the export trade, which had shrunk to a very small fraction, should be re-established; naturally no articles obtained on Lend/Lease or identical thereto would be exported for profit or sold; but it was essential that the United States should not attach any conditions to supplies delivered to Britain on Lend/Lease which would jeopardize the recovery of her export trade. The President thought this would be proper.

W.S.C. to Marshal Tito,* September 15, 1944

GUNFIRE 142

Your complaint of September 5 refers to a single American Air Crew Reserve Unit which is not under our control. The American General Dono-

---

*Josip Broz, known as Tito (1892–1980); leader of the Yugoslav Communists and partisans; from 1943 the British and Americans supported Tito's operations in increasing measure, despite many misgivings; after the war, Tito served as Prime Minister (from 1953, President) of the Federal Republic of Yugoslavia, which in 1948 broke away from the Cominform.

van's organization* wished to send in a Mission to Mihailovic† which had already started. The President on my representations has cancelled this. I do not consider that the facts at all warrant the tone of your note.

On the other hand, I have been increasingly concerned to see how large a portion of our ammunition and supplies is being used against your own fellow-countrymen rather than against the Germans. This, as I told you at Naples,** raises questions of grave difficulty not only now but in the future.

I am much disappointed that you have not implemented the arrangements made at Naples to form a United Yugoslav Government, which His Majesty's Government could recognize officially. This aspect may become much more important should the war cease and negotiations begin. I hope therefore that in making complaints about extremely small matters such as I have mentioned, you will not forget that the much larger matters in which we have done our utmost to help you all this time have not received sufficient satisfaction.

Sir Alexander Cadogan's diary, September 15, 1944[37]

Citadel at 12. P.M., Pres., A. [Eden], and at intervals Morgenthau and Cherwell, talked – or rambled – on a variety of things. It's quite impossible to do business this way. Stayed there for lunch – P.M., Clemmie, Pres., A. and Dick Law. Towards end of lunch, got on to Dumbarton Oaks. Both Pres. and P.M. rambled hopelessly. I tried to pin them down to the point, but they always wandered away. Lunch went on till 4. I came back to Hotel and had tea with Alan Brooke. Drafted a telegram to Washington about Dumbarton Oaks and gave it to A. to show to P.M. That may elicit some definite opinion. Also some notes of other subjects which they touched on this morning. A. went to dine at Citadel. Thank goodness I didn't, as there was to be a showing of the 'Wilson' film, which lasts 2 hours and 40 minutes; so they won't even *begin* talking much before 1 a.m.!

---

* The Office of Strategic Services, forerunner of the Central Intelligence Agency.

† Draza Mihailovic (1893–1946), Serbian officer; head of Chetnik resistance movement in Yugoslavia, and from 1943 Minister of War in the Yugoslav government-in-exile; Allied support was largely withdrawn from him after 1943; executed by Tito's government, 1946.

** Where W.S.C. and Tito had met in August.

[The conference at Dumbarton Oaks, Washington, at which Cadogan was the principal British delegate, had already been meeting for the better part of a month to work out some principles for the new world organization. A good deal of progress had been made; but the Russian delegation was adamant that a permanent member of the Security Council must possess a veto even in matters in which its own interests were involved. Although Cordell Hull had tried to prevent Cadogan from going to Quebec, W.S.C. insisted.

The purposes, shape and methods of this new organization presented serious dilemmas, not least to Canada, for if it were to have a largely regional basis, she would doubtless be dominated by the United States. If the great powers disagreed among themselves and each could exercise a veto, would any useful role be left for a middle-rank country like Canada, which aspired to play a serious part in the affairs of the world? And if the great powers disagreed strongly among themselves, would the UN be condemned to impotence from the outset?]

W.S.C. to C.R. Attlee, Sir J. Anderson and War Cabinet, September 15, 1944

GUNFIRE 169

Following is agreed record of conversation on 15th September.
BEGINS. At a conference between the President and the Prime Minister upon the best measures to prevent renewed rearmament by Germany, it was felt that an essential feature was the future disposition of the Ruhr and the Saar.

The ease with which the Metallurgical, chemical and electric industries in Germany can be converted from Peace to War has already been impressed upon us by bitter experience. It must also be remembered that the Germans have devastated a large portion of the industries of Russia and of other neighbouring allies, and it is only in accordance with justice that these injured countries should be entitled to remove the machinery they require in order to repair the losses they have suffered. The industries referred to in the Ruhr and in the Saar would therefore be necessarily put out of action and closed down. It was felt that the two districts should be put under some body under the world organisation which would supervise the dismantling of these industries and make sure that they were not started up again by some subterfuge.

This programme for eliminating the war making industries on the Ruhr and in the Saar is looking forward to converting Germany into a country primarily agricultural and pastoral in its character.

The Prime Minister and the President were in agreement upon this programme.

(Intd.) OK

F. D. R.

W. S. C. 15/9/44

ENDS.*

W.S.C. to J. Curtin, Canberra, September 15, 1944

GUNFIRE 144

I will certainly receive General Lavarack† and put him in touch with the British Chiefs of Staff.

The only difficulty here has been to persuade the Americans to give us the space and facilities to deploy in the Pacific. Some of them wanted to keep it all to themselves. However I have offered a British Fleet capable of fighting an action single-handed against the whole Japanese Fleet, to share in the main operations, and this has been accepted. We have also requested and obtained a proportionate share for the British long range Air Force in the process of bombing Japan to bits.

The military operations are of a much more complicated character and I will have to inform you later about them. In the first instance, of course, we must clean up Burma by taking Rangoon and cutting the Japanese communications. Thereafter we advance eastward across the Bay of Bengal, engaging the maximum Japanese Army and Air at the earliest moment. There is no question of disturbing MacArthur's command in any way. On the contrary, we shall be able to supply from our main Fleet a satisfactory naval component to guard his left flank.

None of these dispositions will prevent our placing in the Indian Ocean a second substantial Fleet capable of dealing with any detachment the Japanese may make.

---

* Both Roosevelt and W.S.C. soon abandoned this plan.

† Australia's military representative in Washington. W.S.C. acquainted the General with the results of Octagon and showed him before its despatch the telegram reporting them to Canberra. The Australian High Commissioner in Ottawa and New Zealand's Acting High Commissioner were also present at Quebec.

This conference has been a blaze of friendship and unity and can you wonder at it in view of the unparalleled victories being gained by our armies in every quarter of the globe? The above is most secret and for your own personal information. Heartiest good wishes.

W.S.C. to Lord Halifax, September 15, 1944

GUNFIRE 154

I have of course followed the Drew Pearson* incident and I cannot think it is of the slightest importance. He has been described as the champion professional liar of the United States and really might claim to hold the world title. We must beware of a tendency to worry too much about these minor jars. In the United States there is so much free speech that one thing cancels out the other and the great machine crashes on. I do not propose to trouble the President on these points when everything is going so well in all directions.

You had better verify exactly what I said to Parliament about the applicability of the Atlantic Charter to India. The statement was made in the house immediately on my return from Argentia [Placentia Bay] and has been several times referred to by me. It had full cabinet authority and no derogation from it has been approved by His Majesty's Government. The President has been very good to me about India throughout these years and has respected my clearly expressed resolve not to admit external interference in our affairs. A public statement by him might only add to his burdens.

C.R. Attlee to W.S.C., September 15, 1944

CORDITE 279

The War Cabinet were pleased to hear that the atmosphere of the Conference is so good. The news you give us about American acceptance of our views on future strategy in Italy is most heartening and the results

---

* Andrew Russell Pearson (1897–1969), of the *Baltimore Sun*'s Washington bureau; his column was syndicated by some four hundred newspapers. Pearson published articles criticizing British policy in India and the poor morale of the Indian Army. These allegations were taken up in the Senate in Washington and the press in Moscow. The State Depatment had apologized to the British Government but, despite British requests, had not issued a public repudiation.

will, I hope, compensate our Armies in Italy for the secondary role they have been made to play in the last few months.

[When Churchill raised the subject with him, Roosevelt said he would be very glad to have Canadian forces operating in the North or Central Pacific.

It was not yet clear how rapidly the Italian campaign might progress. At Quebec, it was decided that if the Germans retreated rapidly, the Allies should be free to make an attack across the Adriatic to seize the Istrian peninsula and aim toward Vienna. In that event, landing craft due to go to the Bay of Bengal, for operations against Burma, would remain in the Mediterranean. To the British, it was perhaps surprising, and certainly welcome, that the American Chiefs of Staff and President were willing to accept that option. It followed that there would be no further withdrawal of substantial units from Italy for the moment, and the landing craft would remain there until the middle of October, that being the last date for a decision as between the Adriatic and an assault on Rangoon.

Roosevelt and Churchill agreed that Italy had worked her passage. She would now have a larger measure of control over her own government, be allowed to send representatives to London and Washington and eventually take her place among the United Nations.

The two governments accepted General Eisenhower's decision that the various forces under his command should advance into Germany on several fronts. Field Marshal Montgomery had believed that better results would flow from one powerful blow against the Ruhr, and the directive issued from Quebec did draw attention to the advantages of a northern line of approach into Germany.]

W.S.C.'s statement during a joint press conference held with Roosevelt, in the presence of Mackenzie King, at the Citadel, Quebec, September 16, 1944[38]

It is a year since we met here. Well, no one can say that the conference last year was simply of an idle and agreeable character. Out of it came decisions which are now engraved upon the monuments of history. Out of it came arrangements by which our vast armies were hurled across the sea, forced their way on shore in the teeth of the enemy's fire and fortifications, broke up his armed strength, and liberated, almost as if by enchantment, the dear and beautiful land of France, so long held under the corroding heel of the Hun....

A curious feature in this conference has struck me. I read some of the papers when I am over here, these great big papers about an inch thick – very different from the little sheets with which we get on in Great Britain. I read these papers, and I see from time to time suggestions that the British wish to shirk their obligations in the Japanese war, and to throw the whole burden on the United States. And that astonished me very much, because as a matter of fact, the conference has been marked by exactly the opposite tendency. If there was any point of difference which had to be adjusted, it was that we undoubtedly felt that the United States meant to keep too much of it to themselves. But I am glad to say we have arrived at a thoroughly amicable agreement, and that Great Britain with her fleet and her air force and, according to whatever plans are made, her military forces, all that can be carried by the shipping of the world to the scene of action, will be represented in the main struggle with Japan. And we shall go on to the end.

And of course, Mr. Mackenzie King and the Dominion of Canada came up and said that they insisted on having their part assigned to them too. And that is the feeling. It is not a question of people shirking an awkward and painful job. It is a question of a stern resolve of all parties to assert their right to be in at the death, with forces proportionate to their national strength. So that, I think, may be given full publicity. . . .

When I have the rare and fortunate chance to meet the President of the United States, we are not limited in our discussions by any sphere. We talk over the whole position in every aspect – the military, economic, diplomatic, financial. All is examined. And obviously that should be so. The fact that we have worked so long together, and the fact that we have got to know each other so well under the hard stresses of war, make the solution of problems so much simpler, so swift. What an ineffectual method of conveying human thought correspondence is – even when it is telegraphed with all the rapidity and all the facilities of modern intercommunication! They are simply dead blank walls compared to personal contacts. And that applies not only to the President and the Prime Minister of Great Britain, it applies to our principal officers, who at every stage enter in the closest association and have established friendships which have greatly aided the tasks and the toils of our fighting troops.

[At the end of this address, the whole assembly of journalists, more than two hundred of them, broke into spontaneous applause.]

J.R. Colville's diary, September 16, 1944[39]

The Conference ended and the skies cleared for the occasion, hot sun burning down on the terrace and roof of the Citadel. There was a Plenary meeting at noon. After lunch the Chancellor of McGill University and the Senate arrived to confer honorary degrees on the President and the P.M. They, with the Athlones who today returned from their tour, assembled on the roof outside the sunroom for the ceremony. Both the P.M. and the President, the latter wheeled along in his chair by his black servant, were strange spectacles in their academic dress. They both made speeches. Lord Athlone said that both he and the P.M. had been educated "by Degrees".

Then, still on the sun roof, there followed a joint press conference. The battery of photographers and reporters was formidable indeed. The scene was as follows: in the background rose the great bulk of the Château Frontenac; at the end of the parapet hung the flags of the three countries; below ran the St Lawrence, with a few white sails; and around clustered a great crowd, mostly journalists but, interspersed among them, the members of McGill Senate in their academic robes, the Athlones and their Household, Mrs Churchill, Mr Eden, Lord Leathers and the Prof. Facing the mob sat the President, the P.M. and Mackenzie King flanked by splendid mounties and leering G-men. The President spoke first, scarcely audible above the clicking cameras, and then the P.M. gave an impromptu talk which was truly remarkable for its force and eloquence. It was important that he should say nothing which the Republicans could construe as aid for Roosevelt in the forthcoming Presidential elections (they are already playing that tune) and I do not think he did. . . .

The King sent a most cold message in reply to the P.M.'s requests for a fraternal greeting to the Duke of Windsor, whom the P.M. is to see at Hyde Park on Monday. The P.M. dictated to me rather a crushing answer, but, as often, he subsequently had it destroyed and replaced by one more conciliatory.

A. Eden to the Foreign Office, London, September 17, 1944

GUNFIRE 247

I have discussed with the Prime Minister Soviet attitude regarding Bulgaria as reported in telegram Cordite No. 316. Our views are as follows:

Behaviour of Soviet Government is exasperating and disingenuous. Having gone to war with Bulgaria for a few days only, Soviets are now claiming the lead in armistice terms and already planning to obtain co-belligerent status for Bulgaria. These pretensions and manoeuvres cannot fail to be displeasing to H. M. G. who have been at war with Bulgaria for more than four years and who have special relationships with Greece, to whom admission of Bulgaria, her bitterest enemy, to co-belligerent status would be intolerable. . . .

The Prime Minister and I feel that His Majesty's Government should be prepared to accept an arrangement with the Soviet Government which would recognise that the Soviet Union take the lead in Bulgaria and that His Majesty's Government take the lead in Greece. . . .

Further question arises whether we should try to extend the proposed arrangement about Bulgaria to cover the Balkans as a whole. We have already informed the Soviet Union that we recognise that they should take the lead in Roumania while we take the lead in Greece. There remains Yugoslavia. Here we should require the Soviet Government, as part of the general arrangement, to agree that, on matters concerning Yugoslavia, there should be close consultation between us and that it is our common interest that Yugoslavia should be a strong, united, independent and democratic State. As regards Albania, Soviet Union joined us and the U. S. Government in declaring that we stand for the independence of the country, and it should suffice to provide for close consultation between H. M. G. and the Soviet Government.

The State Department did not like our arrangement with the Soviet Government about Roumania and Greece, and will no doubt equally dislike the suggested arrangement about Bulgaria and Greece. The Prime Minister will, however, speak to the President on the subject.

Mackenzie King to W.S.C., September 17, 1944[40]

The Citadel
Quebec

My dear Winston:

No remembrance could have begun to express in like manner the intimacy of the friendship and the completeness of the confidence you have accorded me throughout these years of war as do the little silver models [of the Mulberry harbours], so beautiful in themselves, and which symbolize, so perfectly, the secret of the success of the invasion.

To have received this gift from your own hand, here at the Citadel, where so many of the plans have been worked out, including, if I'm not mistaken, that [?] of the bridging of the Channel, lends to your gift a preciousness quite beyond words. I can only thank you for what it means to me, and will ever mean, but this I do with all my heart.

May God continue to guide, and guard and strengthen you in the service you are rendering the cause of freedom in this war; and, through many years to come – years of peace – spare you to continue, in the service of your fellow-men, to extend in other ways, "the frontiers of life".

Your devoted friend
Mackenzie.

[Perhaps W.S.C. had realized from Mackenzie King's and Cranborne's tributes that the British High Commissioner in Ottawa had done remarkably well there. He had written in May to Malcolm MacDonald, "After all your excellent work I should very much like to submit your name to The King for Knight Crand Cross of the Order of St. Michael and St. George. . . . It may be a help to you in your work in Canada in showing the confidence we have in you." This offer MacDonald declined with thanks, because he wished to continue as "plain Mister."

During the conference Churchill asked him to become Minister of Civil Aviation. On the notepaper of the Château Frontenac, MacDonald refused politely; he felt he should remain in Canada during the next few critical months, for a High Commissioner with some years' experience would perhaps be more useful than a brand-new one.[41]]

Malcolm MacDonald to Lord Cranborne, September 17, 1944[42]

The Conference here is going well from the Anglo-Canadian point of view. The contacts made between our Chiefs of Staff in London and the Canadian Military Mission there before our Chiefs of Staff sailed had been useful in working out general, tentative plans about Canada's part in the Pacific war. So when the Chiefs of Staff arrived here they already had a fair idea of what the Canadians would like and how their desires might be fitted into the general pattern of military action against the Japanese. The exchange of opinions has gone further here. . . .

Mr. Churchill has been at great pains to keep Mr. Mackenzie King and his colleagues informed. Between you and me, his attitude with the Canadians is far better now than it was up to eighteen months ago. He is friendly and generally approachable, gives them lots of confidential information, and is more or less ready to discuss patiently and reasonably any question which they wish to raise. This makes them feel that he regards them as real comrades. They used to admire him enormously, but from a distance and with a certain sense that they were naughty children whom the headmaster saw occasionally with no particular pleasure. They now admire him at least as much as they ever did, not only as a great but forbidding leader, but also as a friend and good companion. Relations between him and them are really excellent. Of course, it doesn't do any harm with them when he indicates clearly, as he did at his meeting with them the other day, that he thinks they have done a really magnificent job and hopes that they will be returned to power again at the next Election!

At the end of the meeting [on September 14] he made a very sincere and moving speech to Mr. Mackenzie King and his colleagues about Canada's war effort and the position of greatly enhanced importance which this has given the Dominion in world affairs. Mackenzie King replied with some equally sincere and moving words about Canada's admiration and affection for Winston. It was a good show.

Mackenzie King's diary, September 17, 1944

Churchill invited me to come back to have dinner with them tonight before they start off for the train. He has been exceedingly thoughtful in that way, never failing to extend an invitation. . . .

When Mrs. Churchill came into the room she said this is our last night here. It is a very special occasion. We must have some little celebration before we start. Mr. King, you must join us in a glass of champagne. I said all right Mrs. Churchill if you say so I will, but it is only because you ask it and because of the occasion.

The dinner was really a very enjoyable one. Churchill sat and talked like one who was father of a family. I have seldom seen him more placid quiet and in a thoroughly contented mood. Most of the conversation was across the table between us. He spoke about the war and a good deal about

De Gaulle toward whom he still entertains feelings of great distrust. . . . He spoke particularly of Canada's part in the war, of how exceptional in every way it was. He raised his glass to me and reached across the table to touch mine, and then was quite eloquent on the relief from bondage, regaining full freedom, etc. It was really quite a little ceremony, all related to the close friendship which we had enjoyed. I recalled that it was 44 years since we had first met. . . . Finally when he was about to arise I lifted my glass, looked across at him and said God bless, guide and guard you. His eyes filled with tears, he rose and when he came across to my side of the table he put my arm in his and spoke about the years we have had together; how faithful a friend I have been; of the little dance we had together at Chequers. I told him if spared we would have yet another in the days of Victory.

The *Globe and Mail*, Toronto, September 18, 1944

Mr. Churchill was wise to dispose in emphatic fashion of unfounded suggestions freely bruited by mischief-makers in the United States that, as soon as Nazi Germany was subdued, Britain would develop a selfish lukewarmness about the war in the Pacific, and leave the whole burden of it to the United States. There was no niggling reservation about his definite pledges that as soon as victory came in Europe Britain would throw all her fighting resources into the Pacific war, and that the only limit to their employment would be the availability of adequate bases and the practicability of furnishing them with necessary supplies which the huge distances of the Pacific Ocean make difficult. . . .

The United States is in the middle of a Presidential election campaign and Canada is to have a Federal election soon. These factors no doubt explain the absence of "pre" or "post" conference oratory. Indeed, in the United States partisans had openly prejudged the conference as an election "build-up," and freely predicted that it would be made the opportunity for the British Leader to do some "carpet-bagging."

Prime Minister Churchill has been most generous in his praise of the United States war effort in the past, as he has been generous in his praise of Canada. His warm feeling for the President and the American people is as well known as his warm feeling toward the Canadian people. Silence cannot cool that feeling. But there was no "carpet-bagging" at Quebec. The British Leader was very careful that no word of his should be misconstrued as an intrusion in domestic affairs.

[The Presidential election being but seven weeks away, Churchill accepted an invitation to spend a couple of days at Hyde Park; a sojourn at the White House or even the British Embassy might well have been exploited by Roosevelt's opponents. As a courtesy to Churchill, the invaluable Harry Hopkins, who had fallen out of favour with Roosevelt some while before, was invited.

It was already clear that Russia would not accept any of the proffered compromises in the matter of the veto. That tricky question was postponed for consideration after the election, as Mackenzie King had strongly advised. Nor was the position without other complications, because the American military authorities had apparently come to the conclusion that the Russian plan was the correct one and would work in the interests of the United States.[43]

Roosevelt promised that, immediately after the election, win or lose, he would visit Britain, France, and the Low Countries.

Most important of all, the atomic project had progressed so rapidly that a bomb of almost unimaginable power would probably be ready by August 1945. The British and Canadian contributions to the enterprise remained substantial, though the main burden fell upon the United States. At Hyde Park, the President and Prime Minister agreed that the utmost secrecy should be preserved. If and when the bomb were finally available, it might perhaps be used against the Japanese; full collaboration in developing atomic power, for military and commercial purposes, should continue after the defeat of Japan, unless brought to an end by joint agreement. Roosevelt and Churchill initialled this paper. It appears that no one else in the American government knew of it, and the partnership ceased soon after the war.

In this instance, as in many others, we know what was decided between Roosevelt and Churchill, whereas the processes by which conclusions were reached are often obscure. On this occasion at Hyde Park, Mrs. Churchill observed that Roosevelt's habits of work differed markedly from those of her husband, who laboured at all hours, whereas the President, though Commander-in-Chief, fixed his attention on the war for perhaps four hours a day. Not long after the war, she dined in London with General Marshall. "He talked much about you & President Roosevelt," she reported to her husband, "with whom it seems he often disagreed & whom he sometimes did not consult – he said that the President would direct his mind like a shaft of light over one Section of the Whole subject to be considered, leaving everything else in outer darkness – he did not like his attention being called to aspects which he had not mastered or which from lack of time or indolence or disinclination he had disregarded. Mind you he did not actually use these words but the gist & I thought much more were implied."[44]]

W.S.C. to A. Eden, September 19, 1944

GUNFIRE 273

I still think that commercial or monetary considerations within the modest limits involved ought not to stand in the way of our meeting U.S. wishes so far as possible* in view of the immense help we are receiving in other directions. There is no reason, however, why the dissatisfaction we feel should not be expressed to the State Department by the Ambassador.

W.S.C. to A. Eden, September 19, 1944

GUNFIRE 284

You remember all the tales Bob Hudson† told us of the seven years famine in Europe, no cattle etc? It seems most important to have independent reports from France, the Low Countries and Germany as to the health and food supply of the population. I believe they will be found very much better off than we have been led to believe. Please get this under way at earliest.

W.S.C. to General Wilson,** September 19, 1944

GUNFIRE 272

Who is responsible for the atrocious lynching [of the chief witness in the trial of the former chief of police] which took place in Rome yesterday?

---

* In respect of a four-year contract which the British wished to make with Argentina for the supply of meat. Cordell Hull had made fervent and prolonged objections.

† Robert Spear Hudson (1886–1957), later 1st Viscount Hudson; British politician; numerous junior ministerial offices, 1931–40; Minister of Agriculture and Fisheries, 1940–45.

** Henry Maitland Wilson (1884–1964), later 1st Baron Wilson and Field Marshal; British soldier; General Officer Commanding-in-Chief, Egypt, 1939; in command of several campaigns in North Africa, Greece, Persia, Iraq; Supreme Allied Commander, Mediterranean, 1944; Head of the British Joint Staff Mission, Washington, 1945–47.

Such scenes reflect not only on the Italian Government but on the responsible military authorities.

[W.S.C. and Mrs. Churchill left Hyde Park that evening and embarked for home on the *Queen Mary* at New York.]

J.R. Colville's diary, September 20, 1944[45]

Lord Leathers, Sir Andrew Cunningham and Pug were among those at lunch, the P.M. being in the best of humours and form. He only clouded over once, when he spoke of de Gaulle and said that of recent years "my illusions about the French have been greatly corroded." . . .

Lord Moran (who is so critical that he runs down everybody in the party, especially the P.M., and so indiscreet that he does so indiscriminately) was obviously much put out by the course of the discussion on morale and courage, the P.M. being vicious in his attacks on the military psychoanalysts and declaring that it was more important to win victory by deploying the maximum number of men in the line than to waste thousands in rearward services for increasing the men's comfort.

Two noteworthy points which came out in discussion were (i) on the Russian front the Germans had to cover about twelve miles on a divisional front whereas in Normandy they had only had to cover four miles. Thus their effort against the Americans and ourselves was more concentrated than against the Russians; (ii) in Europe as a whole we had as many fighting men employed against the enemy as had the Americans. From the American papers one would scarcely suppose any British troops were fighting.

Lord Moran's diary, September 20, 1944[46]

Queen Mary

After a train trip from Quebec, we left New York yesterday, shortly before midnight, and the P.M. will have nearly a week at sea to turn over in his mind what happened at Quebec. On these voyages he really gets going and talks himself out, but he has been taking stock in a sober mood. Looking forward, he sees the future in grey tones; the old familiar buoyant note is wanting.

Moran: 'Did you find this conference less tiring than the Cairo meeting?'

P.M.: 'What is this conference? Two talks with the Chiefs of Staff; the rest was waiting for the chance to put in a word with the President. One has to seize the occasion. There was nothing to tire me. I don't have to work out things. And if they are not in my head I'm very good at handing them on to someone who squeezes the guts out of them for me. But I'm older, Charles. I don't think I shall live long.'

Moran: 'You haven't lost your grip on things.'

P.M.: 'Oh, my head's all right. But I'm very tired. Can't you give me something to pick me up? I wish I could go to the South of France for two or three weeks at Christmas and get the sunshine. You, Charles, could send me. I'd tell them you ordered me a rest. I have a very strong feeling that my work is done. I have no message. I had a message. Now I only say "fight the damned socialists." I do not believe in this brave new world. Why, Charles, tell me any good in any new thing. That is' – and here he put his hand on my arm in a kindly way – 'excepting medicine.'

[The Cabinet on the evening of September 20 unanimously approved a scheme which in most points met the arguments Churchill had advanced; the increases of pay for forces in the Far East had been settled in detail for the three Services and adjusted to give appropriate increases to all ranks. The Cabinet turned down Churchill's proposal that service pay and allowances should be provided for a period of twelve months from the date of demobilization for those who had fought in the Far East and could not find employment.[47]]

W.S.C. to C.R. Attlee, September 21, 1944

GUNFIRE 294

I attach the greatest importance to being able to assure the soldiers who go away from this country to what will be to them a new war on the other side of the world while all the rest come home to take jobs of peace, that they will have special unprecedented treatment on their return and will not be flung on to Dole. Indeed I feel this assurance is essential to peace of mind of these men. The objections you mention do not convince me. A refusal to accept a reasonable offer of employment would of course relieve government from further obligations. Just in the same way as a man who refuses a suitable job at the Labour Exchange cannot claim unemployment benefit. . . .

Moreover the money in question is only in the case of an unemployed man the difference between military pay and the ordinary dole which has been greatly increased. I cannot therefore feel the financial burden would be unduly heavy. Certainly not nearly so heavy as would be the cost of a serious breakdown in the willingness of the men to go to the Far East.

I cannot agree that these matters can be left over till the end of the Japanese war. [Real?] need is to give assurance and comfort now to men who will be going forth. As publication is about to be made without this essential provision I shall hope to [make?] further announcement to Parliament on my return. Meanwhile, I should be glad if facts and figures could be worked out for Cabinet to discuss with me. I am most grateful to my colleagues for their consideration.

Malcolm MacDonald to Lord Halifax [Washington], September 26, 1944[48]

We had a lot of fun at Quebec whilst the President and Prime Minister were there.... By the way he [W.S.C.] had been very unwell and in a towering bad temper for about three weeks before he landed in Canada. As you know, immediately on his return from Italy he had been threatened with another attack of pneumonia. Moran and his unmerry men filled him up with sulpha drugs which (a) cured him miraculously and (b) depressed him horribly. On board ship everybody was shaking their heads and saying what a pity it was that at the moment of the great man's triumph he should behave continuously in the worst possible manner. Then he set foot on Canadian earth and was given wild sing song receptions from Canadian crowds. All the harm that the sulpha drugs had done disappeared and all the good that they had done remained. He was at once in his most friendly and glorious form and remained so throughout the Conference. It was cheering to see him so boyish and gay and at the same time so powerful in intellect....

One evening at dinner someone asked him whether he did not think that the President was silly having all those thugs round him when he drove out in public. Security was of course a proper objective, but it could be carried too far. Winston shook his head very mournfully and exclaimed "Oh Security, Security, what muddles are committed in thy name."

On another occasion he was telling us about the propaganda which had been done amongst the German High Command before D-Day. He described how every kind of lie had been published about the places where we intended to invade Europe. We had let it be known that we were going to attack Norway and Denmark and the Balkans and Italy and the South of France, etc. Then Winston smiled to himself and told us that he had once uttered a "bon mot" on the subject. This was at the first meeting with Stalin in Moscow.* He said, "I said to Joe, 'In war Truth is such a precious creature that she should never be allowed to move about without a strong bodyguard of lies'. Joe liked that very much".

My third offering to you arises out of an occasion when I said – not for the first time – something that Winston disagreed with. We had been talking about Smuts and Botha. I remarked that South Africa was one of those countries with a climate which produced great men. Winston scowled, bit hard at his cigar and thumped the table. "It isn't climate", he said, "that makes great men. It's WAR." He then went into a trance of glorious eloquence in which he described how the churning up process of war threw giants into the places of high responsibility in the affairs of pygmy man.

[Churchill's expenditure was recorded in the usual meticulous fashion: a pair of gloves for $5.20; three dozen white handkerchiefs at $14.98; a tip of £5 to the steward on the *Queen Mary*; and other items, minus an Octagon allowance in the princely sum of £6 1s. 4d. The Prime Minister owed £14. 17s. 6d. He was asked to make his cheque payable to the Treasury, which he did at once.[49]]

* * *

The Warsaw uprising came to its heroic but pitiful end at the beginning of October. Whether Churchill believed at the time that Russia had deliberately allowed the Germans to crush the insurrection is debatable. What is certain is that in Moscow, to which he went immediately with Anthony Eden, Russia's explanation was accepted, as it was often to be on other subjects. They had gone there partly because they knew how markedly Russia's position was strengthening, and at a time when there was no prospect of another summit for several months, and partly to demonstrate to Stalin that the conference at Quebec did not mean that the British and Americans

---

* In August 1942.

were arranging everything significant between themselves or wished to leave Russia in the cold.

Churchill had long felt apprehensive about Russia's purposes, without coming to the firm opinion that they were evil or dangerous. He bullied and chastised the Poles unmercifully at Moscow, believing that if they did not make such terms as they could get, they would receive far worse later on. He was by no means insensible to Stalin's personality, and welcomed (as he put it to the War Cabinet) his "expressions of personal regard which I feel sure were sincere."[50] It was here that the "Percentages Agreement" was made, under which the two leaders agreed that in the countries of south-eastern Europe their countries should have this or that degree of influence; half and half in Yugoslavia, for example, a predominant Russian say in Bulgaria, and a British pre-eminence in Greece. The arrangement was never intended, at least on Churchill's side, to determine the shape of the postwar world. Afterwards, the document was held in Russian circles to constitute a shocking example of old-fashioned imperialism, of the kind in which the U.S.S.R. would never indulge, and was accordingly denounced as a Western fabrication. Only in recent times has it been admitted that the agreement was indeed made. The record of the discussion shows that Churchill recognized the delicacy of putting such a document to Roosevelt, who had repeatedly denounced "spheres of influence" without explaining what was to be put in their place.

That Churchill was trying his best for the Poles, as the Red Army rolled westwards, is undoubtedly true. British treatment of the Polish claims can be defended on the grounds that necessity knows no law, but on few other; and although many have believed that Churchill was clear-eyed from an early date about the Russian danger and the nature of Stalin and his government, the evidence will not support a conclusion so consoling. To be sure, Churchill wished to see the earliest possible Russian entry into the war against Japan, and he was desperately anxious that in Greece, where British sea power and land forces could be brought into play, the position should be held. But there was also the element of illusion. "I have had very nice talks with the Old Bear," he wrote to Mrs. Churchill from Moscow. "I like him the more I see him. <u>Now</u> they respect us & I am sure they wish to work with us. I have to keep the President in constant touch & this is the delicate side."[51]

Roosevelt was duly re-elected, though it is now plain that he was unfit to bear the burden. Churchill's own vitality had diminished but remained remarkable; after all, he reached the age of seventy in the autumn of 1944 and was still working a good part of the day and half the night. Those who saw him after his return from Russia remarked that he seemed rejuvenated. All the same, as the sympathetic American Ambassador in London had noted, the intervals between Churchill's illnesses grew shorter. No doubt each produced its undermining effect. The signs of extreme tiredness manifested themselves in lengthy monologues to the Cabinet and an inability to despatch business. The Prime Minister relied increasingly upon his experience and instinct. In the end, the Deputy Prime Minister felt obliged to type out a letter of protest, to the effect that Churchill had often not read the papers before meetings, showed scant respect for his colleagues' views on civil affairs and was apt to indulge in disquisitions "only slightly connected with the subject matter." Churchill was at first angry. When he showed the letter to his wife, however, she said that she thought Mr. Attlee was entirely right. Churchill replied to him:

> My dear Lord President,
>
> I have to thank you for your Private and Personal letter of January 19. You may be sure I shall always endeavour to profit by your counsels.[52]

Not that exhaustion had destroyed Churchill's nerve or will to act decisively when he saw the way clear. He was determined that Greece should not fall into Communist hands; British troops were sent at the invitation of the Greek Prime Minister; leakages from the State Department produced a painful public row with the United States. Mackenzie King disapproved of the British stance and said he might publish a statement that Canadian troops would not be used. There had never been any such intention, as Churchill swiftly informed him. "It is on such occasions as this that the British Commonwealth should stand together," he telegraphed to Ottawa, pointing out that American landing-ships and aircraft were helping the British forces in Greece.[53] In the event, King did not dissociate Canada from the intervention.

To beleaguered Athens, Churchill and Eden flew at Christmas. They arranged a reconciliation – or in some cases an armed truce – between the factions in Greece, insisting that the British forces would not be pushed out and that their purpose was to ensure that Greece had in due course the chance to decide its own fate. Stalin did not intervene in support of the

Communists, remaining faithful to the Percentages Agreement. This fact impressed Churchill, and undoubtedly inclined him to trust Stalin's promises a few weeks later at Yalta.

* * *

Before then, a crisis of the first order had arisen in Canada. High casualties in the field, the increased strength of the RCAF and the RCN, some decline in the rate of voluntary enlistment, all combined to convince the Minister of National Defence, Col. J.L. Ralston, that the government should now exercise its power to send conscripted men overseas. Most of his colleagues took the view that the system of voluntary enlistment would still meet the need. Ralston's enforced resignation was announced early in November. He was succeeded by Gen. Andrew McNaughton, himself a convinced believer in the voluntary system and until lately in command of the Canadian Forces in Europe. The Prime Minister found himself under strong pressure. Those in favour of conscription argued strongly on grounds of fairness and military need. These were the sentiments of many in anglophone Canada. In Quebec, the solid bedrock of the Liberal government's support in the Federal Parliament, very different views prevailed. King feared something much worse than a violent political quarrel: the possible dissolution of the government and the ruin of Canada's war effort. After his intermittent outbursts against the supposed British desire to impose policies upon Canada, there is something ironic, even sad, about the decision to seek Churchill's counsel in late October[54] – and also something understandable, for he had taken care to air this question of conscription, the most sensitive in Canadian politics, in their talks over several years. That he felt able to broach such a matter by telegram is a testimony to the confiding relations which had developed between them. The message went to London against the wishes of the Under-Secretary at External Affairs (Norman Robertson) and Malcolm MacDonald. Predictably, Churchill declined to give advice.

On November 22, King took the plunge. He announced that some of those conscripted would be sent to serve overseas. In a speech of three hours, he asked Parliament for a vote of confidence, revealing that he had invited Ralston and other ministers past and present to state whether they would form a government. The answer had in each case been "No." After many days of debate, the government was upheld by a comfortable majority. In the event, only about thirteen thousand men went to fight abroad under the new arrangements.

* * *

To the last, the German forces fought with tenacity. The Allied reverse at Arnhem, the slowing down of the advance through France and the Low Countries, the sharp shock of the German counterattack in mid-December, vindicated the cautious view which Churchill had expressed concerning the likely date of the war's end and, far more significantly, strengthened Russia's position. It had taken months to arrange another summit meeting. As before, the British and Americans did most of the travelling. Early in February, Churchill, Eden and the Chiefs of Staff watched a great American warship make its way into the Grand Harbour of Valletta, with the tiny figure of the President visible on the bridge. The Emperor of the West, as the British Minister Resident in the Mediterranean expressed it, was on his way to meet the Emperor of the East. It was not clear how much time either would have for the policies of the powers in the middle.

Preliminary conferences between the Americans and British there in Malta achieved little. The two delegations were housed a good distance apart at Yalta, the resort on the shores of the Black Sea chosen for the conference. We must assume that, as at Tehran, every known device for eavesdropping had been installed in the British and American quarters alike. Again, Roosevelt and Stalin sometimes conferred alone. They arrived at an agreement relating to the Far East, which was then shown to Churchill. It was not compatible with other obligations and in effect gave Russia a territorial reward for entry into the war against Japan – of which, German defeat being still some way off, there was as yet no sign. Despite the advice of Eden and Cadogan, Churchill felt that he must sign. Allied planning for the Pacific then entailed a long campaign of more or less conventional warfare, with amphibious landings and fierce fighting to capture groups of islands. Neither President nor Prime Minister could count upon an alternative. At Yalta, Churchill said to his daughter Sarah, "I do not suppose that at any moment in history has the agony of the world been so great or widespread."[55] He would in some moods confess to deep fears about the immediate future. He realized with dismay and distress that the President was increasingly detached, not least from his British ally. Nonetheless, a good deal was satisfactorily settled, at least on the surface; for instance, it was agreed that France should have a zone of occupation in Germany. This was the result of strong British pressure.

The most important single issue at Yalta was the fate of Poland, which had become a touchstone of Russia's intentions. That Russia would take the eastern part of the old Poland had long since been agreed; that Poland would be compensated in the west at the expense of Germany was also understood, though the boundaries were far from settled; but what mattered was whether the new Poland would be directly controlled by Russia. Stalin promised that free elections would soon be held in Poland, and signed a reassuring declaration concerning the treatment of liberated Europe. His assurances were accepted by the American and British delegations. In Parliament and in the strict secrecy of the War Cabinet's deliberations Churchill proclaimed his confidence in Russia's good faith and Stalin's fidelity to his word. "Our hopeful assumptions were soon to be falsified," Churchill wrote after the war. "Still, they were the only ones possible at the time."[56] In fact, other assumptions were made by some. As a future Prime Minister (Lord Dunglass, later Sir Alec Douglas-Home) remarked in the debate, the Yalta settlement could be accepted as reflecting the facts of power without pretending that it reflected justice.[57] The comparisons with the Munich settlement were understood by Churchill at the time: "Poor Neville Chamberlain believed he could trust Hitler. He was wrong. But I don't think I'm wrong about Stalin."[58] That mood soon changed. All the same, he had taken too nearly at face value Stalin's expressions of esteem, and he did not comprehend more than imperfectly the nature of the Russian tyranny. Others, including Roosevelt, were yet more seriously deluded.

When British troops crossed the Rhine toward the end of March, Churchill went to see for himself. On returning from this brief exposure to the discipline of Montgomery's headquarters he remarked that, if in earlier days he had consorted with the Field Marshal, Mrs. Churchill would have had a much easier life. Supposing this to refer to "his chronic unpunctuality & to his habit of changing his mind (in little things) every minute," she was touched and said she had been able to bear things very well as they were. In that event, asked the Prime Minister brightly, perhaps he need not bother to reform? Mrs. Churchill responded, "Please improve because we have not finished our lives yet."[59]

The behaviour of the Russian government in the next few weeks belied the assumptions upon which the Yalta agreements rested. Perhaps Stalin no longer cared what the British and Americans thought; perhaps he had addressed so many brusque messages to them that he was unaware of the effect. Roosevelt in the last few days of his life reacted vehemently to a telegram from Moscow which in effect accused him and his leading colleagues of deliberate duplicity. Churchill, knowing that he had gone bail for Russia's good intentions and behaviour, told a gathering of Commonwealth statesmen in April 1945 that since Yalta the atmosphere with Russia had so changed that "one might have thought that one was talking to a different country." Nevertheless, he thought they were not far from achieving two grand objectives: to bring the United States into the future world organization and to draw Russia from seclusion into the genial sunlight of the comity of nations.[60]

In the first few days of May came the news of the death of Mussolini, caught and hanged by Italian partisans, and of Hitler's suicide amidst the ruins of the Reich which, in his nihilist fury, he had brought down around him. Millions of German troops surrendered. While all this was going on, Mrs. Churchill was in Russia, fulfilling engagements as chairman of the Red Cross Aid to Russia Fund. It had raised no less than £7 million, chiefly for the relief of suffering among wounded soldiers of the Red Army, and she had given herself to this work unremittingly for years. On the eve of victory, her husband wrote from London, "I need scarcely tell you that beneath these triumphs lie poisonous politics and deadly international rivalries. Therefore I should come home after rendering the fullest compliments to your hospitable hosts."[61]

Parting company with Roosevelt after Yalta, Churchill had felt that the President had "a slender contact with life." When Roosevelt died in harness a few weeks later, Churchill paid unfeigned tribute to him, mourning the loss of someone whose high spirits and courage and dexterity he had admired. Roosevelt's successor, Harry Truman, was unknown to Churchill, had been Vice-President only a few months and despite his predecessor's failing powers had not been brought into serious contact with high strategy or foreign policy. Afterwards, Churchill deeply regretted that he had not followed his first instinct to attend Roosevelt's funeral and make acquaintance with the new President. Churchill tells us that by this stage of the war he was so tired that he had to be carried in a chair up the stairs.[62] He kept worse hours than ever, despatched telegrams of mounting alarm to Truman and in late May asked the Chiefs of Staff to examine in deadly secrecy whether it would be possible to fight Russia. He told them to make one assumption which we must think doubtful (that the Americans would join wholeheartedly in such a process) and another which was staggering (that German forces would have to be used). The Chiefs of Staff duly replied that there would be no practical prospect of winning such a campaign, even on these assumptions. Scandalized commentators have sometimes assumed that Churchill wanted war, or at any rate would not have been averse to war, with Russia. His request that "Operation Unthinkable" should be examined does not signify anything of the kind. Rather, the Prime Minister needed to know whether, should Russia move west and show herself entirely indifferent to the wishes or even warnings of her erstwhile allies, they would be able to resist. It does not mean that he thought such an event likely, still less desirable; but Russian behaviour was such – for example, as manifested by the kidnap of the Polish leaders who had gone to Moscow in good faith, then by their "trial" and sentencing to long terms – that the inquiry to the Chiefs of Staff was entirely justified. Churchill did not know that the Russians had for years been receiving through espionage most secret intelligence, not only about British foreign policy and strategy but also about the atomic enterprises in Canada and the United States; and Stalin's powerful currents of suspicion doubtless ran the more strongly for the knowledge that such information had not been imparted to him.

At San Francisco, a strong Commonwealth team took a leading share in drafting the constitution and procedures of the United Nations Organisation. Amongst them were Mackenzie King and Smuts. From there Anthony Eden, who led the British delegation, telegraphed to Churchill on May 8, the day of victory over Germany, "All my thoughts are with you on this day which is so essentially your day. It is you who have led, uplifted and inspired us through the worst days. Without you this day could not have been."[63] That was well said, and felt by many millions the world over. Amidst all the rejoicing, Churchill asked himself again and again whether the war, won by the narrowest of margins, might lead to an outrageous conclusion; that Germany would be replaced by a Russia as an enemy constrained neither to the east nor to the west. Unwittingly Churchill borrowed from Dr. Joseph Goebbels, of all people, the words he afterwards made famous when he told the new President that an iron curtain had been drawn down upon the Russian front, from the Baltic to the Adriatic. He would have liked the Allied armies to get as far east as possible, and then to stand fast until matters could be thrashed out with Russia in conference. Truman was not convinced by this line of argument.

With victory in Europe the Labour members of the government, to Churchill's regret, insisted upon withdrawing from it; he had hoped that the coalition would remain intact until the defeat of Japan. A general election was accordingly called, the first since 1935. Churchill had felt no enthusiasm for open warfare against the leading Labour figures with whom he had worked well for five years. However, the pugnacious side of his nature prevailed, and it is perhaps a measure of his tiredness that his early broadcasts during the campaign were ill-judged. In one of them he said that no Socialist government could afford to allow free or violently worded expressions of public discontent. "They would have to fall back on some form of Gestapo, no doubt very humanely directed in the first instance."[64] Lord Beaverbrook, deemed to have special insight in such matters, was confident that Churchill would be returned at the least with a solid majority.[65] Almost everybody believed the same thing, including the Labour leaders; but the outcome remained uncertain, because an interval of three weeks intervened between the election and the declaration of the results, during which the votes of millions serving abroad had to be collected and counted.

Churchill therefore went to Potsdam in July accompanied by Attlee, who, though no longer a minister, would succeed him if Labour had won the election. Truman attended his first international conference. Stalin gave away nothing of substance. Churchill still hoped for Russian restraint. "I like that man" he said repeatedly. "I am full of admiration of Stalin's handling of him," remarks Eden's diary. "I told him I was, hoping that it would move him. It did a little."[66] By the time Churchill left for London to await the election results, the western frontiers of Poland were still undecided. When Truman told Stalin that the United States had just tested a weapon of terrible destructive power, the Russian leader gave no sign that he knew much on that subject already, while Churchill grasped with immense relief that possession of the atomic weapon altered the strategic balance with the Soviets. President and Prime Minister agreed that, if Japan refused to surrender in short order, the first atomic bomb should be dropped.

The early election results showed that Labour would win easily. Perhaps thinking of her husband's exhaustion, and anxious that he should not after five years as national leader become a party politician again, Mrs. Churchill remarked to her husband, "It may well be a blessing in disguise." He rejoined, "At the moment it seems quite effectively disguised."[67] Captain Pim, who had run Churchill's incomparable map room, read some of the results to the Prime Minister while he took a bath. With admirable dignity and good humour Churchill said, "This may well be a landslide, and they have a perfect right to kick us out. That is democracy. That is what we have been fighting for. Hand me my towel."[68]

Neither Stalin nor Molotov had paid attention to Churchill's assertion that he did not know whether he would return to the conference or be replaced by Attlee. Unfamiliar with elections of uncertain outcome, they doubtless thought this a piece of polite patriotic deception. Taken aback to discover that Attlee did not have a manservant, Churchill insisted on sending his own valet with the new Prime Minister to Potsdam. The Foreign Secretary, Ernest Bevin, had been looking forward to a holiday by the sea, and instead found himself arguing about the Western Neisse as the frontier of Poland. Churchill always said that he would sooner have broken up the conference than consent to that demarcation, but there was no prospect that the United States would support any stiffer line or that Stalin would surrender any point of substance. The first of the atomic bombs was dropped on Japan early in August and a second a few days later. The Emperor's submission followed. What had been envisaged as a campaign of perhaps eighteen months, involving millions of Allied servicemen and casualties by the hundreds of thousands, had come to an end three months after the defeat of Germany. Burma, the Malay States, Singapore and Hong Kong all returned to British control. But the capacity to maintain empire, even in times of relative stability, depended upon a reputation for invincibility, and it soon became apparent that the raising of the Union Jack would provide no guarantee of a long tenure of power. The same lesson would prove true in French Indochina.

Late on August 14, 1945, Attlee announced over the radio that Japan had been defeated. Churchill was dining that night with colleagues in an hotel, where he had temporarily taken up residence. Someone got hold of a wireless set and placed it on a table so that the Prime Minister's short speech could be heard. These were the unexpected, almost humdrum, circumstances in which Churchill's war came to its conclusion. Reflecting long afterwards upon those days of 1940 when the white-hot glow ran through the island, he said simply, "They were very wonderful" and then how much he wished that certain people could have lived to see the victory: "Not many; my father and mother, and F.E., and Arthur Balfour, and Sunny."[69]*

The war need not have been fought, critics sometimes say, or could have been brought to an early end by agreement with Germany; in a variation, Germany could have been encouraged to attack Russia, in the hope that those two powers would pummel each other to destruction. If all this were true, it would mean that the destruction and sorrow which fell upon many millions were endured for no sufficient purpose. That is not an uncommon verdict upon great wars. The evidence presently available does not allow any such judgment upon the conflict of 1939–1945. There is no convincing argument that the ingredients of a bargain with Germany were in place, even if the moral issue were set aside. It would be necessary to show that if Germany were left alone, or encouraged to attack Russia and then defeated her, invincible might would not have been turned against Britain and the Commonwealth. In short, in order to demonstrate that the decision to fight the war out to the end was mistaken, we must believe that Hitler would have had the intention and the incentive to keep whatever bargain he made; which is not to deny that an abbreviation of the war would have been a benefit of the first order to the Commonwealth, and most of all to Britain.

The combined populations of the Dominions amounted to about 30 million, and that of Great Britain to some 47 million. Great Britain mobilized between 5 and 6 million, the Dominions perhaps 2.5 million, and India, entirely by voluntary enlistment, another 2.5 million. British and Commonwealth war dead, including the civilians killed in air raids on the United Kingdom and losses in the merchant navy, come to rather over half a million, and "casualties" – a category that includes those taken prisoner of war – amounted for Britain and the Commonwealth to about 1,250,000, more than 100,000 of whom were Canadians.

* F.E. Smith, later Earl of Birkenhead; A.J. Balfour, later Earl of Balfour; and W.S.C.'s cousin, the 9th Duke of Marlborough.

The scale and nature of this exertion is one of the supreme facts of the twentieth century, and not the less so because seldom acknowledged. Smuts told the sober truth to his fellow Prime Ministers in 1944:

> It was a wonderful feat to have weathered the storm for four and half years, during two of which we had stood alone. How the British Commonwealth, with its comparatively slender resources, had fought Germany and Italy at a time when Russia was bound by treaty to the enemy, and when Europe was overrun, would stand out in history as one of the most remarkable achievements ever known.[70]

8

"A Magnificent Future": 1952

IN THE DAYS OF DEFEAT, Churchill behaved as Arthur Balfour had done after 1906, leading his diminished band with determination, never complaining about the decision of the people or, even in private, talking of ingratitude. However, he felt acutely the loss of those excitements upon which he had thrived. The red boxes and large staff had gone. His first speech in the new Parliament, measured, eloquent and gallant, "right back in his 1940–41 calibre" as his wife described it, promised support to the Labour government in measures necessary for the national interest and recognized the immensity of the problems to be confronted, domestically and abroad. In private, he took some time to recover equilibrium. Mrs. Churchill recorded that she and her husband seemed "to be always having scenes. I'm sure it's all my fault, but I'm finding life more than I can bear. He is so unhappy & that makes him very difficult."[1] He had already begun to paint again, which helped a good deal; and soon a team was assembled to gather material for his history of the war, no less than six volumes of which appeared at yearly intervals from 1948. He had always intended to do this, as after the first conflict, but now with the advantage that he could tell the story from the position of one who had held the highest office for more than five years. The spinal cord of the narrative was already there: innumerable memoranda dictated to ministers or civil servants or the Chiefs of Staff; about a thousand messages sent to Roosevelt; the records of all the major conferences. He would set out a summary of the main themes to be explored, whereupon the research assistants would put the papers together and draft substantial passages.

Long tracts of the books reproduce documents in full, often a strain on the patience of the reader but an abundant quarry for historians from that day to this. Everything was done by dictation, and the result is best read aloud. When Lord Moran remarked upon a description of Mussolini's conduct, "at once obsolete and reprehensible," Churchill replied, "Ah, the bs in those words, obsolete, reprehensible, you must pay attention to euphony."[2]

Whether Stalin would be minded to restrain Russia's power was something that no one could tell, and a proposition upon which only the more sanguine would have cared to place much money. When Mackenzie King came to London in the autumn of 1945, having yet again led the Liberal Party to victory in the election of that year, he told Churchill in private of the revelations of the Russian spy in Ottawa, Igor Gouzenko. Communists, Churchill commented, were following a religion of their own; they would do anything for their cause, deceive everybody and had no religion beyond that. King said that neither the Commonwealth nor the United States could cope with the Russian situation on its own; the two must be kept together. Churchill rejoined, "That is the thing you must work for above everything else."[3] When he delivered a few months later the famous speech at Fulton, Missouri, about the Iron Curtain, he took care to say that, so far as Russia was concerned, the British aimed at nothing but mutual assistance and collaboration. All the same, war could not be prevented surely, or the United Nations developed, without a special relationship between the United States and the Commonwealth, which would require not only a growing friendship between the two systems of society but intimate relations between their military advisers and joint use of bases all over the world. After all, the United States already had a defence agreement with Canada, and the principle should be extended to the whole Commonwealth. Meanwhile, the facts about Russia's conduct must be faced.

Mackenzie King listened to the speech on the radio. That evening, he telegraphed to the Prime Minister in London:

> To me, it was the most courageous utterance I have ever heard by any public man and one that has been made none too soon. Having in mind what has recently been uncovered in Canada of a certain espionage network and its method of operating, I personally feel that there is only one way to meet a threatening danger and that is to fight it in the open. Churchill has sounded a note of warning to the free nations

> of the world which cannot be heeded too fully. With all that he said of effectively facilitating and strengthening utmost co-operation between the United States and the British Commonwealth I am in complete agreement. I believe that Canadian opinion will be strongly behind Churchill in what he said in his address today.[4]

Attlee sent a noncommittal reply. The government in London distanced itself from the speech; the U.S. government declined to endorse it; Russia, naturally enough, issued a stern denunciation.

Even had the outlook with the U.S.S.R. been a benign one, Churchill would doubtless have preached reconciliation between former enemies. As it was, the threatening prospects gave impetus and urgency to his plea that the revival of Europe must start from friendship between France and Germany. This was something which he could say with greater impact than any man living, since none had done more to bring about Germany's ruin. Italy too must come back to life; Austria must eventually be unshackled; the smaller states must be embraced. All this should lead to a United States of Europe, though Churchill did not have in mind anything comparable with the United States of America and certainly did not intend Britain to be included in such an arrangement. As he remarked at the time, "Nothing will induce me to be a Federalist." Rather, he believed that Britain should be the vital link between Europe, the United States and the Commonwealth. That all three groups, overlapping or interlocking at many points, needed to collaborate became plainer by the month. The Marshall Plan did much to stimulate the economic recovery of Europe, and had a psychological effect perhaps as great as the material. There was no pretence that the forces remaining in Western Europe could stand against a determined Russian advance, unless the atomic bomb were used. In short order, the conviction that ruled Allied thinking at the end of the war – that the prime task would be to contain Germany – had been abandoned. Rarely has so great a power squandered so much goodwill so swiftly as Russia after 1945. The Federal Republic of Germany was established as early as September 1949. Immediately afterwards, the Russians tested their first atomic bomb.

Europe had already begun to take the steps for its own defence, modest enough in the first instance, without which it could scarcely hope for continued American commitment. The North Atlantic Treaty Organisation (NATO), in the creation of which Canada played a leading part, became the foundation of security in Europe, bringing America, Canada and Britain into an alliance that carried forward into this era of precarious truce – it could scarcely be termed "peace" in any fuller sense – the military collaboration forged in war. Little more than a decade earlier, Baldwin had caused a mild sensation by remarking that the Rhine rather than the chalk cliffs of Dover had become Britain's frontier; and now the Elbe was the frontier for the people of Ontario and Illinois, or British Columbia and California.

Early in 1946, after tremulous negotiations in Washington, the British had secured a large American loan, vitally necessary since Lend-Lease had ended abruptly in 1945 and they had waged war with scant regard to cost. Canada provided Britain with yet another massive loan of dollars. These funds were exhausted with alarming speed. Soon it was necessary to devalue the pound heavily against the dollar; measures of austerity, some of them more severe than those which had prevailed in the war, were introduced. Britain's economic exhaustion loomed over the international scene. By fighting three enemies in widely scattered theatres by land, sea and air, she had brought about her own premature demise as a power of the first rank. The American government took over British obligations in Greece in 1947; the British soon abandoned their mandate in Palestine; and even before that had left the Indian subcontinent, now partitioned. This latter event, accompanied by atrocities, the dispossession of large populations and the abandonment of long-standing promises to the Princely states, caused Churchill grief. The process may have been inevitable, but he was well within his rights to point out that these were the consequences which he had always expected to follow if the British withdrew from India precipitately. Though the fact was not immediately apparent, departure from India inevitably brought forward the dates of independence for other British territories in Asia, and at no distant remove in Africa.

Domestically, the Labour government nationalized the railways, the production and supply of gas and electricity, water, part of road haulage and part of the steel industry. This was done to honour a long-held belief that a Socialist government must control the commanding heights (as they were called, somewhat fancifully as it turned out) of the economy. Attlee and his colleagues introduced large measures of social reform, the most important being the National Health Service. A good deal of the groundwork for this had been agreed upon during Churchill's wartime administration, though the scope of the Service which came into being in 1948 went well beyond the earlier preparations. Controls and restrictions abounded.

The Labour government's decision to introduce peacetime conscription, soon raised to two years' service, was strongly supported by Churchill, as was the robust response at the time of the Berlin airlift, when the Russians attempted to close off the access of their erstwhile allies to that city. There followed a heavy program of re-armament, expanded when Chinese forces invaded Korea in 1949. The United Nations responded with force, since Russia was at the time indulging in a temporary boycott of the Security Council, and thus unable to employ the veto. Almost all the cost and losses fell on the United States, although Britain, Canada and other Commonwealth countries made a far from negligible contribution.

By 1950, Attlee and most of his senior Labour colleagues had been in office for ten grinding years. Their massive majority of 1945 dwindled almost to nothing at the election of 1950. Churchill had resisted pressure to resign as Leader of the Opposition and regained much of his old zest for the parliamentary fray. Evidently another election could not be long delayed. British taxation was the heaviest to be found anywhere in the free world. Meat, sugar, cheese, butter, bacon, sweets, bread were all rationed. Expenditure on defence in the financial year 1949–50 had reached more than one-fifth of the total budget, and was rising rapidly, as was the cost of essential imports. "Set the people free," proclaimed Churchill and the Conservatives. Private enterprise must be stimulated; bureaucracy must be reduced; there must be greater incentives to save.

In the general election of October 1951, the Conservative Party returned to office with an overall majority of seventeen, though it had actually received fewer votes than Labour. Churchill became Prime Minister at a time of serious economic crisis within a few weeks of his seventy-seventh birthday. He had suffered a mild stroke in 1949, which was known to very few, but had recovered with customary resilience. His own energy, though the flame burned strongly from time to time, could not be that of ten or a dozen years earlier. What could be achieved in wartime, with the danger imminent and palpable and no serious opposition in Parliament, could not be reproduced in 1951 by a Prime Minister and government with a bare working majority. The problems were intractable to a degree. There was no Lend-Lease conveniently at hand. Even if all this had not been true, he realized that his role as a peacetime Prime Minister must be essentially different from the part he had played during the war. One day soon after Churchill resumed office, Sir Ian Jacob came to lunch at No. 10. The Prime Minister's attention was attracted by sounds outside. He walked over to the window to look. A man with a wheelbarrow was moving coke from a lorry parked nearby, though it would have been more sensible to drive the lorry directly into the courtyard. "Ten years before he would have summoned a stenographer then and there and would have sent a Minute on the subject to the Minister of Fuel and Power (who quite probably was not the right person): 'Pray tell me why . . .' The fact that he sat down again and went on with his lunch without doing anything showed me that he was no longer the same man as he had been."[5]

* * *

The first priority, Churchill reflected, must be to establish relations with President Truman and the Secretary of State Dean Acheson. Louis St. Laurent, who had succeeded Mackenzie King as Prime Minister of Canada, said that a visit to Ottawa would be welcome. The British party, which included the Foreign Secretary (Anthony Eden), Lord Ismay (now Secretary of State for Commonwealth Relations), Lord Cherwell (Paymaster-General), the Chiefs of Staff and the Secretary of the Cabinet, left by sea for New York on December 31. The tangled subjects which they were about to discuss embraced the war in Korea; Persia and Egypt; the atom bomb; the European Defence Community; naval command in the Atlantic; and much else. Above and below those issues lay three questions. How could Russia and China be contained? Could Britain recover economic strength? Would the United States be willing to listen?

In Korea, the United States had so far lost – killed, wounded or missing – 105,000 men; the figure for Britain and the Commonwealth stood at about 3,000. Churchill was acutely conscious of the disparity. For six months, acrimonious negotiations for a Korean truce had dragged along. One of the meetings set a record; it ended in complete disunity after four hours, during two of which neither side spoke a word. By the end of November, however, agreement had been reached in principle on a line for a ceasefire. No one knew whether the talks would be spun out indefinitely, or whether an agreement would be made and then broken? If a truce were established, would it provide the occasion for a transfer of Communist strength from Korea to French Indochina or Malaya? France had the equivalent of ten divisions in Indochina, and the British six divisions in Hong Kong, Malaya and Egypt.

Soon after the expulsion of Chiang Kai-Shek and his forces from the mainland to Formosa, the British had recognized the Communist government in China. The United States had not, and was adamant that China should not be admitted to the United Nations while her aggression against Korea continued. The disagreement was a serious one, which Churchill was anxious to minimize. Eden's view of the merits was different, at least in emphasis. Both knew that the Labour government had agreed in secret that, if heavy air attacks were launched from China against the UN's operations in Korea, the Chinese bases would be bombed. Such action would involve the Royal Air Force, already heavily stretched; and if the war spread, there was no telling where the process might end. After all, Communist China had aligned herself closely with Russia, in both foreign policy and trade. Churchill was by no means sure that China would remain for generations in the Communist grip. For the moment, however, the harmony between Russia and China had to be accepted as a threatening fact.

Earlier in 1951, Persia had nationalized the oil industry and seized the assets of the Anglo-Iranian Oil Company. Several efforts at a settlement had failed. The Prime Minister, Dr. Mohammed Mossadegh, was violently hostile to the British and scarcely less so to the United States. While accepting the principle of nationalization, the Labour government submitted the dispute to the International Court of Justice and, at the end of the year, the International Bank announced that it would send a commission to Persia to ascertain whether the Bank could do something that would encourage a resumption of oil refining. Differences of policy between the United States and Britain were substantial at that stage. The Bank's negotiations failed, and the International Court of Justice later decided that it had no jurisdiction in this issue.

After the British withdrawal from Palestine in 1948, an embattled Israel lived in a state of perpetual tension and intermittent warfare with its neighbours. The Egyptian government denounced the treaty of 1936 with Britain, whose sprawling bases and installations in the Canal Zone were under attack. The situation there had become so serious by mid-December 1951 that Eden was driven to consider the possibility of joint military action by the United States, France and Britain against Alexandria and Cairo. Whether any American administration would have entered into such an operation must remain doubtful. In the event, Churchill asked in Washington, as he was to do again in 1954, that the United States should consider sending a small contingent, perhaps a brigade, to the Canal Zone, in order to give substance to a proposal that an international supervisory force be stationed there. Four powers (Britain, France, Turkey and the United States) would take part. The arrangement never came to fruition, and the plea for the despatch of an American brigade went unheeded in 1952, as it would in 1954.

When Churchill took office at the end of October 1951, he learned a startling fact: Britain had built an atomic bomb. No word of this had been vouchsafed to Parliament; almost all members of the Labour Cabinet had been kept in ignorance; and the very large sums required, estimated at £100 million, had been found by dexterous falsification of the estimates presented each year to Parliament. "And they called me a warmonger!"[6] Churchill said angrily. It now fell to him to decide whether the weapon should be tested. Approving heartily of the decision to build the bomb, he decided that it should, and this was successfully done in the Pacific. The British accordingly found themselves in possession of this new power, thanks to what Churchill later termed "Attlee's somewhat unconstitutional exertions."[7]

As a leading partner in NATO, Canada already had troops in Germany and squadrons in England. Her defence budget, on a three-year program from the spring of 1951, was estimated at $5 billion. It would provide a 100-ship navy and 40 squadrons; 1,400 aircrew from NATO would train each year in Canada; and $40 million were set aside to provide 300 radar sets for the alliance. This enormous expenditure accounted for some 45 per cent of the Federal budget. Little opposition was heard, except in some Québecois circles; and St. Laurent's government possessed an enormous parliamentary majority.

In Europe, an extremely complicated situation prevailed. Economic revival had followed the Marshall Plan. The Federal Republic (West Germany) under Chancellor Konrad Adenauer made rapid strides. Although governments succeeded each other with bewildering rapidity in Paris, momentous steps had been taken in the economic sphere toward integration, especially in the production of coal and steel, with the avowed purpose of putting an end to the bitter rivalry between France and Germany. Over all hung a deep fear of Russia with her band of satellites stretching through Central and Southeastern Europe. The European Defence Community (EDC) was intended to produce what the French Foreign Minister called a "supra-national army gradually but irrevocably superseding national armies," an integral part of the NATO forces. West Germany would re-arm and take part in the new enterprise from the beginning; at a second stage, but with no date specified, a European Defence Minister would be appointed. The six states involved – France, Belgium, the Netherlands, Luxembourg, Italy and West Germany – stated that the Community would mark a step toward the unification of Europe, an essential objective of their governments. Many practical issues remained unresolved, not least for the British with their worldwide commitments and strained resources. Churchill's immediate preoccupation was to see Germany re-arm under safeguards and to ensure that the fighting quality of European forces was raised to a high standard as rapidly as possible. His attitude toward the EDC, shared entirely by Eden, was not welcome to Dean Acheson or Lester Pearson, who mistakenly imagined it to spring from little more than nostalgia.

The partnership between the United States and Britain, difficult enough to manage during the war, was bound to be much more problematic now, the gap in economic and military strength having widened so vastly since the war. As a high official at the Foreign Office, shortly to become Ambassador in Washington, put the point:

> We are on a difficult wicket at the moment because, however we try to disguise it, we are back on the breadline for the third time in six years. The Prime Minister's arrival in the U.S.A. will coincide with another disquieting disclosure about the run on reserves. This will add to the impression already created in the U.S.A. by Persia and Egypt that the British Empire is in liquidation.[8]

Two speeches which he must soon deliver, one in Ottawa and the other in Washington, oppressed Churchill's spirits. The cost of the re-armament program in Britain had already risen from £3.7 billion to £5.2 billion. This was manifestly a greater burden than the country could bear. The last quarter of 1951 showed a balance-of-payments deficit of $940 million; Britain's gold and dollar reserves, standing at $2.3 billion, were expected to drop within six months to $1.4 billion. It was only moderately comforting to reflect that the new government could not be blamed for this state of affairs. Imports would have to be reduced and rations tightened. "Never in my life have I faced an ordeal of this kind," Churchill said as the *Queen Mary* approached New York.

> It is worse than 1940. In Washington they will feel we are down and out. We have to tell them that if the rearmament is not spread out over a longer time the nations of Western Europe will be rushing to bankruptcy and starvation. When I have come to America before it has always been as an equal. If, late in the war, they spoke of their sacrifices we could retort by saying that for a year and a half we fought alone; that we had suffered more losses. They have become so great and we are now so small. Poor England! We threw away so much in 1945.[9]

Churchill arrived in Washington on January 5. The first discussion with Truman and Acheson delighted and revived him. "Oh, I enjoyed it so much. We talked as equals."[10] Over several days, he assured his hosts that Britain would surmount her domestic problems, but must seek help with the re-armament essential for the common cause. He explained the British position in respect of Persia, Egypt and the EDC. Churchill seems to have believed that he would obtain in Washington a reasonable share of what the Americans had done in the atomic field, in which expectation he was promptly disappointed. He did not fail to show to Senator McMahon the original texts of the agreements made at Quebec in 1943, Hyde Park in 1944 and between Truman, Attlee and Mackenzie King in November 1945. The embarrassed McMahon, largely responsible for the Act bearing his name which cut off the flow of most atomic information to Britain from 1946, could only say, "If we had known this the Act would not have been passed." Churchill told him something of the size of the British atomic program and regretted that American legislation had "made so large an undertaking necessary."[11]

In essence, Churchill's purpose – and as it developed from 1953 more than purpose, mission – was to persuade the government of the United States to regard Russia and international communism as a disagreeable fact to be lived with. That policy could succeed only if the west re-armed vigorously. The purposes were to deter Russian aggression or to fight, if the worst came to the worst, on the least disadvantageous terms. But to Churchill's mind such a state of armed stalemate, with its enormous cost and risks, must be accompanied by a willingness to respond to any friendlier mood which might show itself behind the Iron Curtain.

For the immediate future, he argued vigorously against an earlier decision that an American admiral should be appointed as Supreme Commander for the Atlantic. The Prime Minister remembered how nearly Britain had been strangled in 1941 and 1942, and refused to be shaken from the view that the Royal Navy could cope better than the Americans with submarine warfare. The matter was left unresolved in the first round of the talks.

The two governments did agree that they should seek common policies in the Middle East. They reaffirmed that the United States would not use atomic weapons from U.K. bases without British consent. Both countries would do their utmost to help the establishment of a European Defence Community. They recognized that, in the Far East, "the overriding need to counter the Communist threat in that area transcends such divergences as there are in our policies towards China."

Churchill spent two days in New York and then travelled to Ottawa by train.

* * *

Memorandum by L.B. Pearson, December 9, 1951[12]

I had lunch with Mr. Churchill today at Chequers during which, and afterwards, we discussed many things. The only other persons present at the lunch were Mrs. Churchill and his Private Secretary.

The Prime Minister looked old and tired, at least until the luncheon got well under way when he revived and became his normal, sparkling and dramatic self, under the influence, not of my company, I suspect, but of his own natural reaction to an audience, assisted somewhat by champagne, burgundy, port and quantities of brandy. I did my best to keep up with him, in this latter respect at least, but when he suggested after lunch that we now have a scotch and soda, I gave up.

The Prime Minister had much to say about Canada, his memories of the Quebec Conferences, and of Mr. Mackenzie King. He painted a glowing future for our country, even predicting that the centre of power would one day move to the northern half of the American continent. He felt that we would be well advised, however, to maintain a strong connection with the U.K. and the Commonwealth, and cling to the old traditions which would help stabilize our national development. In this respect, he confessed that he had been bitterly disappointed when "Rule Britannia" was ruled out of the Canadian Navy, and he begged me to do something about that when I returned to Canada. He said it was the only request he made of me. To reinforce it, he recited all the verses of "Rule Britannia", and inspired by this, went on to recite several Harrow patriotic songs he had learned sixty years ago. He admitted that Great Britain was not now the powerful country she once was, and probably would not be so again, but she was still the centre of great authority, and he felt that Canada would not be making a mistake in maintaining her historic relationships with London and the past. Of course, Mr. Churchill is still romantic about the past, and in every subject that we discussed, this romanticism cropped up.

I brought up the question of a European Army, and he was emphatic that in its present form Great Britain would not join it; she would fight with European forces, but not in them. He said the proper way to bring European armies together was to maintain their national identities and tie them together as a "bunch of sticks", bound together by common interest in their own salvation, rather than to mix them all up as "wood pulp". He did not believe in the "wood pulp" theory of unity. Britain would certainly fight again with France, if she were attacked, but was not willing to lose herself completely in Europe. He found it difficult to understand how the French, with their strong national and military traditions, were willing to allow their army to be completely absorbed in a European force, or how their soldiers could ever develop a loyalty to such a force. Mr. Churchill seemed somewhat of a romantic reactionary when discussing this subject. He added that he had also told Adenauer his views on this matter while the latter was in London. I mentioned to him the fears of the French that the British would one day withdraw again from Europe and that they were not very sympathetic with the general trend toward European unity. Mr. Churchill said that this was not true, that their association would be close and continuous, but not necessarily organic. He would try to make their friendly and sympathetic position clear to the French when he visited Paris next week.

[The conversation then turned to other topics: the organization and command structure of NATO; Field Marshal Alexander's impending appointment as Minister of Defence in London; the Korean War.]

There would be no change in British policy in the Far East as a result of the change of Government, but there would certainly be no "kowtowing" to the Chinese Red Government, or to any Chinese Government. China was not a great power, and it had been a great mistake to recognize her as such because of American insistence during the war. However, he agreed with me that it would be most unwise needlessly to irritate or offend the Peking Government in present circumstances. That Government, he felt, was not likely to become the tool of Moscow in the long run.

Adverting to Russia, he felt that the danger period would be during the next year or two when we were getting strong. Russia would not, he thought, deliberately provoke a war, but might blunder into one through a miscalculation.

The Prime Minister then reminisced for some time about his contacts with the Russians, and particularly with Stalin, during the war. He would be quite willing to see Stalin again, but would not do so if the Americans objected. What he wanted to do was to try to convince the Russians that he was willing to take up their relationship where they left it off at the end of the war, though he had no illusions as to the difficulty of this. This was the reason why they [the British] had changed their mind and voted for Byelo-Russia for the Security Council rather than Greece. It was evidence that they were not anti-Soviet on every issue, and he had taken pains to see that this attitude was brought to Stalin's attention. . . .

I then brought up the question of his forthcoming visit to North America. Mr. Churchill admitted that he did not know the President very well, though they had got along admirably together at Potsdam until "electoral exigencies" had intervened, and also that on the train to Fulton* they had sat up two nights until 2.00 a.m. playing poker. He then sent for and read to me a telegram which he was just about to send to the President, outlining the arrangements that were proposed for the visit to Washington, and asking whether they were satisfactory. He said in this telegram he would like to make one major speech, and was not sure whether he would call it "Review of the International Position" or "Christmas Day in the Work House". He thought that the latter might be more appropriate from a United Kingdom Prime Minister, but he was willing to leave the matter to the President. This telegram was in Mr. Churchill's best style and the old gentleman chuckled a good deal over it. Eden told me the next day that these jocular references had been deleted from the telegram before it was sent.†

* Harry S. Truman, Vice-President of the United States, 1944–45, and President, 1945–53. He had in February 1946 travelled to Fulton, Missouri, with W.S.C., who delivered there the "Iron Curtain" speech.

† This sentence shows that at least part of the memorandum was not written on December 9.

Mr. Churchill expressed some worry about certain aspects of U.S. policy toward Europe, and he hoped that his trip would be helpful in that it would give him the opportunity to talk to Mr. Truman and others about these worries. The only purpose of this trip, he emphasized, was to establish a good personal and official basis for relations in the years ahead. He realized perfectly that no great decisions were possible, or even desirable, during the visit.

He then expressed keen pleasure at the visit he would be making to Ottawa subsequent to his sojourn in the United States, and added, somewhat to my surprise, that he thought he would go to Toronto also and take a degree at the University there, the name of which escaped him for the moment. The Prime Minister is, indeed, getting old.

He referred to Eden in terms of warm regard and approval, and expressed satisfaction that Eden and Acheson* had met and had gotten on such "good terms". He was happy about his Cabinet which, he said, did not consist primarily of "political personages" but of patriotic and experienced experts,† some of whom had been given "a group of subjects" for which to be responsible.

About 3.30 Mr. Churchill decided it was time for a nap. So, in his boiler suit, cigar in mouth, and glass of whiskey in hand, he walked to the door with me and said a cheerful good-bye.

From J.R. Colville's *Footprints in Time*[13]

After the war, when Churchill was again Prime Minister, he paid several visits** to Canada. One of them had an inauspicious start. He had read in the newspapers that the Canadian Government of Monsieur St. Laurent had decreed that the Royal Canadian Navy should no longer play *Rule Britannia*. Churchill knew *Rule Britannia* by heart. He loved it passionately:

---

* Dean Gooderham Acheson (1893–1971), American lawyer and politician; Under-Secretary of State, 1945–47; Secretary of State, 1949–53.

† Churchill's Cabinet in the early stages had only sixteen members. An unusual number were not career politicians: Sir Walter Monckton (Minister of Labour), Lord Ismay (Commonwealth Relations), Lord Woolton (Lord President of the Council), Lord Leathers (Minister for Co-ordination of Transport, Fuel and Power), Lord Cherwell (Paymaster General), and Lord Alexander (shortly to become Minister of Defence, a post which W.S.C. himself held until March 1952).

** In fact, two.

it represented all that he treasured in the history of the British Empire. So St. Laurent's nationalist measure was a crime akin to blasphemy. A stern, reproving telegram was sent from Downing Street, recalling to me a surviving remnant of my classical education, Juvenal's description of the terrifying missives sent by the Emperor Tiberius from his villa at Capri: *Verbosa et grandis epistola venit a Capreis*. Monsieur St. Laurent was unmoved. He explained in reply that Canada, though deeply conscious of her links with the British Crown, was a free and independent country with her own navy ruling her own section of the waves. Churchill was furious. He tried once more, against the strong advice of Lord Ismay, the new Secretary of State for Commonwealth Relations, and received a second polite but uncompromising refusal. Very well; after his forthcoming journey to the United States in a few weeks' time, he would cancel the plans for a visit to Ottawa. He would show these infamous, republican upstarts what he thought of them.

Wiser counsels prevailed. Lady Churchill said that if he insisted on behaving like a spoilt child, she would not go to America with him. In fact she had a good mind to shut up Chartwell and move off by herself to Brighton.* Others took a firm if somewhat less dramatic stance. Nevertheless it was an ill-humoured, unco-operative Churchill who eventually boarded a special night sleeper at Washington bound for Ottawa. In the morning St. Laurent and his whole Cabinet were assembled at the railway station to greet him. Behind them were the massed bands of the Canadian army, navy and air-force. As the old man stepped down on to the platform, the massed bands struck up *Rule Britannia*. He stood there, hat in hand, with tears pouring down his cheeks; and thenceforward nobody ever dared to utter even the mildest criticism of Monsieur St. Laurent or of Canada.

[The matter of "Rule, Britannia" recurs in these pages. It is indubitably true that Churchill loved those verses and longed to see the symbols of naval power and British association with Canada maintained. His interlocutors responded kindly, believing that they were listening to the sentimental pleadings of an elderly romantic. So they were; but it is always well to remember that Churchill was an artist, building up effects by subtle processes and wily in getting his way. He was quite capable of calculating that his Canadian friends, moved by these petitions and unable to grant them in full, would be the more disposed to meet him on other points.]

---

* This threat should be taken with a pinch of salt; it was a means of bringing W.S.C. to order.

The *Journal*, Ottawa, January 11, 1952

CHURCHILL TAKES OVER THE SHOW

Hearty Prime Minister Winston Churchill came back to Ottawa today to the lift of Canadian cheers. To the delight of the crowd he took over direction of part of the reception at the Union Station.

The sturdy warrior, his cigar glowing, stepped firmly from the train that brought him from New York to the greeting of Prime Minister St. Laurent and other Canadian ministers* at 11.56 a.m.

He inspected a guard of honor with the detailed care of a veteran soldier, and then marched to the entrance off Little Sussex Street. There he was to enter the limousine for the ride to Rideau Hall, where he will be the guest of his friend, the Governor General, Lord Alexander. He was expected to enter the car at once. Instead, he moved past the door held open for him, waving officials, policemen and photographers aside with his cane. He marched through the path he had waved through the group, out into the open square where he stood alone. He swept off his hat as the crowds gathered before him, and on the roof tops about, cheered. He waved his hat to them. He clapped on his hat and waved his cane. He gave the V-sign. He beamed. He was in rare fine form, high good humor. Behind him the deserted group waited anxiously.

In his own good time, Mr. Churchill turned slowly to walk back to the car with Prime Minister St. Laurent at his side. Then, with a last wave, he entered the car and drove away, followed by cheers and given more cheers by knots of people who gathered at street corners on the way to Government House. For them he had a wave and the V-sign.

Lord Moran's diary, January 11, 1952[14]

Government House,
Ottawa

The P.M. has been looking forward to his stay with Alex, who has a great hold over his affections, and his interest was quickened when General

* When St. Laurent introduced Brooke Claxton with the words "My colleague, the Minister of National Defence," Churchill answered, "My colleague too, then."

Templer* arrived in order to be vetted for the command in Malaya†. . . . Alex was quite sure he was the man for this job of rooting out the Communist guerrillas from the jungle and Monty, too, had sent a letter, so we are hopeful that all will go well. Before I went to bed Templer told me he had talked with the P.M. for two hours.

'Winston began: "I am an old man. I shall probably not see you again. I may be sending you to your death." When he said this he almost broke down. And then he said to me: "Ask for power, go on asking for it, and then – never use it." At the end the P.M. smiled: "Here am I talking to you for all this time when I have two speeches on my hands." '

Templer turned to me:

'What is there about this man which no one else has?'

He did not seem to expect an answer, and I had none to give.

[The directive announcing Sir Gerald Templer's appointment as High Commissioner reaffirmed that Malaya would become in due course a fully self-governing country. Law and order must first be restored. He should promote political progress that would further "our democratic aims in Malaya"; this process could not be achieved without a common form of citizenship for all who regarded the Federation of Malay States as the "object of their loyalty."]

From the unpublished memoirs of Brooke Claxton[15]

When Winston Churchill visited Ottawa in January 1952, the restoration of Rule Britannia was one of four things he asked me for while I was seated with him after dinner at Government House. He was in great form and we got along very well together, as we always did. He said, "Now, Minister, I have four very important requests to make of you, which I hope you may find it possible to grant me." First, he said, "Will you leave your three squadrons of magnificent fighters in England as long as you can? The

* Gerald Templer (1898–1979), British soldier; Vice-Chief of the Imperial General Staff, 1948–50; High Commissioner and Commander-in-Chief, Malaya, 1952–54; Chief of the Imperial General Staff, 1955–58; Field Marshal, 1956.

† Where a serious insurrection had been developing for some time. The previous Governor had been ambushed and killed in October 1951.

outgoing government lied to me. They said we had some air defences. We have none at all; the cupboard is empty, the stable is bare. We are undefended except for your three squadrons. They are the only fighters in England that can stand up against the [Russian] MIGS." I agreed to this at once and planned all the subsequent moves so that the three squadrons were the last to move to the Continent. We took our time about getting the station at Marville ready for them so that we stayed on in England until April 1954 and I believe right up to the end of that time were just as important a factor in the defence of England as they were when Winston spoke to me. "Now," he went on, "my second request is for a lot of Sabre fighters. Our own fighters, the Hunter and the Swift, may be very good but where are they? We won't have any in squadron use for more than a year." . . . Here I was able to tell Winston that I had been working on this for some time and I believed that in a few weeks it might be possible to announce an arrangement whereby the Americans would provide the engines and we the rest of the aircraft representing about 70% of the cost. I told him it might run into some hundreds of aircraft and naturally he was very pleased. In fact, in February, a month later, we were able to announce this arrangement. . . .

Actually we were to give Britain 370 Sabres and the United States purchased another fifty from us to bring the total to 420. The gift was hardly noticed in the British press and neither our Prime Minister nor myself received any formal acknowledgement. The same was true about our even greater contribution to air training facilities which was the subject of Mr. Churchill's next request. He went on, "Now, Mr. Minister, my third request is very important indeed. I know that you have been most generous in providing air training facilities for pilots and navigators but we need more. Can you provide us with more spaces?" On this I said that I would be greatly obliged if he would look into this again and let me know if he really felt we should do anything more. Of course, we would be glad to consider it. I told him, however, that my information was that the RAF was steadily not using all the places we were offering. Moreover, I said, my information was also that each group of trainees arrived ten or fifteen short of the places they had accepted. It would then be too late to offer these places to other N.A.T.O. countries or to get our own cadets into them, so that this very scarce and costly training facility would be wasted. There was an over-all deficiency for air training facilities in N.A.T.O. This was a very serious matter indeed. It cost upwards of $65,000 to train a jet pilot and a good part of this cost went on if a vacancy was not taken up. Then I asked him if he knew that more than 60% of the cadets coming out were conscripts of whom only a very small proportion continued on with the RAF after completing their training in Canada. In other words, the RAF was spending our money and using our training facilities to train reserve fliers for the RAF when the N.A.T.O. countries generally were short of front-line air crew. This all surprised him, as he said, and I never heard anything more about the subject. As a matter of fact, I checked up the next day and found the facts were all as I had said. However, he was doing pretty well having got his squadrons and aircraft.

His final request was about Rule Britannia. This was most moving and rather pathetic. He said, "You have a wonderful Navy. I know about its efficiency and its growing strength. Why, it has become one of the great Navies of the world (which, in fact, it has). You must be like I am, a great believer in tradition and you know the Navy was my first love. Won't you allow them to sing Rule Britannia?" I told him that as far as I was concerned they could sing Rule Britannia as much as they liked. I pointed out what had happened was that I hardly thought it appropriate that distinguished visitors, say an American or French admiral, should be received on a Canadian ship with the tune of Rule Britannia. He said, "Oh I did not understand that, but I still think you should use it." I agreed with him emphatically and I assured him, whatever else we did, we would always play it for him.

I had arranged for the RCAF band to play during the Government dinner the next night and I had it play Rule Britannia for him. When Mr. Churchill left the next day I had the band at the station play Rule Britannia as the train pulled out of the station. When he returned at the end of June 1954 I had the RCAF band at the airport play Rule Britannia as his car moved away and each time he thanked me personally.

The *Evening Citizen*, Ottawa, January 14, 1952

"What happens here (in Canada) is of interest and importance to the whole world and important to all who care for freedom and truth", declared Rt. Hon. Winston S. Churchill at a Parliamentary Press Gallery reception Saturday noon. . . .

Hanging on the wall was a picture of Mr. Churchill being presented with a seal cap by gallery officials when he was last here in December, 1941. . . .

"As Mr. Paradis [President of the Press Gallery] has said, I have been a journalist," Mr. Churchill went on. "All my life, when I have been out of public office – and that has been about half my life – I have earned my living by selling words and, I hope, sometimes thoughts as well.

"The Canadian press holds a high and distinguished place amongst the press of what once was called the Empire. If that word slips out (laughter), I won't ask your pardon. That has been so because the Canadian press has stood for fair play in respecting all the decencies known to the British population, enabling us to uphold our society, even if we are not as clever, or as rich, as some other countries."

Memorandum by L.B. Pearson of his discussions with A. Eden, January 13, 1952[16]

In general, Eden expressed considerable satisfaction with the results of the Washington visit. He thinks that he has established better personal relations with Acheson, although he recognizes that there are differences in temperament between them. He is also worried about the Prime Minister, his difficulty in keeping going and his tendency to do things and make statements which his colleagues find somewhat embarrassing. Eden is perfectly frank about this but remains intensely loyal to the Prime Minister. His view is that his colleagues must all do everything they can to help Mr. Churchill to play the great moral and prestige part that he can play, by taking over more and more of his actual work.

[After dinner that evening, Pearson, Eden, Ismay and their advisers talked over a wide range of subjects, from the Atlantic command to the supply of raw materials, the reform of NATO to the Korean armistice, the Japanese peace treaty to Kashmir. At every point, the Canadian attitude was understanding and helpful.

Among the other subjects discussed in Canada, sometimes by officials and on other occasions by ministers, were the supply of Rolls-Royce aero-engines to Canada; the provision of places for the training of aircrew; atomic energy, in which sphere the British had just decided, not before time, to tighten their security procedures; and the organization and prospects of the Commonwealth forces in Korea and Japan.

The four British ministers who met their Canadian colleagues next morning constituted one quarter of the British Cabinet.]

Conclusions of the British Ministers' meeting with the Canadian Cabinet, January 14, 1952[17]

[In addition to W.S.C., Eden, Ismay, Cherwell, Sir A. Clutterbuck* and Sir N. Brook† attended on the British side. St. Laurent presided and welcomed Churchill, who recalled his visit to Ottawa of ten years before, when he had become a member of the Privy Council of Canada.]

ATOMIC WEAPONS

Mr. Churchill stressed the importance of the development and improvement of atomic weapons during the period when the relative strength of the western countries in conventional weapons would not be adequate to afford them protection. The Labour Government in the United Kingdom had made progress in the development of an atomic bomb and the first one produced in the United Kingdom would be tested in Australia during the summer. If it was successful, production could proceed. Apart from its intrinsic importance a successful British bomb might have a substantial influence on the readiness of the United States to exchange information on atomic development. He was very anxious to see an equality of knowledge with the United States which would lead to a more ready exchange of technical information.

The Prime Minister [of Canada] suggested that detailed discussion on atomic energy questions might be left to Lord Cherwell and Mr. Howe.

POLICY TOWARD THE SOVIET UNION

Mr. Churchill said that the policy was to preserve peace or at least a *modus vivendi* with the USSR of as long a duration as possible. This could only be secured from strength. Agreements with the USSR could not be secured on any other basis. The strength of the West was being developed through the North Atlantic Treaty Organisation. It was to be hoped that N.A.T.O. would not be limited solely to preparations for defence but that it might develop into a lasting grouping of Powers which would produce a new effectiveness for the United Nations. The present did not appear to be a propitious time to enter into talks with the USSR but the United Kingdom would be ready at any time to respond to any genuine advance from the Soviet side.

A deterrent factor in the present dangerous situation was that war would be extremely unpleasant for both sides. Both would suffer what they dreaded most at

---

* British High Commissioner in Canada.

† Norman Craven Brook (1902–1967), British civil servant; Secretary of the Cabinet, 1947–62; Head of the Home Civil Service, 1956–62; 1st and last Baron Normanbrook.

the outset: Europe would be overrun and the USSR would be blasted by atomic weapons in all its vital points. This gave some assurance that peace could be maintained. It seemed certain that at best there would have to be a prolonged period of cold war. That, however, was much better than catastrophe.

The Prime Minister enquired whether Mr. Churchill thought that the apparent concessions made by M. Vishinsky* at the United Nations in relation to the banning of atomic weapons and the possibility of inspection gave indication of desire on the Soviet side to see some progress.

Mr. Churchill felt it would present a difficult problem if the Soviet Union were to offer to accept our conditions for the control of atomic weapons since the West was not sufficiently strong at present to do without the protection that their possession afforded. It was the vast superiority of the United States in atomic weapons and the technical improvements they had achieved, that provided a decisive deterrent at present. It was doubtful, however, that the USSR would be prepared to allow *bona fide* and continuous inspection since it would too greatly lift the veil they kept over their affairs.

Mr. Eden said he thought the Vishinsky concessions did represent a positive move. The Western nations would have to expect more of these moves. They were indicative of a growing anxiety on the part of the Soviet Union.

Mr. Churchill said that there was, perhaps, some significance in the Soviet emphasis on the development of fighter planes rather than of bombers. It was a defensive emphasis which revealed anxiety and suggested that fear was an important factor in Soviet actions.

THE FAR EAST

The Minister of National Defence [Mr. Claxton] said he would be interested to hear the views of the United Kingdom Ministers on the position in the Far East, particularly on the prospects in Korea. He felt that the six months of discussion on a cease-fire in Korea had left the United Nations in a much weaker position relatively than when the talks began. The United States commanders in Korea thought that the Chinese genuinely desired a cease-fire. On the other hand, the Prime Minister of Japan was of the opinion that the Communists would not accept one. He thought they would attempt to prolong the present discussions. Even if a cease-fire were achieved, it was not apparent how the United Nations were going to extricate themselves from Korea.

---

* Andrei Vishinsky, Foreign Minister of the U.S.S.R., 1949–53.

Mr. Eden expressed general agreement with Mr. Claxton's comments. He found it equally difficult to see how the Korean episode was to be resolved. He had felt some surprise in the discussions in Washington at the confidence of the United States authorities in their capacity to deal with any possible military developments in Korea next spring.

It was difficult to forecast developments in other parts of South-East Asia. There was no reliable evidence that an extension of hostilities in Indo-China was imminent. There had been a number of reports of preparations by the Chinese but all had been contradicted by other sources. Some of the reports might be instigated by the Chinese Nationalists. He had been pleased that the President of the United States in his Message on the State of the Union had explicitly warned China against the possible consequences of further aggression. He [Eden] had tried to follow that up in his own speech in New York. The French felt that they could hold their position in Indo-China if there were no major aggression as in Korea. If there were any such move they would want the United Nations to take action.

The Secretary of State for External Affairs [Mr. Pearson] said that he was disturbed by M. Vishinsky's statement in Paris in which he claimed that the United States had moved Chinese Nationalist divisions* to Burma and other South-East Asian countries. If any new Communist move were being contemplated, this was the sort of propaganda preparation that might be expected.

Mr. Churchill pointed out that ten of the best United Nations divisions were tied up in Korea, and ten French divisions in Indo-China. The addition of that strength to Western Europe could make a very substantial difference. At the present time, there was not one complete division in the United Kingdom. There were, however, some 250,000 troops in military schools and depots in the United Kingdom, and these were now being armed and trained so that they would have some combatant value in an emergency. He meant to secure that the United Kingdom looked more like the back of a hedge-hog than the paunch of a rabbit. If the Chinese attacked Indo-China it would be necessary for the United Kingdom to reconsider its recognition of the Communist Government of China.

Mr. Pearson asked what divergences there now were between the United Kingdom and the United States on policy in the Far East.

Mr. Eden said that there now only two points of divergence, viz., the United Kingdom recognition of the Chinese People's Government and the proposed treaty between Japan and the Chinese Nationalists. The first was little more than a formal

* i.e., from Formosa, now Taiwan.

point and the United States Government were not now seriously concerned about it. The second was more troublesome. The United States Administration apparently felt very strongly that, in order to satisfy Congressional opinion, they must announce that as soon as the Japanese Peace Treaty was ratified Japan would conclude a treaty with the Chinese Nationalist Government in respect of Formosa. The United Kingdom Government agreed that, once she had achieved her independence, Japan would be free to do as she wished in this matter; but they would have preferred that no public announcement of her intentions should be made in advance. They would not, however, continue to press their objections upon the United States Government.

Mr. Churchill said that, as regards Korea, he was glad that the United States Government were now consulting more fully with other Governments which were contributing to the United Nations Forces.

Mr. Pearson said that seventeen countries had now accepted the draft of the warning declaration about the consequences of a major breach of the armistice terms in Korea.

Mr. St. Laurent pointed out that acceptance of the draft declaration would still leave unsettled a number of important questions on which decisions would have to be taken by the countries contributing to the United Nations Forces in Korea.

Mr. Churchill said that the United Kingdom Government were anxious to avoid raising small points of disagreement with the United States on Far East questions, as they were conscious that the brunt of the military effort in that area was being borne by the United States. In the Middle East, where the United Kingdom were carrying the major part of the load, he hoped that the United States could be persuaded to give some support and assistance. Even token assistance would be valuable. The United Kingdom were carrying out an international responsibility in maintaining free right of passage through the Suez Canal.

MIDDLE EAST

Mr. Eden said that in his discussions in Washington he had agreed with the United States Secretary of State that the Four-Power proposals should be revised and made ready for presentation in a new form possibly including something about the Sudan. It could then be indicated to King Farouk [of Egypt] at the appropriate moment, that these proposals were available for presentation to a Government likely to accord them a favourable reception.

Mr. Churchill said that in so far as the oil dispute in Persia was concerned, the policy of the United Kingdom Government was to salvage what they could from the wreck. Britain could get her oil from elsewhere, but she needed the foreign exchange which she had earned from the Persian oil. Permanent loss of this source of revenue would mean a serious addition to the balance of payments difficulties of the United Kingdom.

Mr. Eden said the International Bank had put forward certain proposals which were acceptable to the United Kingdom but had not yet found favour with Dr. Mossadegh. There seemed to be some possibility, however, that Mossadegh might eventually agree to something along the lines of these latest proposals. In any event it seemed clear that they were the sort of proposals that would afford Mossadegh the best opportunity to reach a compromise with the United Kingdom without losing face provided, of course, he were disposed to do so. Throughout the protracted discussions and negotiations on this problem Mossadegh had shown himself to be an extremely shrewd bargainer. The United Kingdom Government had to ensure that any treatment given to Persia should not be generous to the point where it would prejudice the future of oil concessions held elsewhere by the United Kingdom and the United States. If a satisfactory price could be negotiated, the United Kingdom might be ready to forgo any claim it might have for compensation. Dr. Mossadegh might, however, prefer to stress the compensation feature since it would then be easier for him to reduce or eliminate British control and influence.

EUROPE

Mr. Churchill said that General Eisenhower* had made it abundantly clear that he did not expect United Kingdom military units to join the European army. He was quite content that the United Kingdom should make appropriate military contributions to the N.A.T.O. forces, of which the European army was part. Mr. Churchill thought it not only unnecessary but unworkable that United Kingdom forces should be merged in the European army. He did not see how any Prime Minister of the United Kingdom could contemplate sending six British divisions to the European army in the knowledge that none of these divisions would ever stand shoulder to shoulder in the line. There were the problems of language, customs, armaments and munitions which were very real difficulties. He fully appreciated that the doctrine of European federation appealed strongly to the sense of logic of the French. He himself felt that the United Kingdom should offer every encouragement to the concept of European federation without, however, losing sight of the fact that it was in the interests not only of the United Kingdom, but of international peace that the United Kingdom should maintain her strong Commonwealth ties rather than become an integral part of a European federation.

---

* Then Supreme Commander, NATO Forces Europe.

Mr. Eden pointed out that when the present United Kingdom Government took office, the plans for a European army had already been under discussion for nine months. If the new United Kingdom Government had joined in the discussions at that stage, every detail of the proposed arrangements would have been thrown open for renegotiation and this would have caused further substantial delays.

Mr. Churchill thought it unfortunate that the Labour Government had decided not to participate in the conferences of the Schuman Plan* and the European army.

As a general comment, he felt that the principle of the Grand Alliance had much to commend it, primarily because, as became evident during the Second World War, it enabled several sovereign States to work in the closest harmony without any suggestion that one country might be the vassal of another.

ATLANTIC COMMAND

Mr. Churchill said that, in his opinion, British shipping would face greater dangers in a future war than in the last. Enemy submarines would be much more numerous, faster and armed with even more deadly weapons than before. Anti-submarine vessels would have to be much faster craft, which could not be improvised after war had broken out. Even greater than the submarine danger was probably the mine threat. There had been developed new types of suction mines which were impervious to magnetic minesweeping. These could be dropped rapidly in large numbers and it was difficult to see at this time what effective measures could be taken against them.

The United Kingdom's dangers were much greater than those of the United States or Canada. If the United Kingdom failed to keep its ports open it could not survive. For North America the loss of the battle in the Atlantic would mean the loss of the campaign in Europe. For the United Kingdom it would mean extinction. It was for this reason that he had made every effort to impress on the Americans that it was a matter of practical necessity that the United Kingdom should retain complete naval control in the Eastern Atlantic at the reception end. Executive control of the battle and the convoys should be exercised in the eastern half of the Atlantic by the First Sea Lord and in the western half by the United States Chief of Naval Operations. On almost every occasion they would work in complete harmony. If any differences should arise between them, these could be resolved by the Standing Group who could be advised on policy by an Admiral of the Atlantic. He was, however, most strongly opposed to the creation of a Supreme Allied Commander, Atlantic. He

* Of 1950, which led to the establishment of the European Coal and Steel Community.

was gratified to hear that some members of the Canadian Government shared his views on this question.

Mr. Churchill said that Canada was to be congratulated on the growth of its Navy. It was building up one of the leading navies in the free world. He hoped that Canada, with its expanding resources, would continue to cherish the naval tradition, as it had been cherished for so long in the United Kingdom. A strong Canadian Navy would be of great value, not only for purposes of local defence, but also as a link between North America and Europe.

Mr. Churchill thought that, while the Western countries were becoming stronger, they were not yet necessarily safer. The greatest danger would come in the period just before their strength became really effective. If the Russians made war, they were more likely to do so as the result of miscalculation than by reason of an "incident". In his view the odds were against a war this year, although no one could make an accurate forecast.

The Russians had greatly improved their position by bringing large portions of Europe and all of China under their control without loss to themselves. They might, therefore, think it best to continue as at present. Their leaders appeared to fear war and atomic bombing since these would undermine their control over their people. They seemed more interested in maintaining their power internally than anything else. If, at a later date, the West desired to intensify the "cold war" it might possibly do so by taking steps to make more information available to the Russian people. The West would be in increased danger if there were the slightest sign that the N.A.T.O. countries were not pursuing their defence plans with determination.

ECONOMIC SITUATION

Lord Cherwell said the Americans had been anxious to obtain additional supplies of aluminium. Canada's willingness that the United Kingdom should divert to the United States some of their Canadian supplies of aluminium had made it possible to persuade the United States to allocate to the United Kingdom considerable quantities of steel which would be of great value, both for rearmament and for exports. It was vitally important to maintain United Kingdom exports. For the United Kingdom gold and dollar reserves had fallen seriously in 1951 and it was going to be very difficult to stop them from continuing to decline in the next six months.

Mr. Churchill said that his Government had been faced with a grave financial situation on assuming office. The sterling area was running a large deficit with the dollar area, with Europe and with the rest of the world. The rearmament programme of £4.7 billion would now cost £5.2 billion owing to increased prices. His Government was, however, not going to be afraid to take the unpopular steps that were necessary if national solvency were to be regained. He felt that, if the need for further stringencies were put squarely to the people of Great Britain, they would accept the measures required by the situation. He did not propose to ask for outside help for the purpose of enabling the people of the United Kingdom to avoid discomfort. Rearmament was, however, a different matter; for it was designed to serve the common cause. He was ready to seek external aid to help forward the United Kingdom defence programme. The assistance which the Americans were providing would be a great help to the rearmament effort and the export drive.

Lord Cherwell said that cuts could only be made in domestic consumption, the defence programme or in exports. Consumption had already been cut to the bone. Some of the rearmament programme would have to be postponed.

Mr. Churchill said that he now expected the United Kingdom rearmament programme to take four rather than three years to complete. In the circumstances, his Government was concentrating its efforts on such essential elements of the programme as new types of aircraft and tanks.

From J.R. Colville's contribution to *Action This Day*[18]

Thus although in his second Administration, with age beginning to weigh and zest to flag, there were occasions when he actually used a draft speech prepared for him on some ceremonial or social occasion, he never, to my knowledge, spoke words that were not his own in a political speech delivered as Prime Minister. I remember that on a visit to Ottawa in January 1952, he arrived exhausted after several gruelling days in Washington and New York. He had to deliver a speech at a banquet given in his honour by both Houses of the Canadian Parliament. He had had neither the time nor the energy for his usual meticulous preparation and so I, in despair, drafted an entire speech and took it to him in bed at Rideau Hall. He read it sadly and paid me the compliment of saying it was too good: he would have to use it. Then suddenly, with eyes flashing, he sat up and said that nothing would induce him to play such a deceitful trick on the Canadians. He had never done such a thing, and he never would. So casting my draft and his lethargy aside, he summoned 'a young lady' and launched himself into the dictation of a speech which was entirely his own.

[W.S.C. spoke in the ballroom of the Château Laurier and reached the largest audience which had ever heard a broadcast in North America. All the guests wore sober black except three Roman Catholic prelates in heavy red robes and the head of the Royal Canadian Mounted Police in a scarlet mess jacket. Only three ladies were present: the Mayor of Ottawa, Charlotte Whitton; the MP for Hamilton West, Miss Ellen Fairclough; and Senator Cairine Wilson.

A nice regional balance was maintained in the menu; the trout came from Lake Superior, the beef from "Western Canada."]

Speeches by L. St. Laurent and W.S.C at the dinner given by the government of Canada, Ottawa, January 14, 1952[19]

ST. LAURENT:

It is as Prime Minister of the United Kingdom in this year, 1952, that Mr. Churchill is visiting the United States and Canada at this time. But, in welcoming him to Ottawa, our thoughts go back to his previous visit, just ten years ago

Mr. Churchill, in those dark days, had become far more than the Prime Minister of any one country; for all of us, his voice was the voice of human freedom, and he had become the symbol of the unconquerable spirit of free men and women faced with terrible odds. . . .

The Crown of course is more than the symbol of our association in the British Commonwealth; it is also the symbol of unity in each of our nations. It is in the name of our common King that we discharge in both countries the responsibilities of government.

We have, each of us in our Commonwealth nations, a system of government as free as any on earth; within each nation, however, we place few limits on differences of party, but happily all political parties are as one in their devotion to the Crown and their attachment to the Commonwealth. . . .

In Canada, outside our own boundaries our principal concern is for the closest and the most friendly relations between the United Kingdom and the United States. We acknowledge with gratitude that no man living has done more than you have, to bring about an association of hearts and minds between your father's native land and your mother's native land. And we are all of us confident that your present visit to North America will deepen and strengthen the friendship and the common purpose of Great Britain and the United States which mean so much to us and to the whole free world.

[The following paragraph spoken in French:]

As a Canadian of French descent, I am happy also to greet in you, Prime Minister, a sincere friend of France, a lifelong admirer of French culture and, what is still more significant for us, a statesman as convinced as we ourselves are of the advantages to be derived, for the security of our Western world, from steadfast and unwavering co-operation between the governments and peoples of our two mother countries.

CHURCHILL:

It is ten years almost to a week since I last came to see you in Ottawa. That was indeed a memorable occasion for me with all the burdens I had to bear. It was also an inspiring but formidable moment in the war. With the entry of the United States into the struggle, the pathway to victory seemed, and in fact was, open and sure. But I bore in my heart and conscience the knowledge, which I could not share with you, of immense, shattering disasters which were about to fall upon us throughout the East, as the inevitable consequence of the Japanese onslaught in vast regions where we were weak and ill-prepared to meet it.

I knew and I could feel beforehand the heavy blows that must fall upon us, and the peril to Singapore, the Dutch East Indies, to Burma and to India itself. I had no feeling of self-reproach for not being ready there because between the fall of France in 1940 and Hitler's invasion of Russia in 1941, it had taken Britain and the British Empire – I hope you do not mind my using the word; it is quite a good word in its proper place – it had taken Britain and the British Empire, fighting alone, every scrap of our life and strength to keep the flag of freedom flying until we were joined, as I was sure we should be, by the mighty allies who came to us. But while I spoke to you ten years ago gaily and confidently, and was sure that final victory would be gained, I felt like one about to come under the lash wielded by a strong and merciless arm.

I knew that many months must pass before the United States Navy could regain the control of the Pacific Ocean. I knew that that meant a terrible period for us. We, with your gallant Canadian help, had to fight the Battle of the Atlantic against the U-boats – that might not be entirely overlooked, I think sometimes – whose attack was ever growing in strength and skill, and who were about to take their greatest toll along the American seaboard. An almost unbroken series of misfortunes and defeats lay before us until the battle of Alamein was won by your famous Governor-General*

* Field Marshal Lord Alexander.

and his brilliant lieutenant, General Montgomery, and the concerted descent upon North-West Africa by General Eisenhower's Anglo-American Army, until these great events and these three great men – I think I may say that without getting at all mixed up with party politics – turned the tide once and for all. Until these events occurred we could not see our way safely through our many problems.

Your Excellency, Prime Minister, I have many Canadian memories of the war. My friend General Crerar* was saying the other day how frightened I was – quite rightly – not for myself, but for my responsibilities for the whole Canadian division coming over together through the U-boats and how I thought it might be better for them to land at separate ports in France, but how he and others said they would like to take the risk. So then I said the Admiralty have hardened their hearts; we will make the best arrangements in human power. Not a man was lost. All landed safely in England. And, although the Canadian Army was very sulky and upset at being kept so long in England, we must remember the Canadian Army Corps was the only really formidable force we had in our country during the period when Hitler might easily have decided to throw his effort on to an invasion.

Then, afterwards, I had the honour to see your troops in Italy when I visited the Field-Marshal – I beg your pardon, His Excellency – there, and also to see them when they were about to cross the Rhine. They have a great record in the war and I am proud to be able to remind you of it to-night and to have been associated with you in some of these historic actions.

What is the scene which unfolds before us to-night? It is certainly not what we had hoped to find after all our enemies had surrendered unconditionally and the great World Instrument of the United Nations had been set up to make sure that the wars were ended. It is certainly not that. Peace does not sit untroubled in her vineyard. The harvests of new and boundless wealth which science stands ready to pour into the hands of all peoples, and of none perhaps more than the people of Canada, must be used for exertions to ward off from us the dangers and unimaginable horrors of another world war.

---

* Henry Duncan Crerar (1885–1965), Canadian soldier; Chief of the General Staff, 1940–41; General Officer Commanding, 1st Canadian Corps, 1941–44; commanded 1st Canadian Army, 1944–45.

At least this time in visiting you I have no secrets to guard about the future. When I came last time I could not tell what was going to happen, because I could not make it public. This time I do not know. No one can predict with certainty what will happen. All we can see for ourselves are the strange clouds that move and gather on the horizons, sometimes so full of menace, sometimes fading away. There they are. They cast their shadow, as Mr. Truman said the other night, . . . they cast their shadow on our life and actions.

But this time at any rate we are all united from the beginning. We all mean to stand by each other. Here in Canada, in the United States, in Britain, in Western Europe, all of us are united to defend the cause of freedom with all our strength and by that strength we hope to preserve unbroken the peace which is our heart's desire.

Your Excellency, I have spoken to-night a good deal about the past. Edmund Burke said, "People will not look forward to posterity who never look backward to their ancestors." The past is indeed the only guide to the future. But it is the future which dominates our minds. A great future is yours in Canada. The two world wars of the terrible 20th Century have turned the economic balance of power from the Old World to the New. It is certain that Europe could not have survived without the moral and material help which has flowed across the ocean from Canada and the United States. Now, we have the North Atlantic Treaty which owes much to Canadian statesmanship and to the personal initiative of Mr. St. Laurent. This treaty is not only the surest guarantee of the prevention of war but it is the sure hope of victory should our hopes of preventing war be blasted.

So far this solemn compact has been regarded only in its military aspect, but now we all feel, especially since our visit to Washington, that it is broadening out into the conception of the North Atlantic community of free nations, acting together not only for defence for a specific danger but for the welfare, happiness and progress of all the peoples of the free world. For this we require to do all in our power to promote United Europe and the design of a European Army, including Germany. I have long been an advocate of both these ideas. We shall do all in our power to help them to fruition. That does not mean that Great Britain will become a unit in a federated Europe, nor that her army, already in line upon the continent and to grow steadily, will be merged in such a way as to lose its identity. We stand with the United States, shoulder to shoulder with the European Army and its German element. We stand under the Supreme

N.A.T.O. Commander and we stand ready to face whatever aggression may fall upon us.

Now – now be careful! I am going to do something which I always warn my French friends about. I am going to speak French. The late Lord Birkenhead whom many of you knew said of my French that it was the best in the world. He said: "The French seem to understand it and it is the only French I have ever been able to understand." However, I will follow the example of the Prime Minister, asking for all your kindness and consideration.

In repeating what I have just said –

[W.S.C. then gave in French the substance of the paragraph beginning "So far this solemn compact . . ." before reverting to English.]

Your Excellency, Prime Minister, it was only ten weeks last Friday that I accepted His Majesty's commission to form a government in the United Kingdom. We have hardly yet had time to learn the full facts of our economic position. But what we saw at first sight convinced us of its gravity. By reducing our imports, mainly of food, by £350 million a year, and by other measures, we strove to arrest the evils which were advancing and descending upon us.

We do not intend, we do not want, to live on our friends and relations but to earn our own living and to pay our own way so far as the comforts and standards of the British people are concerned. I can assure you that will be the resolve of the British nation. We gave all our strength to the last ounce during the war, and we are resolved to conquer our problems now that the war is over. The ordeal that lies before us will be hard and will not be short. We shall not shrink from any measures necessary to restore confidence and to maintain solvency, however unpopular these measures may be.

Prime Minister, you have spoken in your most gracious speech, if I may apply the word, your most kindly speech, about the crown; and you have spoken in terms which express our deepest feelings. No absolute rules can be laid down about the methods of government, but on the whole it is wise in human affairs and in the government of men to separate pomp from power. Under the constitutional monarchy, established over the centuries, of Britain and of the Commonwealth, the King reigns but does not govern. If a great battle is lost, parliament and the people can turn out the Government. If a great battle is won, crowds cheer the King.

Thus, while the ordinary struggles, turmoils and inevitable errors of healthy democratic government proceed, there are established upon an unchallenged pedestal the title-deeds and the achievements of all the realms, and every generation can make its contribution to the enduring treasure of our race and fame. You spoke, Mr. Prime Minister, of the crown as the symbol of our united life, and as the link between our vigorous communities spread about the surface of the globe. But perhaps you will allow me to-night to pass from the constitutional to the personal sphere. Besides the crown there is the King. We have a truly beloved King. In constitutional duty he is faultless. In physical and moral courage he is an example to all his peoples. We are proud to pay him our tribute; and this is no formal salute of loyalty but an expression of our deepest natural feelings.

Here in Canada you have had what might be called a wonderful visit. The Princess Elizabeth* and her husband have travelled the length and breadth of what you will not mind my styling the great Dominion. They have left behind them a long and lasting trail of confidence, encouragement and unity.

I claim here in Ottawa that tonight in our gathering we make a valiant and, I believe, unconquerable assertion of the spirit of our combined identity and survival. We have surmounted all the perils and endured all the agonies of the past. We shall provide against and thus prevail over the dangers and problems of the future, withhold no sacrifice, grudge no toil, seek no sordid gain, fear no foe. All will be well. We have, I believe, within us the life-strength and guiding light by which the tormented world around us may find its harbour of safety after a storm-beaten voyage.

This year will mark the 85th anniversary of Canada's confederation. A magnificent future awaits Canada if only we can all get through the present hideous world muddle. When I first came here after the Boer War these mighty lands had but 5 million inhabitants. Now there are 14 million. When my grandchildren come here there may well be 30 million. Upon the whole surface of the globe there is no more spacious and splendid domain open to the activity and genius of free men, with one hand clasping in enduring friendship the United States, and the other spread across the ocean both to Britain and to France. You have a sacred mission to discharge. That you will be worthy of it I do not doubt. God bless you all.

---

* In the following month to become Queen Elizabeth II, on the death of her father, King George VI.

The *Toronto Evening Telegram*, January 15, 1952

The two leading statesmen [Churchill and St. Laurent] were discussing world affairs while eating, and their conversation centred on Russia. Microphones in front of them were open and newsmen in the balcony overlooking the ballroom in the stately Chateau Laurier, where the dinner was held, were taking it all in.

Mr. Churchill in his whimsical manner, quipped that "the Almighty moves in a mysterious way at times, His wonders to perform. He has caused His servant Stalin to bring about, through the N.A.T.O. organization, the most effective union of the west."

Paying glowing tribute to the big part Mr. St. Laurent had played in organizing the North Atlantic community, Mr. Churchill added:

"I understand that your initiative was largely responsible for bringing about this great North Atlantic union, which as a result of our talks will now become more than an instrument of war —"

Mr. St. Laurent quickly interjected: "Oh, no! It was never meant for war —"

Among the newsmen who heard the conversation was Arcadi Ogorodnikov, Tass* correspondent.

Earlier in their conversation, Mr. Churchill asked Mr. St. Laurent if he should say a few words in French when he arose to speak. The Canadian Prime Minister said he thought it would be splendid idea.

"I intend to speak in French myself for a few moments," said Mr. St. Laurent. "It would be fine if you did, too. Many people in Quebec will be listening to your address and they would be very grateful."

Later, after he had spoken briefly in French, Mr. Churchill was loudly cheered. He drew a round of laughs when he joined in the handclapping himself.

Lord Moran's diary, January 14, 1952[20]

All day the P.M. has been working at his speech. He has a feeling that he can add something even now which might make all the difference. I think he must have infected me with his doubts and hesitations. Anyway, tonight when he rose to speak at the dinner given by the Prime Minister of Canada, I was so worked up I might myself have been making the speech. We had no need to be jittery. The fervour of his reception was a tribute, not to anything he had to say, but to his own corner in the hearts of the Canadian

* The Russian news agency.

people. Afterwards he sat all crumpled up, but happy, receiving, like a Pope, the homage of the faithful. They were brought up to him one by one, and he gave them his hand, beaming upon them.

'Now,' he said to me, 'I'm not afraid of the Congress speech. When this speech is safely over it's more than half.'

[The former Prime Minister Arthur Meighen remarked as he left the Château Laurier that night, "I bow in humility before the majesty of his life's performance."]

Sir A. Clutterbuck, British High Commissioner in Ottawa, to Sir P. Liesching, Permanent Under-Secretary at the Commonwealth Relations Office in London, January 23, 1952[21]

The advent of Mr. Churchill was awaited with a mixture of emotions in official circles – lively satisfaction that with all his manifold preoccupations he should have included not a perfunctory one-day trip but a four-day stay in Ottawa in his itinerary, eagerness to hear what he had to say on the international outlook and on the many problems confronting the new Government, curiosity to know whether in spite of advancing years he still retained his masterly grasp of world affairs, and a certain apprehension that from the pinnacle of his wisdom and experience he might talk down to Canadian Ministers and expect them to accept without question any suggestions he might make to them.

We shall be sending a full report on the visit, and all I need say here is that at the end the satisfaction remained, all doubts and apprehensions had been set at rest, great value had been derived from the exchange of views with the Cabinet, and I think I may say a new affection was born for Mr. Churchill himself among those who only knew him before as a remote and somewhat alarming world figure. The visit was thus from a Canadian standpoint a very great success, and from our standpoint I am sure that the impact made on Ministers and their chief advisers will greatly help U.K.-Canadian relations in the difficult year ahead. . . .

These happy results were largely due to the way in which the Prime Minister adapted himself to the change in conditions since he was last here in 1942 [sic]. He and the President were then running the war, and others had to conform to their decisions. Now, though we are still "primus inter pares" in the Commonwealth, the "inter pares" has received a new emphasis. In N.A.T.O., though having a special position through membership of the Standing Group, we are equal partners with Canada. And in economic power, while we have been greatly weakened by the war and by post-war developments, Canada has continued to go from strength to strength. The Prime Minister fully realised that all this made for a distinct change in atmosphere, and in his discussions here he adopted just the right approach – speaking not as one who sought to impose any particular view but as an enquiring friend who was quite ready to give his own views with the utmost frankness but who was genuinely anxious to hear the views of responsible Ministers here. This cordial and candid approach as between equals both relieved and delighted the Canadians – so much so that they forgot their nervousness and even entered into the spirit of the Prime Minister's humorous digs at them for dropping "Dominion", "Empire" and "Rule Britannia". (The Prime Minister was also in very good form at the luncheon which I gave for him at Earnscliffe primarily in order that he might meet my Commonwealth colleagues. He spoke to each of them individually, and they told me afterwards that it had been one of the greatest occasions in their lives.)

There was of course never any doubt about the success of the visit from the public standpoint. Mr. Churchill was cheered by large crowds whenever he appeared in public, and innumerable photographs and news-reels were taken of him. His visit to the Parliament Buildings on the day after his arrival took on the form of a triumphal procession. It seemed that everyone in Ottawa was determined to catch a glimpse of him somehow, and it was obvious to all that the unique regard in which he is held by Canadians throughout the country has been increased rather than impaired by the passage of time.

The Press was full of laudatory articles, and his speech at the State Dinner was reproduced by most newspapers in full. One heard an occasional word of disappointment that the speech contained no new pronouncement of policy, but it was generally realised that it had to be in the nature of an "appetiser" before the main speech to the United States Congress, and it was agreed on all hands that it most admirably served the purpose.

The speech to Congress has also been widely acclaimed and fully met expectations here as a masterly review given in very difficult circumstances.

L.B. Pearson to D. Acheson, January 15, 1952[22]

The Old Gentleman was in good form here, but takes, as you no doubt found out, some time and some champagne to reach that form. When he gets there, however, he is about as brilliantly Elizabethan as ever. There certainly is no one quite like him, and possibly, for the problems of 1952, that is just as well. I have always had the impression that the only atmosphere in which he thrives and produces is that of conflict, and while we are not actually battling on the field at the present time, there is every other kind of conflict to arouse what remaining fire and energy Mr. Churchill possesses. I saw him a bit in England before he came here, and I have seen a great deal of him the last few days, and I got the impression that this fire and energy is not going to last too long (though I may be wrong about this) and that it won't be very many months until Eden takes over. I suspect that you will have mixed feelings about that prospect. I have a high regard myself for Eden's knowledge and experience and good sense in foreign affairs, but his temperament and mannerisms at times make me a little uneasy; especially when he refers to me as "dear" or "my dear". I prefer Ernie Bevin's "my boy".

However, it was not about these things that I meant to write you, so much as to tell you that both the P.M. and Eden spoke in the highest and warmest terms of their reception in Washington. Churchill was very definitely touched by the warmth of that reception and said some extremely nice things here about the President and yourself, and about your views and policies on international problems. This, I thought, was all the more impressive because he admitted that on some matters he disagreed with you, but even here, he was very generous and understanding about the reasons for and the nature of the disagreement. He has certainly, I think, mellowed a good deal since 1945. I suppose that age plus a steady and heavy diet of champagne and brandy does have that effect on one! He himself, of course, has very great qualities of leadership, is a patriotic "Brit" of the old, imperial school, and yet more than once in our talks here he spoke in terms of complete acceptance and admiration of the leadership of the United States and of their resolve to support that leadership. At the same time, he is determined that this support shall be from a country which has its own strong and free voice in the collective counsels and of a kind which deserves the respect of its partners. His attitude on this matter is one, I suppose, which might be followed by us all.

There is not much point in going into the specific subjects the P.M. brought up, because I think he repeated to us the views which he gave you in Washington. In addition, he and Eden, particularly the latter, passed on to us your views on these matters and, from what I can judge, fairly and accurately. The only respect in which the P.M. and his Foreign Secretary seemed to differ themselves was on the Far East, and I am aware of that difference only because I had separate talks with Eden. When they were together before our Cabinet, no divergence of view was indicated. However, it is quite clear that Mr. Churchill would go further in support of your present attitude toward Communist China and Japan's relation to Chiang Kai-Shek than Eden himself is willing to go. You already know this yourself. They are both also very preoccupied with Middle East questions, and here I think Mr. Churchill would go a little faster and farther in trying to enlist your active co-operation than Eden would. . . .

You will be amused to learn that the only other matter about which he pestered US here was the restoration of "Rule Britannia" as the official hymn of the Canadian Navy. We could hardly meet him in this as we switched some years ago to the more appropriate song, "Vive la Canadienne". However, this weighty problem was resolved by agreeing to play "Rule Britannia" whenever a British Admiral boards a Canadian ship, and by playing "Rule Britannia" last night at the State Dinner when Churchill took his place. In return for these concessions, we expect the British to reduce their demands for economic help from, say, a billion dollars to $999 million!

[Eden returned directly to London with a renewed conviction of Britain's need to re-establish her economic and financial independence, and reported to the Cabinet that he had been impressed by the strongly pro-British attitude of the Canadians, though they were also ardent nationalists and deeply conscious of their status of equality with the United Kingdom within the Commonwealth.

Meanwhile, W.S.C. reached Washington by train from Ottawa on January 16. On the next day he addressed both Houses of Congress, assuring them that he was not begging money to make life more comfortable for the British. He dwelt upon the subjects that had been discussed with the Canadian Cabinet: Korea, Egypt and the Canal Zone, the deterrent. The process of re-armament in the United States, Europe and the Commonwealth might well avert the danger of a third world war. The United States must be careful not to let go of the atomic weapon until certain that other means of preserving peace were to hand. If the truce sought in Korea were broken, and the Chinese crossed the Yalu River into North Korea, "our response will be prompt, resolute and effective." That Britain and the United States spoke the same language, Bismarck had once said, was the supreme fact of the nineteenth century. "Let us make sure," Churchill pleaded, "that the supreme fact of the twentieth century is that they tread the same path."

As in Ottawa, W.S.C. pressed his point about naval command in the Atlantic. He uttered what Acheson later called perhaps the most moving plea he had ever heard,[23] begging that command in the eastern Atlantic, the floor of which was "white with the bones of Englishmen," should be entrusted to the Royal Navy. He secured, more or less single-handed, some substantial amendments.

As for the most weighty matter of all, W.S.C. told Truman on January 18 that, in the present circumstances, he would not favour a meeting with the leaders of the Soviet Union; it would be a different story if in the future the Russians indicated that they were prepared to make a genuine effort to reach an understanding with the democracies.

In order to replace W.S.C. as Minister of Defence in London, Lord Alexander reluctantly resigned his office as Governor General of Canada. He was succeeded by Vincent Massey, the first Canadian to hold the post.

The great-grandfather of Lady Randolph Churchill, Lieutenant Reuben Murray, had served with George Washington. The British Prime Minister was accordingly installed as a member of the Society of the Cincinnati, limited to the male descendants of those who had fought in the revolutionary army.]

D. Acheson to L.B. Pearson, January 23, 1952[24]

I also thought that the Old Gentleman was in good form and was thoroughly enjoying himself. Eden told me that Mr. Churchill regarded visits here as a great holiday and an escape from the harassments of office which he took much harder now than he did six years ago. I was interested to see how much his two speeches preyed on his mind – the speech in Ottawa and the speech before the Congress. He referred several times to them as vultures which were hovering over him and depriving him of all power to relax and enjoy himself. However, he seemed to have excellent aids to navigation in escaping from these preoccupations, and the State Department cooperated fully in this. We were very worried as to whether the President for his lunch and dinner and I for my dinner and reception would have exactly the right champagne and brandy to meet his taste. So we asked Ridge Knight, who is a great expert in these matters, to take the situation in hand. This he did, so we had exactly the right brand and year of champagne and a brandy obtained after ransacking New York and Washington.

I thought that the meetings here went well and that they pleased Mr. Churchill. I am delighted at what you told me he said to you about the warmth of the reception and the pleasant words he had to say about the President and me. He and the President got on very well, and the President made it very clear that he not only respected Mr. Churchill greatly, but also that he was very fond of him. Mr. Churchill also said to me that I understood his point of view and his troubles and had been helpful to him on several occasions. . . .

We also had our lighter moments, one of them being when at dinner he made Cherwell get out his slide rule and compute the depth of the inundation which would take place in the dining-room if all the champagne Mr. Churchill had drunk in his life were poured into it. The results were very disappointing to the Old Man. He had expected that we would all be swimming like goldfish in a bowl whereas it would hardly come up to our knees.

9

Farewell to Canada: 1954

In February 1952, not long after his return to London, Churchill suffered a spasm which caused some temporary confusion in his speech. The fact was known to very few; Lord Moran thought this episode might portend a stroke. Churchill himself was distressed, but discounted the possibility that he might move to the House of Lords, while remaining Prime Minister. He recovered rapidly. In foreign affairs, the situation remained threatening and confused. The European Defence Community might or might not come into operation; Russia under the declining Stalin remained bitterly hostile, suspicious, and powerful; there was no prospect that NATO could match her in conventional forces.

Rather more than a year after taking office, Churchill remarked that even in the darkest moments of the war he had never felt the state of the world to be graver.[1] Nonetheless, the position at home began to improve; rationing was relaxed and over a period of years abolished; preparations for the Coronation of Queen Elizabeth II went forward in a mood of hopefulness and increasing confidence. There was little to be done with Russia while Stalin remained supreme but after his death in March 1953, Churchill lost no time in putting to the new President of the United States, Dwight D. Eisenhower, a message which he was to press for the next two years: though the risks of a rebuff or trickery were obvious, the United States and Britain should approach Russia to see whether they could together avoid a race in armaments of ever more frightful cost and destructiveness. It was essential, Churchill argued, that before the British people were asked to bear such a burden, they should be sure that everything possible had been done to avoid another war.

Such a policy would leave Russia in possession of all that she had gained in the latter stages of the war. To that Churchill saw no alternative; but he always believed that in the end Communism would rot from within if contained. Early in 1953, Anthony Eden fell seriously ill. Churchill took charge of the Foreign Office, the only great office of state which he had not previously held, and in a speech of May 11 proclaimed his wish that a meeting with the new Russian leaders should be arranged. Although this ambition was not shared by most members of the Cabinet, or by the new administration in the United States, Churchill was not put off. He believed that, gravely diminished as Britain's material power was, he could still play a substantial part in the world's affairs. His doctor had urged with reason that to superintend the work of the Foreign Office and to be Prime Minister entailed too great a strain. Churchill himself was conscious of diminished vitality; the composition of papers and speeches caused him more trouble than in the old days.

Half the world came to London for the coronation in June 1953. Churchill accepted with pride the Knighthood of the Order of the Garter proffered by the Queen, a distinction that he had felt obliged to refuse from her father, King George VI, after the Conservative Party's defeat in the election of 1945. Entertaining the Prime Minister of Italy at dinner in 10 Downing Street, Churchill did what he seldom did, delivered a speech without notes, and in his most felicitous style. With his special gift for bringing history to life, he explained how the legions of Rome had in crossing the Alps borne treasures more precious than they knew.

A few moments later, still sitting at the dinner table, he suffered a severe stroke. The effects spread in the next few days. He could hardly move, and spoke with some difficulty. He knew that he might have to resign, and was conscious that Eden, his designated successor, who was undergoing an operation in the United States, would not be fit for some months. Lord Moran, it appears, thought the Prime Minister might die within a few days. Churchill had other ideas. "His courage is only matched by an astounding humility which has come over him," wrote his Private Secretary, Jock Colville, "and Lady C. is no less heroic."[2]

By an immense effort of body and will, Churchill recovered sufficiently to resume. He pressed upon the American administration what he called his policy of "double-dealing," of building up the strongest deterrents and simultaneously offering to the Russian leaders the prospect of co-operation. Indeed, he would have liked to suggest that all further research for the perfection of nuclear weapons should be abandoned, provided that the powers would agree to a rigorous system of inspection. For the moment, however, this found no favour with President Eisenhower or the American Secretary of State, John Foster Dulles. At a conference with the British and French in Bermuda at the end of 1953, Eisenhower remarked that whatever dress she wore, Russia was the same harlot underneath and it was America's business to drive her off the streets.[3]

Churchill liked and respected Eisenhower from their many dealings in the war, and put the maintenance of good relations with America far ahead of any other object of foreign policy. If the United States felt unable to join in a summit conference with the Russians, Churchill wrote, he would not flinch from a "solitary pilgrimage."[4] After all, he was an old man, at the end of his political life and expendable. In February 1954, he learned from a report in the *Manchester Guardian* a startling new fact: the United States possessed and had tested the hydrogen bomb, many times more powerful than the weapons which had devastated Hiroshima and Nagasaki. This had been disclosed by Mr. Sterling Cole, Chairman of the Joint Congressional Committee on Atomic Energy. Telephoning in turn the Foreign Secretary, the three Chiefs of Staff and the Secretary of the Cabinet, Churchill discovered that they, like him, knew nothing of this tremendous event which, he told Jock Colville, "would alter the history of mankind, because it would make wars of the old-fashioned kind impossible for this and future generations. Its immediate effect must be to alter our own strategic thinking in Egypt and elsewhere, and perhaps to make easier a rapprochement with the Soviet Union. It was lucky, he concluded, that at least one person in Whitehall read the newspapers."[5]

The power of the new bomb ruled out any effective protection for military installations or the civilian population. Cole had pointed out that Russia, though perhaps a year behind America, also had the knowledge and capacity to produce these weapons. "You can imagine," Churchill wrote to Eisenhower,

> what my thoughts are about London. I am told that several million people would certainly be obliterated by four or five of the latest H bombs. In a few more years these could be delivered by rocket without even hazarding the life of a pilot. New York and your other great cities

> have immeasurable perils too, though distance is a valuable advantage at least as long as pilots are used....
>
> Of course I recur to my earlier proposal of a personal meeting between Three. Men have to settle with men, no matter how vast, and in part beyond their comprehension, the business in hand may be.[6]

Churchill had been advised in the previous year, when he knew nothing of developments in America, that a hydrogen bomb might cost twenty times as much as an atom bomb, but would have an explosive power one hundred times greater. In mid-June 1954, the Defence Policy Committee of the Cabinet agreed that Britain should produce the hydrogen bomb. This decision was shrouded in the utmost secrecy and unknown for the time being to most members of the Cabinet. Churchill still hoped that more information, and perhaps eventually resources, might be shared between the United States and Britain in that sphere. "I am sure you will not overlook the fact," he remarked to Eisenhower, "that by the Anglo-American base in East Anglia we have made ourselves for the next year or two the nearest and perhaps the only bull's eye of the target."[7]

Clearly it was time for another meeting with the President. The revelations about the bomb had changed Churchill's thinking about the strategic importance of the Canal Zone. Arrangements for regional defence in the Eastern Mediterranean were now stronger, and Britain could scarcely afford to keep eighty thousand men in Egypt when she had no regular reserves left at home. The commitment to Malaya remained heavy; it was feared that Communist successes in Indochina might lead to an assault on Malaya through Thailand. Churchill hoped to see a coherent system of alliances stretching across the Middle East and into Southeast Asia. Moreover, disagreements between the United States and Britain had become apparent at Geneva, where a conference grappled for many weeks with the aftermath of the Korean War, but more importantly with the consequences of French military defeat in Indochina. The brunt of the business fell upon Eden, who displayed remarkable diplomatic skills though he held few cards. Newspapers and chancelleries everywhere reverberated to talk of friction between Britain and America.

St. Laurent said that Canada would welcome a visit by Churchill and Eden if they could fit it in after their conversations in Washington, and this was agreed. The British party also included Lord Cherwell, no longer a member of the Cabinet but heavily involved in atomic matters, and Sir

Edwin Plowden, chairman-designate of the United Kingdom Atomic Energy Authority. Churchill stayed as Eisenhower's guest at the White House, and to his surprise and delight, the President at once agreed to talks with the Russians. It appeared by the second day that this might even become a rather bigger affair, with the French, the West Germans, the British and the Americans holding a meeting in London, the opening of which the President himself would attend. These unexpected reactions on Eisenhower's part may well have derived less from conviction than from an anxiety to be pleasing to Churchill. At all events, by June 27 the enthusiasm for a meeting with the Russian leaders had diminished, although Churchill was relieved to find that America would not object if he made his own pilgrimage. The talks about other subjects went better than expected, although with little progress toward a genuine partnership in thermonuclear matters. The British ministers argued successfully that the Geneva Conference should be given more time to reach a settlement. Although Dulles was reported to have spoken to journalists of the handicap imposed upon American diplomacy in the Middle East and Asia by a tendency to support British and French colonial views, nothing was heard to that effect at Washington. The American government said it would use economic help as a means of inducing Egypt to make and keep an agreement, and supported the principle of freedom of transit through the Canal. The two governments agreed that a measure of sovereignty should be granted to West Germany if France failed to ratify the EDC treaty. Previously the one process had depended upon the other. They welcomed a statement by the French prime minister that a decision must be reached, and were conscious that West Germany's Dr. Adenauer had behaved with dignity and patience, at considerable cost to his domestic position, during several years of uncertainty.

The President and Prime Minister issued a communiqué saying that their conversations had been friendly and fruitful. In strict secrecy, Eisenhower was told of the British decision to manufacture the hydrogen bomb. At a luncheon with the American press, Churchill recommended "a real good try" for peaceful co-existence with the Russians, since a conflict would "leave us victorious upon a heap of ruins." He flew to Ottawa on the afternoon of June 29.

* * *

The *Globe and Mail*, Toronto, June 29, 1954

No guests could be more welcome or more honored in this country than Sir Winston Churchill and his Foreign Secretary, Mr. Anthony Eden, who are expected to arrive in Ottawa from Washington late today. While regretting the circumstances which compelled them to visit the United States – and hoping that their task there has been accomplished – we rejoice that it has given them the opportunity to come and see us once more.

Sir Winston's visit is especially welcome, since his failing health had made it seem unlikely we would be seeing much more of him. Yet for all his weight of years, we draw hope and comfort from his very presence among us. Today, as in the dark years of the war, he generates strength wherever he goes.

Canadians, no less than Americans, should understand that Sir Winston and Mr. Eden are not coming to Canada merely because it happens to be close to the U.S. Were that the case, they might as well go to Mexico or Cuba. They are coming to this country for the much more important reason that it is a prominent member of the Commonwealth alliance – an alliance which, it should be remembered, is the only one that includes nations in every part of the world. This alliance has brought together in a very practical fashion in the past, and holds together in a very significant fashion today, races, creeds and even continents that elsewhere are at loggerheads.

Perhaps the most pressing problem of the West today is to establish understanding and effective co-operation with Asia. Properly employed, the British Commonwealth can be a most effective instrument in achieving that end. Britain may not command – no nation does – the friendship of all Asia's countries. But her prestige stands high in those which, at this juncture of history, really matter to the West.

The *Ottawa Journal*, June 30, 1954

CHURCHILL IN OTTAWA: PROUD AND PERKY

At Rockcliffe Airport, to greet him with fond cheers, were an admiring 1,000, led by Prime Minister St. Laurent and the Cabinet. Around the Chateau Laurier another 3,000 to 4,000 crowded back behind the lines of troops along the curbs to give him a roaring welcome. . . .

Only a couple of minutes ahead of schedule, the C-5 drifted over the field, came down, and deliberately loitered at the end of the runway so Sir Winston could deplane at precisely 5.45 p.m. . . .

A tri-service honor guard gave him the general salute, 19 guns boomed, and with Mr. St. Laurent at his side he began a man-by-man inspection of the proudly-polished Navy-Army-RCAF ranks.

"And he's not missing a medal", said an RCAF Air Commodore, as Sir Winston peered knowingly at the rows of campaign ribbons and service decorations on the chests of his honor guard.

"Must know them all", said an Army Major General, "having done a few thousand of these inspections and won a few decorations himself." . . .

When he met Mr. St. Laurent's cabinet, there were tears in his eyes on shaking hands with Production Minister Howe. "I guess we're pretty old pals", volunteered Mr. Howe later, recalling the wartime visits back and forth across the Atlantic. . . .

Then he [Churchill] went to the thick cluster of microphones, and in a steady glare of flash bulbs and TV and movie lights, said:

"We have had a most pleasant journey from Washington in a magnificent Canadian aircraft, after friendly, and I think and trust, fruitful talks with our American friends. Mr. Eden and I are happy to once again be on Canadian soil. While I think our visit will last only a short while, I am sure it will be agreeable and most useful."

Then, looking up from the type-written sheet in his hand, and with a grin, and almost a wink, he said: "Now, look out", and started speaking in French. En Francais, he said how glad he and Mr. Eden were to meet the Canadian Cabinet, then continued, in English:

"I love coming to Canada. Canada is the master-link in Anglo-American unity, apart from all her other glories; God bless your country."

From the unpublished memoirs of Brooke Claxton[8]

As he [Churchill] came to the door of the aircraft and stepped out on the top of the ramp, you didn't need to know him well to see that he was in good form and high spirits, nor did it require that he should give as he did, his famous "V for Victory" sign with the thumb and forefinger. The "V for Victory" sign is vulgar, as is almost everything about Winston – his over-sized cigar, his conscious showmanship, his mouthing, his hats and clothes – all these are vulgar, vulgar in the sense that they are flamboyant, overdone – vulgar like most of the great figures of the age of Elizabeth, among whom I would put first Winston Churchill himself. Only during the time of Elizabeth did many men have the vitality, the creative power, the ebullience, the unquenchable thirst and the unquenchable spirit of Winston Churchill. Anyway, as he came out on the ramp and made his sign, anyone could see he was in high spirits. He made it felt that his mission to Washington must have been a success, brought about by his own work.

One of the most difficult things about these airport arrivals is to get the centrepiece moved on to the centre stage without too much pushing and shouting. After he had shaken hands with Mr. St. Laurent and Sir Archibald Nye,* I guided him to a low dais in front of the Guard of Honour where he took the salute. After inspecting the guard we had him enter an open car. He did not sit in this like an ordinary person but he partly stood up, leaning against the back of the seat, as if he was canvassing for votes. I had told the RCAF band to play Rule Britannia as his car drove away and I gave them the sign by closing my left hand. They played loud enough so that he could hear and it pleased him immensely. A tear or two rolled down his cheeks as he turned to me standing beside the car and gave me a special wave.

[Most of the diplomats accredited to Ottawa awaited W.S.C.'s arrival at the airport although it was announced that the Russian Ambassador could not be present because he would be attending a cocktail party given by his Indonesian colleague.

Because the Governor General's residence was closed for renovations, Churchill stayed at the Château Laurier. That evening, St. Laurent and the Minister of Defence Production, C.D. Howe, dined with W.S.C. in his suite. Colville, who was present, records, "A most secret subject discussed with apparent success."[9] Even now, most of the papers relating to this aspect of the visit are closed; but it is evident that Churchill told the two Canadian ministers of the decision to manufacture the hydrogen bomb in Britain, and sought the help of Canada, which was indispensable. It was doubtless to discuss such deadly subjects that Lord Cherwell had come to Ottawa. Within a few hours, the Canadian Cabinet had granted the British request for tritium, the purpose of which must have been obvious. Meanwhile, most members of the Cabinet in London still knew nothing of all this.]

---

* Archibald Edward Nye (1895–1967), British soldier and diplomat; Vice-Chief of the Imperial General Staff, 1941–45; Governor of Madras, 1946–52; High Commissioner in Canada, 1952–56.

Conclusions of a meeting of the Canadian Cabinet, June 30, 1954[10]

DISCUSSION WITH SIR WINSTON CHURCHILL AND MR. ANTHONY EDEN

The Prime Minister welcomed Sir Winston Churchill, Mr. Eden, Lord Cherwell,* and Sir Archibald Nye, and invited Sir Winston to tell the Cabinet something of the important talks which he and Mr. Eden had been having in Washington.

Sir Winston and Mr. Eden proceeded to explain the discussions and agreements concerning Indo-China, the European Defence Community, and the British base in Egypt. During and after this exposition a number of questions were asked and answered and discussion ranged over these subjects and others. Before concluding, Sir Winston went on to emphasize that he felt the best and perhaps the only defence against the terrible nuclear weapons that had now been developed was the deterrent effect of the power to retaliate in kind, which must be preserved and multiplied.

The Prime Minister expressed his appreciation and that of his colleagues for the remarks of Sir Winston and Mr. Eden.

[Churchill and the members of the British party left the meeting at this point. The Canadian Cabinet then discussed other subjects including the production of tritium for the United Kingdom:]

The Minister of Trade and Commerce [Mr. Howe] stated that Sir Winston Churchill and Lord Cherwell had asked if it would be possible to secure a quantity of tritium for the United Kingdom's nuclear programme. This isotope of hydrogen was a key item for the production of thermonuclear weapons and could only be manufactured in atomic piles of certain types. The United Kingdom would not have a pile suitable for this purpose for several years but understood that the Canadian piles at Chalk River would be suitable. They proposed to ship to Canada sealed material to be irradiated in the Canadian pile. After treatment, the product would be returned to the United Kingdom and the tritium extracted there.

The use of the Canadian pile for this purpose would conflict with its use for other purposes and require a substantial re-arrangement of plans for the use of the pile. The cost of providing this service to the United Kingdom was estimated to be of the

---

* Lord Cherwell had resigned from the Cabinet in 1953, but continued to advise the British government about scientific matters and was about to become a member of the United Kingdom Atomic Energy Authority, established in July 1954.

order of $8 million. It was for consideration whether the request should be met, and, if so, how it would be financed.

In the course of discussion the following points emerged:

a) Canada was already providing material for the U.S. atomic bomb programme on a commercial basis. While there was an understandable reluctance to become involved in the production of hydrogen bombs, there seemed no reason, in principle, why work could not be done for the United Kingdom similar in general nature to that done for the U.S., if the facilities were available.
b) The financial implications of the proposal would have to be worked out in detail. It might be that the mutual aid programme for the next year or two would be such that funds could be provided from that source to meet the cost. On the other hand, the service might be provided on a straightforward commercial basis as was the production of plutonium for the United States.

The Cabinet noted the report of the Minister of Trade and Commerce, and agreed, in principle, that tritium might be produced by Atomic Energy of Canada Limited for the United Kingdom, the financial arrangements for covering the cost of furnishing the service (estimated to be perhaps as much as $8 million) to be settled in due course following further discussions between the two governments.

[Eden had made sustained efforts at Geneva, with a good deal of success, to reach a broad understanding with the leaders of the Asian powers, and especially the Asian members of the Commonwealth. The Canadian delegation there had been consistently helpful and constructive, no easy position to adopt in view of Dulles' attitude. Eden was anxious to thank the Canadian government in person for this co-operation. Canada was one of the three powers later appointed to supervise the arrangements made at Geneva, after much travail, for the future of Vietnam, Laos and Cambodia.

It is not difficult to guess the broad outlines of what W.S.C. and Eden said to their Canadian colleagues concerning the European Defence Community (EDC) or the treaty with Egypt. Beyond that we cannot go, at least for the moment. The subjects discussed were so sensitive that the circulation of a terse record is readily understood. It seems unlikely that no detailed note was kept, but if such does exist it has not yet come to light in Ottawa or London. We are thus driven to rely on the recollections of Brooke Claxton, printed below. These would be of interest at any time, written by a minister of long experience, who knew Churchill well and had shown consistent goodwill toward the British. In the absence of a full official account, that interest redoubles. There is room for a good deal of debate about a number of his assertions; for instance, whatever impression may have been left that morning, there was more to British policy than an ambition to establish a new Anglo-American axis "almost on a bilateral basis." It is true that the British, Churchill even more ardently than Eden, desired a close alignment with the United States in the Far East, Middle East, Europe and elsewhere. The realities of interest, money and power demanded nothing less. A concordance in their Egyptian policies had long been sought, with little success; at Geneva, Eden had pursued lines of policy distinct from those of the U.S. government; and in Europe the last thing W.S.C. or Eden desired was the weakening of NATO. This point was to be demonstrated within a few weeks, after the French refusal to ratify the EDC treaty. As for Claxton's view that Churchill had stayed in office too long, there were plenty who agreed, including some of his colleagues at home. It is, however, an exaggeration to say that he was "preventing his colleagues from governing at all." Had that been true, the Anglo-Egyptian Treaty would not have been made, for it was largely Eden's doing. The same goes for the agreements reached at Geneva later in the summer and the British response, rapid and constructive, to the collapse of EDC in September.]

From the unpublished memoirs of Brooke Claxton

The next morning he came to the Cabinet at 10.30 with Anthony Eden and Lord Cherwell and had an hour and a half meeting with us. He was not wearing his hearing aid and without it could not follow all the conversation. He and Eden gave us a full account of their visit to Washington and discussed operations for the Geneva meeting and the attitude of the Soviet Union. This time as far as I could make out, they did not want anything from us, which is the first such case I remember.

As is usual at such meetings, the Prime Minister said a word of hearty welcome to Mr. Churchill and his group and then asked him if he would like to speak about the meetings he had had in Washington. Mr. Churchill began with a statement taking about twenty minutes, from time to time asking "Anthony" or "Cherwell" to supplement. The main lines were on the international situation in the Far East, South East Asia, the Middle East and in Europe. It struck me that the British position described throughout was quite unrealistic and that the report they gave of American reactions to what they had put forward was compounded of poor reporting and wishful thinking. They spoke as if it would be possible to secure Chinese approval of United States actions in the Far East in return for United States approval of Chinese admission to the United Nations. Such a deal would include not only approval of United States bases in South East Asia, but the build-up of strength by the British and Americans in Malaya, Siam and Burma. It seemed to me that the realities of American politics demanded that the United States government should not put their names to any piece of paper signed by Communist China. Nor would China give up so much in return for recognition at the United Nations. What Churchill and company were talking about was a new United States–United Kingdom axis almost on a bilateral basis. To my way of thinking this would weaken if it did not end EDC and NATO. What Britain should be doing was to strengthen EDC and NATO. Unless this were done I thought the American impulse to withdraw from Europe would gather momentum leaving Britain very much out on a limb. They described the proposed agreement with Egypt to leave the canal zone in detail, speaking of it as a considerable achievement. Eden said that the period of the right to return [to the zone] had been extended. As part of this all-round deal the United States had agreed to extend economic assistance to Egypt. Korea and Formosa were touched upon. They felt that the problems there might soon be ended. A. and H. bombs were so powerful that none could initiate a major war without complete surprise, but whatever the Russians might do at present there was the absolute certainty of a devastating counter stroke by the United States. In this last I agreed. But on the rest we felt as if we were with Alice in Wonderland. Naturally at my last appearance* I was not anxious to create difficulty but I joined Pearson and some of the Canadian group in raising some questions along the lines indicated above. The answers were anything but reassuring. I felt, I think all the Canadians felt, that Winston had stayed on too long. He was occupying the field, making up his mind and deciding on action on information that was incomplete or imperfectly comprehended. He was governing in a fool's paradise and preventing his colleagues from governing at all.

From this meeting I took Winston to the Press Gallery where he had a great time with the boys, with whom he had a couple of scotch and sodas.

---

* Claxton was about to leave the government.

W.S.C.'s press conference, held in the Department of External Affairs, Ottawa, June 30, 1954. Sir A. Nye presided[11]

SIR WINSTON: Sir Archibald and ladies and gentlemen – I am always very glad to meet the Press though in my own country, in England, I prefer Parliamentary question time to this particular method, which is so widely used in the United States. I am very glad to come here. I have been a journalist, beginning my profession before any of you were born, I think, and managed to keep the wolf from the door with no larger weapon than the pen for a good many years. I know how very important it is for journalists to get good information in plenty of time, and to be able to put all the different variants upon it which are naturally compatible with formation of opinion in a free society. . . .

QUESTION: Are the prospects for world peace better now, than before you went to Washington?

SIR WINSTON: Well, I must say I never had a more fruitful visit or more pleasant visit. When we came across the ocean in the aeroplane we saw in the papers that a storm of anger awaited us in the United States, but I didn't see any of that storm at all; on the contrary, the usual kindness, more than usual kindness, in my talks with the President. Of course we have known him a long time. I personally have had very close relations with him in peace and war on all sorts of subjects, for 12 years. I think he is a grand man. I thank God he is where he is now. I'm quite sure that we've done good, because all the little misunderstandings are news, as he himself pointed out, whereas the great underlying foundations, bodies of agreement and of interest between us, are so well known that you really wouldn't get any advantage by repeating them every day. But a difference, of course, is news. And there's no reason why they shouldn't be stated. I see no reason why we shouldn't argue things out together and with all the freedom that there is, if at the same time that we do that, we don't forget the underlying foundations, and what I really hoped we should achieve coming over here was to bring that aspect out.

It ought to be brought out now and again. It certainly has been. I think the feeling and impression given by our visit and by the documents which have been issued will be all over the world – that Britain and the U.S., and now Canada, are all looking at these terrible problems together. We have a very great measure of understanding and agreement between us, and we are not going to let that be broken or disturbed in any way. I am sure that that feeling has been strengthened by our visit and if you ask me what's that got to do with world peace, I think it has everything to do with it. Good, continuous, intimate, trusting relations between Britain, and Canada and the United States are the foundation and the security of world peace. Nothing will deter the aggressor more than the fact that he knows he's got to face the whole of the British Commonwealth and the United States of America. My answer could have been given more shortly in one word – even in one monosyllable – Yes!

QUESTION: Is the proposed South East Asian Pact directed against Communism, or against military aggression by Communists?

SIR WINSTON: Well, of course, it could be interpreted by people who supported the pact, a little bit according to taste; but as far as the British view is concerned, we are concentrating upon the idea of aggression and although we do not consider that we are passed by anyone in our resolute hatred of Communism, we do not exclude the possibility of having to live together for a number of years, and side by side (I liked Mr. Eden's phrase when I heard him use it the other night in the House of Commons, 'peaceful co-existence'). I don't see at all why we should in any way depart from the idea that you may have to live with all sorts of people in this wicked world. I was rather brought up to that idea. It doesn't mean that you are going to be taken in and entrapped by them in any way, but you may have to live side by side. In the present case, if you had to choose between living side by side with people whose system you think produces great evils, very great abuses, a hideous state of society based upon profound fallacies, if you had to choose between living side by side with them, and perhaps bringing about the destruction of the human race by trying to reform them, there might be a lot to be said for letting reforms stand over for the time being. . . .

QUESTION: Sir, as a result of your visit to Washington, do you consider we are nearer to agreement on an exchange of information on atomic subjects?

SIR WINSTON: When you say 'we', is that Britain, the U.S. and Canada? That leaves out Russia, and the question which arises turns on the great proposal which the President of the U.S. made after we had met at Bermuda six months ago, in order to turn the whole of this process in a peaceful direction and to help mankind with it instead of destroying them. You can't say that that idea should die, that hope should die, because Russia has not so far agreed. On the other hand, the question of application and timing, and so on, must be considered in relation to all sorts of other matters which arise, but I think we should persevere.

As to the exchange of information on atomic matters between Britain and the U.S. and Canada, I certainly consider that our visit has coincided with a strong feeling in America that there really is no harm in their telling us what they know the Russians know. I think they can be encouraged to run that risk at any rate.

QUESTION: Are you optimistic about the prospects of a United States of Europe?

SIR WINSTON: I have got another [question] No. 5 down [one which enquired as to the date of Churchill's retirement], which I thought perhaps it wasn't your business to ask, if I may say so, because any idea that I might have on that topic I should first impart to Her Majesty the Queen.

A United States of Europe was a great hope and dream, and I certainly think it's a cause that no one should desert. What a wonderful thing it would be if there were a United States of Europe, if all these historic states – I mean those that are in bondage as well as those that are free – were to be united in a community, preserving all their national characteristics, but gaining this wonderful power and pride that would come from the personality of Europe being presented to the world. I think it would be particularly helpful in regard to the world instrument – the United Nations as it is called now – if instead of being founded as it is on the principle of everybody coming together on even terms, we had had a regional foundation. Europe would have been one, and very likely the British Commonwealth might have been another; the American republic and South America two other regions. The problem of Africa would have to be faced; Asia has several organisms; Russia the Slavonic world. I think then if they all met together and consumed their own smoke in internal discussions and brought their really famous leading men to the front, then these men would be able to meet together on a level much higher than exists at present, and very likely could give the world that guidance that it requires. But anyhow don't let us throw away the United States of Europe, which I pleaded for six years ago when I was out of office, and which now at any rate has a permanent centre at Strasbourg. It is a family and can afford to have many different types in the children but surely they ought to be able to come together to uphold their common safety and to vindicate their common glory.

QUESTION: Sir: Would you comment on accusations in the United States press that Britain is pursuing the same policy in appeasement towards Soviet Russia in Europe as she did towards Hitler over Czechoslovakia?

SIR WINSTON: Well, of course, I am always in favour of the press and a free press very much (I got my living by it as I mentioned earlier in the day) but that carries with it the idea that some of it will say quite nasty things that one disagrees with. But really I think Mr. Eden and I who have at the present moment the responsibility – the principal responsibility – for representing Great Britain, I think we really could afford to treat with contempt the idea that we were animated by a spirit of appeasement, not in the sense of reducing tension, but of seeking to avoid doing our duty. We pursue a two-fold policy, peace from strength. It was very well put in *The Times* newspaper, which I don't always agree with, some time ago, when they said, 'Arm to parley'. That's all part of the idea. People say to me, aren't you asking to have it both ways? If you are trying to build up fighting strength and organization, unity of the great vast confederacy of which we are a part, isn't it impossible to hold out a friendly hand to Russia? Isn't it trying to have it both ways? Well I am trying to have it both ways. I think when the two things hang together as they do there's no harm in trying to have things both ways. In fact you won't get them any other way than having them together. Peace through strength means that you will keep a friendly alternative before the eyes of your principal opponents. I said when I was talking to an even bigger meeting than this of press correspondents* – 500, biggest I've ever seen, but very friendly – that I thought the Russians might very likely be content to have a good time instead of another phase of torture and slaughter such as they've gone through. They haven't had much of a good time, the people of Russia, with whom I have no quarrel – never had, always great sympathy – but I assure you if the capitalist democracies had to go through the sort of life they have to lead, there would be lots to talk about at the general elections which would occur. They have a very hard life in Russia; and I was trying to explain to our

* In Washington.

American friends, why shouldn't they have the kind of fun the democracies everywhere are expecting, now that the primal needs for food are being met? I have every reason to believe that these two policies can be combined, and ought to be combined, and do not conflict with one another; but as for the idea of shirking the other alternative of doing one's duty and facing the consequences, I do feel that that is best treated with the contempt which it deserves. I won't elaborate on that because, as you know, contempt is not contempt if you have to take any trouble in expressing it. It's got to be quite involuntary, and if possible unconscious.

QUESTION: Sir, will you tell us anything of your discussions with the Canadian Government?

SIR WINSTON: Yes, I certainly will. They have been very jolly.

QUESTION: Was there any serious part, apart from the jollity, Sir?

SIR WINSTON: Yes, the jollity consisted in the mood of friendship. The serious part consisted in the very solemn, formidable and complicated issues which we discussed among ourselves as friends and brothers.

QUESTION: Have you any plans for coming back to Ottawa at some time?

SIR WINSTON: Well, I really don't wish to cut myself off from doing so by making quite needless predictions at this stage. When I came here fifty-four years ago for the first time, your population was just over five millions. Now it's just under fifteen millions. And all that has happened in my life! It's extraordinary, wonderful. But if I were coming back I don't think I ought to lay down any limit as to what your population should be. I dare say by the end of the century it may be thirty or forty millions, or more. And what a wonderful thing, what a marvellous thing, what a work you are all engaged in, building up rapidly the life of this vast community, so full and so buoyant . . . with its hitherto unmeasured possibilities, far beyond what you've already discovered. A wonderful reign lies before you in the future, playing your part and serving world causes and never forgetting the Old Country to which you owe so much of the civilization that you enjoy and are spreading throughout the world.

We have rough times behind us, and many difficulties to face in our small island with our vast population, but nothing encourages us more to face these difficulties than the increasingly friendly and loving relations which are growing up between you and us, and between the other great Commonwealth states like Australia and New Zealand; it really enables us to face every problem with a feeling of confidence. I shall not indulge in a major engagement today as to when I shall return, but I should be very sorry if I never saw Canada again.

From the unpublished memoirs of Brooke Claxton

Then we drove to Earnscliffe where he was to have lunch with Sir Archibald Nye. I sat directly across the table from him and we had some amusing talk as he recalled our various meetings and what he had got out of them. He was in tremendous form. I reminded him that our first meeting had been at the Ritz Hotel in London when he was out of office during the war. This would be in July 1917, when having been reduced to the ranks, I was a plain gunner. My mother had me to lunch and traded on having met Winston once or twice to introduce her soldier son "from the Dominions". Winston said, "We were both in the ranks: you of the gunners and I of the unemployed. I hope I was polite. I was not in a very good temper those days. They did not like any of the things I wanted to do."

W.S.C.'s broadcast from Ottawa, June 30, 1954[12]

I have had a lovely welcome from the people of Ottawa this time and it is a great comfort and stimulant to me to feel their warm, spontaneous spirit carrying with it approval of much that I have done in a very long life.

I have always enjoyed coming to Ottawa, and also it might well be Quebec or Toronto or Montreal, and I have often regretted that as on this occasion, time and pressure have prevented me going further afield throughout your vast domain. But I have been all over Canada in my time and I have the most vivid pictures in my mind of many places from Halifax to Kicking Horse Valley and further on to Vancouver, where I caught a lovely salmon, a beautiful salmon, in the harbour in about twenty minutes. In fact I think one of the only important places that I have never visited in Canada is Fort Churchill which was named after my ancestor John Churchill, the 1st Duke of Marlborough, who succeeded the Duke of York, afterwards James II, as Governor of the Hudson Bay Company [sic]. All that part of the world is growing in importance, both commercial and strategic. Nowadays, in fact, a wonderful thing about your country is that there is hardly any part of it where something new and very valuable may not spring to life any day either on the surface of the soil or underneath it.

It is a very large field but well worth looking at very carefully.

It must be inspiring to all of you and especially to those who have the responsibility of the Canadian Government upon their shoulders, to feel that you are the architects and builders of a mighty structure whose future cannot be measured, but which will certainly take its place in the first rank of Sovereign communities.

When all these hopes are fulfilled and all these glories come to you, do not forget the Old Land; do not forget that little Island lost among the Northern mists which played so great a part in your early days and now regards you with so much admiration and pride.

There is also France to which a strong and ancient element in the Canadian people look with the respect which children should show to their parents. It must be a pleasure for French Canadians to feel that the bitter quarrels between France and Britain have passed into history and that we have shared our other perils and sufferings as friends and allies in this fearful twentieth century of strife.

I hope that those buoyant, modern pilgrims – I believe there are nearly a million of them – who have gone forth from the British Isles since the end of the last War to find a new home among you have brought you some knowledge of the place of honour which Canada holds in British hearts. I can bring you good reports from the Old Country. Honour and victory crowned our arms in the most terrible struggles the world has seen. The cost has been heavy in the flower of our race, and in this you too have borne a grievous and splendid part. It has also been heavy in material wealth and opportunities, and very great continuous exertions will be needed from all classes in our country if we are to keep the high position we still hold in the world. . . .

We give our thanks, my friends – we give our thanks to Providence that we have come through so many trials and dangers and that in this period of perplexity and peril we have been granted the aid of the gleaming figure who is Queen of Canada and makes us in all the lands of the British Commonwealth kinsmen because we are Her subjects and thus are able to command the envy and respect of the world.

Au revoir, mes amis Canadiens. C'est toujours un plaisir pour moi de faire un séjour dans votre pays, que j'ose considérer presque comme le mien.

Au revoir et dormez bien. C'est un avenir splendide qui vous attend demain. Bonsoir. Goodnight.

Lord Moran's diary, June 30, 1954[13]

Washington took a great deal out of Winston, and he was already tired when he arrived last night at Ottawa. After his wonderful *tour de force* at Washington we had expected great things, but when faced by a string of questions at the Press conference at noon today he was listless and appeared jaded. At the end he got very sentimental over Canada and her connection with England, but there was more strength and life in his voice when he went on to speak of Canada's future and her boundless resources. She was the master link of Anglo-Saxon [American?] unity. This phrase was hammered out in the air on the way to Ottawa.

When he had done, the spark died out as suddenly as it had come to life, and it was in a very subdued mood that he sat down to luncheon with the High Commissioner. And then, as he put it later, 'with the help of some liquor I came to.' He did not talk a great deal, but seemed at peace. When, however, we returned to the hotel he struck a very bad patch, one of his black moods, sombre and full of dark thoughts. His voice had become querulous. He snapped at Jock [Colville], and bit the head off anyone who came near him. He would be glad when this bloody broadcast was over. He has always got worked up before an important speech, and now to his fears and apprehension was added a rather alarming degree of exhaustion. He seemed all in. He told me he had tingling in his cheeks. Did it mean anything? He asked me to take his temperature. 'I sat in the sitting-room between two fans half an hour ago. If I caught a chill, is it too soon to produce a pain in my chest?' He decided to play bezique, and then got very fussed when they told him there was only half an hour left and he had not yet finished his broadcast.

I left him; there was nothing I could do. The corridors of the hotel were lined with excited people, and from the steps of the hotel a great crowd swelled out into the streets beyond. Washington likes Winston, but it takes him very calmly. These Canadians were different. They were wildly excited. He belonged to them, and they had a feeling that they might never see him again, and that he had descended into Ottawa out of history to say 'Goodbye' to them. I went to his car, which was open, and put up the windows, and as I was doing this there was a burst of cheering. He was flushed and perspiring freely as he came down the steps after his broadcast; he paused to wave to the crowd and then clambered clumsily into the big Cadillac.

All the way to the Country Club, where he was to dine as the guest of the Canadian Prime Minister, crowds lined the road, waving frantically and smiling their affection. As his car drove off there was loud cheering, and I could see that Winston was greatly moved. I ran back to my car, and as the cheering grew in volume Winston levered himself out of his seat in the well of the car and with some difficulty perched himself on the body behind. There, with his hat in one hand, he held up the fingers of the other in the victory sign. Anthony had followed his example, and from my car some way behind they had the appearance of two marionettes acknowledging the cheers of the people with sharp, jerky movements of their arms. When the crowd thinned and the cheering died down Winston felt the chill night air, and putting on his hat subsided into the well of the car. Then as the car passed through a village there was more cheering and more crowds, and once again he hoisted himself, so painfully, on to the body of the car.

During dinner Winston became very happy. The broadcast was over, and he had not broken down. That had always been at the back of his mind. He had dreaded it, feeling that it would be something of a disgrace. Anyhow, he had got through and now he could relax. Mr. St. Laurent, who sat on his right, looked a very tired man and made little attempt to talk to the P.M. But Winston was full of life and fun and beamed on everyone. The chicken broth particularly pleased him; he could not get it made like that at home, and they had paid him the compliment of providing the particular brand of champagne he likes – Pol Roger. At times he seemed to sit in a kind of stupor. Then he would wake up and raise his glass to Howe, and talk with great animation. He said he did not want the party to break up; he was very happy. Anthony leant over; they were getting late, he said, they must set out for the airfield soon. Winston took no notice. It was a quarter-past eleven before we left the ground at Ottawa. In the air Winston kept talking of the kindly greeting the people of Ottawa had given him. 'I purred like a cat,' he said, 'I liked it very much.'

[Endless trouble had been taken by the Canadian government. Enquiry had revealed that Churchill would like champagne at dinner and hock at lunch; he would bring his own cigars but would "smoke any Havana or Jamaica with pleasure." The same care had been lavished upon the menu at the Country Club; Gaspé salmon was followed by braised beef tenderloin.]

From the unpublished memoirs of Brooke Claxton

Mr. St. Laurent was by no means in good sorts and talked very little to Winston [at the dinner of June 30]. Winston was too deaf to engage in conversation across the wide table. I had him virtually to myself for the whole dinner.

Winston was in terrific form. I have never heard him talk better or more continuously. If I did have something to say, he was prepared to listen as if he was interested. Mostly I had him talk about himself, a pleasure he shares with the rest of humanity.

I asked him about his tremendous output of work. I supposed that the main source of his strength was his enjoyment of everything he did. He agreed but spoke about periods of depression from which he was able to escape through change of occupation and sometimes of scene. He had begun his habit of going to bed in the afternoon relatively young. There was no rule about this but he generally found it worked. Asked how much alcohol contributed to his energy output, he said he imagined "a very considerable lot." "I am a steady drinker" he said. "I begin early in the morning, but not much at a time." What does he mean by "not much?" Having seen him keep up a pretty steady diet of two ounces of scotch or brandy every hour or so during the day and night, I wondered "Is that much?" He found red wine did not agree with him but white wine did.

Asked about his book production he said that his principal steady occupation was writing. He was first and foremost a book maker. Everything he did, he did in a way which would enable him to make a book about it whenever he had, as it were, a spare moment. This had started by his combining the job of war correspondent and soldier in the Sudan and Africa. He was politician and journalist at one and the same time throughout his whole mature life. He asked me if I had read many of his books. I said "Yes." He said, "How many?" I said "I should guess about thirty." He said, "Oh, there are many more than that. Which did I like best?" I said I thought "The World Crisis", particularly if I remembered correctly the volume dealing with the period from 1916 to 1918. He was pleased, saying that this was, he thought, his best work.

He spoke flatteringly about the Canadian Armed Forces and the great strides we had made in training, weapons, development and unification.

When we were reaching the dessert he had a talk with Mr. St. Laurent. This went on for some time and then he turned to me and said: "What's this I hear? I find your Prime Minister in dreadful sorts, his spirits are low. Are you really proposing to leave the Cabinet tomorrow? This has upset him very much, much more than you think. You and Abbott and Chevrier.* How old are you?" I said "Fifty-six." He said, "A very young man. I'm eighty† and I would not leave for anything. I enjoy it too much. You will find business dreadfully dull. Is this to make money?" I said, "Partly, but having had eleven years in the government, more than eight of them in defence, it was high time they got someone else." He said, "They should give you another portfolio, eight years is too long, particularly for so exacting a portfolio." I said, "No other portfolio would be interesting after defence." He said, "But there is always politics itself. Then you can write and have a good time." He really gave me quite a going over, all in the most flattering way.

Before this he had asked me next time I was in England to come and stay with him at [Chartwell]. He closed this phase of the conversation by saying, "Well, I think it's most upsetting and sad. When you come to England you must stay with me, but I shall give you only the second best champagne."

Sir A. Nye to the Commonwealth Relations Office, London, undated[14]

Visit to Ottawa of Sir Winston Churchill and Mr. Eden, June 29–30, 1954.

This thirty-hour visit was an outstanding success from all points of view. Sir Winston enjoyed a remarkable and moving personal triumph. He impressed the Canadians with his grasp and vigour. Mr. Eden's contribution was likewise recognised and acclaimed. The weather was kind and the general public turned out, in numbers most unusual in Canada, to cheer the two visitors wherever they went.

Canadian opinion held that the mission to Washington had been timely and well worth while, and that Anglo-American differences could not have been healed as well in any other way. The visit to Canada was regarded as both courteous and useful. The willingness of the Prime Minister to

---

* Respectively, Ministers of Finance and Transport. The three resignations took effect on the next day, July 1.

† Not quite; W.S.C. was then five months short of his eightieth birthday.

broadcast and give a press conference and of Mr. Eden to appear on television was much appreciated.

A feeling has grown up in Canada that, where the United Kingdom and United States differ on Far Eastern policy, the balance of wisdom usually lies with the United Kingdom statesmen, however much the balance of power lies with the United States. Editorial comment since the visit has been sceptical about United States pronouncements against the admission of the Peking Government to the United Nations and on Far Eastern policies generally, and steadfastly friendly towards the efforts of Sir Winston and Mr. Eden to seek out a realistic *modus vivendi*.

L.B. Pearson to N.A. Robertson,* July 7, 1954[15]

The background of my letter to Anthony Eden† ...is Sir Winston Churchill's desire, as expressed to President Eisenhower, for a very early high level meeting with Malenkov, before he retires from Downing Street. President Eisenhower, anxious to be considerate and polite to his guest, did not do very much to discourage such an idea and this had worried not only the State Department but Anthony Eden. The latter expressed his worries to me in Ottawa in a very private and personal way because obviously he would not wish Sir Winston or the Americans to know how he felt about the desire so ardently held by his chief. Nevertheless, we both agreed that a visit of this kind would be bad and might be disastrous. In the first place, to whom would Sir Winston talk? There is no Stalin now in Moscow. Secondly, he is really not physically and mentally strong enough to stand a serious discussion with the Communists. The Washington and Ottawa visits were personal triumphs for him but the atmosphere was warm and friendly, everything was done to make him comfortable in body and mind, and he was surrounded by goodwill. There would be none of this in Moscow, or indeed at a neutral capital. Indeed, the Communists would probably press him hard and do their best to break him down. For

* Norman Alexander Robertson (1904–1968), Canadian civil servant and diplomat; Under-Secretary for External Affairs, 1941–46, 1958–64; Secretary to the Cabinet, 1949–52; High Commissioner in the U.K., 1946–49, 1952–57; Ambassador to the United States, 1957–58.

† This letter, rehearsing the same anxieties, shows that W.S.C. had mentioned casually to St. Laurent the possibility of a meeting with the Russian leaders, an idea the Canadian Prime Minister sprinkled with "rather cool water."

these and other reasons, I am sure that everything that <u>can</u> be done should be done to prevent such a visit. . . .

I suppose you have gathered from the press that Sir Winston received a tremendous welcome in Ottawa. I have never seen anything to equal it, except possibly the visit of the Queen. The old gentleman reacted vigorously to his reception and was in magnificent form but he is now certainly an old gentleman.

The *Ottawa Journal*, July 2, 1954

Prime Minister Churchill broke away from his escort, and the crowd from the police lines, in a mutually affectionate and sentimental farewell Wednesday night at Rockcliffe Air Station.

Sir Winston, with a surprisingly brisk turn of speed, popped from the limousine in which he had ridden from the state dinner at the Country Club, and trotted down the roped-back line of more than 1,000 of his admirers who had come to say goodbye. He shook restraining hands off his sleeves, and in a tottering run went half-way down the long line, shaking hands. As he turned toward the waiting plane that flew him to New York to catch the Cunarder Elizabeth, the crowd bulged through the police and RCAF service line and a score of hands reached for him.

He was all but embraced a couple of times, and in turn took two or three strangers by the shoulders to give them an affectionate shake. Tears ran down his pink old cheeks. Some in the crowd wept as openly and unashamedly.

Defence Minister Claxton who had been trotting along at his heels began singing "For He's a Jolly Good Fellow", and more than 1,000 willing voices took it up.

Together Mr. Claxton and Prime Minister St. Laurent called and led three rousing cheers for Sir Winston, who stood there in the half light – the TV arcs were focused in the opposite direction – an unlighted cigar jutting defiantly from a stiff jaw and let emotion have its way. He quickly recovered composure, and was grinning when they herded him into the glare of the lights before a nest of microphones.

When he had flown in Tuesday evening, he had spoken from a bit of type-written paper. When he left Wednesday night, he had his spontaneous say.

"It has been a short but wonderful visit", he beamed, "and I can't begin to tell you how much I have enjoyed it. As an aged Privy Councillor I have been honored to sit with your Cabinet and can report they take their responsibilities most seriously. I am very proud to be in the rare position of a Canadian Privy Councillor, enjoying Cabinet confidences. Canada is playing a great part in today's world under your remarkable and distinguished Prime Minister. Canada stands high in influence and authority in the councils of the nations.

"I know you will continue playing your part in keeping bright the shield of freedom and justice."

There was a roaring cheer, and as it died individual voices could be heard crying "Come back again Winnie . . . we all love you."

Smiling, handsome British Foreign Secretary Eden quickly stepped into the circle of light and quickly stepped out after saying: "Both the Prime Minister and I have found this visit a refreshment and an inspiration."

Then for a silent moment Sir Winston and the crowd stood staring at each other, adrift for a moment on a sentimental ocean of memory.

It was the same old love affair it had always been; the people and their "Winnie", and "Winnie" and his people.

Then he was gone up the ramp to stand for a moment, hat in hand, his grey wisps of hair blowing wildly in the night wind, at the open door.

At 10.45 p.m., 30 minutes late, the big RCAF C-5 taxied out into the darkness, Sir Winston's face pressed against one of the windows, and the crowd still calling their goodbyes.

Envoi

RETURNING TO ENGLAND on the *Queen Elizabeth*, Churchill judged that the President had crossed a gulf of thought by making up his mind that Communism was not something that must at all costs be wiped out, but something to be lived with. In Parliament, Eden had spoken of the need for "peaceful co-existence" between the Communist and free worlds. Shortly after the British party left Washington, Eisenhower said much the same thing, adding a warning that this doctrine must not lead to the appeasement which would compel any nation to submit to foreign domination. Churchill expressed his hearty agreement.

That Eden should have confided his anxieties to Lester Pearson at Ottawa is a testimony to the close relationship which flourished between them; indeed, Pearson was probably the only minister in any country to whom Eden would have spoken in such a fashion. Before Pearson's letters to Norman Robertson and Eden had even been written, W.S.C. had despatched a message to Moscow proposing an early meeting. The Cabinet had not been consulted, and several members talked of resignation. But for the moment the notion of a conference faded away at the end of July, when Russia suggested instead a gathering of all European governments to consider the establishment of a system of collective security.

* * *

Churchill's vitality declined by slow stages. At his best, he brought to political business a blend of knowledge, authority, magnanimity and insight that none could match. He could still make a fine speech; but such occasions became rarer and the effort greater. His wit and sense of the comic remained. It is difficult to read without laughter the letter he sent to his wife after the Minister of Pensions came to Chartwell. Britain's economic position had improved notably since 1951, and an increase in pensions was soon to be announced. Not altogether tactfully, in view of the fact that his host would shortly reach the age of eighty, the Minister expatiated upon the burdens imposed by the elderly:

> and cast a critical eye on me. He told me about his Father who was stone blind for 20 years and kept alive at gt expense by 3 nurses till he died reluctantly at 91; and of course the Death Duties were ever so much more than they wd have been if he had only been put out of the way earlier. I felt vy guilty. But in rejoinder I took him in to my study and showed him the 4 packets of proofs of the History of the ES Peoples wh bring 50,000 dollars a year into the island on my account alone. 'You don't keep me, I keep you.' He was rather taken aback.[1]

In July, Churchill had told Eden that he would resign toward the end of September. The date had been settled and altered more than once, and within a few weeks Churchill changed his mind again. This situation became trying in the extreme to Eden and other senior colleagues, for the Prime Minister seemed to waver capriciously, almost mischievously. To judge from all his statements, private as well as public, W.S.C. clung to office because he still hoped for a meeting at high level with the Russians, when the horrifying power of the new weapons available to both sides might perhaps convince all that war between the great powers had – so to speak – outlawed itself. As he expressed it in a solemn speech about deterrents and defence, delivered a few weeks before he retired, humanity might by a process of sublime irony reach a stage where safety would be the sturdy child of terror, and survival the twin brother of annihilation: "The day may dawn when fair play, love for one's fellow men, respect for justice and freedom, will enable tormented generations to march forth serene and triumphant from the hideous epoch in which we have to dwell. Meanwhile, never flinch, never weary, never despair."[2]

Churchill's hope of a summit was in the end denied; the Russians showed no keenness and the Americans scarcely more. At a meeting of the Cabinet in mid-March 1955, Eden asked outright whether the possibility of such a meeting made any difference to the date agreed between them for Churchill's retirement. It was unprecedented in his experience, the Prime Minister replied, to discuss such matters in Cabinet; he would "be guided by what I believed was my duty and nothing else, and . . . any Minister who disagreed could always send in his resignation. The poor Cabinet," Churchill explained to Clementine,

> most of whom knew nothing about the inner story, seemed puzzled and worried. Of course, as you know, only one thing has influenced me, and that is the possibility of arranging with Ike for a top level meeting in the near future with the Soviets. Otherwise I am very ready to hand over responsibility . . . if it is clear that Ike will not in any circumstances take part in the near future in a top level meeting, that relieves me of my duty to continue.[3]

The plans for the European Defence Community, so long discussed, had collapsed in September 1954 with the French refusal to ratify. Thereupon the British announced that they would in all save the most extreme circumstances maintain a substantial armed force on the continent of Europe for the next fifty years. In practice, this confirmed what was already in place, and the long-drawn agony over the EDC had given emphasis to what Churchill, Eden and other British ministers had said to their American and Canadian counterparts. The new arrangements tied the British to the defence of Europe in a formal and obvious way. Lester Pearson, soon to be Prime Minister of Canada, said in private that he had never been so deeply moved as when Eden announced the British offer, for now the United Kingdom had found it possible to reconcile its links with Europe with those in the wider world. With Britain playing its part in Europe and the United States standing massively in NATO, Canada could feel content about the future and look forward to it with confidence.[4] West Germany was to regain a good deal of her sovereignty and re-arm on a substantial scale, though under some constraints, an outcome which would have seemed unthinkable a few years earlier. As Churchill had remarked to St. Laurent in that unguarded moment at dinner early in 1952, Stalin had brought about an unwonted unity in the West.

Lady Churchill had been anxious for years that her husband should retire but knew what the decision meant: "It's the first death – and for him, a death in life."[5] Churchill himself, as he used to express it, always liked to stay in the pub until closing time. After painful exchanges with Eden, it was settled that he would go early in April 1955.

The Queen wrote to him:

> My confidence in Anthony Eden is complete and I know he will lead the country on to great achievements, but it would be useless to pretend that either he or any of those successors who may one day follow him in office will ever, for me, be able to hold the place of my first Prime Minister, to whom both my husband and I owe so much and for whose wise guidance during the early years of my reign I shall always be so profoundly grateful.

The response from Churchill, who was devoted to the monarchy in principle and to the Queen in particular, recalled his service under the five previous sovereigns and measured the decline of his country's strength from the Augustan age – as it appeared to him in retrospect – of the nineteenth century. There is something touching and affecting about Churchill's tribute to the Queen, every syllable of which came from the heart:

> we could not claim the rank we hold were it not for the respect for our character and good sense and the general admiration not untinged by envy for our institutions and way of life. All this has already grown stronger and more solidly founded during the opening years of the present Reign, and I regard it as the most direct mark of God's favour we have ever received in my long life that the whole structure of our new-formed Commonwealth has been linked and illuminated by a sparkling presence at its summit.[6]

* * *

Shortly after he succeeded Churchill, Eden called a general election, which the Conservative Party won by a comfortable majority. Churchill himself was returned to Parliament, and again in 1959. Despite the frictions, he had handed over his charge to Eden with goodwill. Thereafter he played a reducing part in public life. The four volumes of *A History of the English-*

Speaking Peoples, drafted before the war but now substantially revised, appeared to general acclaim. He continued for some years to paint, suffered several strokes and other misfortunes of old age and felt grieved by a good deal which he saw around him, especially Britain's rapid diminution in authority and confidence.

Churchill died, seventy years to the day after his father, on January 24, 1965. Not long before, dining with a faithful friend, he had quoted from a favourite poet:

> We tarry yet, we are toiling still,
> He is gone and he fares the best,
> He fought against odds, he struggled up hill,
> He has fairly earned his season of rest.[7]

* * *

Three hundred thousand people filed past Churchill's coffin as it lay in Westminster Hall. The famous and powerful gathered from every part of the world for the funeral in St. Paul's Cathedral. Immense crowds thronged the streets. By the Cenotaph stood a group of men and women from the Resistance movements of western and northern Europe. Asked who they were and what they did, they replied, "We were unknown then, we shall remain unknown now."[8]

Churchill believed that Britain was on the whole the best place in the world. Not far behind came the United States and Canada, the overseas countries that, with France, played the largest part in his life. He visited Ottawa for the first time in the days of Queen Victoria and for the last in the reign of her great-great-granddaughter Elizabeth II. The sandy-haired young man who lectured about the Boers had become by 1954 the rubicund Prime Minister, celebrated everywhere and admired in most places, who had seen Canada grow in population, economic strength, military power, international presence; the country whose goodwill he sought to enable the manufacture of weapons so destructive that all might in the end see the sense of forgoing them.

In his ninetieth year, Churchill had received with pleasure a message from Alberta. A group there wished to establish a Sir Winston S. Churchill Society, which would spread knowledge of what he had done and enable coming generations to learn something of his example. The Society has flourished in Edmonton ever since, as do similar bodies elsewhere in Canada and many other countries. Some of Churchill's admirers are moved by love of his speeches and books; others by his prescience, or personification of defiance in one phase and forgiveness in another, his capacity to range around the circumference of an issue while penetrating its heart. Few will fail to recognize in Churchill what the philosopher Emerson sought in genius, "that stellar and undiminishable something."

Acknowledgements

Over many years, the staffs of Library and Archives Canada (LAC) at Ottawa and of The National Archives in London have provided indispensable help in the search for documents and I am glad of this opportunity to salute their expertise and helpfulness. Material covered by Crown copyright in Canada and the United Kingdom is reproduced by permission. LAC has also allowed use of the papers of W.L. Mackenzie King and L.B. Pearson. I am most grateful to Mr. John Claxton for access to the unpublished memoirs of his father, and to the proprietors of the many Canadian newspapers which are quoted in this book. I also record warm thanks for the goodwill of Durham University Library (Archives and Special Collections), where the papers of the Rt. Hon. Malcolm MacDonald are housed, and of Churchill College, Cambridge, which, in addition to Sir Winston's own vast archive, holds a wonderful range of other material.

For leave-to-print extracts from published works, I am obliged to the holders of the copyright in A. Danchev and D. Todman, eds., *War Diaries 1939–45: Field Marshal Lord Alanbrooke* (published by Weidenfeld & Nicholson, London, 2001); D. Dilks, ed., *The Diaries of Sir Alexander Cadogan* (Cassell, 1971); J.R. Colville, *The Fringes of Power* (Hodder & Stoughton, 1985); Lord Moran, *Winston Churchill: The Struggle for Survival* (Constable, 1966); *The Memoirs of General The Lord Ismay* (Heinemann, 1960; used by permission of the Random House Group Ltd.). Mrs Joan Bright Astley has most kindly permitted the reproduction of material from *The Inner Circle* (1971), and Mrs. David Bowes Lyon has with equal generosity allowed me to print extracts from the book by her late father, Sir John Colville, *Footprints in Time* (Collins, 1971).

David Dilks

Notes

LAC denotes Library and Archives Canada, Ottawa.

TNA denotes The National Archives, London (formerly the Public Record Office).

Books cited in these notes were published in London except where otherwise indicated.

INTRODUCTION

1 W.S. Churchill, *The Second World War*, vol. 4 (Reprint Society edition, 1953), p. 72.

2 A.M. Browne, *Long Sunset* (1995), p. xi.

3 *Boswell's Life of Johnson* (Oxford University Press, new edition, 1953), p. 417

CHAPTER ONE

1 W.S. Churchill, *My Early Life* (Odhams edition, 1947), p. 5.

2 E. Marsh, *A Number of People* (1939), p. 154; hereafter cited as Marsh.

3 R.S. Churchill, *Winston S. Churchill*, vol. I (1966), p. 543.

4 CHAR 28/26/80-82, Churchill College, Cambridge.

5 CHAR 28/26/83-86, Churchill College, Cambridge.

6 CHAR 28/26/88-93, Churchill College, Cambridge.

7 R.S. Churchill, *Winston S. Churchill*, vol. 2 (1967), p. 2.

8 W.S. Churchill, *My Early Life*, p. 358.

8 M. Soames, *Clementine Churchill* (2002), p. 103; hereafter cited as Soames.

CHAPTER TWO

1 P. Williamson, ed., *The Modernisation of Conservative Politics: The Diaries and Letters of William Bridgeman, 1904–1935* (1988), pp. 233–34.

2 W.S. Churchill, *Great Contemporaries* (Odhams edition, 1947), p. 106.

3 M. Pottle, ed., and M. Bonham Carter, *Lantern Slides: The Diaries and Letters of Violet Bonham Carter, 1904–1914* (1996), pp. 414, 382; hereafter cited as Pottle and Bonham Carter.

4 M. Pottle, ed., *Champion Redoubtable: The Diaries and Letters of Violet Bonham Carter, 1914–1945* (1998), p. 239.

5 Marsh, p. 149.

6 Soames, p. 46.

7 Marsh, p. 243.

8 Soames, p. 49.

9 Pottle and Bonham Carter, p. xxvi.

10 Unpublished article in Beaverbrook papers, House of Lords Record Office, G 5/2.

11 Soames, pp. 114, 66, 108, 78.

12 Mackenzie King's diary, Library and Archives Canada, Ottawa (hereafter LAC), MG 26 J 13.

13 M. Pottle, ed., *Champion Redoubtable*, p. 25.

14 ibid., p. 52.

15 Soames, p. 205.

16 ibid., p. 156.

17 J. Wallach, *Desert Queen* (London, 1996), p. 300.

18 Mackenzie King's diary, Sept. 18 and 26, Oct. 4, 1922; LAC MG 26 J 13. The diary is filed in strict order; accordingly, I have not repeated this reference for later entries.

19 ibid., Nov. 7, 1924.

20 ibid., May 3 and Oct. 18, 1926.

21 The National Archives (formerly the Public Record Office), London (hereafter TNA); file R 40/12833. The details of W.S.C.'s earnings are contained in an enveloped marked "Semi-official correspondence."

22 B.E.C. Dugdale, *Arthur James Balfour*, vol. 2 (1936), p. 337.

23 W.S.C. to Lord Beaverbrook, July 20, 1929, Beaverbrook papers C/86.

24 CSCT 2/21/1, Churchill College, Cambridge.

25 CSCT 2/22/2-5, Churchill College, Cambridge.

26 M. Gilbert, ed., *Winston S. Churchill*, vol. 5, *Companion Part 2*, p. 42.

27 CSCT 2/22/6-11, Churchill College, Cambridge.

28 M. Gilbert, ed., *Companion Part 2* (see note 26, above), p. 47.

29 R.S. Churchill, *Twenty-One Years* (1965), p. 74.

30 M. Gilbert, ed., *Companion Part 2* (see note 26, above), p. 51.

31 CSCT 2/22/12-15, Churchill College, Cambridge.

32 M. Gilbert, ed., *Companion Part 2* (see note 26, above), p. 56.

33 CSCT 2/22/16-21, Churchill College, Cambridge.

34 M. Gilbert, ed., *Companion Part 2* (see note 26, above), p. 55.

35 CSCT 2/22/22-27, Churchill College, Cambridge.

36 CSCT 2/22/28-29, Churchill College, Cambridge.

37 M. Gilbert, ed., *Companion Part 2* (see note 26, above), p. 64.

38 CSCT 2/22/30-36, Churchill College, Cambridge.

39 R.S. Churchill, *Twenty-One Years*, p. 77.

40 CSCT 2/22/37-38, Churchill College, Cambridge.

41 M. Gilbert, ed., *Companion Part 2* (see note 26, above), pp. 85–87, 105–06.

42 W.S.C.'s article "Wall Street"; Churchill papers, CHAR 8/590, Churchill College, Cambridge.

43 M. Soames, *Speaking for Themselves: The Personal Letters of Winston and Clementine Churchill* (1998), p. 349.

CHAPTER THREE

1 Mackenzie King's diary, Dec. 30, 1941.

2 W.S. Churchill, *Great Contemporaries*, pp. 201–2; Soames, p. 281.

3 P. Williamson, ed., *The Modernisation of Conservative Politics*, p. 234.

4 W.S. Churchill, *Great Contemporaries*, p. 119.

5 W.S. Churchill, *The Second World War*, vol. I (Reprint Society edition, 1950), p. 44.

6 W.S. Churchill, *My Early Life* (Odhams edition, 1947), pp. 11, 110–11, 125.

7 M. Gilbert, ed., *Winston S. Churchill*, vol. 5, *Companion Part 2*, pp. 361–62.

8 P.J. Grigg to W.S.C., April 10, 1931, and reply, April 15; these and many other papers relating to W.S.C.'s income tax are to be found in IR 40/12833, TNA.

8 M. Gilbert, ed., *Companion Part 2* (see note 7, above), p. 391.

10 Lord Birkenhead, *The Prof in Two Worlds* (1961), p. 134.

11 Soames, p. 290.

12 J.A. Stevenson to G. Dawson, editor of *The Times*, March 2, 1932, Dawson papers 76, Bodleian Library, Oxford.

13 Notes headed "Toronto speech," CHAR 9/99B, Churchill College, Cambridge.

14 W.S. Churchill, *My Early Life*, p. 302.

15 Mackenzie King's diary, Oct. 18, 1926.

16 DO 35/2181, TNA.

17 I owe this to the late Viscount Boyd of Merton, who as a young man knew W.S.C. well and later served as a minister in his administration of 1951–55.

18 Lord Tweedsmuir to Baldwin, Feb. 3, 1937, Baldwin Papers 97, Cambridge University Library.

19 Soames, p. 142.

CHAPTER FOUR

Mackenzie King's diary is held at the Library and Archives Canada, Ottawa, with the reference MG 26 J 13. It has not seemed necessary to repeat this reference for the many extracts from the diary printed in Chapters Four to Seven.

The telegrams exchanged between London and the British party attending the conference at Placentia Bay are to be found in W.P. (41) 203, Cab 121/149, at The National Archives, London.

1 Lord Moran, *Winston Churchill: The Struggle for Survival 1940–1965* (1966), p. 324; hereafter cited as Moran.

2 W.S. Churchill, *The Second World War*, vol. 1, p. 532.

3 Moran, p. 259.

4 Parliamentary Debates, House of Commons, 5th series, vol. 362, col. 54.

5 Lady Diana Cooper, *Autobiography* (1979), p. 559.

6 M. Gilbert, *"Never Despair": Winston S. Churchill 1945–1965* (1988), p. 1075.

7 J.R. Colville, *The Fringes of Power: Downing Street Diaries, 1939–1955* (1985), p. 196 (hereafter cited as Colville); W.S. Churchill, *The Second World War*, vol. 3 (1952), p. 602.

8 Soames, p. 266.

9 ibid., p. 325.

10 J.R. Colville in J.W. Wheeler-Bennett, ed., *Action This Day* (1968), p. 112.

11 Earl of Avon, *The Eden Memoirs: The Reckoning* (1965), p. 351.

12 D. Dilks, ed., *The Diaries of Sir Alexander Cadogan* (1971), p. 675; hereafter cited as *Cadogan*.

13 Colville, p. 262.

14 W.S. Churchill, *My Early Life*, p. 111.

15 R.C. Brooks to Lord Beaverbrook, Sept. 26, 1962, Beaverbrook papers G/15/3.

16 Colville, p. 258.

17 D. Dilks, "The Twilight War and the Fall of France: Chamberlain and Churchill in 1940" in Dilks, ed., *Retreat From Power*, vol. 2 (1981), p. 58.

18 Lord Lothian to Lord Halifax, May 26, 1940, FO 371/24/92, TNA.

19 Mackenzie King to W.S.C., May 30, 1940, MG 26 J1, vol. 286, LAC.

20 W.S.C. to Mackenzie King, June 5, 1940, Prem 4/43B/1, TNA.

21 Lord Halifax to Lord Baldwin, Dec. 28, 1940, Baldwin papers 174, f. 202, Cambridge University Library.

22 Colville, p. 266.

23 ibid., pp. 283, 329, 341.

24 Broadcast messages exchanged between Mackenzie King and W.S.C., June 2, 1941, CHAR 9/157, Churchill College, Cambridge.

25 J.R. Colville in *Action This Day* (see note 10), p. 89.

26 M. MacDonald to Lord Cranborne and enclosures, Aug. 1, 1941, and reply of Aug. 11, DO 121/68, TNA.

27 Lord Cranborne to M. MacDonald, Aug. 11, 1941, DO 121/68, TNA.

28 M. MacDonald to Lord Cranborne, Aug. 1, 1941, DO 121/68, TNA.

29 W.S.C. to Mackenzie King, in a telegram from the Dominions Office to M. MacDonald, July 26, 1941, Cab 120/20, TNA.

30 M. MacDonald to Lord Cranborne and enclosures, Aug. 1, 1941 (see note 26).

31 M. MacDonald to Lord Cranborne, note with covering letter, Aug. 8, 1941, DO 121/68, TNA.

32 *Cadogan*, p. 395.

33 J.M. Martin to Minister for Information, AVENUE Nos. 36 and 37, Aug. 16, 1941, embodying an article by H.V. Morton, which had been read and amended by W.S.C., Cab 120/22, TNA.

34 TUDOR No. 3, Aug. 6, 1941, Cab 120/24, TNA.

35 *Cadogan*, p. 396.

36 C.R. Attlee to W.S.C., ABBEY No. 12, Aug. 6, 1941, Cab 120/25, TNA.

37 Mackenzie King's diary, Aug. 6, 1941.

38 *Cadogan*, p. 401.

39 Cab 120/24, TNA.

40 M. Gilbert, "*Finest Hour*": *Winston S. Churchill, 1939–1941* (1983), pp. 1158–59.

41 ibid., p. 1159.

42 *Cadogan*, pp. 398–99.

43 Notes of a meeting held in the Prime Minister's cabin in HMS *Prince of Wales*, Aug. 11, 1941, COS (R) 6, WO 193/326, TNA.

44 The telegrams exchanged between W.S.C. and London, Aug. 8–17, 1941, are conveniently collected in W.P. (41) 203, Cab 121/149, TNA.

45 Mackenzie King's diary, Aug. 12, 1941.

46 M. MacDonald to the Dominions Office, received Aug. 13, 1941, Cab 120/20, TNA.

47 W.S.C. to the Prime Ministers of the Dominions, Aug. 24, 1941, Prem 3/485/3.

48 Report on the discussions between the British and U.S. Chiefs of Staff, Aug. 15, 1941, Cab 121/49, TNA.

49 WM (41) 84th Conclusions, Aug. 19, 1941, the most secret parts of the record being contained only in the Secretary's Standard File, Cab 65/19; W.S.C. to Smuts, Serial No. T 794, Nov. 8, 1941, Prem 3/476/3; W.S.C. to the Prime Ministers of the Dominions, Aug. 15, 1941, Prem 3/485/3, TNA.

50 Mackenzie King's diary, Aug. 21, 1941.

51 ibid., Aug. 21, 22 and 24, 1941.

52 C. Eade, ed., *The War Speeches of Winston S. Churchill*, vol. 2 (1965), pp. 59–66; hereafter cited as Eade.

53 Telegram No. T530, Aug. 31, 1941, Prem 3/156/6.

54 Mackenzie King's diary, Aug. 25, 1941.

55 ibid., Aug. 28, 1941.

56 M. MacDonald to the Dominions Office, Aug. 28, 1941, DO 121/68, TNA.

57 Eade, vol. 2, pp. 67–69.

CHAPTER FIVE

As before, the extracts from Mackenzie King's diary are to be found, in date order, at LAC, with the reference MG 26 J 13.

The telegrams sent to W.S.C. and other members of the British party visiting the United States and Canada, the TAUT series, are held at TNA in files Cab 120/30-32.

Telegrams sent in the other direction, the GREY series, are contained in Cab 120/28-29.

1 W.P. (41) 228, Cab 66/19, TNA.

2 W.S.C. to Lord Athlone, Sept. 12, 1941, Prem 4/44/10, TNA.

3 *The Memoirs of Lord Chandos* (1962), p. 264.

4 W.S. Churchill, *The Second World War*, vol. 3 (1952), pp. 487, 474.

5 ibid., p. 477.

6 M. Soames, ed., *Speaking for Themselves*, p. 461.

7 W.S.C. to A. Eden, Dec. 20, 1941, GREY No. 28, Cab 120/128, TNA.

8 J.W. Pickersgill, *The Mackenzie King Record*, vol. I (Toronto, 1960), p. 317; hereafter cited as Pickersgill.

9 Moran, pp. 16–17.

10 Eade, vol. 2, pp. 71–72.

11 W.S. Churchill, *The Second World War*, vol. 4 (1953), p. 179.

12 Mackenzie King's diary, Dec. 25, 26 and 27, 1941.

13 De Gaulle to W.S.C., TAUT No. 241, Dec. 27, 1941, Cab 120/31, TNA.

14 Sir J. Anderson to W.S.C., TAUT No. 211, Dec. 26, 1941, ibid.; M. Gilbert, ed., *The Churchill War Papers*, vol. 3, 1941 (2000), p. 1705.

15 RG 2, Vol. 4654, LAC.

16 Mackenzie King's diary, Dec. 29, 1941.

17 Moran, pp. 18–20.

18 Prem 4/71/2, TNA.

19 Pickersgill, pp. 326–27.

20 Lord Halifax to M. MacDonald, Dec. 29, 1941, MAC 14/8/6, MacDonald Papers, University of Durham.

21 Debates, House of Commons, Dominion of Canada, Session 1941–42, vol. 4, pp. 4478–82.

22 This record was made by Saul F. Rae, then serving as a Third Secretary in the Department of External Affairs; RG2, vol. 30, LAC.

23 K. Reinhardt, "Moscow 1941" in J. Erickson and D. Dilks, eds., *Barbarossa* (Edinburgh, 1994), p. 216. For an estimate of German losses of some 4 million by early March 1942, see Sir R. Campbell (Lisbon) of the Foreign Office, citing evidence from Romanian officers, FO 371/32985, TNA.

24 Mackenzie King's diary, Dec. 30, 1941.

25 Moran, pp. 19–20.

26 Prem 4/71/2/ TNA.

27 Mackenzie King's diary, Dec. 31, 1941.

28 Moran, p. 20.

29 C.R. Attlee to W.S.C., TAUT 442, Jan. 9, 1942, and reply, GREY 296, Jan. 11, Cab 120/32, TNA.

30 J.B. Astley, *The Inner Circle* (1972), p. 78.

31 Eade, vol. 2, pp. 184–85.

CHAPTER SIX

1 D. Lloyd George to Lady Milner, Jan. 21, 1942, Violet Milner papers 45, C422/2, Bodleian Library, Oxford.

2 W.S. Churchill, *The Second World War*, vol. 4 (1953), p. 88.

3 M. Pottle, ed., *Champion Redoubtable*, p. 239.

4 W.S. Churchill, *The Second World War*, vol. 4, pp. 178–87.

5 ibid., p. 187.

6 *The Memoirs of Lord Chandos*, p. 287.
7 W.S. Churchill, *The Second World War*, vol. 4, p. 173.
8 Soames, p. 352.
9 J.R. Colville in *Action This Day*, p. 69; Soames, p. 255.
10 J. Connell, *Auchinleck* (1959), pp. 472–73.
11 *Cadogan*, p. 461.
12 J.B. Astley, *The Inner Circle*, p.85.
13 The Earl of Birkenhead, *Halifax* (1965), p. 537.
14 W.S. Churchill, *The Second World War*, vol. 4, p. 556.
15 Memorandum by C.R. Attlee and Sir Kingsley Wood, Feb. 5, 1943, W.P. (43) 56, Cab 66/34, TNA.
16 Minutes of a meeting with Dominion representatives, May 20, 1943, Prem 3/443/2, TNA.
17 Pickersgill, p. 502.
18 ibid., pp. 509–12.
19 M. Pottle, ed., *Champion Redoubtable*, p. 247.
20 Lord Baldwin to T. Jones, Feb. 24, 1943, A6, Jones Papers, National Library of Wales, Aberystwyth.
21 M. MacDonald to the Dominions Office, July 17, 1943, Prem 3/83/2, TNA.
22 W.S.C. to Mackenzie King, July 17, 1943, Prem 3/83/2, TNA.
23 W.S.C. to Mackenzie King, July 18, 1943, same file.
24 M. MacDonald to C.R. Attlee (Dominions Secretary), Aug. 6, 1943 (circulated to the War Cabinet on Aug. 14 as W.P. (43) 368), Prem 3/83/2, TNA.
25 The main telegrams on this subject are in Prem 3/366/2: MacDonald to W.S.C., July 21, 1943, and reply, July 23; Roosevelt to W.S.C., July 24; W.S.C. to Mackenzie King, July 25 and reply, same date.
26 A. Danchev and D. Todman, eds., *War Diaries 1939–1945: Field Marshal Lord Alanbrooke* (2001), p. 437; hereafter cited as Danchev and Todman.
27 The telegrams are filed in Cab 120/94-102, TNA; for W.S.C.'s telegrams from Quebec see CHAR 20/129, Churchill College, Cambridge, and for W.S.C.'s Personal Minutes of Aug., 1943, CHAR 2/104/2.
28 W.S. Churchill, *The Second World War*, vol. 5 (1954), p. 512.
29 W.S.C. to the Minister of Information, Aug. 10 and 15, 1943, WELFARE 27 and 122, Cab 120/94; Minister of Information to W.S.C., CONCRETE 114, Aug. 11, Cab 120/98; *The Times*, Aug. 27, "Mr. Churchill and U.S. Propaganda Films."
30 Vol. 5, p. 77.
31 *The Memoirs of General the Lord Ismay* (1960), p. 309.
32 W.S. Churchill, *The Second World War*, vol. 5, p. 513.

33 M. MacDonald to C.R. Attlee, Aug. 30, 1943, circulated to the War Cabinet as W.P. (43) 399, Cab 66/40, TNA.

34 Mackenzie King's diary, Aug. 8, 1943; M. Gowing, *Britain and Atomic Energy, 1939–1945* (1964), pp. 107–11, 122–26, 155–77, 184–5.

35 Mackenzie King's diary, Aug. 10 and 11, 1943; W.S.C. to C.R. Attlee and A. Eden, WELFARE 55, Cab. 120/94, TNA.

36 J.B. Astley, *The Inner Circle*, pp. 108–9; hereafter cited as Astley.

37 RG2, vol. 5679, LAC.

38 W.S.C. to Mackenzie King, Aug. 14, 1943, MG 26 J1, vol. 338, LAC.

39 Prem 3/139, TNA.

40 Danchev and Todman, eds., p. 442.

41 ibid., p. 443.

42 C.R. Attlee to W.S.C., Aug. 14, 1943, CONCRETE 201, Cab 120/99, TNA.

43 I owe this to Sir Douglas Dodds-Parker, who heard it from W.S.C.

44 Moran, p. 109.

45 W.S.C. to Mackenzie King, covering a copy of the Articles of Agreement, Aug. 19, 1943, MG 26 J1, vol. 338, LAC; M. Gowing (see note 34), p. 172.

46 Danchev and Todman, eds., p. 444.

47 Prem 4/73/1, TNA.

48 Eden, *The Reckoning* (see Chapter Four, note 11) (1965), pp. 402–3.

49 Danchev and Todman, eds., p. 446.

50 W.S. Churchill, *The Second World War*, vol. 5, p. 86.

51 Danchev and Todman, eds., p. 447. The records of the meetings of the Combined Chiefs of Staff with the president and W.S.C., and the final report of the CCOS, are in Cab 99/23, TNA.

52 CHAR 2/477, Churchill College, Cambridge.

53 Stalin's message of Aug. 25 and the War Cabinet's favourable reaction are contained in CONCRETE 569 and 570, Cab 120/100.

54 Eden, *The Reckoning* (see note 48, above), p. 404.

55 Cab 120/106, TNA.

56 *Foreign Relations of the United States: The Conferences at Washington and Quebec, 1943*, p. 1182.

57 Prem 4/73/1, TNA.

58 Danchev and Todman, eds., pp. 450–51.

59 Prem 3/366/1, TNA.

60 Eade, vol. 2, pp. 502–9.

61 CHAR 20/94A/106, Churchill College, Cambridge.

62 W.S.C. to C.R. Attlee and A. Eden, Sept. 2, 1943, WELFARE 577, Cab 120/96, TNA.

63 WELFARE 607, Sept. 4, 1943, Cab 120/97, TNA.

64 Soames, p. 376.

CHAPTER SEVEN

1 W.S. Churchill, *The Second World War*, vol. 4., p. 173.

2 J.W. Wheeler-Bennett, ed., *Action This Day*, p. 96.

3 Soames, pp. 379–85.

4 ibid., p. 386.

5 I owe this to the late Nicholas Lawford.

6 V. Massey, *What's Past Is Prologue* (Toronto, 1963), p. 393; for the text of Halifax' speech, Jan. 24, 1944, see DO 35/1204, WC 75/9, TNA.

7 M. MacDonald to Dominions Office, Jan. 27, 1944, annexed to a memorandum by Cranborne, 'Lord Halifax' speech in Toronto', Jan. 29, WC (44) 67, Cab. 66/46; and High Commission, Ottawa, to Dominions Office, Feb. 1, DO 35/1204, TNA.

8 Manuscript note by W.S.C., April 13, 1944, on a report in the *Evening Standard*, London, of the previous day; Cranborne to W.S.C., April 29, and W.S.C.'s manuscript note thereon, same date; all in Prem 4/84/1, TNA.

9 Eade, vol. 3, p. 121.

10 *Documents on Canadian External Relations, vol. 11, 1944–45*, pp. 1241–45.

11 J.W. Holmes, *The Shaping of Peace*, vol. 1 (Toronto, 1979), pp. 149–50; minutes of the meetings of Prime Ministers, especially those of May 1, 2, 3 and 5, 1944, Prem 4/42/5, TNA.

12 *The Annual Register: 1944*, pp. 126–27.

13 R.R. James, ed., *Winston S. Churchill: His Complete Speeches 1897–1963* (1974), vol. 7, p. 6926.

14 W.S. Churchill, *The Second World War*, vol. 5 (1954), p. 72.

15 CHAR 20/171, Churchill College, Cambridge.

16 *The Fringes of Power*, p. 509; hereafter cited as Colville.

17 Danchev and Todman, eds., pp. 587–88.

18 The CORDITE series is contained in Cab 120/149-51, and the GUNFIRE series in Cab 120/152-3, TNA; many of the telegrams are also to be found in CHAR 20/257, Churchill College, Cambridge.

19 Colville, pp. 509–10.

20 ibid., p. 510.

21 Danchev and Todman, eds., p. 589.

22 Colville, pp. 511–12.

23 C.R. Attlee to W.S.C., CORDITE 122, Sept. 11, 1944, Cab 120/149, TNA.

24 Prem 3/54/9; Brooke's revised table showed that on Sept. 10, 1944, the British and Commonwealth divisions numbered 30, with 20 Independent Brigades; the U.S.A. 34 and 6; and other Allied forces 11 and 13 (Brooke to W.S.C. Sept. 13, same file).

25 Danchev and Todman, eds., pp. 590–91.

26 pp. 152–53.

27 Ismay, pp. 373–74.

28 Danchev and Todman, eds., p. 591.

29 Moran, pp. 177–78.

30 Danchev and Todman, eds., pp. 591–92.

31 Minutes of first plenary meeting, Sept. 13, 1944, Prem 3/329/14, TNA.

32 Conclusions of the Canadian Cabinet's meeting, Sept. 6, 1944, RG 2, vol. 2636, LAC; Mackenzie King's diary, Sept. 13.

33 Prem 3/329/6, TNA.

34 pp. 165–66.

35 Colville, p. 515.

36 Danchev and Todman, eds., pp. 592–93.

37 *Cadogan*, p. 665.

38 Eade, vol. 3, pp. 208–11.

39 Colville, pp. 515–16.

40 The original is held in Prem 4/75/2, TNA; the typed version of this manuscript letter in King's papers, MG 26 J1, vol. 356, is imperfect.

41 W.S.C. to M. MacDonald, May 24, 1944, and MacDonald to W.S.C., Sept. 15, MacDonald papers, University of Durham, 13/5/17-18.

42 DO 127/53, TNA.

43 W.S.C. to A. Eden, Sept. 18, 1944, GUNFIRE 264, Cab 120/153, TNA.

44 Soames, p. 447.

45 Colville, pp. 517–18.

46 Moran, p. 183.

47 C.R. Attlee to W.S.C., CORDITE 381, Sept. 21, 1944, Cab 120/151.

48 MacDonald papers 14/8/46, University of Durham.

49 CHAR 1/384, Churchill College, Cambridge.

50 W.S.C. to the War Cabinet, Oct. 17, 1944, Prem 3/355/13, TNA.

51 Soames, p. 399.

52 Attlee's letter and W.S.C.'s reply can be found in Attlee papers 2/2, Churchill College, Cambridge.

53 M. Gilbert, *"Road to Victory": Winston S. Churchill 1941–1945* (1986), pp. 1101–2.

54 Mackenzie King to W.S.C., Oct. 22, 1944, MG 26 J1 vol. 356, LAC.

55 Soames, p. 402.

56 W.S. Churchill, *The Second World War*, vol. 6 (1956), p. 329.

57 Parliamentary Debates, House of Commons, 5th series, vol. 408, col. 1306.

58 Diary of Dr. Hugh Dalton, Feb. 23, 1945, Dalton Papers, British Library of Political and Economic Science, London; the remark quoted is endorsed on the typescript in Dalton's handwriting.

59 Soames, p. 405.

60 Minutes of the "British Commonwealth Meeting," April 6, 1945, BCM 9 (45) 4th meeting, DO 35/1479, TNA.

61 Soames, p. 412.

62 W.S. Churchill, *The Second World War*, vol. 6, p. 471.

63 Gilbert (see note 53, above), pp. 1350–51.

64 Eade, ed., vol. 3, p. 479.

65 Beaverbrook to Harry Hopkins, June 29, 1945, Beaverbrook papers G/11/4, House of Lords Record Office, London.

66 Eden, *The Reckoning*, p. 545.

67 W.S. Churchill, *The Second World War*, vol. 6, p. 536.

68 *Sir Winston Churchill: Tributes broadcast by the B.B.C.* (1965), p. 60.

69 Moran, p. 324.

70 Meeting of Dominion Prime Ministers, May 1, 1944, PMM (44), 2nd meeting, Prem 4/42/5, TNA.

CHAPTER EIGHT

1 Soames, p. 429; for W.S.C.'s speech of Aug. 16, 1945, Eade, vol. 3, pp. 513–25.

2 Moran, p. 429.

3 Mackenzie King's diary, Oct. 26, 1945.

4 Mackenzie King to C.R. Attlee, March 5, 1946, MG 26 J1, vol. 400, LAC.

5 Sir Ian Jacob in *Action This Day*, p. 188.

6 Moran, p. 352.

7 M. Gilbert, *"Never Despair": Winston S. Churchill 1945–1965* (1988), p. 1091.

8 Memorandum by Sir R. Makins, Nov. 29, 1951, FO 371/90938, TNA.

9 Moran, p. 353.

10 ibid., p. 355.

11 ibid., p. 359; record of W.S.C's conversation with Senator McMahon, Jan. 8, 1952, Cab 21/3057, TNA. This file contains the records of the British party's visit to Washington and Ottawa.

12 Pearson Papers, MG 26 N1, LAC.

13 pp. 132–33.

14 Moran, p. 363.

15 Claxton Papers, MG 32 B-5 222, LAC.

16 MG 26 N1, vol. 19, LAC.

17 Prem 11/161, TNA, with additions from *Documents on Canadian External Relations*, vol. 18, 1952, pp. 1085–92.

18 J.W. Wheeler-Bennett, ed., p. 72.

19 The text of St. Laurent's speech is to be found in his papers, MG 26 L, vol. 285, LAC, and of W.S.C.'s in Prem 11/161, TNA. The printed text has been amended from the recording made by the CBC.

20 Moran, pp. 364–65.

21 DO 35/3888, TNA.

22 Acheson Papers, Harry S. Truman Library, Independence, Missouri; I am grateful to the Hon. Geoffrey Pearson for providing me with copies of this letter and the reply.

23 D. Acheson, *Sketches from Life of Men I Have Known* (1961), p. 68.

24 See note 22.

CHAPTER NINE

1 M. Pottle, ed., *To Hope: The Diaries and Letters of Violet Bonham Carter 1946–1969* (2000), p. 117.

2 J.R. Colville to Lord Beaverbrook, June 25, 1953, Beaverbrook papers C/89, House of Lords Record Office, London.

3 Colville, pp. 682–83.

4 M. Gilbert, *"Never Despair": Winston S. Churchill, 1945–1965*, p. 828.

5 J.R. Colville in *Action This Day*, p. 122.

6 M. Gilbert (see note 4), pp. 959–60.

7 ibid., p. 995.

8 Claxton Papers, MG 32 B-5 222, LAC.

9 Colville, p. 695.

10 RG 2, series 16, vol. 20, LAC.

11 United Kingdom Information Office, Ottawa, Release No. 61, DO 35/6126, TNA. The printed text has been amended from the recording made by the CBC.

12 Release No. 63, ibid.

13 Moran, pp. 569–71.

14 DO 35/5267, TNA.

15 Pearson Papers, MG 26 N1, vol. 19, LAC.

ENVOI

1 M. Gilbert, *"Never Despair": Winston S. Churchill, 1945–1965*, p. 1044.

2 This speech, delivered in Parliament on March 1, 1955, mirrors closely what W.S.C. had already put in private to the Prime Ministers of the Commonwealth in February.

3 M. Soames, *Speaking for Themselves* (1998), pp. 589–90.

4 N. Pritchard (of the British High Commission in Ottawa) to Sir S. Garner, Commonwealth Relations Office, Oct. 14, 1954, FO 800/757, TNA.

5 Soames, p. 493.

6 M. Gilbert, *"Never Despair,"* pp. 1126–28.

7 The friend was Jock Colville and the poet Adam Lindsay Gordon.

8 S. Churchill, *A Thread in the Tapestry* (1967), p. 16.

Index

Note: Page references in **bold** type indicate the presence of a biographical note. A page number followed by "n" (as in 50n) refers to a footnote on that page. Forms of names for the most part reflect usage in the main text.